AF521278

Revisiting Myanmar's Present Through Its Past

Revisiting Myanmar's Present Through Its Past

Foreword by

Dr. Arvind Gupta

Edited by

Brig Vinod Anand and Cchavi Vasisht

Vivekananda International Foundation

PENTAGON PRESS LLP

Copyright © Vivekananda International Foundation, New Delhi, 2023

All rights reserved. No part of this publication may be reproduced, stored in a retrieval system, or transmitted in any form or by any means, electronic, mechanical, photocopying, recording or otherwise, without the prior written permission of the Publisher.

First published in 2023 by

PENTAGON PRESS LLP
206, Peacock Lane, Shahpur Jat
New Delhi-110049, India
Contact: 011-64706243

Typeset in Adobe Garamond, 11 Point
Printed by Avantika Printers Private Limited

ISBN: 978-93-90095-83-4 (HB)

Disclaimer: The views and opinions expressed in the book is the individual assertion of the Author. The Publisher does not take any responsibility for the same in any manner whatsoever. The same shall solely be the responsibility of the Author.

www.pentagonpress.in

CONTENTS

FOREWORD

On 01 February 2021, the Myanmar armed forces under Senior General Ming Aung Hlaing staged a coup and placed Daw Aung San Suu Kyi behind bars. With all hopes of democracy shattered once again, the country was plunged into yet another bout of violence, uncertainty and despair. Two years after the coup, the prospects of normalcy returning to the country remain bleak. The National Unity Government (NUG) and its armed wing known as the People's Defence Forces (PDF) and many Ethnic Armed Organisations (EAOs) are putting up a strong resistance to the military's repression. The reports coming out of the country suggest that the resistance is strong and growing.

The Russia-Ukraine war has changed the international environment radically in the last year. The international community is distracted by larger issues. The focus on Myanmar has been diluted. There is no credible initiative on Myanmar on the cards. While ASEAN has been watching the situation helplessly, the Chinese influence in the country continues to grow.

India cannot remain a mute spectator to the developments in Myanmar. It shares a long and unstable land border with the country. The people of India's Northeast and those in Myanmar share deep ethnic, linguistic and historical ties. India is executing several infrastructure projects in Myanmar. Recent developments have slowed down their progress. Instability in Myanmar has a deep impact on India's security. The crisis in Myanmar has already caused several thousand Myanmarese to cross into India. This is in addition to the illegal migration triggered by the Rohingya crisis that erupted a few years ago. Myanmar is also India's maritime neighbour.

The Vivekananda International Foundation has paid continuous attention to Myanmar. In 2021, we published a comprehensive book on India's Myanmar strategy. To understand the genesis and implications of the February 2021 military coup, the VIF invited a number of experts and scholars to share their understanding and perspectives on the nature of developments in Myanmar. I am grateful to all the authors for their contributions. Brig Vinod Anand (retd.), Senior Fellow at the VIF, and Ms Cchavi Vashist, Research Associate, VIF, have edited the book. Brig Anand is a long-term watcher of Myanmar developments, while Cchavi is a young researcher specialising in Myanmar studies. The contributors also make suggestions which would be useful for Indian policymakers. It is our hope that this book will contribute to a better understanding of the recent developments in Myanmar.

New Delhi
02 March 2023

Dr. Arvind Gupta
Director, VIF

EDITOR'S NOTE

The February 2021 military takeover has had adverse impact on the country's political, economic and social landscape, which was undergoing a democratic transition. It was a step back in the democratic journey the country had embarked upon since adopting the 2008 military-drafted Constitution. The military extended the emergency rule on 01 February 2023, and the elections which were to be held as per the 2008 Constitution mandate was further deferred. Unlike the earlier two military coups, the opposition forces (National Unity Government, People's Defence Forces and Ethnic Armed Organisations) reacted sharply to the military takeover. A nationwide Civil Disobedience Movement (CDM) was launched after the imposition of military rule. It has been over two years, and the forms of resistance against the military have increased in intensity and magnitude. As a result, the rural and urban areas and most of the western and northern regions face an unstable environment that is dominated by conflict and turmoil.

The military adopted a strategy of annihilating the opposition forces and declared them as "terrorist organisations". However, the resistance or conflict is not just between the military and opposite forces. There are the following three sets of conflict patterns-between the military and the NUG armed wing known as People's Defence Forces (PDF), including various local defence forces, and between the military and the Ethnic Armed Organisations (EAOs). To understand the military takeover in Myanmar, it is important to revisit the country's political, economic and socio-cultural realities. And this volume attempts to delve into the history behind the rise of the military, the opposition forces, the EAOs and the economic, social and political conditions of the country. Finally, Myanmar's relations with the major international players, China, Russia, India, Japan and ASEAN, are also explored.

Section One: Political Organisation of the Country

Since its independence in 1948, the military has held power in its hands and believes that it is the guarantor of Myanmar's national unity and integrity. The military, because of its organisational capacity, cohesion and access to resources, believes that it cannot be challenged. To respond to the current crises, the military has used conventional methods and its 'Four Cut Strategy'. The worst has been the airstrikes and use of anti-personnel landmines, which have caused increased civilian casualties.

The National Unity Government (NUG) came into existence in April 2021 as a response against military rule. The NUG is composed of the ex-politicians elected in the November 2020 elections. They formed the Committee Representing Pyidaungsu Hluttaw under the political roadmap outlined in the Federal Democracy Charter of NUG, which has consequently rejected the military-drafted 2008 Constitution. Therefore, it is essential to look at the rise of the opposition forces, their charter, as well as their weaknesses. Here it is important to reflect on the role of Daw Aung San Suu Kyi, who has been at the helm of political affairs in the country's march towards democracy. Suu Kyi has been sentenced to 33 years of imprisonment, potentially keeping her out of politics.

Further, it is essential to look at the history of the various EAOs in Myanmar, from their origin to their current positions. The majority of the EAOs have been attempting to unite forces to fight against the military. Similarly, it is interesting to note that few of EAOs are exercising a degree of control in their region's political and administrative affairs—for instance, the United Wa State Army, the Arakan Army and so on. Amid the rising number of clashes, the military is trying to negotiate with some ethnic armed groups under the National Cease-fire Agreement. Though in the past 70 years, numerous peace talks have been held, yet the same has not borne substantive results. In the earlier two coups, the military promised greater representation to the EAOs but failed to deliver on its promises. Even the previous NLD government failed to bring together EAOs. Therefore, there are a few EAOs, who also do not trust the NUG and its processes. It is, therefore, crucial to look at the history of these EAOs and their relationship with the military as well as the civilian government.

Section Two: Economic and Socio-Cultural Development

After decades of isolation, Myanmar's economy had been viewed as one of the most promising since the 2010s, with an annual growth rate of 5 to 8 per cent. However, the coup has caused negative impact on this growth. According to a

January 2023 report, the World Bank estimated that the country's economy would grow by only 3 per cent through September 2023 due to the effects of the pandemic and the overthrow of the civilian government. Myanmar's currency, the kyat, has been devalued, there is inflation, and the prices of commodities have increased. The exports have dried up, and the foreign exchange holdings are below previously estimated, with major investments withdrawn following the FATF ruling of blacklisting Myanmar in October 2022. In this background, this section highlights the country's economic developments and major infrastructure projects, especially since its democratic transition. Here issues of poverty, health and gender are also discussed.

Section Three: Security Issues

The conflict resulted in widespread displacement of people within and outside the country, leading to the refugee problem in Thailand, Bangladesh and India. Furthermore, the United Nations (UN) has raised the alarm about the widespread crisis in Myanmar due to the military coup and the COVID-19 outbreaks. During the current crisis, another issue which has received attention is the condition of the religious minorities in the country. Being a Buddhist-dominated country, other religious communities, such as Christians, Muslims, and Hindus, are facing persecution and humiliation in the country.

Another important security concern is the consistent challenge of narcotic substances, which in turn has contributed to the finances of both the military and EAOs. Further, the Global Climate Risk Index puts Myanmar among the most at risk from the climate crisis. The environmental activists fear that the military will scale up logging, the teak trade, palm oil plantations and the exploitation of natural resources, such as jade. These natural resources in the past have supported military regimes even under international sanctions.

Section Four: Myanmar's Relations with the Major Partners

China, Russia, Japan and ASEAN are important players in the region. Therefore, in this section, the genesis and evolution of these nations' ties with the Myanmar military are discussed in detail. With Indonesia taking up ASEAN chairmanship in 2023, there are hopes for bringing Myanmar back into the ASEAN fold. As far as the elections are concerned, the international responses have not been encouraging. The UN Special Representative Thomas Andrews decried that the likely elections would be a "fraud." The USA, Malaysia and European Union have openly called the elections a sham and warned that the vote under military rule would not be free and fair. On the other hand, Thailand, China and Russia have provided certain legitimacy to the military rulers by supporting them and supplying arms.

Section Five: India-Myanmar Relations

The section on India-Myanmar relations explores the evolution of relations between the two countries in the past 75 years. Some of the changing dynamics in the relations between the two countries are also discussed. Special attention has been given to the borderlands and how stable borders can be reimagined. It is vital to understand the complexities of the relations between India and Myanmar as the two share 1643 km of borders with close ethnic ties shared by the people across the borders.

Section Six: The Way Forward

The question of what lies in the future is raised because even if the military continues to hold power, the legitimacy and prestige it had earlier will not return. The continuation of protests and conflict and the success of the silent strikes and attacks from the opposition forces have made it clear that the people are against the military. Therefore, the number and intensity of clashes are bound to increase in 2023. Also, there have been signs of weaknesses in military strength in terms of manpower because of a rising number of defections. There has been no constructive dialogue held so far between the military and opposition elements. Further, the people of Myanmar are unwilling to go back to the system of government that existed under the 2008 military constitution. Though the elections are predicted to take place in the near future, the legitimacy of the same is questioned. Further, in March 2023, the military dissolved the NLD and 39 other political parties as they failed to register under the new law. Being Myanmar's western neighbour, India is closely watching the situation in the country and making efforts to keep the ties going forward with the government as well as stand with the people of Myanmar in their fight to restore democracy.

New Delhi
01 March 2023

Brig Vinod Anand
Cchavi Vasisht

LIST OF CONTRIBUTORS

Angshuman Choudhury is an Associate Fellow at the Centre for Policy Research, New Delhi. He is also a member of the Indo-Pacific Circle. Prior to this, he was a Senior Researcher at the Institute of Peace and Conflict Studies, New Delhi, where he coordinated the South East Asia Research Programme. He is a former GIBSA Visiting Fellow at the German Institute for International and Security Affairs, Berlin. He primarily works on Myanmar, Northeast India, Southeast Asia, Indian foreign policy, and patterns of armed conflict. He has additional interests in identity, citizenship regimes, and forced displacement, with a focus on Assam and Rakhine State.

Anurag Sharma is a Senior Research Associate at the Vivekananda International Foundation (VIF) in India. He completed his MPhil in Politics and International Relations at Dublin City University in Ireland in 2018. His thesis is titled "The Islamic State Foreign Fighters Phenomenon and the Jihadi Threat to India". Anurag's main research interests are Terrorism /Counter-Terrorism and the Internet, Cyber Security, Countering Violent Extremism/Online (CVE), Radicalisation, and Foreign (Terrorist) Fighters.

Cchavi Vasisht is a Research Associate at Vivekananda International Foundation. She has submitted her PhD at Jawaharlal Nehru University. Her doctoral research focuses on understanding entrepreneurship from a gendered lens in Nepal's Kathmandu and Rautahat districts. She has been awarded the UGC NET Senior Research Fellowship to pursue her research work. She completed Masters of Philosophy from the Centre for South Asian Studies, where she understood international surrogacy from a sociological perspective within South Asia. She completed her Master of Arts in Sociology from the same university.

Prof Chaw Chaw Sein has been Head of the International Relations Department at the University of Yangon since 2006. She was promoted to the post of Professor in 2011 and now taking charge of both International Relations and Political Science at the University of Yangon. She works as an advisor to the Union Civil Service Board and Advisory Group for establishing the Diplomatic Academy of the Ministry of Foreign Affairs. She is also a member of the University Administrative Board and sits on the editorial board for Asia Research Journal and Universities Research Journal.

Amb Gautam Mukhopadhaya joined the Centre for Policy Research as a Senior Visiting Fellow in June 2019 after a career in the Indian Foreign Service, during which he served in various capacities in Indian Embassies and Missions in Mexico, Cuba, France, and the United Nations; the Ministry of Defence of India (2002-05); and eventually as India's Ambassador to Syria (2006-08), Afghanistan (2010-13) and Myanmar (2013-16). He also re-opened the Indian Embassy in Kabul in November 2001 as Charge d'Affaires after the ouster of the Taliban in Afghanistan in November 2001. His other current affiliations include an association with the NITI Aayog's 'NITI Forum for the North East' as an Advisor and Chair of a CII Task Force on economic ties with Cambodia, Laos, Myanmar and Vietnam (CLMV countries).

Khin Zaw Win is currently the Director of the Tampadipa Institute, working on policy advocacy and capacity building since 2006. His current engagement includes a plural and inclusive future, federalism and international relations. He served under the Department of Health, Myanmar, and the Ministry of Health, Sabah, Malaysia and did the Masters in Public Policy programme at the National University of Singapore. He has held a fellowship with the Friedrich Ebert Foundation (New York office) and was also a UK FCO Chevening Fellow at the University of Birmingham. He was also a prisoner of conscience in Myanmar for "seditious writings" and human rights work from 1994 -2005.

Naing Ye Zaw is a development professional working in Non-Governmental Organisations in Myanmar. His areas of research interest include education reform, peace-building, youth empowerment and development.

Dr Nazia Khan is currently a Research Officer cum Project Coordinator at the Centre of Excellence in Public Policy and Government (CoEPPG), IIM Kashipur. Her doctoral thesis, "Religious Extremism in Sri Lanka and Myanmar: A Comparative Study" was completed at the Centre for South Asian Studies, School of International Studies, Jawaharlal Nehru University, New Delhi. She has also published articles in the International Review of Social Sciences and Humanities,

South Asia Monitor and Mainstream and book reviews in Contemporary South Asia and the Journal of Law and Religion.

Amb Pankaj Saran is a former diplomat with forty years of experience in foreign, strategic and national security affairs. He has served in key positions within the Government of India in the Prime Minister's Office, the National Security Council Secretariat, the Ministry of External Affairs and Indian Missions abroad. He served as India's Ambassador to Russia from 2016 to 2018 and India's High Commissioner to Bangladesh from 2012 to 2015. He has served in different capacities in the Prime Minister's Office under five different Prime Ministers for nine years between the period 1995 to 2012, contributing to decision-making at the highest levels in a diverse range of sectors. From 2018 to 2021, he served as the Deputy National Security Adviser for Strategic Affairs under Prime Minister Narendra Modi, dealing with regional and global strategy formulation. He is presently Convenor of NatStrat, a Delhi-based independent Centre for Research on Strategic and Security Issues and a commentator on security and strategic issues.

PK Khup Hangzo is an Associate Fellow at the Vivekananda International Foundation, focusing on the intersection of national security and climate change. He also coordinates the Climate Change Expert Group at VIF. Mr Hangzo has a master's degree in Strategic Studies from the S. Rajaratnam School of International Studies (RSIS), Nanyang Technological University (NTU), Singapore. He acquired this degree in 2010 through the Research Analyst Study Award, a fully funded scholarship offered by NTU. He also has previous work experience as a Research Analyst and an Associate Research Fellow at the Centre for Non-Traditional Security (NTS) Studies at RSIS, NTU, Singapore, from 2008-2014. Mr Hangzo's research interests at RSIS included ethnic conflicts, insurgencies, and the geopolitics of transboundary rivers.

Dr Prabir De is a Professor at the Research and Information System for Developing Countries (RIS), New Delhi. He is also the ASEAN-India Centre (AIC) Coordinator at RIS. He has over three decades of full-time research and teaching experience in India and abroad. He graduated from the Scottish Church College in Calcutta in economics honours, he did his Master's in economics from Calcutta University and PhD in economics from Jadavpur University, Calcutta. He was a Visiting Fellow of the Institute of Developing Economies (IDE-JETRO), Japan; the Asian Development Bank Institute (ADBI), Tokyo; Korea Institute for International Economic Policy (KIEP), Seoul; and Visiting Senior Fellow of the United Nations Economic and Social Commission for Asia and the Pacific

(UNESCAP), Bangkok. He has also served as a national jury member for the EXIM Bank's national award for best PhD thesis. He is the Founding Editor of the Journal of Asian Economic Integration, published by Sage, and also the Journal of Land Ports and Border Economy, published by Routledge.

Amb Preet Mohan Singh Malik has been a member of the Indian Foreign Service since 1962. He was posted in Gangtok from October 1967 to April 1970 at the political office for India to Sikkim and Bhutan. He has also served as India's Ambassador to Bahrain, Cuba, and Myanmar and as High Commissioner to Tanzania with concurrent accreditation to the Seychelles and Malaysia, with concurrent accreditation to Brunei. He has worked at the permanent missions of India to the European office of the United Nations (UN) in Geneva, where he was also a delegate to the Disarmament Conference and on the governing body of the International Labour Organization. He was a deputy permanent representative at the UN Mission in New York. He specialised in economic diplomacy, covering both bilateral and multilateral areas.

Amb P S Raghavan is a former Indian diplomat and former chairman of India's National Security Advisory Board. He is a Distinguished Fellow at the VIF.

Radhika Daga is an independent scholar and consultant with policy research organisations in the Indian subcontinent region. She has worked in policy planning, and research with India's leading think tanks, including Institute for Defence Studies and Analyses (IDSA) and Vivekananda International Foundation (VIF). She was also a consultant with the Myanmar Institute for Peace and Security, Myanmar, where she worked in the security and conflict sector. She is well-travelled and is mapping the cultural harmony in diversity across South and Southeast Asia. Radhika holds an MA in Defence and Strategic Studies from Panjab University. She wrote her Master's thesis on "The Geopolitical Relevance of Into-Pacific" and has extensively published on various media and academic portals over the years.

Prof Rajaram Panda is a leading expert of Japan. He has remained engaged in the study of Japan in important dimensions of Japan such as history, foreign policy, security and strategic issues, including maritime security, cultural diplomacy, economic and trade/investment issues in India-Japan relations, and Japan's domestic issues. Prof Panda holds a PhD from the Japanese Studies of the School of International Studies, Jawaharlal Nehru University (1981), an M.Phil (1976), Masters in History from Ramjas College, University of Delhi, 1972 and a B.A.

(Hons) from Gangadhar University, Sambalpur, 1970. Dr Panda has been a recipient of the Odisha Government Scholarship, UGC Research Associateship, ICSSR Post-doctoral Fellowship, Asahi Shimbun Foundation Fellowship, Japan Foundation Fellowship, Lok Sabha Research Fellowship, and ICCR India Chair Professor at Reitaku University, Japan. Presently, he is a Senior Fellow at the Nehru Memorial Museum and Library, Ministry of Culture, Government of India.

Amb Rajiv Bhatia is a Distinguished Fellow at Gateway House and a former Ambassador of India. As Director General of the Indian Council of World Affairs (ICWA), he played a key role in strengthening India's Track-II activities. While in the Indian Foreign Service (IFS), he served as Ambassador to Myanmar and Mexico and High Commissioner to Kenya and South Africa. He is a prolific columnist and a regular speaker on foreign policy and diplomacy in India and abroad. He holds a Master's degree in political science from Allahabad University. His recent books India-Myanmar Relations: Changing Contours (Routledge 2016) and India-Africa Relations: Changing Horizons (Routledge 2022) has received critical acclaim.

Dr Shrabana Barua is a Research Fellow at the Indian Council of World Affairs, New Delhi. Before this, she was a faculty member at the Department of Political Science at Hindu College, University of Delhi. Her research focuses on geopolitical and security issues in South and Southeast Asia as well as Chinese infrastructural developments in the region. Her PhD is from the Centre for International Politics, Organization and Disarmament (CIPOD), School of International Studies, Jawaharlal Nehru University. Her doctoral thesis was titled 'Infrastructure Diplomacy as a Tool for Influence by China and India: A Case Study of Myanmar'.

Prof Sreeradha Datta teaches International Affairs at O.P Jindal Global University presently. Earlier, she was a Senior Fellow and Centre Head of Neighbourhood Studies Vivekananda International Foundation. She is also a non-resident Senior Fellow with the Institute of South Asian Studies, National University of Singapore, Singapore. She has also served as Director of Maulana Abul Kalam Azad Institute of Asian Studies, Kolkata and has held fellowships with Institute for Defence Studies and Analyses. Her research interests include South Asia and India's extended neighbourhood, regionalism and cross-border issues. Her latest edited volume on Bangladesh on a New Journey Moving Beyond Regional Identity will be published shortly. Some of her works include Act East Policy and Northeast India and an edited BIMSTEC: The Journey and Way Ahead and co-edited Bangladesh at 50: Development and Challenges. That apart, she has written Caretaking Democracy:

Political Process in Bangladesh, 2006-08, Bangladesh: A Fragile Democracy, The Northeast Complexities and its Determinants, and edited Changing Security Dynamics in South East Asia and a few other monographs covering Bangladesh, South-East Asia, Myanmar. She has also published over 160 articles in journals, edited volumes, newspapers and academic websites.

Sreeparna Banerjee is a Junior Fellow at the Observer Research Foundation, Kolkata, with the Strategic Studies Programme. She works on the political and strategic affairs of two Southeast Asian countries, Myanmar and Thailand. Her core focus is on the Rohingya issue within the Bay of Bengal region. She is also pursuing doctoral studies on the displaced Rohingyas based in Bangladesh camp areas from WBSU and earlier taught at Basanti Devi College, Kolkata. Her research interests are in gender studies and identity politics.

Dr Srikanth Kondapalli is the Dean of the School of International Studies and a Professor of Chinese studies at Jawaharlal Nehru University, New Delhi. He was Chairman of the Centre for East Asian Studies, SIS, JNU from 2008-10, 2012-14, 2016-18, 2018-20 and in 2022. He is also the Ministry of Defence Chair Professor for the Chair of Excellence in Defence and Strategic Studies. He is educated in Chinese studies in India and China with a PhD in Chinese Studies. He learnt the Chinese language at Beijing Language & Culture University and was a post-Doctoral Visiting Fellow at People's University, Beijing, from 1996-98. He was a Visiting Professor at National Chengchi University, Taipei, in 2004, a Visiting Fellow at China Institute of Contemporary International Relations, Beijing, in May 2007, an Honorary Professor at Shandong University, Jinan in 2009, 2011, 2013, and 2015, 2016, 2017 and 2019; at Jilin University, Changchun in 2014 and at the Yunnan University of Finance and Economics, Kunming in 2016 and 2017, a Non-Resident Senior Fellow at People's University since 2014 and a Fellow at Salzburg Global Seminar in 2010. He is a distinguished fellow at several think tanks, including Vivekananda International Foundation and Institute for Peace and Conflict Studies. He is the Editor of JNU SIS *International Studies* Journal (being published by Sage).

Prof Swapna Bhattacharya is an MA Sanskrit (Visva-Bharati), PhD, South Asian History (Heidelberg), former Professor and Head, Department of South & Southeast Asian Studies, Calcutta University (Director, CSSEAS, 2003-2005), specialised herself in Myanmar (including Language), Bangladesh, Northeast India and German History. She taught (1986-2017) South & S.E. Asian History, Politics and Religion, and lectured in the Departments of History and Buddhist Studies at the Institute of Foreign Policy Studies and P.G. Course in Human Rights.

Toe Aung is a Chevening Scholar studying at the University of Essex, United Kingdom. He specialises in human rights, international human rights law and transitional justice in the Southeast Asia context.

Amb (Dr) V S Seshadri joined the Indian Foreign Service in 1978 and served in several diplomatic posts. He was India's Ambassador to Myanmar from 2010 to 2013. Dr Seshadri has contributed a number of research articles on trade and other international economic issues, as well as on Myanmar. He is currently associated as a Senior Fellow with the Delhi Policy Group.

Brig Vinod Anand has served in the army for over 36 years, a significant part of which he has spent in North East India. He was posted in Nagaland, Manipur and Mizoram, where he dealt with issues relating to countering insurgency along the borders with Myanmar. He has authored a number of papers on issues relating to Myanmar military and bilateral relations. He has also written papers on defence cooperation with the ASEAN countries as also on geopolitics and developments in South China. He has authored several monographs and book chapters on Central Asia and the countries of South Asia. In addition, he has authored edited volumes on defence planning and geopolitics. He has been earlier a Senior Fellow at the Institute of Defence Studies and Analysis in New Delhi and later at the United Services Institution in New Delhi. Presently, he is a Senior Fellow with Vivekananda International Foundation.

Win Maw is a Senior Officer at an international NGO based in Yangon, Myanmar. He holds a Master's degree in Public Administration. He keenly observes political developments in Myanmar, particularly in areas bordering India and China.

Yadanar Soe is a community development worker and scholar from Myanmar. She works for civil society strengthening, improving public services through evidence-based policy advocacy, governance, and challenging structural inequalities.

SECTION ONE

Political Organisation of the Country

1

Nuances of Power-sharing, Conflict and Consensus in the Light of *Dhamma*: Myanmar at the Crossroad

Dr Swapna Bhattacharya

ABSTRACT

In the recent as well as in the distant past, Myanmar experienced similar political crises as it faces today; but overcame the hurdle "to start anew". This became possible due to the unique inner strength of this wonderful country, where conflict leads to consensus with the help of the Army, Sangha and civil society. Though through different ways, the two major and closest/trusted neighbours, India and China, contributed immensely, for without a strong and stable Myanmar, peace will be in danger in Asia. The benefits of socio-political advancements, economic openings and constitutional reforms [new constitution of 2008, replacing the old one of 1974) through the SLORC (1988)–SPDC (1997)]-USDP 2010 (Union Solidarity and Development Party successor to the Union Solidarity and Development Association) reached not only the Army (Tatmadaw), elites of society, political parties, students, intellectuals, Buddhist monks and Buddhist welfare organisations, urban-based people from the world of trade, but also common people from villages and beyond. I could witness this change during my several academic visits to the country between the years 2005 and 2016, placing in contrast to my first-ever visit in the year 1995. At every stage in the history of Myanmar, the Army (Tatmadaw) played an immensely constructive role in the state-building process; indeed, the formation of BSPP—Burma Socialist Programme Party—and the drafting of the 1974 Constitution would not have been possible otherwise in those turbulent days of the high insurgency. The transition from U Nu government to General Ne Win-led military government in 1962 happened to be relatively "peaceful", when compared to similar events elsewhere. The 1945-born BNA (Burma National Army) had its genesis in the BIA (Burma Independence Army) and the BDA (Burma Defence Army). The chapter will explain with examples (short description of Subhash Chandra Bose-led INA movement) how

Myanmar, in its long journey of state building, found a trusted strategic-spiritual partner in the Indian people with whom they shared a common perception of the protection of Dhamma, the righteous path and moral principles. Taking the period from the 13th CE (Mongol invasion of Pagan 1287) to the 18th CE (1784 Rakhine conquest by king Bodawpaya of Konbaung dynasty), this chapter further address how powerful Myanmar kings with their bases in the dry zone/tattabhumi (Upper Myanmar/Upper Burma), the Suvannabhumi, maritime-trade based Lower Burma (Pegu or Hamsavati) and the littoral Rakhine (Arakan) maintained strong armies which caused sleepless nights to rulers in Siam (Thailand) in the East, Manipur on the West and China in the North. All these may sound ludicrous today, yet, the spiritual-military achievements of kings like Dhammazedi (1472-92), Min Kyi Nyo (1486-1531), Bayinnaung (1551-1581), Thalun (1635; Thalun moved from Pegu to Ava) and the first king, Alaungpaya, of Konbaung dynasty (Konbaung dynasty 1752-1885) have to be read carefully to appreciate the formidable strategic potential of the pre-colonial Myanmar State with its strong rural economic foundation and external trade. This chapter also discusses the history of the Rakhine expansion (1430-1630). The Buddhist virtues of dana (donation), metta (loving-kindness, Sanskrit Maitri) and Upekkha (equanimity) constantly contributed towards the legitimisation of royal power and expansion of the Army. While such a process of "State from above" is a universal phenomenon, in the state-building process "from below", the Myanmar monks have left the noblest example of wisdom and sacrifice unparalleled in the world.

Understanding Myanmar

This chapter, simple and descriptive, is an attempt to narrate a few little-addressed aspects of the State in pre-colonial Myanmar from the Indian perspective. The presentation here is narrative in nature. A detailed discussion of socio-political and constitutional developments as they took shape in recent times—up to 2012—can be found in one of my recent articles.[1] My latest book, *Rabindranath Tagore and Myanmar: India's Look East Policy and India-Myanmar Relations*,[2] may help readers understand how Gurudev Tagore, who visited Myanmar in 1916, 1924, and 1927, respectively, deeply admired the country's liberal societal structure, based on the tradition of Theravada Buddhism. Gandhiji and Dr. B. R. Ambedkar, among many other thinkers and statesmen of our country, held the same respect and love for the people of Myanmar.

During the 1950s, Myanmar was one of the most front-ranking nations in Asia, and the world at large, respected for her neutrality, anti-imperialist posture and commitment to Theravada Buddhism.[3] This tradition of Myanmar's foreign policy, taking Asian partners like India, ASEAN countries, China, Japan and others into her fold, continue with the same magnanimity. Indeed, Myanmar has a balanced relationship of mutual respect with all countries near and far. In the past, Myanmar had to cope with several political crises but overcame the hurdle "to start anew". This became possible due to the unique inner strength of this wonderful country, where conflict leads to consensus[4] involving the Army, Sangha and civil society.

The benefits of economic openings and constitutional reforms visible from 1990 onwards reached not only the Army (*Tatmadaw*) and elites of society or political parties but also common people from various professions and associations. I witnessed the changes during my several visits to the country between the years 1995 to 2016. At every stage, government institutions, major Buddhist institutions and the Army (*Tatmadaw*) played an immensely constructive role in the state-building process; indeed, the formation of the BSPP (Burma Socialist Programme Party) and the drafting of the 1974 Constitution would not have been possible in those turbulent days of the high insurgency. The transition from U Nu government to General Ne Win-led military government in 1962 happened to be relatively "peaceful", when compared to similar events elsewhere.

The ancestors of the Myanmar people (Burmese) were not only the Pyus. There were other branches, like Saks, Kadus, Kanrans, etc., about whom many sources are available.[5] On account of their origin from the *Sakya* clan, they were highly revered in the entire Hindu-Buddhist realm. After all, Buddha belonged to the lineage of the Sakyas. The first king of Myanmar, Abhiraja, who founded Tagaung in 850 B.C., came from Kapilavastu, the home of the Sakyas. Archaeological remains of the Pyu civilisation (Beikthano, Halin Sri ksetra) speak of the existence of a highly urbanised culture at the crossroad connecting China with India.

The seventh-century Chinese pilgrim, Hsuan-Tsang, mentioned Sri Ksetra as a prosperous Buddhist kingdom. These ancestors of the Myanmar people (Burmese) believed in specific values which were deeply rooted in Theravada Buddhism of very pure nature. However, at the same time, with the increasing popularity of the urban trade generated Mahayana faith, liberal social norms penetrated into early Myanmar society. Immigration from the coastal Indian trade centres,[6] located in modern Indian states of Tamil Nadu, Andhra Pradesh and Telangana, continued with the increasing popularity of the worship of Gods and Goddesses of the Hindu-Buddhist pantheon. The coastal state of Orissa also played an extremely significant role in such people-to-people relations between India and Myanmar.

The people also adopted a rule-based society, as portrayed in the Myanmar *Dhammathats*.[7] The popularity of Lord Vishnu, as reflected in the art and architecture of ancient Pagan, shows the degree of identification of the Myanmar kings with the universal element of the *Bhakti* cult. In contrast, the popularity of stories from the *Mahabharata*, the *Ramayana* and the *Bhagavatgita*[8] inspired them to fight *Dharamjuddhas* with remarkable dignity and courage.

To appreciate the spirit of consensus, one has to be familiar with the Buddhist mindset of the people and the pluralist nature of Myanmar (Burmese) society. There is a saying, "To be a Buddhist is to be a Burmese."[9] Not only pagodas, but the country also has numerous temples, mosques and churches everywhere. The history of Myanmar at every stage has left an unprecedented imprint of constructive indifference, which can be explained by the term *Upekhha* or equanimity. This helps an individual as much as institutions to overcome "extreme" or difficult situations. Such practices contribute to neutralising the differences within society through dialogue. However, when it comes to an unwanted encroachment into her territory, vigorous measures seemed to be the only way to preserve internal peace and secure the border.

There are four keywords in the title of this chapter: Power-sharing, Conflict, Consensus and *Dhamma*. The "shared-power" derives its strength from the "shared value", which then operates critically, leading to a national consensus. Buddhist knowledge community provided the superstructure built based on the paradigm of the pivotal role that Asoka and Gotama Buddha, played in the domain of kingship. Myanmar kings were perceived as protectors of *Dhamma*, and therefore called Dhammaraja.[10] The traditional concept of "World Conqueror" or universal ruler found expression in the title *Cakkavatti.*

The traditional Myanmar administration had a strong base of local government. Indeed, British rule (1886–1948) superimposed a central authority, creating a vacuum in the politico-religious space, that is, the monarchy-patronised Sangha. The virtues of *metta* (loving-kindness), *upekkha* (equanimity) and *dana*[11] (sharing of wealth) provided and still today provide the people of Myanmar with a unique identity.

As has been made clear, the present exercise is to share my very impartial view of the history of the State of Myanmar, which carries a very rich legacy of continuity of dynastic rule. From a methodological viewpoint, instead of "Upper Myanmar-Lower Myanmar dualism" in the form of "Bamar-Mon"/*Tattabhumi, Suvannabhumi* (parched land / Dry zone-Golden land) dualism,[12] or, for that matter, "Bamar-Rakhine dualism", or even "Bamar-non Bamar dualism" in the form of "Mainland-Frontier Area dualism", I see the state formation as a continuum, a process, where the structure is multi-centred, competitive, but not always combative.

Going through the history of Myanmar, one finds many examples where kings forgave defeated enemies, returned their lands, or even integrated erstwhile enemies into the army or administration. This happened in the case of Manipur-Upper Myanmar's historical intercourse through war and peace. Indeed, with the disintegrated Shan groups, similar and various other integration processes became more a norm than the exception. Having worked for many years on the state formation in the Romano-Germanic world, one can see many analogies between Europe, for example, post-Carolingian Germany and Italy and Asia, medieval Myanmar and India.[13] Politico-spiritual process of legitimisation through symbols of worship in pilgrimage centres and the act of getting hold of images/symbols—like worship of the Mahamuni or possession of the Holy Lance (German Heilige Lanze), writings of Eulogies (Sanskrit *Prasastis,* or in the context of Myanmar, *Ayedawbon Chronicle*) under royal patronage[14]—made the very foundation of a pre-modern state stronger in all its moorings.

Writing and rewriting chronicles, purifying and reforming the Order became a routine or even compulsion. As a result, the masses with various ethno-linguistic origins were "impressed" and integrated rather than feeling "conquered". The Konbaung dynasty continued this tradition with a "Look West Policy" (towards India). The constant change of their capital was due to pressure from the North. If one follows the history of colonial struggle[15] one can see this continued, despite tremendous provocations by colonial rulers. Continuity in this relation has been shown excellently by Rajiv Bhatia[16] in his book, *India Myanmar Relations: Changing Contours.*

I have followed my method of selecting sources, all of which are secondary sources written in English. The books published by the Myanmar Historical Commission bought fresh and hardly-addressed facts. My academic interactions over almost three decades with many scholars, diplomats, members of think tanks, scholarly monks, and students from the universities of Dagon and Yangon in Myanmar have considerably enriched my understanding of their country. Another enriching experience has been my academic dialogue on *Dhamma* with senior monks of Myanmar origin who settled in various Myanmar monasteries across our country.[17] Equally enriching were my visits to various archaeological sites across Myanmar, which stand witness to an age-old relationship of immense value.

Pre-colonial State in Myanmar: Some Narratives of Conflict and Consensus

Driven by the cold and dry weather of Tibet and Nepal, the Tibeto-Burman people of the great Sino-Tibetan family of languages came down to settle in the fertile lands of the rivers Irrawaddy, Chindwin, Salween, Sittang, Yangon, Great Tenasserim and Kaladan. Not only the Pyus, but it was also the Mons, who were earlier called *Telangs,* who had a significant share in making the great Pagan Empire.

Widely known is the story of the Pagan king, Anawrahta or Aniruddha[18] (1044-1077), his conquest of the Mon kingdom of Thaton (1057) in Lower Myanmar and his initiation to pure Theravada Buddhism. His successors like Kyanzittha (1084-1111), Alaungsithu (1111-67) and Narapatisithu (1173-1210) contributed brilliantly to building a pluralist-centralized state in the very heart of Asia. However, the Pagan Empire on the bank of the Irrawaddy River fell mainly due to the invasion of the Mongols, who had already conquered Yunnan in the 1250s and subsequently directed their expedition towards Pagan from the 1270s onwards.

The Shans, who belong to the Tai group (Tai-Chinese linguistic family) and ancestors of the Shans of Myanmar, inspired by the Mongol conquest, proceeded toward Pagan. Three Shan brothers, named Yazathingyan, Athinkhaya and Thihathu, ruled over three governorships of Pagan—Sagaing, Pinya and Myin Saing. The Shan kingdom of Tali–Fu was so powerful that it came very close to "overthrowing the Chinese Tang dynasty"; equally formidable were Nanchao and Ngai–Lao, who "often raided the Chinese in the old days.[19] So, it is no wonder the Pagan rulers had to adjust to the two formidable rivals, the Mongols and the Shans.

In 1364, a leader named Thadominbya built Ava (Inwa) near Sagaing, located at the confluence of the Irrawaddy and Myitnge rivers. This location enabled the Ava kingdom to control the richest rice-growing region, Kyaukse.[20] The Ava rulers Minkyiswa Sawke (1368-1401), Mingaung the First (1401-22), Narapati the Great (1443-69), and Mingaung the Second (1481-1502), undoubtedly had a huge share in making a strong centralised state structure.

The Mon-dominated, *Suvannabhumi* (*Ramannadesha*) was a major commercial centre in Lower Myanmar. The Mons belonged to the Mon-Khmer family of languages. Their co-brethren are found in various parts of modern South and Southeast Asia, Cambodia in particular. In India, they are represented by the Munda group of central and eastern India. The Mon king, Binnya U, established

Pegu in 1369. His son Razadarit's (1385-1423) assertive rule brought three Mon countries—Pegu, Moulmein and Bassein—together. Martaban and Syriam were the two other major ports. In 1363, the Siamese forced Binnya U to leave Martaban.

The disintegration of the Mon kingdom of Dvaravati in central Siam was caused by the Tai–Chinese, though the Siamese belong to the same ethno-linguistic family. The famous commercial centre, Pegu, is almost identical to the name of the famous Mon king, Dhammazedi (1472-92), who was actually a monk. But, at the request of the Mon queen, Shin Saw Bu, he took off his yellow robe and accepted the throne of Pegu. Prior to it, a king named Binnyakyan (1450-53) had ruled before Queen Shin Saw Bu.

The Shwedagon Pagoda attracted special attention under these rulers. The height of the Pagoda was raised repeatedly. Myanmar looked at Sri Lanka for necessary and timely inspiration. Even a visit to Sri Lanka became urgent. A group of monks were sent there, ordained after having a dip in the holy river of Kalyani. On their return to Pegu, *Kalyani Sima*[21] was established. The Kalyani Inscription of 1479 stands witnesses to this pilgrimage. This major commercial centre (Pegu) remained with its national and international glory under the reign of Binnaran I (1426-46), Binnyaran II (1492-1526), and Takayutpi (1526-39).

A major blow came over Pegu when king Tabinshweti (1531-50) of the Toungoo royal family took the city, making it a part of his kingdom. His predecessor Min Kyi Nyo (1486-1531), after securing recognition from Chiengmai, had already consolidated his power over the capital at Toungoo. Unless the Shans could be checked, nothing could be done. Therefore, he captured Kyaungbya, killing the Shan Governor. The naming of his capital "Dwayawadi"[22] perhaps indicates his keen interest in using the legacy of the lost kingdom of Mons, *Dvaravati*.

Tying of the marital knot with Ava Princess legitimised his control over the economically most coveted canal area of Kyaukse and numerous villages in and around the Ava-Toungoo area. He died in 1531. This kind of power struggle continued through vigorous military expeditions. As a result, Bayinnaung (1551-1581) could capture Ava (1555) from the Shans. Afterwards, defeating Mons (1566), he built a new city called *Hanthawaddy* (Sanskrit Hamsavati). The Bayinnaung recaptured the Tai kingdom of Ayuthaya (1569), making Siam a vassal state of his Empire.[23]

To quote Nicholas Tarling from his *The History of Southeast Asia*, "guns were successfully integrated into the infantry and elephant units."[24] In the politico-spiritual sphere, Bayinnaung's act of donating *hti* (umbrella) to Shwedagon and securing the tooth relic of Buddha from Sri Lanka awarded him a very special position. After his death in 1581, one of his sons and crown prince, Nandabayin, became king and ruled from 1581 to 1599.

Let me give a short description of the Second Ava Dynasty, which is often called "Restored Toungoo Dynasty". There was a *myosa*-ship called Nyaungyan in the central part of Meiktila district. The Lord of this *myosa*, Nyaungyan Min (1600-1605), became the first ruler of this second Ava dynasty. The word "myosa" literally means "the eater of the town",[25] indicating someone who benefits from the share of his fiefdom by appointing agents. There were challenges on the way to achieving unification of the entire country and bringing it under a single umbrella in order to combat several emerging power centres.

However, Naungyan Min's son, Anaukpetlun[26] (1605-28), by virtue of his military might, was able to pacify Toungoo, Prome and Syriam. The port of Syriam at this point in time was under the control of a Portuguese adventurer, Philip De Brito.[27] He was so ambitious that he dreamt of "conquering", not only the port city of Syriam but also the entire country. Remaining in touch with the friars representing the Archbishop of Goa, De Brito went on looting pagodas, plundering the wealth and casting the bronze from the bells into cannons. The strategic friendship that De Brito made with the king of Toungoo, Natshinnaung, could not help him. For his ambitious plan of becoming king of the whole land (Myanmar), he had to pay the price of his life. Natshinnaung was also executed. Anaukpetlun was not against Christianity as such, but was against the idea of conversion and pillage of pagodas.

King Thalun of this dynasty was crowned at Pagu as king in 1629. After moving back to Ava in 1635, he received another coronation. Interestingly, Ava bore the Indian name *Ratanapura* meaning "the city of jewels". After all, Myanmar is a country of gems and jade, besides forests, minerals and rice. Thalun's rule made further progress in centralising the already consolidated power structure and maximising human resources.

Of various social (hereditary) categories or groups like *ahmudan, kyun athi* and others, the most important were the *ahmudan*—crown-service groups or 'carrier of obligation'.[28] Through recruitment and restructuring of the *ahmudan*, a disciplined unit arose out of the infantry. The *athi* were free servicemen. But, they could be called to offer their services as 'military auxiliaries',[29] if the state required. The cavalry was also rearranged on the basis of their respective regional attachment. The Myosa system was exercised at the central and provincial levels. Steps were taken by the Second Ava or Restored Toungoo dynasty to reform Sangha, integrating it into the State polity and economy. Monks were to follow their Vinaya rules strictly; after all, Myanmar is famous for Vinayadhara monks.

In the delta region, we see a very short revival of Mons. The legitimacy of the Mon king named Smim Htaw Buddhaketu was derived from the concept of "Future Buddha" (*minlaung*). The Kaunghmudaw Pagoda in Sagaing was built on the model of Sri Lanka's Mahacetiya. Under king Alaungpaya (1752-1760), the country saw the last battle with Mons. The word "Yangon" means "where victory was achieved". In many ways, the Alungapaya or Konbaung dynasty laid the foundation of post-colonial Myanmar.[30] They ruled with the same power of legitimacy and consensus as the Myanmar kings had ruled earlier. Mahabandula, the great general, fought so bravely, yet Arakan (Rakhine State) and Tenasserim were annexed, and the humiliating Treaty of Yandabo was signed in 1826.

In the period between the First 1824 and the Third 1886 War (Anglo-Burmese Wars), a massive transformation of the country was visible. Society became more conscious of living in a rule-based world, rather than in conflict and chaos. Sangha–Royalty relations revived with the active patronage of the kings. Myanmar kings (from Mindon Min to the last king Thibaw), started opening doors to the West, including Britain.

Contact with India, the land where *punnya* (merit) could be acquired and knowledge could be widened, became the most desired destination for drawing the strategy to combat the "common enemy". In 1829, King Bagyidaw appointed a committee to write a chronicle of the kings of Myanmar. This was obviously to remind all concerned about the great tradition of continuity in power, knowledge and wisdom. The committee consisted of 'learned monks, learned Brahmans, and learned ministers'.[31] The outcome is known as *The Glass Palace Chronicle of the Kings of Burma.*

The Rakhine State (Arakan) of Myanmar has a brilliant history of continuity in Theravada Buddhism and rich cultural life of thousands of years.[32] At the same time, many traditions like Mahamuni worship and Mahamuni Mela and reform,[33] like the one by Samgharaja Saramedha (19th century) carry the legacy of a spiritual bond between the Buddhists of India, Bangladesh and Myanmar.[34] The history of the Rakhine expansion over Chittagong covers the period between 1430 and 1630. There was a strong provincial government in Chittagong functioning smoothly under the administration of the Rakhine Myanmar kings. They used the title *Ánauk Bhuran*—meaning 'king of the West 'on their trilingual coins: Rakhine, Bengali and Persian.[35]

That there was a friendly relationship between the Rakhine kings and kings of the Ava dynasty can be read in the encounter between Man Khari (1434-1458) and king Narapati of Ava (1443-1469) when both met at the Rakhine Yoma and reassured each other to remain committed to their mutual friendship.[36] By following very well-thought diplomacy, the Rakhine kings Man Pa (1531-1553), Man Raja Kri (1570-1630), and Man Phalaung (1571-1593) put up a sound resistance to the Mughals so that the Mughals could not capture the port of Chittagong. The same skilled diplomacy, cultural policy and liberal practices displayed by the Ava-based rulers were visible in the Rakhine-Myanmar kingdom when the kings patronised the Bengali talents at their court.[37] When king Bodawpaya (1784) came to Mrauk-U and took the Mahamuni image to install it in his new capital, Mandalay, he must have had many reasons. The First Anglo-Burmese was fought on this front in the years 1824-1826.

Concluding Remarks

The history of the YMBA (Young Men Buddhist Association), GCBA (General Council of Burmese Association), GCSS (General Council of Sangha Sametggyi), and the Saya San Rebellion of 1930-32 is widely known.[38] As I have shown in my book *India Myanmar Relations 1886-1948*, the members of the Jugantar, Anushilan and Ghadr party affiliates and associates drew major inspiration from this non-compromising spirit of Myanmar nationalism. The *Dobama-Asiyone* or the Thakin movement started from the 1930s onwards[39] and also had a great impact on the Indian nationalists; Netaji Subhas Chandra Bose, who made Yangon the centre of his struggle for a free India, was one of them. The Japan-returned Thirty Comrades (Bogye Aung San, U Nu, U Ne win and others) remained united and continued their mission to get early freedom. There appeared to be many problems in reaching a consensus due to differences in ideological orientation.[40]

The birth of the Anti-Fascist People's Freedom League (AFPFL) in 1944 broadened the scope of ideological accommodation, but the global political situation was getting ever so complex. As a result, the original plan of a kind of "coordinated struggle" of the INA (Indian National Army) and BIA (Burma Independence Army) by leaders like Dr. Ba Maw and Subhas Chandra Bose, perhaps in agreement with Bogye Aung San, suffered a big blow. Born in 1941 in Bangkok, the BIA was renamed 1942 the BDA (Burma Defence Army) in 1942, but it was again renamed the BNA (Burma National Army) in 1945.

The changed strategy of Bogye Aung San and his colleagues was to leave the Japanese side by extending a hand of cooperation with the British forces, and the government was only strategically planned to get early independence without any pre-conditions, for example, joining the Commonwealth. It is interesting to read in Maung Aung Myoe's[41] profile of *Tatmadaw* within the background of this extremely challenging phase of the 1940s.[42] Extremely bitter experiences of World War II taught the people of Myanmar to have a strong defence policy with a strong *Tatmadaw*.

In the midst of all these challenges, the guiding spirit of *metta* between the Myanmar people and Indians living in Myanmar was visible as we see no clashes between the BNA and the INA.[43] We have much to learn from the people of Myanmar and their history. The knowledge world is an important component of the *Act East* Policy,[44] in which Myanmar plays the most pivotal role. My recent article on the exchange of knowledge between the universities of Calcutta and Yangon[45] may be interesting in this context. The time has come for us to look at Myanmar as a strong economic-academic partner placing our two countries in the oceanic (maritime space) perspective as well as overland connection. The study of the "lost" ethno-linguistic–cultural contact between Myanmar and India should be invigorated. My short essay included in a Document on *Act East Policy* published by the Syama Prasad Mookerjee Research Foundation, New Delhi, to celebrate 20 years of Mekong Ganga Cooperation[46] may be of some interest in this regard.

ENDNOTES

1. Bhattacharya, Swapna. "Myanmar's Own Way to Democracy, Peace and Reconciliation: Introspective Observations from a Friend of Myanmar." In *Searching for Non-Western Roots of Conflict Resolution: Discourses, Norms and Case Studies*, edited by Shantanu Chakrabarti (New Delhi: Knowledge World Pvt. Ltd., 2013): 138-150.
2. Bhattacharya, Swapna. *Rabindranath Tagore and Myanmar: India's Act East Policy and India–Myanmar Relations* (Kolkata: Firma KLM Pvt. Ltd., 2019).
3. Bhattacharya, Swapna. "History of Buddhism in Myanmar: Interpretation from Indian Perspective." *Journal of the Asiatic Society of Bengal* 47, no. 4 (2005): 65-81.
4. Pye, Lucien W. *Politics, Personality and Nation Building: Burma's Search for Identity* (New Haven and London: Yale University Press, 1962).
5. Bhattacharya, Swapna. "Pre-colonial Myanmar: Narratives of State Power, Symbols, Languages and Norms", Sectional President's Address. In *Proceedings of the Indian History Congress 77th session,* (University of Kerala, Thiruvananthapuram 2016): 766-776. Aligarh: Indian History Congress, 2017.
6. Ba Han. "Emergence of the Burmese Nation." *Journal of the Burma Research Society* 48, no. 2 (Dec. 1965): 25-38.
7. Aung Than Tun. "Myanmar Dhammathats: Paradigm of Social Framework." In *Texts and*

Contexts in Southeast Asia Part II. Proceedings of the Texts and Contexts in Southeast Conference 12-14 December 2001: 101-125. Yangon: Universities Historical Research Centre, 2003.

8. Charney, Michael W. *Powerful learning and the Throne in Burma's last Dynasty 1752-1885*, Ann Arbor: Centre for South & Southeast Asian Studies, The University of Michigan 2009.
9. Bechert, Heinz. "To be a Burmese is to be a Buddhist: Buddhism in Burma." In *The World of Buddhism*, edited by Heinz Bechert and Richard Combrich, 147-158. London: Thames & Husdon, 1993.
10. Charney, Michael W. *Powerful learning and the Throne in Burma's last Dynasty 1752-1885*, Ann Arbor: Centre for South & Southeast Asian Studies, The University of Michigan 2009, 201.
11. Spiro, Melford E. *Buddhism and Society: A Great Tradition and its* Burmese *Vicissitudes* Berkeley: University of California Press, 1970.
12. Aung-Thwin, Michael and Maitrii Aung Thwin. *A History of Myanmar since Ancient Times: Traditions and Transformations* (London: Reaktion Books, 2012): 123-127.
13. Bhattacharya, Swapna. "Comparative diplomatic in the Latin West and early medieval Bengal: a brief Overview." In *Copper Parchment & Stone: studies in the Sources for Landholding and Lordship in Early Medieval Bengal and Scotland*, edited by John Reuben Davies and Swapna Bhattacharya (Glasgow: University of Glasgow, 2019): 138-150.
14. Thaw Kaung, "Bayinnaung in the *Hanthawadi Hsinbyumya Shin Ayedawbon* Chronicle." In *Essays in Commemoration of the Golden Jubilee of the Myanmar Historical Commission.*, 1955-2005: 22-43. Yangon: Myanmar Historical Commission, Ministry of Education, Union of Myanmar, 2005.
15. Bhattacharya, Swapna. *India-Myanmar Relations 1886-1948* (Kolkata: K.P. Bagchi & Company, 2007).
16. Bhatia, Rajiv. *India-Myanmar Relations: Changing Contours* (New Delhi: Routledge, 2016).
17. Bhattacharya, Swapna. "Regional Representation of Myanmar Buddhism in Northern, Eastern and North Eastern India: Trends, Traditions and Future Course." In *On the Trail of Buddhism in Asia: Reflections on Tradition and Practice,* edited by Suchandana Chatterjee and Susmita Bhattacharya (N. Delhi: Pentagon Press, 2016): 12-39.
18. Stadtner, Donald M. *Secret Sites of Burma: Myth and Folklore in an Evolving Spiritual Realm* (Bangkok: River Books, 2011).
19. Sai Aung Tun, "The British Administration in the Shan States." In *Essays in Commemoration of the Golden Jubilee of the Myanmar Historical Commission*, 1955-2005 (Yangon: Myanmar Historical Commission, Ministry of Education, Union of Myanmar, 2005): 228.
20. Aung-Thwin, Michael and Maitrii Aung Thwin. *A History of Myanmar since Ancient Times: Traditions and Transformations* (London: Reaktion Books, 2012).
21. Ray, Niharranjan. *An Introduction to The Theravada Buddhism in Burma: A Study of Indo-Burmese Historical and Cultural Relations from the Earliest Times to The British Conquest* (Bangkok: Orchid Press, 2002).
22. Harvey, G.E. *History of Burma: From the Earliest Times to March 10 1824: The Beginning of the English Conquest* (London: Frank Cass & Co. Ltd., 1967): 124.
23. Seekins, Donald M. *Historical Dictionary of Burma (Myanmar)* (Lanham: Rowman & Littlefield, 2017): 106.
24. Tarling, Nicholas. *The Cambridge History of Southeast Asia*. Vol. 1. (Cambridge: Cambridge University Press, 1992): 390.
25. Taylor, Robert H. *The State in Myanmar* (London: Foundation Books, 2009): 27.
26. Harvey, G.E. *History of Burma*, 185.
27. Khin Maung Nyunt. *Selected Writings of Dr. Khin Maung Nyunt* (Yangon: Myanmar Historical Commission, 2004): 84.

28. Thant Myint U. *The Making of Modern Burma* (Cambridge: Cambridge University, 2001): 32.
29. Taylor, Robert H. *The State in Myanmar*, 33.
30. Desai, W.S. *A Pageant of Burmese History* (Calcutta: Orient Longmans Ltd., 1961).
31. Pe Maung Tin and G. H. Luce translated. *The Glass Palace Chronicle of the Kings of Burma*, translated by Rangoon: Rangoon University Press (1960), 9.
32. Maung Htin Aung, *A History of Burma* (N. York: Columbia University Press, 1967): 197.
33. Bhattacharya, Swapna. "Buddhism in Arakan: Some Observations." In *Script Identity Region: A Study in Sylhet Nagri*," edited by Anuradha Chanda, 63-78. Kolkata: Dey's Publishing & Maulana Abul Kalam Azad Institute of Asian Studies (MAKAIAS), 2013.
34. Bhattacharya, Swapna. *The Rakhine State (Arakan) of Myanmar: Interrogating History, Culture and Conflict* (N. Delhi: Manohar & MAKAIAS Kolkata): 2015.
35. Bhattacharya, Swapna. *The Rakhine State (Arakan) of Myanmar*, 27.
36. Leider, Jaques. "On Arakanese Territorial Expansion: Origins, Context, Means and Practices." In *The Maritime Frontier of Burma: Exploring Political, Cultural and Commercial Interaction in the Indian Ocean World, 1220-1800*, edited by Jos Gommans and Jaques Leider. KNAW: Royal Netherlands Academy of Arts and Sciences (Amsterdam: KITLV Press, Leiden, 2002): 130.
37. Bhattacharya, Swapna. "Myth and History of Bengali Identity in Arakan." In *Maritime Frontier of Burma*, edited by Jaques Leider and Jos Gommans, 199-212.. KNAW: Royal Netherlands Academy of Arts and Sciences (Amsterdam: KITLV Press, Leiden, 2002).
38. Bhattacharya, Swapna. *India Burma Relations 1886-1948,* chapters 5 & 6.
39. Maung Maung, *Burma and General Ne Win* (London: Asia Publishing House, 1925): 66.
40. "Political Situation in Myanmar from World War II to 1947." In *Myanmar Politics 1958-1962*, Yangon: Myanmar Historical Commission, Ministry of Education, Union of Myanmar vol. 1 (2006): 5-9.
41. Maung Aung Myoe. *Building the Tatmadaw: Myanmar Armed Forces since* 1948 (Singapore: Institute of Southeast Asian Studies, 2009): 59-62.
42. U Thet Tun. *Selected writings of retired Ambassador U Thet Tun* (Yangon: Myanmar Historical Commission, 65-82: 2004).
43. Bhattacharya, Swapna. *India-Myanmar Relations 1886-1948*, 346.
44. Ganguly, Anirban. "Modi and India's Civilizational Quest." In *The Modi Doctrine: New Paradigms in India's Foreign Policy,* edited by Anirban Ganguly, Vijaya Chauthaiwale and Uttam Kumar Sinha, 183-191. New Delhi: Wisdom Tree, in association with Syama Prasad Mookerjee Research Foundation, 2016.
45. Bhattacharya, Swapna. "Pali and Buddhist Studies at the Universities of Calcutta and Yangon: A Mixed Narrative of Knowledge-Sharing, Colonial Patronage and Linguistic Nationalism in India and Myanmar." *Bengal Past and Present*, 138 (2019): 1-17
46. *Vision of Act East & 20 Years of Mekong-Ganga Cooperation [MCG]* 20 July 2020. *Webinar Outcome Document* (Syama Prasad Mookerjee Research Foundation, New Delhi).

2

The Importance of Being Aung San Suu Kyi

Amb Rajiv Bhatia

ABSTRACT

This chapter attempts to decipher the political impact, moulded by a strange mélange of magic, on the people and the military's distrust of Aung San's daughter. Without understanding the powerful Aung San Suu Kyi phenomenon, it is impossible to internalise the complex dynamics of Myanmar politics in the past four decades. This analysis sheds light on her difficult relationship with three generations of military leaders—Ne Win, Than Shwe, and Min Aung Hlaing—and explain why and how the lady rose, fell, and rose again to end up in army detention (February 2021) and eventually solitary confinement (June 2022). In this critical examination of Suu Kyi's pragmatic approach towards the army and the other stakeholders in the polity, her lineage, political philosophy, leadership style, and personality flaws comes under objective scrutiny. Another segment of the essay analyses the external perceptions of Suu Kyi, Myanmar's best-known political figure in modern history, covering her fluctuating equations with the West and Asia particularly. A sub-section also touches on how India connected with her—and she with India. The overarching purpose is to evaluate Aung San Suu Kyi's role so far and reflect on her future and that of democracy in Myanmar.

Introduction

For an in-depth exploration of the Myanmar polity today, understanding the nature and impact of the role of Daw Aung San Suu Kyi (ASSK) is of critical importance. The last phase of Ne Win's rule and post-Ne Win decades in Burma's history has been moulded by the perennial conflict between the Army and the people. The latter, always stamped by diversity and ethnic differences, made it clear nevertheless that they desired to determine their own destiny and political governance. This has not been acceptable to the Army leadership, stretching from

General Ne Win to Senior General Min Aung Hlaing. This epic conflict which began in 1987 and continues unabated in August 2022 (at the time of writing) features a central figure representing the bulk of the people of Myanmar. Every time they got an opportunity to vote their preferences freely – 1990, 2012, 2015, and 2020, they chose the ASSK-led National League for Democracy (NLD). Therefore, she is vital to comprehending developments in the past three and half decades and determining what awaits the nation in the next five years.

"Suu Kyi's time in politics," wrote Rodion Ebbighausen, "has been full of contradictions, surprising twists and disappointed expectations."[1] The rise, fall, resurrection, return to detention again, and future of the most famous personality from Myanmar offer a fascinating study. On 15 August 2022, Aung San Suu Kyi facing house arrest/imprisonment/solitary confinement since 1 February 2021, was sentenced to another six years in prison after a Myanmar court found her guilty of corruption cases. A press report cryptically commented, "The 77-year-old veteran leader of Myanmar's opposition to military rule has been charged with at least 18 offences ranging from graft to election violation, carrying combined maximum jail terms of nearly 190 years."[2] Yes, the figure 190 years has been quoted correctly!

So, who is she—a true heroine or a villain? What explains her hold on the people? What are the moral values and political philosophy that drives her? Besides attempting to answer these questions, this essay aims to trace her political trajectory, pointing to her leadership style with a mix of strengths and vulnerabilities, to situate her in the wider international context in order to assess her changing relations with the nation's external partners; and to particularly examine her relationship with India. The author hopes, in the end, to pinpoint some clues as to how the current political stalemate may head towards a resolution, reflecting if she could still contribute to that process.

A Long Political Journey

It is proposed to examine ASSK's long political journey below, classifying it into five distinct phases.

First Phase

As a political actor, her innings began soon after her unexpected and unplanned return to Burma in April 1988 to look after her ailing mother. However, her relationship with her people began much earlier, through her lineage as the daughter of Aung San—the Father of modern Burma, the founder of the Army, the war hero who negotiated independence and prepared to lead the nation but fell to assassins' bullets in July 1947. He was 35. In a family of three children—two boys and one girl, the magic and burden of Aung San's legacy should normally have been passed on to a son in the typical Asian fashion. But destiny desired otherwise: the younger brother drowned in a pond at a young age, and the elder brother refused to get involved in politics. The mother's illness drew the daughter away from the comfortable life of a woman married to an Oxford scholar to the gathering storm of protests and demonstrations organised by students and other sections of society. It was an impassioned revolution by the people against a brutal army dictatorship and authoritarianism of the kind the nation had not experienced before. The people were in a frantic search for a national leader. Gradually, they discovered her. She, too, connected well with them after resolving her own dilemmas and setting her own terms. One of the most famous advocates of democracy and human rights of our times was thus born accidentally, one who would shape the trajectory of Burma/Myanmar for a long time.

Her extensive tours in the country and active campaigning helped the NLD immensely. "Wherever she went, north, south, east or west, Suu was met by vast crowds who hailed her as their ruler, their saviour, their redeemer."[3] The famous incident at Danubyu on 5 April 1989, when she showed incredible *sang froid* in facing down the soldiers who were at the point of opening fire to kill her, helped build her reputation for personal courage and resoluteness in fighting for her mission. "It was this incident," wrote Peter Popham, "which, more than any other, created the mystique of Aung San Suu Kyi, while at the same time in this land of a zero-sum game, effectively dismantling that of the army." In the people's minds, she emerged as "her father's daughter", the worthy child of the redoubtable Aung San who had defied both the British and the Japanese to prevail in the teeth of challenge and adversity.[4]

This first phase of ASSK's political activism lasted till July 1989, when she was placed under house arrest and barred from participating in the first free and fair multiparty elections held in May 1990. Her party won 80 per cent of seats, establishing her as the unquestioned leader, even in absentia.

Second Phase

In the next 20 years (1990–2010), the second phase of her political life, she could taste freedom, albeit under restrictions, for about five years only. Senior General Than Shwe was her chief protagonist for much of this period, and General Khin Nyunt was an important communication link. In this era, the Army charted its course through the 'Roadmap to Discipline-flourishing Democracy' (2003), the Saffron Revolution (2007), and the framing and adoption of the Constitution (2008), while ruling the country with an iron fist, endeavouring to open the economy as well as conducting a dialogue with key international partners, and consolidating bilateral cooperation, where possible.

Expounding her core philosophy, Suu Kyi put forward her view while accepting the Sakharov Prize on 1 January 1990. "It is not power that corrupts but fear," she asserted, adding: "fear of losing power corrupts those who wield it and fear of the scourge of power corrupts those who are subject to it." In the same speech, she endorsed Nehru's description of Mahatma Gandhi: "The essence of his teaching was fearlessness and truth, and action allied to these, always keeping the welfare of the masses in view."[5]

Soon after arriving in Yangon as India's Ambassador in August 2002, my wife and I had the opportunity to meet Daw Aung San Suu Kyi at a small, informal reception hosted by the US Chargé d'Affaires, at her residence. The Burmese leader was already an international celebrity, having bagged some of the most prestigious awards the world can bestow: the Sakharov Prize (1990), the Nobel Peace Prize (1991), and the Jawaharlal Nehru Award for International Understanding (1993). We were introduced by our host. Daw Suu Kyi talked to us with effortless ease, informality, and charm, conveying a message of warm friendship for India where she noted, she had "many friends."

My second meeting was on a one-to-one basis. It took place on 30 January 2003, after special permission was granted to me to call on her at her famous residence—24 University Avenue—when she was under house arrest. This entailed a substantive discussion on a range of issues relating to Myanmar's politics, economy, and foreign policy as well as the emerging trends in India-Myanmar relations as New Delhi strove to implement its 'dual-track policy' of building ties with the military government while continuing to support the cause of democracy and ASSK. She understood and appreciated what India was doing. She had a realistic perspective on the future of politics in her country. Her calmness and stoicism, her determination to do some good for her people, and her optimistic outlook on the future could not be missed.

During much of the era of rule by the State Law and Order Restoration Council (SLORC) and the State Peace and Development Council (SPDC), Suu Kyi remained, whether free or not, the principal figure sworn to opposing the military rule and holding aloft the flame of democracy and human rights. People continued to believe in her, whether they saw or heard her or not. The generals could not figure out if intimidation, pressure, violence, or dialogue, or a combination of these options could neutralise her politically. The more they tried, the more the people and the international community supported her, being ever conscious of her vital relevance as the one who held the key to resolving the Myanmar conundrum.

The incident at Depayin on 30 May 2003 was another crude attempt by the elements close to the ruling combined to cause physical harm to her, but she prevailed again. Earlier, she faced another, much bigger, challenge as Michael Aris, her husband, diagnosed with cancer, lay on his deathbed in 1999. The regime refused him permission to visit Myanmar when he could. She was unable to visit him and be with him due to her genuine fear that she would not be allowed to return to her beloved country. The conscious choice to passionately continue the struggle for her people at the expense of her family must have been a very painful decision. Still, it further endeared her to her people enormously.

As the century's first decade neared its end, the generals led by Senior General Than Shwe devised a plan to transition the country to a new political system of limited democracy. The Army's political party—the Union Solidarity and Development Party (USDP)—won the November 2010 elections and formed a government headed by President Thein Sein, a retired general-turned-civilian leader. The military had learnt its lesson from the 1990 elections. The NLD was barred from the elections this time. But the overarching ASSK factor could not be reduced to irrelevance. She still enjoyed popular support at home and a massive following in the world's chancelleries, media, and civil society.

Third Phase

The third phase ran from 2011 to 2015. This was when the NLD, under Suu Kyi's leadership, demonstrated its political resilience. Responding to the Army's overtures, it agreed to work within the confines of the 2008 constitution, however stifling they were. The result: the green light was given for the NLD to participate in the by-elections for 44 seats held in April 2012. The party won 43 seats, sending its leader and other members into the parliament. They were a step closer to governance and slowly began learning to work with the Thein Sein government.

Among the nation's critical issues were the imperative need for ethnic reconciliation, the revival of the economy, and the building of international partnerships that could help the country turn the corner after decades of brutal military rule. While extending support to President Thein Sein up to a point, Suu Kyi transmitted a simple message consistently to her people and the world:

yes, some positive change has occurred, but the real change would happen only when genuinely elected representatives of the people would wield power. In other words, without the involvement of the NLD, the ruling dispensation cannot be representative and democratic.

I met Daw Suu Kyi twice during this period. In November 2012, she visited India. I moderated her interactive meetings with a select group of guests from the realm of politics, academia, business, and media at Hyderabad House in New Delhi. She stressed again and again that her country lacked "the rule of law" and democracy. My next meeting with her was in March 2013. As the Director General of the Indian Council of World Affairs (ICWA), I led a delegation of scholars to Myanmar. We had a candid and productive conversation with her at her MP's home in Naypyitaw. I asked her if she planned to help the government in its endeavour to secure ethnic reconciliation. She replied that she was awaiting an invitation from the government. The dialogue, already underway, was not a "roadside tea shop" where she could drop in on her own, she added.

During the Thein Sein presidency, the NLD's principal plank was constitutional reform. The 2008 constitution had too many shortcomings that prevented the realisation of full democracy. The Army had designed it that way. First, the provision to bar a person with a spouse or a child having foreign citizenship from the presidency was targeted against only a single individual—Aung San Suu Kyi. It was unfair and undemocratic. Second, three key ministries (defence, internal security, and home affairs) were reserved for the military's nominees, thus creating a government within the government. Third, the procedure to amend the constitution required a 75 per cent majority support in parliament, thereby giving to the Army a virtual veto power because 25 per cent of the parliamentary seats were reserved for serving military personnel. No matter how hard ASSK campaigned for constitutional change, this goal proved elusive. The Army perhaps hoped that a frustrated NLD would again refuse to participate in the elections, but the party refrained from repeating the past mistake. Demonstrating its inclination for pragmatism, it took part in the November 2015 elections.

Once again, the results were in favour of Suu Kyi, with the NLD winning a clear majority of the seats in both chambers of parliament—the House of Representatives and the House of Nationalities. The party was thus in a position to secure the presidency and form the government for the first time. Suu Kyi stood tall as a political leader; her position was validated by a landslide at the polls. Her weaknesses looked insignificant. Peter Popham wrote, "She has astonished everyone, friends and enemies, for a long time, by her resilience and determination. Now she stands on the brink of achieving her great goal; she may do so again."[6]

The post-election period witnessed intensive negotiations involving ASSK on the one hand and the military as well as other political figures. She was denied the highest post, the presidency, and had to accept becoming the state counsellor, a kind of de facto prime minister. It was a compromise said to be crafted by Senior General Than Shwe who seemed to retain much influence with the current ruling elite.

Fourth Phase

From March 2016 to January 2021, the NLD shared power with the military as part of the cohabitation model outlined in the Constitution. It was thus not the era of NLD rule; rather it was the time when the party that had been in opposition to military rule strove to govern the country in collaboration with the military. It was a novel experience for both sides.

Having failed to persuade the generals to accept her as the President, Suu Kyi arranged the election of a party confidante as the new president and began playing the role custom-designed for her—as the state counsellor who also held the charge of several ministries. The NLD's first priority was to push for ethnic reconciliation by convening the 21st-century Pangalong conference. In the beginning, this initiative drew much media attention, but in the end, the Government achieved little, even less than what President Thein Sein had been able to secure. The wide gulf between the ideas of ethnic minorities, especially the Ethnic Armed Organisations (EAOs), and the *tatmadaw* leadership and also the chasm of mutual trust were an ugly reality. Suu Kyi tried hard to build consensus around the concept of 'Federal Union' but the gulf proved unbridgeable. She failed where no previous government had succeeded.

Other elements of NLD's agenda included constitutional reform, elimination of corruption, and continuation of economic reforms started by the previous government. Modest successes were achieved, but gradually the nation under Suu Kyi's stewardship was overwhelmed by a set of grave developments relating to the Rohingya question, particularly from 2017 onwards.

A deeply complex challenge with a long history, the relationship between the Muslims of the Rakhine state (Rohingyas) and the Buddhists continued to be marked by escalating tensions and conflict. Against this backdrop, attacks by the Arakan Rohingya Salvation Army (ARSA) on police and military facilities in

August 2017 triggered an extraordinarily strong response in the form of the 'Four cuts' strategy adopted by the Army. The result was a merciless crackdown, killings, rapes and devastation culminating in the exodus of over 700,000 Rohingyas to neighbouring Bangladesh.

This tragic drama unfolded when Buddhist-Muslim relations in the country, in general, were under increasing stress. Rightist Buddhist groups were in ascendance. The Burmese people's psyche was one of siege from within. Severe condemnation of the Government that came from the West and Islamic nations over the handling of the Rohingya community drew Suu Kyi and the military closer together. At every forum and occasion, she was in the forefront defending the indefensible actions of the Army, arguing that violence came from both sides; there was wild exaggeration in the accusations against the armed forces; there was no intent of genocide; and, where necessary, internal investigations would be a sufficient response.

Her defence of the Army action at the International Court of Justice (ICJ) crystallised several trends in one go: the Western media identified Suu Kyi as their main target; her past record as the icon of human rights and the goddess of democracy was blackened; her domestic support became stronger than before, and the Army appeared content using her as their shield against external condemnation. To many in foreign countries, the heroine of the past emerged as the villain of the present. However, at home, she was the 'Amay Suu' (Mother Suu), stoutly defending the Motherland. That she was responding to the crisis as a patriotic Burmese and a devout Buddhist who viewed the Rohingyas as outsiders, a non-Burmese race, was implied and understood by all. She never used the R-word, perhaps hoping that the nightmare would go away on its own.

True to the past pattern, the NLD secured another decisive victory when the general elections were held in November 2020. It was a bigger triumph than the one in 2015. The astute playing of the Rohingya card by Suu Kyi had paid off domestically. But the expectation that a grateful military would now be more cooperative with the NLD was not fulfilled. On the contrary, the Army suffered from a sense of deep insecurity, fearing that a stronger NLD in the parliament and Suu Kyi in her 'Mother of Myanmar' role would be uncontrollable in her zest to dismantle the political architecture built by the 2008 Constitution.

The Army's political party, USDP, stunned by its defeat again, came up with the notion that the election was largely fraudulent. A large number of complaints were filed with the election commission. The latter failed to take them seriously. After waiting for several weeks, the Army, backing the USDP, opened direct discussions with the NLD through a secret channel. Thanks to a revealing report by Reuters, the world came to know about the serious political drama that unfolded in the capital in the last week of January 2021. On 28 January, a military team led by Lt-Gen Yar Pyae presented to the NLD "at least three demands: reschedule the February 1 opening of parliament, disband the election commission, and re-examine the vote under military supervision."[7] The answer given by the NLD negotiators led by Kyaw Tint Swe was negative on all three points. There was no give by the party; hence there was no deal with the military. "You are going too far, very rude and insolent," warned the Army representatives. Shortly thereafter, the green light was given for the staging of a new coup d'état. It took place on 1 February 2021.[8]

Fifth Phase

February 2021–August 2022 (at the time of writing) represents the period of severe tensions and conflicts in Myanmar polity. The people's reaction to the coup ranged from peaceful protests to violent opposition, the formation of the parallel government named the National Unity Government (NUG), and attacks on troops by people's militias. The *tatmadaw* responded with a sustained and massive crackdown, resulting in the killing of thousands and imprisonment of a huge number of opponents.[9] The result was a stalemate; the military government failed to browbeat the opposition, while resistance remained strong but unable to prevail. The Ethnic Armed Organisations (EAOs) walked the middle ground, demonstrating how the polity stood seriously fractured in multiple ways.

Andrew Selth pointed out that the "security situation in Myanmar is now more complex and dangerous than it has been since the multiple crises of the 1950s, and there is no resolution in sight".[10] Presenting a similar interpretation, Yun Sun observed that a divided opposition faced a military that is "a highly unitary, monolithic, and hierarchical organisation". She explained:

> *This does not mean that the military can easily conquer the resistance and defeat the insurgency .... But it does mean that the resistance has a long way to go before it could effectively match and counter, let alone defeat, the military.*[11]

Meanwhile, Suu Kyi was deprived of her freedom again. Having been sentenced to several years of imprisonment on trumped-up charges, she spent time under house arrest. In June 2022, she was transferred to solitary confinement in a jail in Naypyitaw. Several reports indicated that her household effects, personal staff, and the pet dog, Taichito, were transported from her former official residence in the capital to her Lakeshore home in Yangon. This triggered speculation that, eventually, she may be brought back there, thus completing the circle of her political trajectory.

Five Questions

The foregoing analytical capture of the Burmese leader's epic political journey from 1988 to 2022 leads us to address the five frequently asked questions about her. Given below are answers based on our deep research and reflection.

1. *Her legacy:* What does she stand for and what has she achieved? Briefly, a lot. The people of Burma rose against Ne Win before she came into the picture, but her role was critical in welding the divergent groups of the regime's opponents into a powerful movement, establishing the NLD and providing increasingly a single-point leadership. She was both the face and the brain of the 27-year-long (1988–2015) struggle against the junta. Her personal sacrifices, courage, conviction, and commitment were phenomenal. This is what earned her the world's recognition and the gratitude of her people. This is what explains her repeated victories at the polls. In the eyes of her people, she proved herself as the worthy daughter of Aung San.

   As part of the government, when she shared power with the military, she set priorities, strove to achieve NLD's goals, and succeeded only partially, while showing that she could have secured more if she had been given full authority.
2. *The 'R' challenge*: By international standards and in the eyes of her most foreign admirers, supporters and friends, Suu Kyi failed miserably in tackling the complex Rohingya issue. She "fell from grace", turning herself from a lovable heroine into a pariah. The much-eulogized defender of human rights, they said, cared little for the human rights of the large Rohingya community in Myanmar. But a closer examination presents a different perspective. 'I am a politician, not an icon,' she repeated on several occasions. In a 2017 interview, she was quizzed by BBC journalist Fergal Keane if the former was an "amalgam of Mahatma Gandhi and Mother Teresa" and was "closer to Margaret Thatcher." She replied in the negative adding: "I am just a politician. I am not quite like Margaret Thatcher, no, but on the other hand, I am no Mother Teresa, either. I have never said that I was. Mahatma Gandhi, actually, was a very astute politician."[12]

   Suu Kyi knew where her Burmese people stood. She simply could not afford to alienate them as well as the military. Her pragmatism led to the retention of popular support at home, grudging support by the Army (which did not last long), and the opprobrium of the international community.

3. *Her worldview*: Suu Kyi's mixed background – the daughter of a famous Burmese leader, higher education abroad (India, UK), wife of a British academic, and exposure to the world's capitals—shaped her worldview. In his recent political biography of Suu Kyi, Michal Lubina portrayed her, with some justification, as "a hybrid politician", a product of the East and the West. He wrote:

   "Aung San Suu Kyi understands the way the Western world operates and wants to implement some—not al—of its civilisational achievements in Myanmar. But she is not Western, she is a hybrid politician, someone in between worlds ... Deeper inside, there lies the uncomfortable truth that human rights, democracy, rule of law, etc., matter differently to the Burmese than to Westerners."[13]

   Reviewing Lubina's book, Rodion Ebbighausen commented that as "a hybrid politician", Suu Kyi "chose to retain her influence in the firm belief that she would continue to fight for human rights, democracy and the rule of law, at least in the sense of how she understands these concepts."[14]

   While in the opposition, Suu Kyi worked effortlessly with the West securing its wholehearted cooperation and support for the nation's struggle for democracy. When she worked with President Thein Sein, but at the same time opposed him on crucial issues, she signalled that she would run a better foreign policy than his.

   As the government leader, she first enjoyed a brief honeymoon with the Western powers. Still, as they spurned her government over the 'R' issue, she turned to China, demonstrating what she had always claimed before that she could cultivate better ties with Beijing than the military. Her equations with other Asian powers were of a mixed kind as several of them suspected her Western links and questioned her Asian-ness.

   "The February 2021 coup," observed Shantanu Roy-Choudhury, "further complicated an already complex web of relations and dynamics both within Myanmar and externally, relating to the Indian and Chinese engagements with the country".[15] While discussing the impact of the coup on ASEAN, Barry Desker referred to the regional grouping's Myanmar dilemma. He pointed out that ASEAN's influence lay in "its capacity to persuade the Myanmar military authorities, not in the presence of rules which may or may not be enforced". He predicted correctly, "This will be a long game and a testing time for ASEAN".[16]

4. *Relationship with India:* There is no doubt that Suu Kyi enjoyed a special relationship with India. Guided by Lord Buddha, inspired by Mahatma Gandhi, and influenced by Jawaharlal Nehru, she could count several Indian Prime Ministers ranging from Rajiv Gandhi to Dr. Manmohan Singh and Narendra Modi, among her admirers and supporters. The Indian intelligentsia and media loved her but realpolitik came in the way. She wanted unrestricted support from the Indian government for her political struggle. India's national interests that lay behind its 'dual-track policy' since 1991 did not allow it. She articulated her reservations through private channels, except once, when at the end of delivering the Nehru Memorial Lecture in Delhi in November 2012, she spoke from her heart and observed:

   "*I was saddened to see that we had drawn away from India, or rather that India had drawn away from us during our very difficult days, but I always had faith in the lasting friendship between our countries based on lasting friendships between our two peoples.... Governments come and go, and this is what democracy is all about, but people remain.... Burma has still not reached the goal of democracy and in this last, I hope, and most difficult phase India will stand by us and walk by us as we proceed on the path that they were able to proceed upon many years before us.*"[17]

   Once she came to power and showed a clear inclination to move closer to China in a bid to balance the West, New Delhi had to be even more attentive to its ties with the military. The October 2020 visit of Foreign Secretary Harsh Shringla and Army Chief General M.M. Naravane to Myanmar, when the delegation interacted separately with Senior General Min Aung Hlaing and Daw Suu Kyi was an essay in fine diplomatic calibration.[18] Since her detention, India has repeatedly called for the freedom of all detainees and prisoners and Myanmar's return to democracy. This was particularly noticed during Foreign Secretary Shringla's visit to Myanmar in December 2021.[19]

5. *Her political future*: At 77, what is Suu Kyi's political future? This is the most important question and also the most difficult one to answer. Some argue that Myanmar has moved on beyond the Suu Kyi versus Generals divide.[20] Others claim that the anti-junta struggle has now no place for her. After the military takeover once again, Rodion Ebbighausen asserted

that "the role Suu Kyi could play in the future seems to be out of her hand."[21] Ardeth Maung Thawnghmung has developed a set of nine different scenarios to explain what may happen in the future.[22]

Conclusion

A considered view, steeped in objectivity and tinged with optimism, suggests that Myanmar is still not through with Daw Suu Kyi. She is the queen who continues to rule the hearts of a majority of her people. The Army can keep her shackled for as long as it wants but whenever it is ready to craft a political solution to the governance issue, the Generals will need to return to her, consult with her and carve out a place for her.

In July 2022, Prak Sokhonn, Cambodia's Deputy Prime Minister, Foreign Minister and ASEAN's Special Envoy for the Myanmar issue, expressed optimism about the possibility of meeting Suu Kyi. This was apparently based on an assurance received from the highest level in the Myanmar government. Sokhonn observed what he planned to "ask, or discuss with her, was about her view on the future of Myanmar, how she saw the way out of the crisis, how her political influence could have weight on the political process, the political dialogue that could lead to peace and reconciliation."[23]

Another important clue: UN Secretary-General's Special Envoy for Myanmar, Noeleen Heyzer, met Senior General Min Aung Hlaing on 17 August 2022, on her first visit to the country since the February 2021 coup. She requested him the opportunity to meet Aung San Suu Kyi, reportedly stating, "I want to have an opportunity to meet with her as soon as possible, both because I care about her personally, and I believe she is a critical stakeholder for my dialogue with all parties concerned."[24] Ms Heyzer also requested that Suu Kyi be allowed to return home. Responding to this demarche, the Senior General stated, "I will consider the matter...after the verdict is done. We did not impose strong charges on her and showed mercy even though we were able to do more."[25]

While alive, Aung San Suu Kyi cannot be ignored or excluded as far as Myanmar's political future is concerned. Naing Khits aptly portrayed Suu Kyi's life as a story of transition "from a pro-democracy fighter to a prisoner, from a prisoner to the country's elected leader, from the elected leader to a prisoner again." This commentator poignantly added, "She is thin but strong. She is old but determined. She is alone but mindful. She is locked but peaceful."[26] And when she is gone, history will judge her as the most influential figure of her time in a country with two names—Burma/Myanmar.

ENDNOTES

1. Rodion Ebbighausen, "Who is Myanmar's Aung San Suu Kyi," *DW,* 01 February 2021, available at https://www.dw.com/en/who-is-myanmars-aung-san-suu-kyi/a-56406128, last accessed on 10 September 2022.
2. "U.N. Special Envoy to Visit Myanmar Amid 'Deteriorating Situation," *Reuters*, 16 August 2022, available at https://www.usnews.com/news/world/articles/2022-08-16/u-n-special-envoy-to-visit-myanmar-amid-deteriorating-situation, last accessed on 10 September 2022.
3. Peter Popham, *The Lady and the Peacock: The Life of Aung San Suu Kyi of Burma* (RHUK, 2013), 232.
4. Ibid, 207.
5. Aung San Suu Kyi, "In commemoration of winning the 1990 Sakharov Prize for Freedom of Thought," *IOWA State University*, 01 January 1990, available at https://awpc.cattcenter.iastate.edu/2017/03/21/freedom-from-fear-1990/, last accessed on 10 September 2022.
6. Peter Popham, 2016
7. Poppy McPherson, "Rude and insolent': fraught talks preceded Myanmar's army seizing power," *Reuters,* 09 February 2021, available at https://www.reuters.com/article/us-myanmar-politics-reconstruction-insig-idUSKBN2A9225, last accessed on 10 September 2022.
8. For details of the reasons that triggered the coup, see Subir Bhaumik, "Return of jackboots in Myanmar: Major implications for region," *South Asia Monitor,* 01 February 2021, available at https://www.southasiamonitor.org/index.php/spotlight/return-jackboots-myanmar-major-implications-region, last accessed on 10 September 2022.
9. According to the Assistance Association for Political Prisoners (AAPP), 246 people were killed, 15,239 were arrested and 12,142 were still detained, as of 26 August 2022. "Daily Briefing in Relation to the Military Coup," *AAPP*, 26 August 2022, available at https://aappb.org/?p=22863, last accessed on 10 September 2022.
10. Andrew Selth, "Myanmar's annus horribilis," *theintepreter, Lowy Institute*, 09 December 2021, available at https://www.lowyinstitute.org/the-interpreter/myanmar-s-annus-horribilis, last accessed on 10 September 2022.
11. Yun Sun, "One year after Myanmar's coup, old and new resistance is undermined by divisions," *Brookings,* 01 February 2022, available at https://www.brookings.edu/blog/order-from-chaos/2022/02/01/one-year-after-myanmars-coup-old-and-new-resistance-is-undermined-by-divisions/, last accessed on 10 September 2022.
12. Cited by M.M. Myat, "Is politics Aung San Suu Kyi's vocation," *Palgrave Communication* Vol. 5, 50 (2019), available at https://doi.org/10.1057/s41599-019-0258-1, last accessed on 10 September 2022.
13. Micha³ Lubina, *A Political Biography of Aung San Suu Kyi: A Hybrid Politician,* (London: Taylor and Francis, 2020): 119–120.
14. Rodion Ebbighausen, "Book Review: Making Sense of Aung San Suu Kyi Kyi's Policy," *Journal of Current Southeast Asian Affairs*, vol. 40(2) (2021): 374, available at https://journals.sagepub.com/doi/pdf/10.1177/1868103420980463, last accessed on 10 September 2022.
15. Shantanu Roy-Chaudhury, "Myanmar's February Coup–Implications for India and China," *Centre for Air Power Studies,* New Delhi, CAPS (InFocus 06/2021), available at https://capsindia.org/wp-content/uploads/2021/08/440efba6-c61d-4c72-8043-ac8fc11ce9e3-1.pdf, last accessed on 10 September 2022.
16. Barry Desker, "ASEAN's Myanmar Dilemma," *RSIS*, 24 May 2021, available at https://www.rsis.edu.sg/rsis-publication/rsis/aseans-myanmar-dilemma/?doing_wp_cron=

1658247599.28087592 12493896484375#.YtbalnbMK5d, last accessed on 10 September 2022.

17. Rajiv Bhatia, *India-Myanmar Relations: Changing contours (*New York, Routledge, 2015): 139.
18. For details, see "Visit of Chief of Army Staff and Foreign Secretary to Myanmar," *Ministry of External Affairs.* 5 October 2020, available at https://www.mea.gov.in/press-releases.htm?dtl/33092/Visit+of+Chief+of+Army+Staff+and+Foreign+Secretary+to+Myanmar+October+45+2020, last accessed on 10 September 2022.
19. For details, see "Visit of Foreign Secretary Shri Harsh Vardhan Shringla to Myanmar," *Ministry of External Affairs,* 23 December 2021, available at https://mea.gov.in/press-releases.htm?dtl/34723/Visit+of+Foreign+Secretary+Shri+Harsh+Vardhan+Shringla+to+Myanmar+December+2223+2021, last accessed on 10 September 2022.
20. Philipp Annawitt, "Myanmar Has Moved Beyond Aung San Suu Kyi vs. the Generals," *The Diplomat,* 25 January 2022, available at https://thediplomat.com/2022/01/myanmar-has-moved-beyond-aung-san-suu-kyi-vs-the-generals/, last accessed on 10 September 2022.
21. Rodion Ebbighausen, "Who is Myanmar's Aung San Suu Kyi," *DW,* 01 February 2021, available at https://www.dw.com/en/who-is-myanmars-aung-san-suu-kyi/a-56406128, last accessed on 10 September 2022.
22. For details, see Ardeth Maung Thawnghmung, "Back to the Future? Possible Scenarios for Myanmar," *Fulcrum.* 12 March 2021, available at https://fulcrum.sg/back-to-the-future-possible-scenarios-for-myanmar/, last accessed on 10 September 2022.
23. "ASEAN special envoy plans third trip to Myanmar; hopes to use Aung San Suu Kyi's influence to end violence,", *Channel News Asia*, 21 July 2022, available at https://www.channelnewsasia.com/, last accessed on 10 September 2022.
24. RFA Burmese, "UN envoy calls for end to conflict after meeting Myanmar junta," *RFA*, 17 August 2022, available at https://www.rfa.org/english/news/myanmar/un_envoy-08172022183805.html, last accessed on 10 September 2022.
25. "Myanmar's Suu Kyi could return home after verdicts, junta chief says," *Reuters*, 19 August 2022, available at https://www.reuters.com/article/us-myanmar-politics-suu-kyi-idAFKBN2PP1D6, last accessed on 10 September 2022.
26. Naing Khit, "Can Aung San Suu Kyi Survive Myanmar Junta's Latest Attack," *The Irrawaddy,* 24 June 2022, available at https://www.irrawaddy.com/opinion/commentary/can-aung-san-suu-kyi-survive-myanmar-juntas-latest-attack.html, last accessed on 10 September 2022.

3

Myanmar Army: No Back to the Future, Transform or Perish

Brig R K Bhonsle

ABSTRACT

The political history of Myanmar (Burma) [till 1989] is marred by long periods of military or para-uniformed entities in government and a short five-year period [2015-2020] of the National League of Democracy (NLD) led by Daw Aung Suu Kyi, the democracy icon. Since 1962, when the military first seized power, there have been intermittent attempts for an elected government controlled by the military such as the Burma Socialist Programme Party (BSPP) from March 1974 to 1988 or the National Unity Party (NUP), its successor. In 1990 when the NLD first won a landslide victory, the military nullified elections and the State Law and Order Restoration Council [SLORC] continued for a second stint. Sensing the necessity to project a democratic front in a changing world, in April 2008, the military formed the Union Solidarity and Development Party (USDP), which swept the elections in November 2010 in which the NLD did not participate. As per the 2008 Constitution, the military held 25 per cent of seats in the parliament, thus ensuring attempts to change state structure through the legislature. 2010 to 2015 was a period of glasnost, so to say, when NLD leader Aung Suu Kyi was released from house arrest gradually and the Party participated in elections in 2010, winning a majority to form the first democratically elected government in Myanmar. There was much elation that democracy had finally taken root in Myanmar.

However, when the NLD swept the polls in November 2020, the familiar insecurity of the Tatmadaw of losing control of the government and of the commander in chief Senior General Min Aung Hlaing's ambition to be President saw the coup on February 01, 2021. A familiar structure for governance with a civilian interface, State Administrative Council (SAC) was formed. Unlike in the past, however, the people of Myanmar, who had tasted the fruits of freedom, initially raised a civilian protest movement and then took to armed resistance. Numerous People's Defence Forces (PDF) were formed, directly targeting the military across multiple regions and states supported by Ethnic Armed Organisations (EAO) that have been waging war with the Myanmar military for decades. The Tatmadaw, known for brutality against the minority, such as the Rohingya in Rakhine and the "Four Cuts," strategy unleashed a brutal campaign using air, artillery and helicopter strikes. Yet, the poorly armed and sparsely trained PDF could not be suppressed. The result two years on is a stalemate, and on 31 January 2023, the military is forced to postpone elections. Clearly, the Tatmadaw cannot expect to "steamroll," the people of Myanmar today as in the past. The military in Myanmar will need a radical transformation to adjust to the new realities. Will this happen remains to be seen.

Overview

01 February 2021 was another defining day in the long history of Myanmar's military interventions in usurping state authority. Myanmar Army rolled in, cracking down on leaders of the civilian government led by the National League for Democracy (NLD), alleging fraud in elections held on 08 November 2020, in which the party had won an overwhelming majority. As a result, observers of the country saw a repetition of history.

What was behind the necessity of a coup when the military had ample control over parliamentary affairs through 25 per cent of seats held by officers of the *Tatmadaw*, the Myanmar Armed Forces, is unclear. The Commander-in-Chief of the *Tatmadaw* Senior General, Min Aung Hlaing, is reported to have held talks with the NLD leadership, including party chair Aung San Suu Kyi. What were the main differences, and why had the military sought absolute power will come out in due course as the history of the black day for democracy is exposed in the years ahead.

Possibly the bargain was over top posts—President, Vice-President, Speakers of the two Parliaments and so on. Importantly, the position of State Counsellor and hitherto Foreign Minister Aung Suu Kyi may also have been a point of contention. Whatever the differences, the NLD did not relent. Some observers have blamed the Party for undue obduracy in the face of past legacy.

That a coup was coming was evident as on 26 January—Army spokesman Brigadier General Zaw Min Tun warned that the military would "take action" if the election dispute was not settled. He asked the Election Commission to investigate discrepancies in the voters' list and was ambiguous of what the military would do otherwise. On 28 January, the Election Commission nominated by the then government led by the NLD rejected allegations of vote fraud. The writing seemed to be on the wall. The crackdown began as the military imposed a state of emergency, and powers were transferred to Senior General Min Aung Hlaing, head of the *Tatmadaw*. Popular leaders of the NLD, then officially the State

Counsellor Daw Aung San Suu Kyi and President U Win Myint, apart from other party officials, were arrested and placed under detention.[1]

Thus began another military takeover in the series of coups that marred the history of the country. However, this one would be different. The military possibly expected that after token resistance, it would be able to take control as it had done a few times earlier, the last being almost three decades back in 1988. This belief proved facetious.

Professional militaries plan operational campaigns with last-minute detail. Whether the *Tatmadaw* did so prior to the illegal intervention, despite flagging a clause in the 2008 Constitution, is not clear. Possibly the army command was confident of suppressing democracy activists led by the NLD and other parties, negotiating with Ethnic Armed Organisations (EAO) and controlling the national space within a few weeks, if not months. The military had aligned parties such as the Union Solidarity and Development Party (USDP) in tow and unrolled a plan for holding fresh elections which has since been tweaked many times.

The surprise for the *Tatmadaw* as well as possibly close observers of internal developments in Myanmar was the rise of a strong resistance movement which had a civilian veneer gradually emerging into a militant composure spread across the country and, importantly, led by the majority of Bamar ethnicity. The intensity of the resistance has built up over the past year and a half and many have likened the situation to a soft civil war.[2] In terms of military capability measured in weight of arms and munitions, the opposition resistance movement appears weak. Still, moral strength seems to be the driving factor as more people join the mass armed rebellion.

The response of the *Tatmadaw* to the resistance has been brutal, again a legacy of the past. Employing a scorched earth policy, burning villages, and massive use of air and artillery, the Army has now raised pro-government militias to beef up local support for the harsh campaign. In growing signs of desperation and to send a strong signal to the resistance, the State Administrative Council (SAC)—the civilian face of the military—executed four political activists on 25 July 2022 for involvement in armed insurrection.[3] This was the first execution since 1988 and was carried out despite a strong appeal by Cambodia, Chair of the Association of South East Asian Nations (ASEAN), amongst others, but the military was unmoved.[4]

Whatever the outcome of the present state of civil war in Myanmar, the *Tatmadaw* will have to transform. Will this be a soft avatar as in Pakistan or

Thailand though models here are too disparate to be applied without some caution, a post-1988 all-powerful *Tatmadaw* does not appear likely. On the political front, is the military willing to compromise on the principle of unity and agree to a federal structure that it has resisted over decades is another unknown.

What is amply clear, however, is that the process envisaged by Senior General Min Aung Hlaing for transition to a legitimate civilian government is suffering setbacks and realising this, the same national emergency has been extended for another six months.[5] To understand the process of transition, looking at the present internal conflict in the light of the history of anti-*Tatmadaw* resistance may provide some perspectives and are being attempted herein with a note that the past need not be a mirror if the glass is shattered.

State of Play: "Civil War," in Myanmar: Raison d'être of Military Take Over

A rational reason for a military takeover can be the collapse of the political system, abject incompetence of civilian administration or overwhelming national security challenges. Very clearly, none of these existed in Myanmar on 01 February 2021, the day of the coup. Elections had been held successfully and the result was widely accepted by the people, the civil administration, and international observers. There were murmurs in the military-supported parties as the USDP had been routed. A newly elected parliament was to assemble on the day when Senior General Min Aung Hlaing decided to take over.

The explanation offered was flawed elections that had led to danger to the "state". In general, while continuing to provide this as a reason for the takeover, the military now also claims a guardian role. "*Tatmadaw* (Myanmar's military) must continue to take a leadership role in the country's politics and maintain its oversight position as the "guardian" of the country," the military says.[6]

A year and a half later, this was stated in a meeting held by the coup leader and the present head of the State Administration Council (SAC). This quasi-government body is the front for the military, packed with serving and retired military officers. The General claimed that the military is essential for peace and stability. However, the overall objective of the *Tatmadaw* is an "absolute grip on power". The public's rejection of this self-ascribed role is evident from the level of political, economic, and military resistance to the coup outlined in the following section.

The Resistance—Political Track

From a virtual void, resistance to the military coup in Myanmar is today well organised and has a political, governance and military face. The Civil Disobedience Movement (CDM) was the first to offer organised opposition, which emerged from civil servants and students who took to the streets in the first week of February after the initial shock of the takeover.[7] Members of the deposed parliament soon came together to form the Committee Representing Pyidaungsu Hluttaw (CRPH) a political front to oppose the military. In April 2021, the CRPH announced the formation of a National Unity Government (NUG), including an ethnically diverse cabinet.

The NUG is backed by the National Unity Consultative Council (NUCC), which includes political parties, EAOs, civil society organisations and strike committees and is seen as representative. By May 2021, the People's Defence Force (PDF), the military arm only loosely aligned with the NUG started forming in various parts of the country with the first fighting in the Sagaing Region and the Chin States bordering India. In September 2021, the NUG declared a People's Defensive War against the military.[8] The NUG now operates as a shadow government with ministerial portfolios including defence and security, foreign policy and so on claiming to operate as a parallel to the State Administration Council.

Though the NUG lacks recognition from a foreign government, there have been some meetings held with officials. A key one is by the Foreign Minister of Malaysia, Foreign Minister Saifuddin Abdullah in May 2022 with the NUG shadow Foreign Minister Zin Mar Aung. US State Department officials, and Deputy Secretary of State Wendy R. Sherman also held a meeting with NUG shadow Foreign Minister Zin Mar Aung in Washington on the sidelines of the summit of ASEAN leaders with US President Joe Biden.[9] These meets were a signal to the SAC which responded by denouncing them.

Military Track

In the military guerrilla sphere, Myanmar's EAOs have been resisting the *Tatmadaw* for decades and some continued to do so either directly or by supporting the PDFs in varied forms. The PDFs spawned across the country, mainly in the Bamar belt in Central Burma, the Irrawaddy Valley and beyond.[10] As per the so-called Ministry of Defence of the NUG, there are some 259 PDFs with approximately 80,000 to 100,000 members. Of these, 15,000 or less than 20 per cent are said to be armed.[11]

A second layer is 250 township-based forces referred to as the Local Defence Forces (LDFs). As per the NUG, there are 401 LDFs, of which 354 have links with the NUG.[12] These are possibly in the form of cells, and the NUG transformed them into PDFs, which may roughly be seen as companies and platoons. The LDFs, such as the Yangon Urban Guerrilla Army (YUGA), mainly carry out assassination attacks and counter the military as well as vigilante groups affiliated with it.

The resistance to the *Tatmadaw* initially commenced in the form of ambushes and raids on Myanmar Army convoys and picquets in remote areas such as the Northern Sagaing and Magwe regions and the Chin State. Gradually, the areas under control have been expanded. As per Nay Phone Latt, an influential blogger, the PDFs control almost 90 per cent of the areas in this belt though this claim could not be independently verified and could be an exaggeration, but operations for gaining domination are also expanding in the Mandalay and Tanintharyi regions.

Another tactic of the resistance is attacks in urban centres such as Yangon, Bago, Ayeyarwady and Naypyitaw. The YUGA, for instance, launched the "Nann Htike Aung Operation", targeting regime administrations across the country.[13] Clearly, the assassination of officials merely for being supporters of the coup regime is not justified. However, the resistance claims these are essential in terms of the defence of political rights.

Despite the large mass of resistance of the PDFs, the limited number of arms and lack of coordination at the regional or national level imply that their operations will continue to remain uncoordinated pockets of resistance, lacking the impact of a national-level uprising. However, morale appears to be high as to the military appeals for the surrender of the estimated 50,000 to 100,000 PDF members across the country; only around 30 have surrendered, as per the *Irrawaddy* quoting military sources.[14] Suffice it to say, there is a high degree of threat to free movement and operations of the Myanmar Army in many areas.

The NUG lacks the budget to arm the PDFs and has projected a requirement of at least USD 10 million each month. The NUG has raised funds by issuing bonds and selling shares and also receives donations from the public. The property of the military in areas under its control is also being auctioned to raise funds. Resistance forces in the anti-regime strongholds of the Sagaing Region and Kayah State have also claimed that they are producing homemade weapons and are asking for public support to keep their arms production going as they continue their fight against the regime.[15]

While the NUG has sought international support claiming widespread atrocities by the Army, there has been no response so far. "To date, we have received no material assistance from the international community. We call again for the international community to listen to the will of the people of Myanmar and help end this military reign of terror against the people," Dr. Sa Sa, NUG spokesperson and Union Minister of International Cooperation, said in an online press conference. "Material support is the fastest way to end this crisis and to free Myanmar," he added.[16]

Despite the shortfall in weapons and related support, the intensity of fighting can be roughly gauged by claims made by the NUG's Ministry of Home Affairs and Immigration. A report stated that between 07 May and 06 June 2022, in 593 clashes and 107 bomb and mine attacks, 2,063 junta soldiers were killed and 539 wounded, as reported by the *Irrawaddy*, which stated that it could not independently verify the figures. The maximum number of encounters was reported in the Karen State with 211, followed by Sagaing Region with 175 and 10 mine attacks. Maximum civilian suffering has been reported from the Sagaing and Magwe regions and Chin State.[17]

Role of the Ethnic Armed Organisations

The EAOs which did not join the Nationwide Ceasefire Agreement (NCA) are also actively resisting the *Tatmadaw*. While there were only minor clashes prior to the coup, such as in the Kachin State, they have intensified. The groups confronting the military earlier were the "Karen National Liberation Army in Kayin State; the Kachin Independence Army in Kachin State; and the Shan State Army in Shan State".[18] The EAOs are also providing training and a limited number of arms to the PDF. Taking advantage of military preoccupation with the PDFs in the Irrawaddy Valley and other areas, several EAOs like the Arakan, Kachin, Karen, Shan, and Wa forces, have expanded their organisation and reach.[19]

The Arakan Army (AA) claims to administer most of Rakhine State and has set up a "government," independent of the military's SAC. A coalition of the Chin National Front and the Chinland Defence Force is making plans to establish a new government for the "liberated" areas of Chin State. The Kachin Independence Army (KIA), and the United Wa State Army (UWSA) and their allied EAOs, have expanded their control in Kachin State and Shan State.[2021]

While the NUG has strong public support, especially among the Bamar ethnic majority, the diverse anti-coup movement, which includes a range of ethnic and religious minority organisations and armed groups, has failed to fully unify because of residual distrust between the NLD, civil society, and ethnic minority communities.[22]

Myanmar Army's Response

The Myanmar Army is familiar with counter-militancy operations, which are based on the use of maximum force in fighting the EAOs for decades. For the record, the total strength of the Myanmar Army is 375,000, but Lowy Institute cites estimates of 100,000-120,000 fighting strength that can be mobilised.[23] However, in recent years the military was on the defensive in many areas and even suffered heavy casualties in fighting in the Rakhine State against the newly-raised AA in the year preceding the coup. The military, including some of the local commanders, had also developed economic interests in areas of control, including the highly profitable jade mining.

At the apex level, the *Tatmadaw* runs large corporations, while former military generals and their progeny control private companies. An activist group, Justice for Myanmar, claims that "133 businesses fully or partially controlled by the Myanmar military, 174 directors of those business, and 112 businesses from which the military derive significant income". The military, after the takeover, has added 32 state-owned enterprises which were previously under civilian ministries to its fold.[24] This has softened the fighting edge of the military, and in the initial months, it has faced a challenge in overcoming resistance, but the Army is unlikely to relent in the near future.

The first action taken by the SAC against the resistance was to declare them as terrorist groups, thus ruling out negotiations after pressure from the ASEAN and other international agencies. The military-formed government also enacted a new police law with constitutional powers.

The response of the Army against the PDFs was on established lines using a heavy hand by deploying the Light Infantry Divisions (LID), a mobile force which is generally held as a reserve for launching offensives using brute force tactics. Many of the LIDs have been accused of human rights violations, including against the Rohingya in Arakan in 2017, which had led to over 700,000 refugees migrating to Bangladesh and an international uproar with a case for international crimes launched by The Gambia in the International Court of Justice (ICJ) which has been accepted for trial.

The LIDs have independent artillery and are supported by air and attack helicopters by the Myanmar Air Force. Heavy use of the airstrikes has led to concerns about relations with Thailand. Myanmar Air Force Chief General Htun

Aung had to apologise to his Thai counterpart after a Myanmar military fighter jet intruded into Thai airspace while targeting a post that the KIA had taken over.

Apart from static units and the use of LIDs in offensive operations and realising the need for countering the PDF at the local level, multiple vigilante groups have been raised, such as Pyu Saw Htee and the Thout.[25] So far, Myanmar military has armed 77 Pyu Saw Htee groups in Sagaing Region alone. Additionally, pro-junta administration staff, as well as Ma Ba Tha ultranationalist Buddhist monks have been provided military training and weapons. For instance, a People's Security Force (PSF) involving the police, the people's militia, the fire service, volunteer civilians, political parties and members of the Youth Buddhist Association (YMBA) has been organised to fight the resistance in the urban areas including the commercial capital Yangon.

Pro-resistance media claims that Myanmar's military has been seriously depleted by desertions and casualties and new recruits are reluctant to join due to heavy hand being used against civilians, particularly their own kith and kin, in the Bamar belt, which is the main recruitment zone of the *Tatmadaw*. The NUG also claims that there is a drop in the optees for "Defence Services Academy, Defence Services Technological Academy and Defence Services Medical Academy," which has led to a relaxation in age by six months to 19 years.[26]

The traditional factor for motivating the soldiers to undertake civilian control and law and order was to instil a belief that a civilian government is not capable of managing the country's sovereignty as well as the majority Buddhist identity, which does not seem to gel any longer. This could be due to the intensity of fighting with the PDF and the EAOs as well as resentment against military actions against the public—the main factor remains indeterminate for now. The NUG, on the other hand, claims that youth prefer to join the PDF as well as the EAOs. Around 100 soldiers, including officers, reportedly defected to the AA since the coup.[27]

Role of the International Community

Myanmar Army is known to treat the international and regional community with impunity when faced with opposition. Thus, the ten-member ASEAN bloc's five-point plan has failed to move forward after it was first mooted in April 2021 in the presence of Senior General Min Aung Hlaing. Banning representatives of the SAC from ASEAN meetings has also not helped. While the USA and Western nations have employed political and economic sanctions as a weapon to leverage the regime, China and Russia have provided a shield of sorts in the UN Security Council, amongst other bodies.

Russia is the key supporter of the junta as Moscow too feels isolated after the Ukraine war. Thus, Russian Foreign Minister Sergei Lavrov was in Myanmar on his way to the ASEAN meet in Cambodia in August 2022. Russian Ministry of Defence has hosted Senior General Min Aung Hlaing a number of times. Of the six new Su-30 jet fighters ordered by the Myanmar Air Force, two were delivered in March 2022. Russian pilots and technicians have been deployed in Myanmar until the warranty period is over.[28]

Chinese and Russian diplomatic and military support is expected to sustain the SAC and the *Tatmadaw* in the months ahead. On the other hand, India which has very significant political, security and diplomatic interests in Myanmar, has maintained calls for negotiations between the opposing sides and an end to violence.

The Past as the Future: Will the Military Succeed in the 21st Century?

The military coup on February 2021 may have surprised many, but close observers of the Myanmar Army have held the past record of the military's penchant to intervene to control political power in the country as a reminder that "democratisation" from 2011 onwards may have been just a façade and the *Tatmadaw* leadership did not accept the devolution of power to political parties which had widespread support such as the NLD.

A brief recount of the Myanmar Army's dalliance in seizing power would be essential to understand the repetition in February 2021. The first time the military seized power in a coup was in 1962, and ruled the country through a Revolutionary Council. In December 1973, a referendum was held on a new constitution which was massively rigged as per a close observer of the Myanmar situation, Bertil Lintner, thus, 90.19 per cent approval was claimed for the new constitution promulgated on 03 January 1974.

Lintner records that 451 contested seats were won by the Burma Socialist Programme Party (BSPP) with an officially declared 94.61 per cent turnout when elections were held in February and March 1974. The one-party rule continued through successive elections. The BSPP won all the 464 seats it contested in 1978, all the 475 it contested in 1981 and all the 489 it contested in 1985.[29] Elections were also supposed to have held in parts of the country which were not even controlled by the government but controlled by various armed rebel movements.

Over the years, public discontent brewed, leading to the 1988 pro-democracy uprising, which was brutally crushed by the then military junta. The State Law and Order Restoration Council (SLORC), a front, was formed to run the country dominated by uniformed officials. The political façade was provided by the pro-military entity, the National Unity Party (NUP), a replacement for the BSPP. The formation of the NLD after the August-September 1988 uprising was a defining event. It quickly gained popularity, winning the 27 May 1990 elections with a landslide victory capturing 392 of the 485 seats it contested in urban as well as rural areas, while the NUP got a mere 10 seats. The junta claimed that the popularity of the military was restricted to urban areas, which was refuted by the all-round gains made by the nascent NLD.

However, the landslide victory of the NLD led to nullifying the elections on 27 July through "Announcement 1/90" by the SLORC, which declared that only the junta "has the right to legislative power"—and that "the representatives elected by the people" would merely be "responsible for drafting a new constitution for a future democratic state." A crackdown on the NLD was imminent, and leaders, including chairperson Daw Aung Suu Kyi, were jailed while many fled the country to India and Thailand.

The 1990 elections could be seen as a precursor of sorts for the elections held in November 2020, where the pro-junta parties faced a similar rout. One of the important lessons drawn by the military from the 1990 elections, which have a bearing on the proposal by the SAC for elections in 2023 or later, is that of the proportional representation system. It was seen that the NUP had garnered over 20 per cent of the popular vote but could gain very few seats due to the first-past-the-post electoral system in Myanmar; thus, Senior General Min Aung Hlaing has proposed a proportional representative system.[30]

In 1993, a new platform was formed, the Union Solidarity and Development Association, which was renamed the Union Solidarity and Development Party (USDP) in 2010, comprising mainly former military officers. It was almost a mirror image of the NUP. In the following years, a so-called "National Convention", mostly of non-elected representatives handpicked by the military drafted a new constitution which was completed in April 2008. The military, which had renamed itself the State Peace and Development Council (SPDC), announced that the constitution had been approved by 92.4 per cent of the voters. A defining feature of the new Constitution was the reservation of 25 per cent of seats in parliament for serving members of the *Tatmadaw*. These moves had come in response to the 2007 Saffron Revolution, international pressure, and the desire for economic growth.[31]

The USDP swept the elections held in November 2010 in which the NLD did not participate. A "civilian" government was formed comprised mainly of retired military officers under U Thein Sein, a former senior general with oversight by Than Shwe, the military supremo.[32] Many saw a new transformation in Myanmar, and some in the Western media hailed Thein Sein as "Myanmar's Gorbachev". Yet the reins of power remained with Senior General Than Shwe. Notwithstanding that, the same impression of Myanmar transforming towards the democratic path gained ground.

In November 2015, when the NLD secured 255 of 330 contested seats in the Lower House and 135 of 168 contested seats in the Upper House, it was believed that the transformation of Myanmar into a democracy was well on the way. The USDP won only 30 and 11 seats, respectively. The military appointed 56 seats in the Upper House and 110 in the Lower House. The SPDC Chairman, Senior General Than Shwe, intervened to accept the result by the military. Yet, when in November 2020, the NLD won 258 seats in the Upper House and 138 in the Lower House, defeating the USDP, which won 26 and 7 seats in the Upper and Lower House, respectively, the military saw red and took over the state power.[33]

Conclusion

More than a year and a half after Myanmar's military junta seized power in a coup, the military's concerted offensive operations have failed to crush anti-regime resistance forces and consolidate power. The violent deadlock between the military government and multiple opposition groups shows no signs of easing, and the people of Myanmar remain trapped in an escalating political, economic, and humanitarian crisis. These resistance groups now present a powerful front of grassroots-level insurgency that is hampering operations by the *Tatmadaw*. The power dynamics between the military and anti-regime resistance forces is existential for both sides. Thus, the deadlock is expected to continue with much pain and loss of blood for both sides.

Min Aung Hlaing has been working on switching the country to a proportional representation (PR) system for the next election, which the regime plans to hold in 2023 after the NLD won landslide victories in both elections held under the first-past-the-post system.[34] Elections, if held under this mandate, are expected to be bloody and may result in propping up a regime that is seen as a front for the military. However, the acceptability of such an order by the EAOs and their political fronts remains a question mark.

Thus, how this confrontation ends is unclear for now. Although a federation is the best option for a country as diverse as Myanmar, in the long term, the military is unlikely to agree to it and has been resisting it for decades. Myanmar's junta spokesman, Major General Zaw Min Tun, for instance, with reference to the virtually autonomous body in the Wa region neighbouring China, said the regime agrees in principle to United Wa State Party (UWSP) demands that the Wa region be upgraded to a "self-administered state". "In principle, we have a general policy to grant higher status regarding the Wa".[35] Clearly, there is no light at the end of the tunnel for Myanmar.

ENDNOTES

1. Chiara Torelli and Emily Griffith, "Myanmar Conflict Briefing," *AOAV* (2022), available at https://aoav.org.uk/2022/myanmar-briefing-report/, last accessed on 22 August 2022.
2. The Geneva Academy's Rule of Law in Armed Conflict portal, RULAC, has designated the intensity of the armed violence in Myanmar, as well as the levels of organisation of the armed actors involved, as meeting the threshold to qualify as an intrastate armed conflict as per Myanmar Conflict Briefing. By Chiara Torelli and Emily Griffith on 01 February 2022, available at https://aoav.org.uk/2022/myanmar-briefing-report/, last accessed on 22 August 2022.
3. Zubaidah Abdul Jalil, "Myanmar: Military executes four democracy activists including ex-MP," *BBC*, 25 July 2022, available at https://www.bbc.com/news/world-asia-62287815, last accessed on 22 August 2022.
4. "Myanmar extends state of emergency for another six months," *The Print*, 01 August 2022, available at https://theprint.in/world/myanmar-extends-state-of-emergency-for-another-six-months/1064261/, last accessed on 22 August 2022.
5. Ibid.
6. "Junta Watch," *The Irrawaddy*, 09 July 2022, available at https://www.irrawaddy.com/specials/junta-watch/junta-watch-coup-leader-says-military-still-needed-in-politics-another-asean-snub-and-more.html, last accessed on 22 August 2022.
7. "Myanmar Study Group: Final Report- Anatomy of the Military Coup and Recommendations for U.S. Response," *USIP* (2022), available at https://www.usip.org/publications/2022/02/myanmar-study-group-final-report, last accessed on 22 August 2022.
8. Chiara Torelli and Emily Griffith, 2022.
9. "Malaysia foreign minister meets counterpart from Myanmar shadow government in Washington," *Reuters*, 15 May 2022, available at https://www.reuters.com/world/asia-pacific/malaysia-foreign-minister-meets-counterpart-myanmar-shadow-govt-washington-2022-05-15/, last accessed on 22 August 2022.
10. Burma is divided into seven regions dominated by the Bamar ethnic majority and seven states inhabited primarily by ethnic minorities.
11. Ye Myo Hei, "One Year On: The Momentum of Myanmar's Armed Rebellion," *Wilson Centre*, May 2022, available at https://www.wilsoncenter.org/sites/default/files/media/uploads/documents/ASIA_220519_1YearOn-BRIEF_V1r2.pdf, last accessed on 22 August 2022.
12. Ibid

13. "Six Myanmar Regime Officials Assassinated in Yangon in Last Four Days," *The Irrawaddy,* 18 July 2022, available at https://www.irrawaddy.com/news/burma/six-myanmar-regime-officials-assassinated-in-yangon-in-last-four-days.html, last accessed on 22 August 2022.
14. "Junta Watch: Regime Shrugs Off Outcry on Executions; Claims Troops Uphold Human Rights, and More," *The Irrawaddy*, 18 June 2022, available at https://www.irrawaddy.com/specials/junta-watch/junta-watch-regime-shrugs-off-outcry-on-executions-claims-troops-uphold-human-rights-and-more.html, last accessed on 22 August 2022.
15. "With No Int'l Support, Myanmar Resistance Groups Seek Public Funds for homemade weapons," *The Irrawaddy*, 19 July 2022, available at https://www.irrawaddy.com/news/burma/with-no-intl-support-myanmar-resistance-groups-seek-public-funds-for-homemade-weapons.html, last accessed on 22 August 2022.
16. "Myanmar's Shadow Govt Urges Int'l Community to Step Up Support," *The Irrawaddy*, 23 June 2022, available at https://www.irrawaddy.com/news/burma/myanmars-shadow-govt-urges-intl-community-to-step-up-support.html, last accessed on 22 August 2022.
17. "Civilian Suffering in Myanmar Northwest Highest as Regime War Crimes," *World News Net*, 2022, available at https://theworldnews.net/mm-news/civilian-suffering-in-myanmar-northwest-highest-as-regime-war-crimes-continue, last accessed on 22 August 2022.
18. "Myanmar's Troubled History: Coups, Military Rule, and Ethnic Conflict," *Council for Foreign Relations*, 2021, available at https://www.cfr.org/backgrounder/myanmar-history-coup-military-rule-ethnic-conflict-rohingya, last accessed on 22 August 2022.
19. "Myanmar Study Group: Final Report–Anatomy of the Military Coup and Recommendations for U.S. Response," *USIP*, 2022, available at https://www.usip.org/publications/2022/02/myanmar-study-group-final-report, last accessed on 22 August 2022.
20. "Is Myanmar's Military on Its Last Legs," *CSIS,* 21 June 2022, available at https://www.csis.org/analysis/myanmars-military-its-last-legs, last accessed on 22 August 2022.
21. USIP, 2022.
22. Ibid.
23. P.K. Chakravorty, "Myanmar's Armed Forces (*Tatmadaw*)," *VIF*, 2017, available at https://www.vifindia.org/article/2017/november/29/myanmar-s-armed-forces-tatmadaw, last accessed on 22 August 2022.
24. "2021 Justice For Myanmar releases list of military-owned businesses, their directors and significant business associates and calls for immediate targeted international sanctions," *Justice for Myanmar,* 04 February 2021, available at https://www.business-humanrights.org/en/latest-news/justice-for-myanmar-releases-list-of-military-owned-businesses-their-directors-and-significant-business-associates-and-calls-for-immediate-targeted-international-sanctions/, last accessed on 22 August 2022.
25. "Six Myanmar Regime Officials Assassinated in Yangon in Last Four Days," *The Irrawaddy,* 18 July 2022, available at https://www.irrawaddy.com/news/burma/six-myanmar-regime-officials-assassinated-in-yangon-in-last-four-days.html, last accessed on 22 August 2022.
26. "Junta Watch: Military Bends Rules to Fill Ranks; Loyal Monk Promoted," *The Irrawaddy*, 02 July 2022, available at https://www.irrawaddy.com/specials/junta-watch/junta-watch-military-bends-rules-to-fill-ranks-loyal-monk-promoted-and-more.html, last accessed on 22 August 2022.
27. "Over 100 Junta Soldiers Defect to Arakan Army in Western Myanmar", *The Irrawaddy*, 14 June 2022, available at https://www.irrawaddy.com/news/burma/over-100-junta-soldiers-defect-to-arakan-army-in-western-myanmar.html, last accessed on 22 August 2022.
28. "Myanmar Regime Takes Delivery of Two Su-30 Fighter Jets From Russia," *The Irrawaddy*, 04 July 2022, available at https://www.irrawaddy.com/news/burma/myanmar-regime-takes-delivery-of-two-su-30-fighter-jets-from-russia.html, last accessed on 22 August 2022.
29. "Myanmar Military's Long History of Electoral Fraud," *The Irrawaddy*, 19 July 2022, available

at https://www.irrawaddy.com/opinion/guest-column/myanmar-militarys-long-history-of-electoral-fraud.html, last accessed on 22 August 2022.

30. Ibid.
31. Chiara Torelli and Emily Griffith, 2022.
32. "Myanmar Military's Long History of Electoral Fraud," *The Irrawaddy*, 19 July 2022, available at https://www.irrawaddy.com/opinion/guest-column/myanmar-militarys-long-history-of-electoral-fraud.html, last accessed on 26 August 2022.
33. Ibid.
34. "Junta Watch," *The Irrawaddy*, 09 July 2022, available at https://www.irrawaddy.com/specials/junta-watch/junta-watch-coup-leader-says-military-still-needed-in-politics-another-asean-snub-and-more.html, last accessed on 26 August 2022.
35. "Myanmar Regime Unlikely to Grant Wa Statehood: Analysts," *The Irrawaddy*, 06 June 2022, available at https://www.irrawaddy.com/opinion/analysis/myanmar-regime-unlikely-to-grant-wa-statehood-analysts.html, last accessed on 26 August 2022.

4

Understanding Ethnic Armed Movements in Myanmar Through the Decades

Angshuman Choudhury

ABSTRACT

Ethnic armed movements have played a central role in shaping postcolonial Myanmar in more than one way. They have not only served as litmus tests for the Burmese state as an entity that underwent tectonic structural changes through the decades after independence but also moulded the fluid relationship between the 'centre' and the 'peripheries'. At the same time, these movements have decisively influenced Myanmar's political economy, which in turn, has shaped the way various politico-security actors have operated through the decades. Ethnic Armed Organisations (EAOs), as they are most commonly referred to in Myanmar, continue to directly impact Burmese politics even today. They continue to offer important templates of ethno-political autonomy and democratic federalism that often counteract the Burmese state's powerful centralising and majoritarian tendencies.

This chapter will analyse the aforementioned aspects in detail. This, it will do by analysing a set of handpicked EAOs whose histories and current politico-security trajectories reflect the dominant patterns of ethnic armed movements in Myanmar. While there are multiple elements to dissect within ethnic armed movements in the country, this chapter will focus on three specific ones: ethnic autonomy and federalism, ceasefires, and international (or cross-border) dynamics. These elements will be analysed primarily within a historical timeframe, with a focus on the period starting from the late 1980s/early 1990s. Finally, this chapter will contextualise this analysis within the current post-coup dynamics in Myanmar so as to offer a prognostic understanding of ethnic armed movements in the country.

Introduction

In modern Burmese history, 1946 and 1947 were two crucial and in many ways, decisive years. Events that transpired during these years shaped Burma's political fortunes in more ways than one. In fact, so definitive was this period in Myanmar's history that it contains the key to fully comprehending the meaning and significance of what is happening in the country today, more than seven decades later. During these two years, even as a powerful Burmese elite fought for independence from British colonial rule, a dizzyingly complex and diverse ethno-political landscape took shape. This tapestry of numerous, and often clashing, socio-political aspirations became the normative foundation of the modern Burmese nation and its core political economy. Not just that, the events of this period also created a set of endemic conditions for how Burma, as a country located at the crossroads of two sub-continental worlds and constituted by influential sub-national polities, was to engage with other countries in the region.

In March 1946, at the cusp of Burma's independence from colonial rule, Kachin, Shan and Chin ethnic leaders gathered in the small town of Panglong located at the centre of what is today Shan State. They were there to deliberate over several meetings upon the political fortunes of their respective communities within an independent Burma. In other words, they were there to exercise their distinct agency in shaping what postcolonial Burma would look like as a nation-state. In material terms, they sought certain guarantees for their ethnic minority communities to ensure that the independent Burmese state and its majority Bamar constituencies do not eventually invalidate their unique identities and indigenous rights.

The Bamar side was keen on ensuring that the minorities, politically, remained a part of the soon-to-emerge union with some degree of constitutional permanence. This brought into sharp relief a fundamental divergence between how the majority and minority blocs envisioned postcolonial Burma and saw themselves within it. Something that the Kachin representative at Panglong said in response to an argument posited by Thakin Nu (also known as U Nu), a senior Bamar political figure who later became independent Burma's first Prime Minister, about the ostensible divide-and-rule policies of the British Government, captured the minoritarian anxiety about a majoritarian Burmese state:

> "What have the Burman people done toward the hill peoples to win their faith and love? Did not a section of the Burmese public who, while saying that we all belong to the same race, blood and home, call in Japanese and cause the hill peoples to suffer? If, therefore, the Burmese want unity with the hill peoples, they must change."[1]

The memory of the more-than-titular victory that the Kachins, Shans and Chins secured by signing the Panglong Agreement in 1947 were critical to the trajectory of ethnic politics in modern Myanmar. The deeply-entrenched historical position of the Panglong Agreement has also been central to the transformation of unarmed ethnic movements into armed ones, wherein the failure of the Bamar-dominated state to deliver guarantees of the pact, in conjunction with the emergence of an apathetic civilian administration and then a violent military state, gradually militarised the ethnic peripheries. That several ethnic groups picked up arms against the Burmese state may also be seen within a certain historical continuum straddling a fraught colonial past that generated narratives of victimhood and violence.

This weaponisation of discontent and victimhood in the post-independence decades not just shaped the internal political and social nature of ethnic minority societies but also the very character of the Burmese state. At the same time, it perpetuated the politico-territorial exclusivity of ethnic borderlands as indigenous spaces, a reality that the colonial empire itself was deeply conscious of. The Burmese state and its like-minded external allies often saw these peripheral spaces as "ungoverned" and "anarchic" as opposed to the "governed" and "peaceful" Bamar heartland; in reality, most of these spaces, through the post-independence decades, remained under the continuous de facto control of ethnic armed entities that were able to create and sustain stable administrative structures with great ease and non-interference.

The history of armed ethnic movements in modern Burma is a history of engagements and disengagements, manifested in the form of civil-military conflict and ceasefires, respectively. While conflict generated displacement and impoverishment, ceasefires often produced a strange limbo wherein elites on both sides were able to amass material benefits while the general population lived under the shadow of negative peace. This produced a peculiar political economy that birthed a powerful set of rebel elites for whom durable peace was less profitable than protracted ceasefires. At the same time, it added to the economic and political heft of the country's all-powerful military, colloquially known as '*Tatmadaw*'.

A central element of this political economy, especially in Burma's northern rebel worlds, was the black and grey economies of contraband production and smuggling, which remains deeply enmeshed in state and non-state networks. This included a cross-border economy of extraction and trade in rare-earths and timber with China and, unsurprisingly, a sprawling underground ecosystem dealing in arms and narcotics. In fact, Burma's northern ethnic rebel worlds are intrinsically tied to drug production and smuggling networks based in and around the infamous Golden Triangle area of northeast Burma, Laos, and Thailand. This underground conflict economy largely rests on rent-seeking, warlordism and violence and hence, has a direct correlation to underdevelopment. In that sense, the Burmese case exhibits some of the key identifiers of civil war economies in the existing literature: parasitic, illicit, and predatory.[2] Another defining element of Myanmar's ethnic armed conflicts and the attendant political economy of ceasefires is group fragmentation, which is noticed in several other cases of protracted civil wars.

This chapter will analyse these characteristic micro features of ethnic armed conflict in Myanmar, as well as the macro drivers of political, social, economic and cultural discontent that sustain armed struggle amongst Burma's myriad ethnic minorities. It will try to outline the key patterns of engagement and disengagement between these movements and the Burmese state and their consequences on the country's fractured political economy. It will use specific Ethnic Armed Organisations (EAOs) to showcase dominant trends, patterns, narratives and discourses. The main period of analysis will be 1946-1990.

Troubled Beginnings: Rise and Fall of the Panglong Spirit

The process of ethnic identity formation and consolidation in Burma did not begin or end in the colonial period; it predated the empire and was firmly rooted even before the arrival of Europeans in Southeast Asia in the 17th and 18th centuries. Normatively, ethnic identity formation in Burma is best understood as a relational process that is conditioned by historical group perceptions about the self and the other. Thus, the idea of the "habitus", articulated and defined by, among others, James Weber and Pierre Bourdieu, may be useful in unpacking how social relations and behaviour created lingering ethnic identities through pre-colonial, colonial and postcolonial Burma. Colonial governance distorted the arc of ethnic identity formation, as arbitrary socio-demographic categories were slapped onto the complex ethnic landscape of Burma. These ascriptive policies of the empire had such a powerful impact that otherwise fluid ethnic categories became ossified, taking a life of their own and turning into permanent, often non-negotiable, political markers. In that sense, ethnic identity formation in Burma became anchored in "cultural differences that are identified through repeated interactions and gradually perceived as politically important".[3]

Burma's postcolonial ethnic milieu needs to be placed within this context. On 12 February 1947, the landmark Panglong Agreement was signed by General Aung San and twenty-three representatives of the Chins, Kachins and Shans. Just a month earlier, he had signed an agreement for Burmese independence with British Prime Minister Clement Atlee. So, for Burma, independence from colonial rule and ethno-political reformulation went hand-in-hand. Panglong was not just a pact but a core political framework for the Burmese state itself. So decisive was this day in the history of postcolonial Burma, that 12 February is still celebrated as "Union Day". The exact terms of negotiations varied. For example, the Shan *saophas* (traditional leaders) managed to secure a right to secede from the union, while the Kachins got their own state without that right. However, the bare-bones term was clear for most of the ethnic representatives, that is, association with the union was contingent upon two key interlinked aspects that are still fundamental to minority politics in Burma—autonomy and federalism. Hence, even before Burma officially got independence from the British, a big chunk of its ethnic minority peoples had successfully carved out their exclusive politico-territorial spaces in the union.

For the core Bamar political elite that had organised itself within the Burma Independence Army (BIA) and later the AFPFL, led by General Aung San and Thakin Soe, and U Nu became recognised, the importance of engaging with ethnic minorities, who had become potent socio-political forces within the emerging Burmese "national" polity. They quickly realised that without the political concurrence of these ethnic minorities, independent Burma would disintegrate into many pieces. It is this imperative that ultimately gave birth to the Panglong Agreement, which despite its shortcomings, set the foundational framework for progressive and inclusive ethno-politics in modern Burma. At its core, it also laid out what a federalised Burma could look like, where ethnic peoples have the agency to decide their own political and economic fortunes. Josef Silverstein has rightly called it a "key document in the post-war, pre-independence relations between the hill peoples and the Burmese".[4]

Yet, Panglong 1947 was a grossly limited pact, both quantitatively and qualitatively. First, it was signed by representatives from just four ethnic groups, that is, Shan, Kachin, Chin and Bamar. This means dozens of other influential ethnic groups, such as the Karens, Mons, Karennis, Rakhine and Kayah, were left out of the crucial process of transfer of power from the colonial to the postcolonial Burmese state. This is shown by the parallel negotiations and undertakings of the excluded ethnic groups. For instance, in the same month that Panglong was signed, the Karens, under the leadership of the radical Saw Ba U Gyi, formed the Karen National Union (KNU) and demanded the creation of a separate "Karen State" at a conference in Rangoon. This was the first time an ethnic minority in Burma had formally iterated its distinct political aspirations using an organisational vocabulary.

Second, it was rife with vague and broad provisions, which lacked anchors for implementation or legal guarantees. In that sense, it was a pre-constitutional and extra-legal agreement that was largely non-enforceable. Beyond this, it was a stillborn baby of Burmese independence—handicapped by the unfortunate circumstances of history. On 19 July 1947, Aung San, who was generally regarded by ethnic minorities as a relatively more trustworthy Bamar figure than others, was assassinated in Rangoon. While Aung San himself had majoritarian impulses, which became clear during the negotiations, his sudden death shook the very foundations of the Panglong spirit. His successor, U Nu, simply could not secure the trust of the minorities the way the General had managed to. Further, as Matthew Walton has pointed out in his seminal study of the Panglong Agreement, the ethnic minority sides themselves had serious credibility and circumstantial issues that would later jeopardise the whole process.

However, the Panglong spirit, which had certainly begun to fray at the edges after Aung San's death, would really collapse only in the later 1950s. A major flashpoint behind this was the gradual realisation amongst ethnic minorities that the Bamar side was not serious about the guarantees of the agreement. The 1947 Constitution was structurally designed to favour the Bamar majority, evinced by the number of seat representatives from the community occupied in the Chamber of Deputies and Chamber of Nationalities. General Ne Win's violent 1962 coup was the straw that broke the camel's back, but even before that, the Burmese union, fragile from the very start, had begun to fall apart. This slow-but-visible collapse was driven and accelerated not just by the untenability of the Panglong process but also by a set of low-intensity insurgencies that sprang up right after independence in defence of both ideologies and ethnic nations driven by, among others, the Communist Party of Burma (CPB), People's Volunteer Organisation (PVO), the Karens, the Karennis, and the Arakanese. Amongst these, the Karen insurgency organised under the Karen National Defence Organisation (KNDO) was the most formidable. It created the preconditions for widespread ethnic rebellion in postcolonial Burma by exhibiting to a large minority constituency that Myanmar was a Bamar-dominated nation in which the gun was the only effective way to reclaim political agency and protect unique identities.

Imagined Nations: Beginnings of the Karen and Kachin Revolts

The period between 1948 and 1950 is one of the critical contradictions. On the one hand, it saw the rise of the first ethnic armed movements in the non-Bamar areas outside the Irrawaddy plains. On the other, it marked the emergence of a

Rangoon-based Burmese regime that was politically and militarily assertive in the face of insurgencies. This head-on clash between the administrations of independent Burma's first Prime Minister, U Nu, and the various armed groups set the tone for the civil conflict that has characterised the country since. Notably, this was also when the modern Myanmar military, colloquially referred to as the '*Tatmadaw*', began taking shape. Initially, the *tatmadaw* was a fragile tapestry of Bamar, Karen, Kachin and Chin battalions, out of which large chunks of the Bamar were left-leaning. It soon defected to join hands with the Communist insurgents. Eventually, the ethnic minority battalions, except for the Chins, also joined their respective rebellions. Interestingly, it was commanded by an ethnic Karen officer known as General Smith Dun, who is famously known as the "Four-Foot Colonel". Just a year after independence, as the Karen revolt broke out, Dun was fired and replaced with his deputy, General Ne Win, who was to later grab power in an infamous coup in 1962 and rule Myanmar for more than 25 years. This was one of the several critical events that marked the reversal of the Panglong spirit of ethnic inclusivity in post-independence Burma.

The Karen and Kachin cases, given their quantitative and qualitative potency, are aptly illustrative of the broad patterns of ethnic armed politics that took a firm grip in Burma soon after independence. Both reveal the dominant trends of engagement, disengagement, consolidation, fragmentation and profitability that characterised Myanmar's myriad EAOs through the decades. Most importantly, the Karens and Kachins were some of the first ethnic groups to rebel against the Rangoon Government based on the key objectives of ethnic self-preservation and political autonomy. They displayed strategic resolve and fortitude, including the capability to stage frontal attacks against key Government targets in urban centres and the countryside and even capture and hold territory. Besides, the Karens and Kachins became the source of support and encouragement for other small ethnic nationalities, such as the Karennis and the Mons. This is a pattern that has endured through the decades and is even seen in the civil warscape that emerged in Myanmar in the period after the February 2021 coup.

The year 1949 was a crossover one for independent Myanmar, as that is when several ethnic rebellions broke out in full colour. Among them, the Karen insurgency was the most potent. Arguably, it posed the biggest military threat to the Rangoon Government at that time. In fact, it showed that "ethnic divisions were of more concern" to the U Nu Government than ideological insurgencies led by other Bamar-led groups, such as the CPB and PVO.[5] On 30 January 1949, weeks after the massacre of hundreds of Karen civilians in the town of Mergui and another village north of the national capital, the KNDO attacked the Rangoon suburb of Insein, triggering an aggravated military response by Government forces and Bamar-led anti-Karen rioters in several places. The urban battle, which spilled over into Rangoon proper, lasted for 112 days in total, during which the rebels also managed to attack the Mingdalon Air Force base. It was during the Battle of Insein that the Myanmar military used the air force against ethnic insurgents for the first time. Despite the ethnic Karens in the *tatmadaw* defecting to the rebel side, the battle culminated in a Government victory, with the Karen insurgents forced to flee towards the Thai-Myanmar border across the Irrawaddy delta.

Subsequently, they set up their main base in the town of Taungoo between Rangoon and Mandalay. Here, the KNU set up a broadcasting station to relay propaganda and multilingual Christian hymns, displaying the first signs of a permanent rebel presence within enclosed grounds. By June 1949, the Karens had created a fighting force called the Kawthoolei Armed Forces (KAF). Just a year later, the *tatmadaw* chased the rebels out of Taungoo further east, forcing them to set up base at Mawchi, just fifty kilometres from the Thai border in the Karenni area. It is here that the KNU started to undertake cross-border bartering of high-value, locally-mined tungsten in exchange for arms and ammunition. This political economy of border trading in rare-earths was to become a defining feature of Burma's rebel worlds in the decades to come. Soon, the rebels moved base again, this time settling in the small market town of Papun, situated by the bank of the Yunzalin river. In Papun, the Karens created their first "state", calling it by the mythical name of "Kawthoolei". In July 1950, during the first open Karen congress, a common administration for all Karen "liberated areas" was declared under the so-called "Kawthoolei Governing Body", which could be shortened to the rather awkward acronym of "KGB". The first real signs of a rebel administration in post-independence Burma had emerged. Incidentally, right after this historic congress, the KNU Chairman, Saw Ba U Gyi, was gunned down by *tatmadaw* forces near the Thai border, majorly demoralising and dissipating the rebellion. Subsequently, the KNU fought what academics have called a "protracted rearguard operation", engaging in attritional battles with the *tatmadaw* from their bases in Karen State.[6]

The Kachin revolt began almost at the same time, with the highly-decorated and battle-hardened commander of the *tatmadaw's* 1st Kachin Rifles, Naw Seng, defecting to the Karen side when ordered to attack the Karen-held town of Taungoo in February 1949. While the Kachins had been given their own state after Panglong 1947, which resulted in many of them maintaining their loyalty to the U Nu administration, Naw Seng aspired for sovereignty for his people. After the Battle of Insein, his mixed Kachin-Karen force headed north towards Shan State, incorporating smaller rebellions, such as those of the Pa-Os, and eventually capturing the Shan capital of Lashio. After months of fleeing the *tatmadaw* through northern Shan state, he finally reached some Kachin villages to the east of Kutkai where he formally raised the so-called "Pawngyawng National Defence Force (PNDF)", named after his desired mythical name for the independent Kachin homeland, much like "Kawthoolei" for the Karens. This was also where the famous red-and-green Kachin flag, with the traditional *dah* (machete) at the centre, was unfurled for the first time. Soon, Naw Seng's rebellion melted away as Government forces forced him to flee across the Sino-Burmese border to Yunnan.

So, while both the Kachin and Karen revolts largely failed to secure their key politico-strategic objectives and the Rangoon Government prevailed, they created a structural framework and political template for ethnic armed struggles in modern Burma. Moreover, they brought to the fore the nationalistic imaginations of the ethnic minorities and gave them semiotic markers and vocabularies in the form of mythical names and flags. To use Benedict Anderson's framing, the KNU and Naw Seng manifested the "imagined communities" that their peoples had fostered for a long, which was to have a lasting effect on the ethno-political mindscape of Myanmar. At the heart of these ethnic discontents lay Rangoon's aggressive and predatory political and economic policies of imposing a Bamar (or Burman) identity on ethnic minority groups and extracting high-value natural resources from their territories. This created a sense of both cultural and economic displacement in ethnic minority regions, which remained impoverished and volatile while the Bamar heartland witnessed development and stability. This core asymmetry between Myanmar's minority and majority regions continued to feed the conflict cycle for decades.

Tug-of-war: Rebel Consolidation and Counter-consolidation

For Myanmar's ethnic armed groups, the period between 1950 and 1988 was one of consolidation, expansion and stabilisation. This period may be divided into several "cycles" as Martin Smith does in *State of Strife: The Dynamics of Ethnic Armed Conflict in Burma*—normalisation of insurgent orders, escalation of violence following the breakdown of trust after Ne Win's 1962 coup, internalisation and intensification, and expansion.[7] The period began with the complete collapse of the Panglong spirit triggered by pre-existing structural factors and transformation of the Burmese state from a civilian multi-party democracy to a one-party, socialist dictatorship. As the Rangoon regime upped its ante, so did the rebels. Thus, this was a period of intense push-and-pull and cyclical rationalisations, wherein greater state repression justified stronger rebel pushbacks, which in turn, generated the conditions for even harsher state repression and militarism.

During the 1950s, the U Nu Government, while espousing a diverse union, acted in ways that deepened and broadened the process of 'Burmanisation' by invalidating ethnic aspirations—such as by carving out an arbitrarily-drawn Karen State, ignoring demographic realities. This "politics of contradiction" that Rangoon displayed diluted the trust that some ethnic minorities had placed in the postcolonial Burmese state.[8] Thus, we see a rapid ballooning of the EAO space during this period. As the Communist insurgency picked up steam on the side, the U Nu administration lost not only effective territorial control of large swathes of territory, but also the general political legitimacy to rule. This set off a series of events that put Ne Win in charge of a 'caretaker Government' in 1958, which in turn, created the perfect conditions for new rebellions to take shape. However, even before that, new rebel formations mushroomed across the ethnic minority regions in the southeast and north.

In 1957, the Karennis, under the leadership of Saw Maw Reh, set up their own EAO known as the 'Karenni National Progressive Party (KNPP).' Then, in 1958, Nai Shwe Kyin established the New Mon State Party (NMSP), while rejecting the ceasefire between the Mon People's Front (MPF) and the Rangoon Government. It was also in 1958 that a nascent Shan insurgency took shape along the Thai border, owing to U Nu's resistance against growing demands amongst Shan youth groups for ethnic autonomy even as the constitutional right to secede given to the Shans kicked in. In March 1960, a group of Shan students formally established the Shan State Independence Army (SSIA) in Möng Yawn, close to the Thai border. Notably, the Shan army at that time consisted mostly of ethnic Wa troopers under the command of Bo Maung—the same Wa who went on to later break away from the CPB and establish the biggest EAO in Myanmar. In 1960, another EAO far down south in Rakhine State, known as the Arakan National Liberation Party (ANLP), was formed.

Then, in 1961, the Kachins, disenchanted by the majoritarian attitude of the U Nu caretaker regime and a longstanding desire for a sovereign homeland, formed the Kachin Independence Army (KIA) near Lashio. Through the next two decades, the KIA grew into a formidable armed group, controlling vast stretches of territory in Kachin State and securing a large war booty through sustained control of jade mines in the region. Once Ne Win consolidated power after the 1962 coup through his Burma Socialist Programme Party (BSPP), the majoritarian, socialist dictator began "[suppressing] non-Burman cultural and political identities, epitomised by the banning of minority languages from state schools", which then "drove a new wave of disaffected ethnic minority citizens into rebellion."[9]

In 1963, he initiated a new type of counterinsurgency (COIN) strategy called the 'Four Cuts', which aimed at depriving the EAOs of food, funds, intelligence and recruits, and also resulted in large-scale displacement of civilians.[10] The *tatmadaw* began to use this aggressive COIN approach in the countryside, leading to rebel retrenchment and widespread civilian displacements. In 1975, the Ne Win regime used it against the KNU and then against the KIA. In fact, there is unambiguous evidence that the *tatmadaw* continues to deploy the 'Four-Cuts Strategy' in the civil war battlefield even today.[11] However, regime forces failed to achieve comprehensive victories, and several EAOs continued to expand or preserve their territorial domains. The *tatmadaw's* ineptitude in fighting guerrilla forces across hilly terrain was a major reason behind this.

During the late 1950s and 1960s, the drug trade in the infamous Golden Triangle sector in Myanmar's north-eastern borderlands began to get intertwined with ethnic rebellions. Not just that, during these years, a complex web of transnational relationships between Burma's ethnic armed actors and external entities began to emerge, such as those between the Shan rebels and US-backed Kuomintang (KMT) forces who had fled to Shan State after the Communist takeover of mainland China. In many ways, the KMT, generously armed by the US Central Intelligence Agency (CIA), tried to use the Shan insurgency to mask its presence inside Burma. In January 1961, the KMT was routed out of Shan State by a joint Chinese-Burmese offensive. The Burmese rebel groups also began to form strategic relationships with the Thai security establishment. This was largely due to deep geographical proximity between both sides and a larger US-backed, Bangkok-supported approach of instrumentalising the rebels as a bulwark against the spread of communism in the region. For the EAOs, this relationship was a material boon, as they could procure arms, ammunition, and other materials from across the border in Thailand.

The following years witnessed a further expansion of the EAO spaces, with several other ethnic groups establishing their own rebel organisations. While some of them were created by fusing existing formations, others were born independently. For example, the Kokang-led Shan State Army (SSA) was formed by a merger between the SSIA and the Shan National United Front (SNUF) in 1964, while the Chin National Front/Army (CNF/A) was raised autonomously in 1988. One oft-ignored aspect of this period is the attempt by the EAOs to create alliances with a broader agenda to engage in joint warfare against the *tatmadaw*. Till 1975, at least seven such rebel coalitions, such as the Democratic Nationalities United Front (DNUF) and United Nationalities Liberation Front (UNLF), were created, but none endured. This is an important historical fact, as it reveals the unifying tendencies of ethnic rebel groups based on the recognition of the need to pool resources and leverage against a powerful common enemy. Importantly, EAO alliance-building was also a direct outcome of weakening trust between ethnic minorities and the Bamar-led pro-democracy organisations. This tendency, in fact, is seen even in the current period, evinced by the formation of super-groups like the United Nationalities Federal Council (UNFC) and the Federal Political Negotiation and Consultative Committee (FPNCC) after the Thein Sein Government began a notional peace process in 2011.

On 10 May 1975, the EAOs, under the KNU's leadership, raised their own coalition after the Ne Win regime, just a year before, had floated a new constitution, which was perceived as anti-minority in nature, and the U Nu-led National United Liberation Front (NULF) failed to achieve meaningful outcomes. Representatives from thirteen EAOs formed the National Democratic Front (NDF) in Manerplaw, Karen State. It was a rebel alliance that was arguably far better organised than its predecessors. Notably, the NDF was tied together by a mutual defence pact, wherein the members were meant to assist each other in case of a Government attack. Manerplaw, hemmed by rugged mountains on one side, became a safe haven for the EAOs who wanted a common base to strategise and plan attacks against the *tatmadaw*. Its proximity to the Thai border also allowed the groups to build cross-border networks of mobilisation for logistical and other forms of support. According to Silverstein, the NDF's formation marked a new phase of the civil war.[12] In July 1992, the NDF published a document titled 'Manerplaw Agreement to Establish a Federal Union of Burma', which outlined their collective desire to build a federal union. Thus, the first proper political manifesto for a federal democratic union from the rebel side came out of Manerplaw, and that agenda sustains to this date. It reveals the core aspiration of Burma's ethnic minorities, that is, to secure meaningful autonomy for themselves within a larger democratic and equitable union of different ethnic nations.

Shifting Tides: Ceasefires, Fragmentations and Territorial Consolidation

By the 1980s, the military had started to broaden and deepen its operations against

EAOs. In 1984, it specifically began to stage yearlong frontal offensives against EAOs, especially the Karens, instead of staggered dry season limited defensive attacks. This began to have serious effects on Burma's rebel-world, and groups began to feel the pressure. Combined with other economic, strategic factors, and geopolitical pressures, the rebel-scape began to fracture. As Silverstein points out, the 1980s also saw the majority-versus-minority gap widen, as Ne Win's regime projected, through sustained one-sided propaganda, that the ethnic minorities were a threat to national security, especially the security of the Bamar heartland. This diluted the credibility of the ethnic armed struggle in front of a larger national audience. Notably, this period also witnessed widespread splintering in the rebel-worlds. Critical intra-EAO differences were, in fact, becoming increasingly common through the decades leading up to the 1990s. In some cases, they were triggered by ideological and cultural differences (such as in the Karen and Wa/Kokang cases), while in others, more material drivers were at play. In retrospect, these splits only helped the military reinforce its political and strategic dominance over the country by weakening rebel opposition.

The fracturing of the ethnic rebel-worlds was compounded by the return of a militaristic coup regime in 1988 in the form of the State Law and Order Restoration Council (SLORC) following widespread pro-democracy protests in the Bamar heartland. However, 1988 marked a unique moment in Burma's modern history; one could argue it for the civil war, it was a crossover year. The SLORC initiated a host of economic reforms, including moves to liberalise the economy and signing economic pacts with powerful neighbours, such as India and China. It also undertook notional political reforms, such as permitting elections in 1990. These produced new economic and geopolitical dynamics, which began to change the fundamental nature of the civil war landscape from one of open military-centric to a more diffused ceasefire-centric engagement. In 1989, one of the biggest rebels' splintering took place when the mighty CPB collapsed after an internal mutiny triggered by a complex set of longstanding structural and more immediate circumstantial factors, dissipating into several smaller ethnic minority-led EAOs. Among them was the so-called Wa-led, Pangshang-based Burma National United Party/Army (BNUP/BNUA), which soon became the United Wa State Party (UWSA), the largest and most well-armed EAO in Myanmar since then. The Kokangs formed the Burma National Democratic Alliance Army (BNDAA), which later became the Myanmar NDAA (MNDAA).

A new EAO ecosystem was born in Myanmar's northern borderlands. The south-eastern rebel-scape also witnessed intense fracturing during this period. By

1994, the Karen rebel base in Manerplaw had become vulnerable following a lethal split between the Christian and Buddhist Karens, which was fully exploited by the SLORC. The KNU splintered, and the Democratic Buddhist Karen Organisation/Army (DBKO/A) was born. It was then given control of Karen State by the SLORC, in a textbook divide-and-rule strategy to weaken the entire movement. In January 1995, a joint DKBA-*Tatmadaw* force launched a massive military assault on the Karen rebel base in Manerplaw. Unable to withstand this formidable offensive, the Karens and other NDF rebels razed and abandoned Manerplaw, with the KNU switching to guerrilla warfare staged from mobile bases elsewhere.

It is within this complex, fluid and often volatile context that one needs to place the emerging ceasefire regimes of the late 1980s and 1990s, especially the ones that mushroomed after 1988. These ceasefires, spearheaded from the military's side by the then Military Intelligence (MI) chief, General Khin Nyunt, were more long-lasting than the previous ones, which were arbitrarily agreed upon by the BSPP and EAOs. According to observers, the SLORC and its successor State Peace and Development Council (SPDC) negotiated ceasefires with 40 groups by 2010. The MNDAA was the first to enter into a ceasefire with the Rangoon regime, ironically right after it was born out of the CPB. The UWSA followed in quick succession. Then, the KIA and the NMSP ceased fire in 1994 and 1995, respectively. With the exception of the KIA, no other EAO had a formal, written ceasefire with the junta. This informal ceasefire ecosystem gave both the military and EAOs a mutually-agreeable, quasi-official space to consolidate their territorial domains and expand their profit-making networks. Even for the KIA, the ceasefire "allowed a war-weary movement to retain their arms and to administer a sizeable part of Kachin State, the so-called Kachin State Special Region-2."[13] In that sense, these post-1988 ceasefires "caused a major transformation of Myanmar's ethnic borderlands" by creating newfound space for peace, rehabilitation, reconstruction and development of civil society.[14] The Yangon regime designed the whole "Special Region" regime to placate the rebels by quasi-regularising territory controlled by them. For many of the EAOs, this newfound stability and quasi-formalisation of political authority became a way to strengthen their rank and file and boost their coffers. As Ashley South notes, "The ceasefire groups were allowed to retain their arms and granted de facto autonomy, control of sometimes extensive blocks of territory, and the right to extract natural resources in their territories".[15]

At the same time, these ceasefires were not accompanied by permanent peace agreements that could offer genuine political solutions to the ethnic conflict.

Instead, they became a way for the military regime to push the EAOs into a corner and co-opt them into the *tatmadaw's* security wheel through the Border Guard Forces (BGF) system. Specifically, this meant renewed belligerence in the form of fresh deployment of *tatmadaw* battalions in EAO-controlled territory, which led to land seizures, forced labour and extortion. As David Brenner's work on the KNU and KIA has shown, many of these ceasefires created friction between the elites and non-elites within the EAOs, particularly as older group leaders accumulated most of the benefits from the financial packages that accompanied ceasefires.[16] He argues that the infamous breakdown of the KIA-*Tatmadaw* ceasefire in 2011 was a direct result of such tensions between the elites and the non-elites as well as the older and newer generation of leaders. Thus, intra-EAO dynamics played decisive roles in the emergence and collapse of ceasefire regimes in Myanmar. At the same time, ceasefires themselves became a marker of factional splits within ethnic groups. This was the case with the Karens, wherein several KNU splinter groups went ahead and signed ceasefire agreements with the *tatmadaw.*

The diverse micro ceasefire regimes in the post-1988 period paved the way for the broader Nationwide Ceasefire Agreement (NCA) regime in 2011, which in turn, created conditions for the multi-stakeholder peace process that the Thein Sein administration started and the Aung San Suu Kyi Government took forward under the banner of the '21st Century Panglong' process. However, the NCA failed to cover most of the northern EAOs, and only served to divide Myanmar's ethnic rebel-world into two camps, which often adversely affected the negotiation process.

Funding War and Peace: The Political Economy of Conflict and Ceasefires

In Burma, the ethnic armed conflict cannot be seen as isolated from economic processes that both buttressed and generated cycles of violence. As Catherine Brown argues, it is only through a 'political economy' approach that one can acknowledge that "the functions of violence can include short- and long-term economic goals, securing resources, ethnic dominance, security as well as the powerful expression of identity and political aspirations."[60] Thus, one may conclude that in Myanmar, economic aspirations were not just funding political wars. Still, they also actively became the principal reason why some individuals or groups went to war in the first place in many cases. It may happen, as scholars have argued, that the structural nature of an ethnic insurgency undergoes transformative shifts as 'greed' replaces 'grievance'.[17] In most cases, it is consistently an admixture of both that generates and sustains state violence and insurgent counter-violence (or vice-versa).

In the pre-1988 period, the EAOs had to identify a whole range of financial sources to fund themselves, many of which fell squarely in the shadowy realm of the black economy. This primarily includes the production or extraction of rare earths, narcotics, timber, and other high-value goods (such as exotic animals). Control over these underground economic networks, in fact, became a primary flashpoint of the ethnic armed conflict as both the *tatmadaw* and the EAOs jostled to assert their monopolies over them. In a way, whoever controlled these networks was also able to control the levers of violence and strategic dominance. Effectively, these contrabands encouraged the birth of warlordism, which in many cases, substituted the original struggles for ethnic autonomy. At a time when the Burmese national economy slid down the abyss of impoverishment due to gross mismanagement and constant instability, the black economy became a negative substitute for "development". Thus, the political economy of Burma's ethnic civil war, which continued to feed into cycles of violence year after year, was as destructive as the actual military offensives.

Opium was the single largest contraband in the Burmese conflict ecosystem. Scholars have argued that the booming, highly predatory opium industry that developed in the infamous 'Golden Triangle' region of northeast Myanmar was, for a long time, the country's "sole financial success [during] years of economic decay and authoritarian rule" and "played a decisive part in the protracted violence and subsequent humanitarian emergency that has caused large numbers of the area's ethnic minorities to flee."[18] Initially, it was introduced in the region in the mid-1950s as a way to finance the KMT's war effort. The *tatmadaw* itself, largely through its militias in the border regions, was involved in the opium trade in the northern border-worlds, most of which was spearheaded by the drug kingpin and so-called "Opium King", Khun Sa. Later, by the mid-1970s, the CPB began to tax opium shipments passing through its territory, thus establishing a profit-making template for other rebel groups. This then means that the CPB's successors, such as the UWSA, too harnessed the drug trade to finance themselves. A large part of this went not into financing a war per se, but in "state-building efforts" emerging out of the ceasefires brokered after 1988.

A key pillar of Myanmar's conflict economy was the "ceasefire economy"—a web of economic interests, both licit and illicit, that emerged from the stability and informal amnesty agreements agreed upon between the *tatmadaw* and the EAOs. Both sides benefited from the absence of violence, as they took the opportunity to expand their illicit economies and profit-making networks. There is clear evidence to show that the SPDC, despite its stated anti-narcotics stand, dipped its hands into the high-value opium production business in Shan State, which ballooned rapidly after the post-1988 ceasefires. In fact, the EAOs in these borderlands were able to proliferate and deepen their illicit economic networks by exploiting the Rangoon regime's desire to consolidate its authority in these areas by providing a range of "services"—such as money laundering, official protection, taxation rights, etc.—to them. The ceasefire economy in the northern areas was also inherently tied to the Chinese market across the border, which became the major consumer of certain contrabands from Burma. For instance, following the ceasefire with the KIA in 1994, "both private sector and Government groups entered into agreements with primarily Chinese companies to exploit [Myanmar's] plentiful resources in jade mining, rubber plantations, and dam projects."[19] In the face of restrictions imposed on the KIA's jade-mining business, which had been feeding its coffers for long, the EAO switched to cross-border timber smuggling. All this resulted in rapid depletion of these resources through deforestation and over-mining.

It is, therefore, clear that the rebel economy and the state's interests relied on each other for sustenance, especially in the post-1988 period, with external interests—such as Chinese commercial interests acting as predatory consumers. Some scholars have called this "collaborative exploitation" by all parties as "ceasefire capitalism".[20] Economic drivers remain important even today, as the *tatmadaw* reasserts its forceful mandate over the country through the State Administration Council (SAC) and the ethnic armed movements enter a whole new phase of war and peace.

Conclusion

Myanmar's ethnic minorities began their fight for their rights and autonomy more than seven decades ago. A lot of water has flown under the bridge since then. Rebel leaders have grown old and tired, with their younger successors continuing the wars in ways markedly different from the past. The Government in Yangon too has undergone tectonic shifts in styles of leadership, models of governance and ideological character. Yet, EAOs remain central to the complex and sometimes violent process of state-making in Myanmar. This became clear not only when the quasi-civilian Thein Sein-led Government created the NCA process but also when the elected Suu Kyi Government gave prime importance to the process of national reconciliation through its flagship peace process. After decades of violence, destruction, extraction and displacement, the Burmese state seemed to have finally realised, at least on principle, that without fulfilling ethnic minority aspirations, Burmese nation-building would remain incomplete.

However, the February 2021 coup has reversed this impulse to a great degree. EAOs, such as the KIA and KNU, which had dodged high-intensity conflict for years, are now engaging the military from the front and providing tactical support to other civilian militia groups, such as the People's Defence Forces (PDF), in their area.[21] Yet, we see the political authority that the EAOs managed to secure in the past decades through strategic and economic engagement with the central Government still looming large over the 'national' landscape. The military still believes that it is unwise to engage the well-armed EAOs in direct battle, because of which it has tried to offer selective ceasefires to them.[22] Further, we see a universalisation of the original ethnic minority aspiration—conspicuous in the Panglong Agreement of 1947 and the Manerplaw Agreement of 1992—of building a 'federal democratic union.' The National Unity Consultative Council (NUCC), a coalition body that emerged after the putsch and includes both majority and minority political organisations, EAOs and civil society organisations, has taken this up in a formal capacity.[23]

Thus, in the renewed nationwide struggle to reform the Burmese political landscape, lessons learnt from the ethnic minority movements continue to occupy a central position. How various parties ultimately incorporate them into a unified national manifesto and utilise the existing networks of mobilisation to create a new and inclusive social, economic and political framework remains to be seen.

ENDNOTES

1. Prime Minister U Nu, cited in Bertil Lintner, *Burma in Revolt: Opium and Insurgency since 1948* (Routledge, 1994), 78
2. Karen Ballentine and Jake Sherman, *The Political Economy of Armed Conflict: Beyond Greed and Grievance* (Boulder, Co.: Lynne Rienner Publishers, 2003)
3. Matthew J. Walton, "Ethnicity, Conflict, and History in Burma: The Myths of Panglong," *Asian Survey* Vol. 48, no. 6 (2008): 889-910
4. Josef Silverstein, "Politics in the Shan State: The Question of Secession from the Union of Burma." *The Journal of Asian Studies,* Vol 18, no. 1 (1958): 43–57
5. Jessica Harriden, "'Making a Name for Themselves: Karen Identity and the Politicization of Ethnicity in Burma," *Journal of Burma Studies,* Vol 7, no. 1 (2002): 84-144
6. Ashley South, "Burma's Longest War: Anatomy of the Karen Conflict", Special Report, *Transnational Institute and Burma Centre,* Netherlands (2011), available at https://www.tni.org/en/briefing/burmas-longest-war-anatomy-karen-conflict, last accessed on 12 January 2023.
7. Martin Smith, *State of Strife: The Dynamics of Ethnic Conflict in Burma* (Singapore: Institute of Southeast Asian Studies, 2007); also see Susanne Prager Nye, "Ethnic Conflict and State Building in Burma", *Journal of Contemporary Asia* 39, no. 1 (2009): 127-135

8. Josef Silverstein cited in "Making a Name for Themselves", 115
9. Ashley South, "Ceasefires and Civil Society: The Case of the Mon" in Mikael Gravers (ed.), *Exploring Ethnic Diversity in Burma*, Nordic Institute of Asian Studies (2007): Chapters 6, 10
10. Saw Naw Sheera Ralph and Stephanie Olinga-Shannon, *Fifty Years in the Karen Revolution in Burma: The Soldier and the Teacher* (Ithaca: Southeast Asia Program Publications, an imprint of Cornell University Press, 2020)
11. "Myanmar's Military Junta Reintroduces the 'Four Cuts' Strategy against Civilians," *The Chindwin*, 07 October 2021, available at https://www.thechindwin.com/myanmars-military-junta-reintroduces-the-four-cuts-strategy-against-civilians/, last accessed on 12 January 2023
12. Josef Silverstein, "Civil War and Rebellion in Burma," *Journal of Southeast Asian Studies* 21, no. 1 (1990): 114–34
13. David Brenner, "Ashes of Co-Optation: From Armed Group Fragmentation to the Rebuilding of Popular Insurgency in Myanmar," *Conflict, Security & Development,* Vol 15, no. 4 (March 2015): 337-358
14. Tom Kramer, "'Neither War Nor Peace': Failed Ceasefires and Dispossession in Myanmar's Ethnic Borderlands," *The Journal of Peasant Studies,* Vol. 48, no. 3 (2020): 476-496
15. Ashley South, "Burma's Longest War: Anatomy of the Karen Conflict", Special Report, *Transnational Institute and Burma Centre,* Netherlands (2011), available at https://www.tni.org/en/briefing/burmas-longest-war-anatomy-karen-conflict, last accessed on 12 January 2023
16. David Brenner, *Rebel Politics: A Political Sociology of Armed Struggle in Myanmar's Borderlands* (Cornell University Press, 2019)
17. South, "Burma's Longest War", 23
18. Catherine Brown, "Burma: The Political Economy of Violence," *Disasters* 23, no. 3 (1999): 234-256.
19. Jenny Hedström, "Myanmar in Transition: China, Conflict, and Ceasefire Economies in Kachin State," *The Swedish Institute of International Affairs,* (2019): 10
20. Brenner, "Ashes of Co-Optation", 338
21. "Myanmar Resistance Forces Unite Under KNU Leadership in Mon State," *The Irrawaddy,* 11 October 2022, available at https://www.irrawaddy.com/news/war-against-the-junta/myanmar-resistance-forces-unite-under-knu-leadership-in-mon-state.html, last accessed on 12 January 2023
22. Robert Bociaga, "Ethnic Armed Groups Eye Post-Coup Myanmar," *The Diplomat*, 31 May 2022, available at https://thediplomat.com/2022/05/ethnic-armed-groups-eye-post-coup-myanmar/, last accessed on 12 January 2023
23. Su Mon Thazin Aung, "Myanmar's Quest for a Federal and Democratic Future: Considerations, Constraints and Compromises," *ISEAS* (18 March 2022) available at https://www.iseas.edu.sg/articles-commentaries/iseas-perspective/2022-28-myanmars-quest-for-a-federal-and-democratic-future-considerations-constraints-and-compromises-by-su-mon-thazin-aung/, last accessed on 12 January 2023

REFERENCES

Bellamy, Alex J. "The 21st Century Panglong: Myanmar's New Hope For Peace." *IPI Global Observatory,* 31 August 2016, available at https://theglobalobservatory.org/2016/08/myanmar-21st-century-panglong-aung-san-suu-kyi/, last accessed on 12 January 2023

Brenner, David. *Rebel Politics: A Political Sociology of Armed Struggle in Myanmar's Borderlands.* Cornell University Press, 2019 available at http://www.jstor.org/stable/10.7591/j.ctvfc55nc, last accessed on 12 January 2023.

____ "Ashes of Co-Optation: From Armed Group Fragmentation to the Rebuilding of Popular

Insurgency in Myanmar." *Conflict, Security & Development* 15, no. 4 (March 2015): 337-358.

Brown, Catherine. "Burma: The Political Economy of Violence." *Disasters* 23, no. 3 (1999): 234-256

Core, Paul. "Burma/Myanmar: Challenges of a Ceasefire Accord in Karen State." *Journal of Current Southeast Asian Affairs* Vol. 28, 3 (2009): 95-105

Gravers, Mikael. "Disorder as Order: The Ethno-Nationalist Struggle of the Karen in Burma/Myanmar—a Discussion of the Dynamics of an Ethnicized Civil War and Its Historical Roots." *Journal of Burma Studies* 19, no. 1 (2015): 27-78

Harriden, Jessica. "'Making a Name for Themselves:": Karen Identity and the Politicization of Ethnicity in Burma." *Journal of Burma Studies* 7, no. 1 (2002): 84-144

Hedström, Jenny. "Myanmar in Transition: China, Conflict, and Ceasefire Economies in Kachin State." *The Swedish Institute of International Affairs* (2019)

Htung, Yaw. "Armed Conflicts between the Kachin Independence Organization and Myanmar Army: A Conflict Analysis." *Thammasat Review,* Vol. 21 (2018): 234-252

"Introduction to United Nationalities Federal Council (UNFC)." *UNFC,* 2007, available at https://www.burmalibrary.org/en/introduction-to-united-nationalities-federal-council-unfc, last accessed on 12 January 2023

Kramer, Tom. "'Neither War Nor Peace': Failed Ceasefires and Dispossession in Myanmar's Ethnic Borderlands." *The Journal of Peasant Studies,* Vol 48, no. 3 (2020): 476-496

Lintner, Bertil. *Burma in Revolt: Opium and Insurgency since 1948.* Routledge, 1994

____ *The Rise and Fall of the Communist Party of Burma.* Cornell Southeast Asia Program, 1990

"Manerplaw Agreement to Establish a Federal Union of Burma." Myanmar Peace Monitor, 31 July 1992, available at https://www.mmpeacemonitor.org/images/2013/Background/PDF/Manerplaw_Agreement_to_Establish_a_Federal_Union_of_Burma.pdf, last accessed on 12 January 2023.

Meehan, Patrick. "Fortifying or Fragmenting the State? The Political Economy of the Opium/Heroin Trade in Shan State, Myanmar, 1988–2013." *Critical Asian Studies* 47, no. 2 (March 2015): 253-282

"Myanmar's Military Junta Reintroduces the 'Four Cuts' Strategy against Civilians." *The Chindwin,* 07 October 2021, available at https://www.thechindwin.com/myanmars-military-junta-reintroduces-the-four-cuts-strategy-against-civilians/, last accessed on 12 January 2023

Myint-U, Thant. *The River of Lost Footsteps: A Personal History of Burma.* London: Faber and Faber, 2008

Nyein, Susanne Prager. "Ethnic Conflict and State Building in Burma." *Journal of Contemporary Asia,* Vol. 39, no. 1 (2009): 127-135

Ralph, Saw, Sheera, Naw, and Olinga-Shannon, Stephanie. *Fifty Years in the Karen Revolution in Burma: The Soldier and the Teacher.* Ithaca: Southeast Asia Program Publications, an imprint of Cornell University Press, 2020

Silverstein, Josef. "Politics in the Shan State: The Question of Secession from the Union of Burma." *The Journal of Asian Studies* 18, no. 1 (1958): 43–57

____ "Civil War and Rebellion in Burma." *Journal of Southeast Asian Studies* 21, no. 1 (1990): 114–123

South, Ashley. "Burma's Longest War: Anatomy of the Karen Conflict." Special Report, *Transnational Institute and Burma Centre,* Netherlands (2011) available at https://www.tni.org/en/briefing/burmas-longest-war-anatomy-karen-conflict, last accessed on 12 January 2023

____ *Ethnic Politics in Burma: States of Conflict.* London: Routledge, 2009

____ "Ceasefires and Civil Society: The Case of the Mon." In *Exploring Ethnic Diversity in Burma,* edited by Mikael Gravers. Nordic Institute of Asian Studies, 2007

Smith, Martin. *State of Strife: The Dynamics of Ethnic Conflict in Burma*. Singapore: Institute of Southeast Asian Studies, 2007

____ *Burma: Insurgency and the Politics of Ethnicity*. Dhaka: University Press, 1999

Walton, Matthew J. "Ethnicity, Conflict, and History in Burma: The Myths of Panglong." *Asian Survey* 48, no. 6 (2008): 889-910

"The Politics of Pressure: The 1990's and the Fall of Manerplaw." *The Museum of Karen History and Culture*, undated, Burma Library

Yun, Liu. "Building Peace in Myanmar: Birth of the FPNCC." *Asia Dialogue*, 06 October 2017, available at https://theasiadialogue.com/2017/10/06/building-peace-in-myanmar-birth-of-the-fpncc/, last accessed on 12 January 2023

Zaw, Aung. "The Battle of Insein Never Really Ended." *The Irrawaddy*, 09 February 2009, available at https://www2.irrawaddy.com/opinion_story.php?art_id=15080&page=2, last accessed on 12 January 2023.

Zaw, Min Oo. "Understanding Myanmar's Peace Process: Ceasefire Agreements." Swiss Peace, 2014

SECTION TWO

Economic and Socio-Cultural Developments

5

Myanmar's Integration with the World: Emerging Trends and Way Forward

Dr Prabir De

ABSTRACT

Located at the crossroads of Asia, Myanmar is a "double track" land bridge, possessing rich culture and tradition, vast natural resources, access to the ocean, a relatively young population, and a market with wide-ranging investment opportunities. Like India, Myanmar is highly heterogeneous and diversified in terms of ethnicity and culture. Myanmar has a unique spatial location; it is a neighbour of two large countries of the world—China and India. Myanmar embarked on a path of political and economic reforms, paving the way for unlocking the country's large economic potential till the Myanmar Army took control of the country on 1 February 2021. The undoing of the reforms started then. Today, Myanmar is one of the worst-performing countries in Asia. Myanmar's economy is heavily fragile and contracting, with reform reversals weakening the growth outlook. This chapter discusses Myanmar's participation in regional integration programmes and argues why greater integration with the neighbours would be of paramount importance in building the country's economy. One of the conclusions of this chapter is that peace-building and restoring democracy may help Myanmar to build a stronger partnership with its neighbours.

Introduction

Located at the crossroads of Asia, Myanmar possesses rich culture and tradition, vast natural resources, access to the ocean, a relatively young population, and a market with wide-ranging investment opportunities. Like India, Myanmar is highly heterogeneous and diversified in terms of ethnicity and culture. Myanmar has a unique spatial location, surrounded largely by two large countries of the world, namely, China and India. Myanmar embarked on a path of political and economic reforms, paving the way for unlocking the country's large economic potential till the Myanmar Army took control of the country on 1 February 2021. The undoing of the reforms has started since then. Today, Myanmar is one of the worst-performing countries in Asia. Myanmar's economy is heavily fragile and contracting, with reform reversals weakening the growth outlook.[1]

Myanmar's disadvantages are a non-democratic government, relatively small population size, missing institutions, inadequate trade capacity, insufficient infrastructure, a narrow trade basket and lack of skilled human resources. At present, Myanmar's underdeveloped infrastructure, unavailability of sufficient skilled human resources and poor connectivity with neighbouring countries seriously limit Myanmar's participation in the regional and global economies. On the other, owing to its strategic position, Myanmar connects Asia's three big markets—the Association of Southeast Asian Nations (ASEAN), China, and India. Improving infrastructure, both national and international, is assumed to be essential for the country's prosperity, continued growth, and, most importantly, global integration.[2]

However, the first and foremost condition is to bring back peace in the country and then establish democracy in the country. Today, Myanmar suffers triple crises: first, pandemic-induced economic downturn; second, political unrest; and third, country-wide violence. It is risky to do business with Myanmar since there are sanctions in Myanmar by the European Union (EU), the United States of America (USA) and Australia.[3] Several countries are closely monitoring the situation in Myanmar, and at the same time, they remain committed to supporting their people.

Nonetheless, the processes of global integration represent both challenges as well as opportunities for Myanmar, so far as the country's growth prospects depend increasingly on the external economic environment (De and Raichaudhury, 2018). In particular, policies of multilateral organisations such as the WTO, the World Bank and IMF, UN bodies such as UNESCAP, regional development banks such as ADB, regional associations/blocs such as ASEAN, SAARC, BIMSTEC and GMS, and countries like China, India, Thailand and Japan have an important bearing on the process of development of Myanmar.

In view of the above, this chapter discusses Myanmar's participation in regional integration programmes and argues why greater integration with the neighbours would be of paramount importance in building Myanmar's economy. The rest of this chapter is described as follows. Section 2 briefly discusses the current economic profile of Myanmar. Section 3 reviews the patterns of Myanmar's trade partners and presents an overview of Myanmar's current state of the regional integration process, followed by a discussion on trends in foreign direct investment in Myanmar in Section 4. Finally, conclusions are drawn in Section 5.

Myanmar's Economic Performance

With a 54-million population and a GDP of USD 65 billion (USD 238 billion in PPP terms), Myanmar is still not well connected with its neighbours as well as globally. Table 1 illustrates the basic economic profile of Myanmar for 2015 and 2021. With falling growth, Myanmar's GDP in PPP terms contracted in 2021 when compared to 2015. This is a major sign of economic distress in the country. The country's per capita income in PPP terms has declined over time, thus indicating a falling quality of life for the common people of Myanmar. About 40 per cent of the country's population is still living below the poverty line in 2022.[4] At the same time, the country has been facing high inflation of basic food items. Thus, controlling inflation is a big challenge for the Myanmar government.

Table 1: Basic Economic Profile of Myanmar

Sl. No.	*Indicators*	*2015*	*2021*
1	Population, total (million)	53.90	53.80
2	Rural population (% of total population)	65.90	68.55
3	Urban population (% of total)	34.10	31.45
4	GDP, PPP (current international billion $)	282.95	238.34
5	GDP (current US$ billion)	62.60	65.09
6	GDP per capita (current US$)	1161.49	1209.93
7	GDP per capita, PPP (current international $)	5249.74	4430.22
8	GDP annual growth, (%)	7.29	–17.91
9	Trade (% of GDP)	47.32	53.10
10	Exports of goods and services (current US billion $)	13.01	18.42
11	Exports of goods and services (% of GDP)	22.98	28.29
12	Imports of goods and services (current US billion $)	16.61	16.15
13	Imports of goods and services (% of GDP)	30.94	24.81
14	Tariff rate, applied, simple mean, all products (%)	4.21	3.68
15	Total reserves minus gold (current US$ billion)	4.35	7.23
16	Inflation, consumer prices (annual %)	10.80	8.83
17	Ease of Doing Business Global Rank*	171	165
18	Logistics Performance Index Global Rank**	113	137

*For the year 2019; **For the year 2018
Source: World Development Indicators (WDI), the World Bank

A vast population of Myanmar lives in rural areas (69 per cent in 2021) and is yet to have access to basic socio-economic facilities such as health, education, electricity, etc. The rising share of the rural population and declining urban population suggest that economic distress and lack of jobs might have forced reverse migration from urban to rural areas amidst ongoing internal conflicts.

There was a slight improvement in foreign reserves during 2015 and 2021 due mainly to declining imports. However, given economic sanctions and restrictions, a shortage of foreign reserves is unavoidable in the country, which has forced the government to impose currency controls. On the other hand, the black market of foreign exchange has gone up heavily in the country. In other words, there are high signs of collapsing kyat. Although the official exchange rate against USD is around 2,100, the Myanmar kyat is now unofficially trading at a record low of 4,500 per USD.

Trade openness has improved during 2015 and 2021—53.10 per cent in 2021 vis-à-vis 47.32 per cent in 2015. To meet the rising domestic demand, Myanmar has given priority to exports. The share of exports in GDP has increased from 23 per cent in 2015 to 28 per cent in 2021. Globally, Myanmar is among the bottom league of countries in both *Ease of Doing Business* and *Logistics Performance Index* indicators.

It goes without saying that Myanmar's growth and integration process is held up primarily due to internal political unrest, armed conflicts, violence and insurgency. Until these are resolved, Myanmar continues to experience free fall and isolation. At the same time, Myanmar requires rapid growth to feed its development works and save the country from food and energy security threats. The country has to make wholehearted efforts to bring political stability through peace and reconciliation. It would then help Myanmar to achieve economic progress in a gradual manner through macroeconomic stability, regulatory reforms, infrastructure and human resources development, and promotion of international trade, among others.

Myanmar's future does not appear to be promising. The World Bank noted: "Myanmar's economy is projected to grow 3 per cent in the fiscal year ending in September 2022, following an 18 per cent contraction last year. Weak economic activity is indicative of the range of constraints facing the Myanmar economy. These include a sharp rise in the prices of imported inputs and consumer goods, partly attributable to the war in Ukraine; elevated levels of domestic conflict; electricity outages; and persistent logistics and financial sector disruptions. Recent policy shifts have added to challenges for businesses. Burdensome trade licence requirements, the abandonment of the managed float exchange rate regime, and the imposition of foreign currency surrender rules have resulted in shortages of key imported inputs and inhibited exporters. Uncertainty among businesses has increased due to the rapid issuance of new policy instructions, including exemptions to previously imposed restrictions, followed by subsequent attempts to revoke those exemptions." (World Bank, 2022)

The Myanmar government must bring reform momentum to bring peace, stability and better governance, and a favourable business environment. An overarching priority for the new government would, therefore, be to strengthen the global integration process further.

Myanmar's Trade Partners and Current Engagement in Regional Blocks

Geographical Patterns of Myanmar's Trade

Surrounded by major emerging markets such as China and India, Myanmar has relatively diversified trade partners. Table 2 (a, b) presents the distribution of the volume of export and import among Myanmar's top 10 trade partners for 2001, 2011 and 2021. Among the top 10 trade partners of Myanmar, China occupies the first position, both in export and import. Other major trade partners are Thailand, the EU and Singapore. In the destination market, Myanmar's export has been highly concentrated in the top 10 partners. Over 90 per cent of Myanmar's exports in 2021 was directed to the top 10 export partners, which has steadily increased from about 78 per cent in 2001. China is Myanmar's major import source. Myanmar's imports from China doubled in 2021 compared to 2011 (see Table 1(b)). The concentration of Myanmar's imports from the top 10 sources is also visible and similar to export. The top three import sources are China, Singapore, and Thailand.

India is one of its top ten trade partners of Myanmar. Over time, Myanmar's trade with India increased from less than USD 50 million in 1991 to over USD 4 billion in 2007 and then declined to about USD 1.5 billion in 2021. Illustrated in Figure 1, the trend of bilateral trade was influenced by Myanmar's exports to India till 2013, when India stopped importing pulses from Myanmar as a single source country. Thereafter, Myanmar's imports from India exceeded that of the exports till 2019. However, the trend has reversed since 2020, and Myanmar has successfully restored the trade surplus with India due mainly to India's announcement of duty-free import of pulses till 31 March 2022, which was further

Table 2: Trends in Myanmar's Top 10 Trade Partners

(a) EXPORT

	2001		2011		2021	
	Value (US$ million)	*Share* (%)*	*Value (US$ million)*	*Share* (%)*	*Value (US$ million)*	*Share* (%)*
China	86.62	1.34	1,515.28	18.60	4,470.85	29.49
Thailand	942.88	14.56	3,216.93	39.48	3,492.85	23.04
EU	175.33	2.71	90.32	1.11	2,325.94	15.34
Japan	98.03	1.51	310.01	3.81	907.80	5.99
India	2,461.50	38.02	929.21	11.41	858.00	5.66
USA	506.22	7.82	8.11	0.10	593.08	3.91
Malaysia	81.02	1.25	190.45	2.34	303.97	2.01
Korea	58.54	0.90	206.99	2.54	295.93	1.95
Vietnam	11.98	0.19	85.27	1.05	224.47	1.48
Singapore	653.00	10.09	396.85	4.87	213.53	1.41
World	6,473.95		8,147.27		15,159.52	
Share of Top 10 in World, %		78.39		85.30		90.28

*Share in total export

(B) IMPORT

	2001		2011		2021	
	Value (US$ million)	*Share* (%)*	*Value (US$ million)*	*Share* (%)*	*Value (US$ million)*	*Share* (%)*
China	211.88	10.58	2,303.66	26.58	4,205.76	29.15
Singapore	339.70	16.97	2,529.65	29.18	2738.80	18.98
Thailand	179.25	8.95	760.82	8.78	2068.13	14.33
Indonesia	75.20	3.76	360.02	4.15	1205.46	8.35
Malaysia	276.84	13.83	281.34	3.25	852.61	5.91
India	122.24	6.11	310.98	3.59	574.24	3.98
EU	45.38	2.27	169.24	1.95	470.11	3.26
Vietnam	36.34	1.82	59.36	0.68	336.60	2.33
Korea	111.94	5.59	541.21	6.24	304.24	2.11
Japan	170.96	8.54	400.52	4.62	300.27	2.08
World	2001.96		8667.95		14428.23	
Share of Top 10 in World, %		78.41		89.03		90.49

**Share in import

Source: Calculated based on DOTS, IMF

Figure 1: Trends in Myanmar's Trade with India

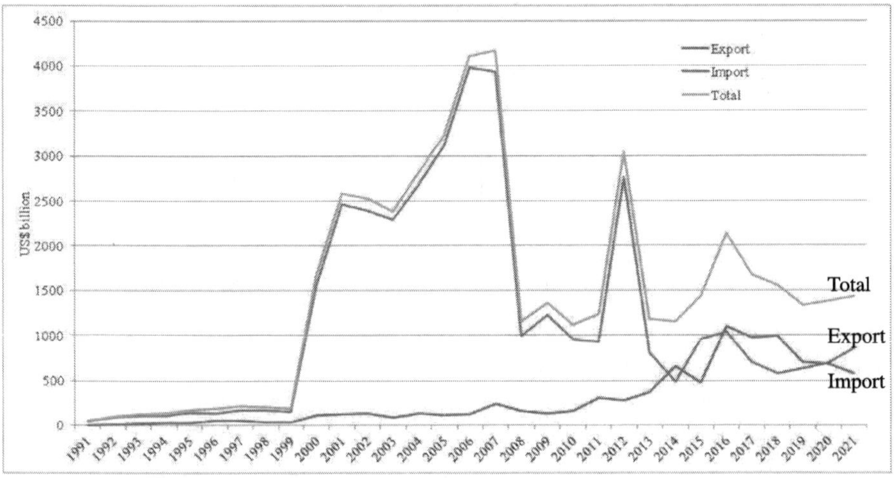

Source: Calculated based on DOTS, IMF

extended to 31 March 2023. However, India's exports to Myanmar have slowed down due to Myanmar's mandatory requirement for an import licence. Myanmar's major exports to India are timber and wood articles, whereas India's major exports to Myanmar are pharmaceuticals, consumer goods, automobiles, iron and steel items, etc.

What emerges is that China and Southeast Asian countries are Myanmar's major trade partners, whereas Japan, India, the EU, the USA and Korea are Myanmar's potential markets, which need to be nurtured, and trade shall be promoted with these countries through effective trade facilitation measures. It seems that Myanmar's trade is likely to fare significantly worse than its peers due to a lack of an appropriate business environment and the failure of institutions which are needed to facilitate trade in the country. Myanmar's trade could rebound if it can surmount substantial development challenges by further implementing across-the-board reforms and strengthening trade relations with neighbours such as India.

Trade Reforms

Myanmar ratified the WTO Agreement on Trade Facilitation in 2015 and has notified its category A, B, and C commitments to the WTO. Furthermore, Myanmar has set up the National Trade Facilitation Committee and endorsed the National Trade Facilitation Action Plan in 2018, which was updated in 2019. Unlike other countries, Myanmar does not impose pre-shipment inspection requirements on imports. Myanmar does not have any non-preferential rules of origin. Imports to Myanmar require preferential rules of origin for imports under the ASEAN Trade in Goods Agreement (ATIGA) and other free trade agreements (FTAs) to which Myanmar is a signatory. Myanmar does not have any anti-dumping, countervailing, or subsidy legislation and has notified the WTO. The Safeguard Law was enacted on 29 December 2019 and has already entered into force in 2021.

Myanmar's Current Engagement in Regional Integration Process

The process of regional integration moves forward with the formation of the free trade area, customs union, common market and finally, economic union (Viner, 1950; Balassa, 1961). The beginning of the economic integration process involves lesser coverage of economic activities. Moving forward all the way from partial scope (e.g., preferential trade agreement) to economic union generates more economic as well as political integration (Figure 2). The Regional Trade Agreements (RTA), formed mainly through an FTA, establishes free trade areas gradually. Customs Union, Common Market and Economic Union follow next.

Proliferation of RTAs has witnessed unprecedented growth in the history of world trade. RTAs have been formed under Article 24 of GATT, or enabling clause or Article V of GATS. As of 31 December 2022, some 582 notifications of RTAs (counting goods, services and accessions separately) had been received by the WTO, of which 355 RTAs were in force. Following the notification of the RTA between Mongolia and Japan in June 2016, all WTO members now have an RTA in force.[5] Over 50 per cent of world trade is carried through regional/preferential trading routes every year.[6]

Myanmar is an original member of the WTO (GATT). Myanmar has granted the MFN treatment to all its trading partners. According to Myanmar's *Trade Policy Review*: "Myanmar has bound 18.4 per cent of its tariff lines (all tariff lines under WTO agriculture) with the simple average final bound rate at 87.3 per cent. Myanmar undertook specific commitments under the GATS in tourism and travel-related services and did not list any exemption to the principle of MFN treatment in its GATS commitment."[7] Merchandise trade in Myanmar is governed under the Sea Customs Act (1878), Land Customs Act (1924), the Export-Import Law 2012, and the Tariff Law (1992). The acts and laws are administered by the Ministry of Finance and the Ministry of Commerce.

Before the military coup in 2021, Myanmar adopted or amended various trade- and investment-related laws, including the Myanmar Investment Law, 2016;

the Myanmar Companies Law, 2017; and the Myanmar Competition Law. In 2019, the Consumer Protection Law 2019 was enacted. Intellectual property laws, Industrial Design Law and Trademark Law, Patent Law, and Copyright Law were introduced in 2019. As noted in Myanmar's latest *Trade Policy Review*, Myanmar has not been party to any dispute settlement proceedings at the WTO as a complainant, respondent, or third party. During the review period, it made a number of notifications concerning, inter alia, first-time notifications for import licensing, customs valuation, sanitary and phytosanitary (SPS) measures, and technical barriers to trade (TBT).[8]

On the regional front, Myanmar has an active participation in ASEAN and ASEAN's FTAs with third countries (Table 3). Myanmar is part of the ongoing negotiation of the BIMSTEC FTA. Myanmar is also a member of the RCEP. In parallel, Myanmar has received GSP (EU and Norway) and GSTP (developing countries) benefits. Myanmar is also a member of SASEC and GMS; both were already made operational and driven by ADB. Myanmar has shown interest in joining BBIN and SAARC.

Table 3: Myanmar's Participation in Regional Blocks

RTAs		*Non-RTAs*
List of RTAs in Force	*Negotiations on-going*	
• ASEAN - Australia - New Zealand • ASEAN - China • ASEAN - India • ASEAN - Japan • ASEAN - Korea • ASEAN Free Trade Area (AFTA) • RCEP • Global System of Trade Preferences among Developing Countries (GSTP) • Global System of Preferences (GSP)	• BIMSTEC	• SASEC • GMS • MGC • BBIN* • SAARC*

*Proposed
Source: Author's own based on De (2018)

Figure 2: Level of Regional Integration

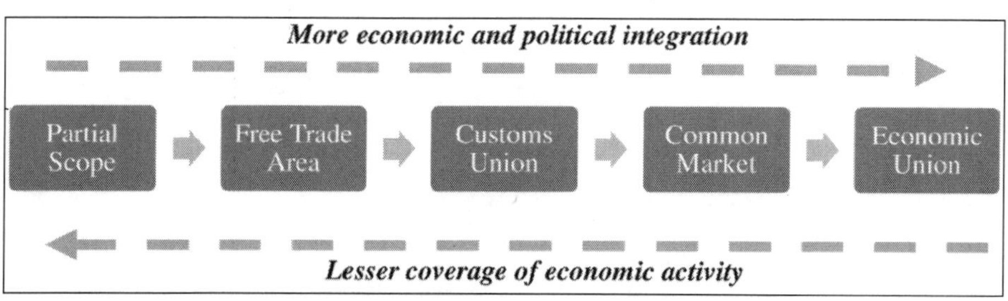

Table 4: Myanmar in RTAs

ASEAN - Australia and New Zealand	
Title	Agreement Establishing the ASEAN-Australia-New Zealand Free Trade Area
Type	Free Trade Agreement & Economic Integration Agreement
Date of entry into force	1 January 2010 for Australia, Brunei Darussalam, Malaysia, Myanmar, New Zealand, the Philippines, Singapore, and Viet Nam
Transition for full implementation for Myanmar	2021/2024/2025
Coverage	Goods and services
WTO consideration status	Factual presentation not distributed
Myanmar's merchandise trade with Australia & New Zealand (2011/12)	Australia: 0.8% of total imports; 0.1% of total exports New Zealand: 0.2% of total imports; 0.003% of total exports
WTO document series	WT/REG284/N/1 and S/C/N/545, 9 April 2010
ASEAN – China	
Title	Agreement on Trade in Goods (under the 2002 Framework Agreement on Comprehensive Economic Cooperation between ASEAN and the People's Republic of China)
Type	Partial Scope Agreement & Economic Integration Agreement
Date of signature/entry into force	Goods: November 2004/January 2005
Services: Jan 2007/July 2007	
Transition for full implementation for Myanmar	2015
Coverage	Goods and services
WTO consideration status	Factual Abstract distributed (goods) Factual presentation not distributed (services)
Myanmar's merchandise trade with China (2011/12)	30.8% of total imports; 24.2% of total exports
WTO document series	WT/COMTD/N/20, 21 December 2004; S/C/N/463, 2 July 2008; WT/COMTD/51, 21 December 2004
ASEAN – India	
Title	Agreement on Trade in Goods (under the Framework Agreement on Comprehensive Economic Cooperation between ASEAN and the Republic of India, 2003, as amended in 2009)
Type	Free Trade Agreement

Date of entry into force	1 January 2010 for Brunei Darussalam, Myanmar, and Vietnam
Transition for full implementation for Myanmar	2018/2021
Coverage	Goods
WTO consideration status	Factual presentation not distributed
Myanmar's merchandise trade with India (2011/12)	3.6% of total imports; 11.4% of total exports
WTO document series	WT/COMTD/N/35, 23 August 2010
	ASEAN – Japan
Title	Agreement on Comprehensive Economic Partnership among Japan and Member States of ASEAN
Type	Free Trade Agreement
Date of entry into force	1 December 2008 (Singapore, Japan, Viet Nam, the Lao PDR, and Myanmar)
Transition for full implementation for Myanmar	2026
Coverage	Goods
WTO consideration status	Factual presentation not distributed
Myanmar's merchandise trade with Japan (2011/12)	5.6% of total imports; 3.5% of total exports
WTO document series	WT/REG277/N1, 14 December 2009 and WT/REG277/N2, 27 July 2011
	ASEAN - Korea
Title	Agreement on Trade in Goods (under the 2005 Framework Agreement on Comprehensive Economic Cooperation among the Governments of the Republic of Korea and ASEAN)
Type	Free Trade Agreement & Economic Integration Agreement
Date of signature/entry into force	Goods: August 2006/January 2010 Services: November 2008/May 2009
Transition for full implementation for Myanmar	2018
Coverage	Goods and services
WTO consideration status	Factual presentation not distributed
Myanmar's merchandise trade with Korea (2011/12)	5% of total imports; 2.4% of total exports
WTO document series	WT/REG287/N/1; WT/COMTD/N/33; S/C/N/559; S/C/N/560, 8 July 2010. S/C/N/559/Add.1; S/C/N/560, Add.1, 3 May 2011

Source: Myanmar (2021)

(a) ASEAN

Myanmar became an ASEAN member in 1997 and was its chair in 2014. ASEAN has been planning to realise an ASEAN Economic Community (AEC) by 2025. ASEAN aims to establish a single market and production base in the ASEAN region, with a free flow of goods, services, skilled labour, and capital. ASEAN currently has component agreements on goods (ATIGA), services (AFAS), and investment (ACIA).[9] Under the ATIGA, ASEAN members are bound to apply a tariff rate of 0–5 per cent for goods originating within ASEAN, with flexibility granted to LDCs, including Myanmar. As noted in Myanmar's *Trade Policy Review*, Myanmar's average tariff under the ATIGA was 0.6 per cent in 2012[10]. The basic principle for granting origin status to a product is 40 per cent regional/local content as Rules of Origin (RoO). Besides, Myanmar has introduced several trade facilitation measures, opened a Trade Portal, and ratified the WTO Trade Facilitation Agreement (TFA).

(b) ASEAN RTAs

As an ASEAN member, Myanmar participates in ASEAN's preferential agreements with Australia and New Zealand, China, India, Japan, and Korea (Table 4). Being a member of ASEAN, Myanmar is a member of the Regional Comprehensive Economic Partnership (RCEP) with ASEAN FTA partners such as Australia, China, India, Japan, Korea, and New Zealand. The framework is to cover trade in goods, trade in services, investment, economic and technical cooperation, competition, intellectual property, dispute settlement, and other issues.

(c) BIMSTEC

The Bay of Bengal Initiative for Multi-Sectoral Technical and Economic Cooperation (BIMSTEC) is a forum to facilitate and promote trade, investment, and technical cooperation among countries around the Bay of Bengal, such as Bangladesh, Bhutan, India, Nepal, Sri Lanka, Myanmar, and Thailand. Myanmar joined the BIMSTEC on 22 December 1997. It has 14 broad sectors for cooperation. In 2004, BIMSTEC agreed to establish a BIMSTEC Free Trade Area and signed the Framework Agreement on goods, services, and investment. Article 3 of the Agreement provides that goods, except those included in the Negative List, will be subject to tariff reduction or elimination according to different time frames.

Myanmar had tariff reductions and eliminations for its fast-track products before June 2011, and the tariffs on its normal-track products are to be reduced or eliminated before June 2017. The trade negotiation has been ongoing. Myanmar is central to the BIMSTEC integration process. BIMSTEC has received a renewed thrust in recent years, particularly from India, and aims to strengthen economic integration through connectivity projects. BIMSTEC's potential in enhancing trade among member-countries lies in geographical contiguity and a common coastal link with the Bay of Bengal and the eastern coast of the Indian Ocean.[11]

(d) GSTP

Global System of Trade Preferences among Developing Countries (GSTP) is a preferential trade agreement which aims to increase trade among developing countries. Myanmar signed the GSTP in 1988, which entered into force on 19 April 1989.[12] Myanmar has received GSTP preferences from almost all developing countries, such as China and India.

(e) GSP

Generalised System of Preferences (GSP) is a preferential tariff system among a group of countries which are also members of the WTO. Normally, preferences are extended to LDCs by developed countries and/or middle to high-income countries. Myanmar is a beneficiary of a number of Generalized System of Preferences (GSP) schemes, including those accorded by Australia, Belarus, Canada, the European Union, Iceland, Japan, Kazakhstan, New Zealand, Norway, the Russian Federation, Switzerland, Turkey, and the USA. The EU reinstated GSP treatment for Myanmar in July 2013, granting retrospective benefits to Myanmar's exports from June 2012. Norway reinstated GSP treatment in January 2012.

(f) GMS

The Greater Mekong sub-region (GMS) programme, driven by the Asian Development Bank (ADB), is one of the important sub-regional cooperation programmes in Asia. In 1992, Myanmar, together with Cambodia, Lao PDR, Thailand, Vietnam, and Yunnan Province of China[13], launched the GMS programme to enhance economic linkages across their borders.[14] The GMS programme covers nine priority sectors, including ambitious GMS economic corridor projects. Myanmar falls on the GMS East–West Economic Corridor.

(g) Other Arrangements

After serving as an Observer for several years, Myanmar joined the ADB's South

Asia Sub-regional Economic Cooperation (SASEC) programme on 21 February 2017 as a full member. Myanmar became the seventh SASEC member-country, following the original four founding partners in 2001—Bangladesh, Bhutan, India, and Nepal—and Maldives and Sri Lanka in 2014. Myanmar is also an active member of the Mekong-Ganga Cooperation (MGC). MGC is an initiative by India and five ASEAN countries, namely, Cambodia, Lao PDR, Myanmar, Thailand and Vietnam, for cooperation in tourism, culture, education, as well as transport and communications. It was launched in 2000 at Vientiane, Lao PDR. Myanmar is also a member of Bangladesh-China-India-Myanmar (BCIM), which is also known as the Kunming Initiative. Launched in 1997 in Kunming, China, the BCIM initiative is still known as the Track II initiative and is presently inactive.

Myanmar has shown interest in joining BBIN and SAARC. To enhance bilateral trade with neighbouring countries, Myanmar has signed MOUs on establishing bilateral joint trade commissions with Bangladesh, India, Thailand, and Vietnam. Myanmar has 14 main border trade points with four neighbouring countries. Myanmar has signed border trade agreements with China, India, Bangladesh, Thailand, and Lao PDR, of which border trade with China and Thailand is very active.

Trends in Foreign Direct Investment Inflows

Foreign Direct Investment (FDI) is considered to be an important source for achieving greater and faster economic growth. The role of FDI in economic activities is more important since multinational enterprises engage in various activities, including trade, in the FDI-recipient economies. The FDI, as well as domestic investment, in Myanmar, is governed by, inter alia, the Myanmar Investment Law, 2016; the Myanmar Investment Regulations, 2017; the Myanmar Companies Law, 2017; the Myanmar Partnership Act, 1932; etc. The Myanmar Special Economic Zone Law, 2014, and the Myanmar Special Economic Zone Rules entered into force on 23 January 2014.

Myanmar used to receive an increasing amount of FDI till the military coup in 2021. From 2010 onwards,[15] FDI inflow to the country increased from less than USD 1 billion in 2010 to over USD 4 billion in 2015 and then declined to USD 2.8 billion in 2019 (Figure 2). The sharp rise in FDI inflow started in 2010 when Myanmar introduced a new FDI policy and a new law to facilitate FDI in the country. A surge in FDI is an important development in an economy, indicating a higher level of economic engagement with the world. However, due to the economic sanctions and political isolation, Myanmar has faced a sharp decline in

FDI inflows. *Nikkei Asia* reported, "FDI in Myanmar, first depressed by the COVID-19 pandemic and then by the political unrest that spread after the February military takeover, has fallen to eight-year low, official numbers show".[16] Today, FDI inflows contribute just 2.3 per cent to the country's GDP, which was, half a decade ago, even less than 2 per cent (Figure 3).[17]

FDI is mainly concentrated in the oil and gas, power, transport and communications, and manufacturing sectors. Before the military coup in 2021, most of the FDI originated from Singapore, followed by China and Hong Kong. As reported in Myanmar's *Trade Policy Review*, the stock of FDI in 2019 was more than USD 34 billion.[18]

Figure 3: Foreign Direct Investment, Net Inflows (BoP, current US$)

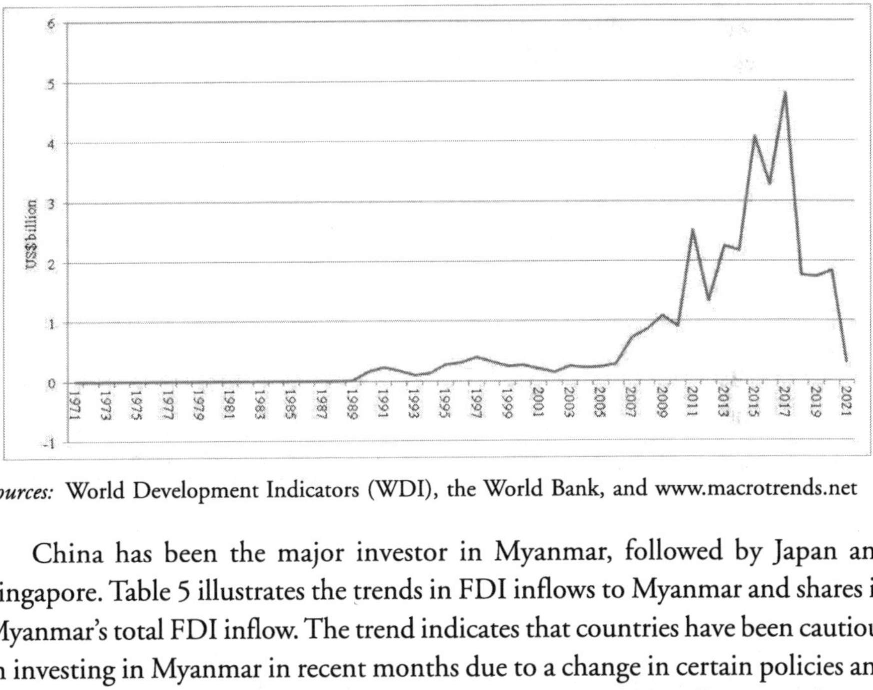

Sources: World Development Indicators (WDI), the World Bank, and www.macrotrends.net

China has been the major investor in Myanmar, followed by Japan and Singapore. Table 5 illustrates the trends in FDI inflows to Myanmar and shares in Myanmar's total FDI inflow. The trend indicates that countries have been cautious in investing in Myanmar in recent months due to a change in certain policies and the uncertainties in Myanmar Investment Commission (MIC).[19] As a result, FDI inflow, according to the Directorate of Investment and Company Administration (DICA) Statistics, to Myanmar declined in 2016-17. As Myanmar starts taking reforms and strengthening the country's legal system, FDI inflow is likely to go up.[20]

The total amount of FDI stock till 2021 has reached about USD 78 billion, consisting mainly of manufacturing enterprises, with oil and gas companies bringing in one-third of total investment. However, the year 2010 was the turning point of Myanmar's FDI flow. Table 5 illustrates the distribution of FDI flows during the period 2010-11 to 2016-17. During the period 2010-11 to 2016-17, the cumulative stock of FDI inflow was USD 51.18 billion, wherein power, oil and gas, and transport and communications are the country's top three major sectors, which together have attracted over 75 per cent of total FDI inflows to the country. Next is the manufacturing sector, which has attracted USD 5.78 billion in FDI in the same period. Hotels and tourism, real estate, and mining are the most promising sectors in Myanmar, each of which has attracted over USD 1 billion in FDI during the period 2010-11 to 2016-17.

India is one of the top investors in Myanmar. As on 30 September 2022, a total of 36 Indian enterprises have received approval of USD 774 million from the Myanmar government.[21] Several Indian star companies have been investing in Myanmar, such as Adani, Zydus Pharma, OVL, etc. However, investment has slowed down mainly due to restrictions imposed by the current military government.

Figure 4: Foreign Direct Investment, Net Inflows (% of GDP)

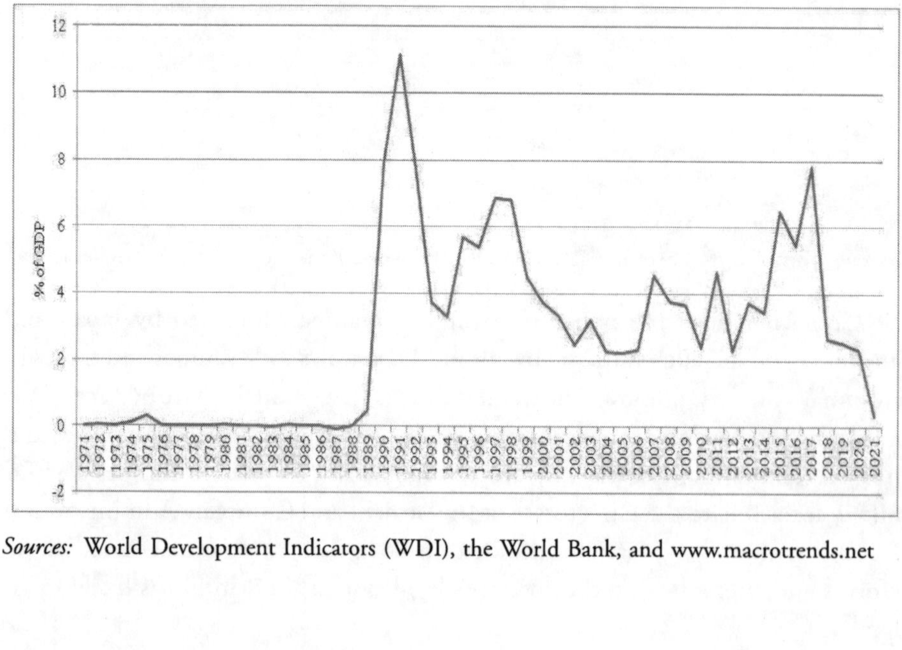

Sources: World Development Indicators (WDI), the World Bank, and www.macrotrends.net

Table 5: Trends in Top 10 Country-wise FDI Inflows

(US$ million)

Year	*China*	*India*	*Japan*	*Malaysia*	*Korea*	*Singapore*	*Thailand*	*UK*	*Vietnam*	*Hong Kong*	*Total*
2010-11	8269.23	*	7.14	76.75	2676.40	226.17	2146.00	799.00	*	5798.28	19998.97
2011-12	4345.73	73.00	4.32	51.86	25.57	*	*	99.83	18.15	*	4644.46
2012-13	231.77	11.50	54.06	4.32	37.94	418.23	1.30	232.70	329.39	84.84	1419.47
2013-14	56.16	26.04	55.71	616.11	81.21	2300.12	529.07	156.86	142.00	107.10	4107.06
2014-15	511.42	208.89	85.74	6.72	299.59	4297.19	165.68	850.76	175.40	625.56	8010.53
2015-16	3323.85	224.22	219.79	257.22	128.09	4246.88	236.17	75.31	4.68	224.67	9481.28
2016-17	447.40	*	51.07	10.18	25.80	2626.72	106.28	7.43	2.20	187.60	3521.52

Share in Total FDI Inflow

(%)

Year	*China*	*India*	*Japan*	*Malaysia*	*Korea*	*Singapore*	*Thailand*	*UK*	*Vietnam*	*Hong Kong*	*Total (9)*
2010-11	41.35	0.00	0.04	0.38	13.38	1.13	10.73	4.00	0.00	28.99	100.00
2011-12	21.73	0.37	0.02	0.26	0.13	0.00	0.00	0.50	0.09	0.00	23.09
2012-13	1.16	0.06	0.27	0.02	0.19	2.09	0.01	1.16	1.65	0.42	7.03
2013-14	0.28	0.13	0.28	3.08	0.41	11.50	2.65	0.78	0.71	0.54	20.35
2014-15	2.56	1.04	0.43	0.03	1.50	21.49	0.83	4.25	0.88	3.13	36.14
2015-16	16.62	1.12	1.10	1.29	0.64	21.24	1.18	0.38	0.02	1.12	44.71
2016-17	2.24	0.00	0.26	0.05	0.13	13.13	0.53	0.04	0.01	0.94	17.32

*Zero or negligible FDI inflow

Source: Directorate of Investment and Company Administration, available at http://www.dica. gov.mm/en/data-and-statistics Last accessed on 25 January 2022

FDI in an increasing order in Myanmar's infrastructure sector may generate higher growth in the medium to long run. Although FDI flow depends largely on country-specific factors, Myanmar at the present moment does not show an optimistic scenario in FDI inflow which can lead to higher growth. For example, the physical infrastructure sector (construction plus transport and communications plus industrial estates) has received only USD 6.5 billion FDI, out of a total of USD 51.18 billion during the period 2009-10 to 2016-17 (Table 6). Apparently, the bulk of the FDI went into export-seeking sectors in Myanmar. For example, oil and gas and power sectors have attracted over 60 per cent of FDI stock in Myanmar, where most of oil and gas actually has been exported to China and Thailand. Infrastructure development is crucial for Myanmar's trade and growth. Channelising FDI into the infrastructure sector would pave the way for higher trade and growth in the country.

Table 6: Distribution of FDI Flows, 2010-11 to 2016-17

(US$ million)

Sector	*2010-11*	*2011-12*	*2012-13*	*2013-14*	*2014-15*	*2015-16*	*2016-17**	*Total (2010-11 to 2016-17)*	*Share^ (2010-11 to 2016-17) (%)*
Agriculture	138.75		9.65	20.27	39.67	7.18		215.52	0.42
Livestock & Fisheries			5.60	96.02	26.86	8.25	86.69	223.42	0.44
Mining	1396.08	19.90	15.33	32.73	6.26	28.92		1499.22	2.93
Manufacturing	66.32	32.25	400.72	1826.98	1502.01	1065.00	883.14	5776.42	11.29
Power	8218.52	4343.98	364.20	46.51	40.11	360.10	605.67	13979.09	27.31
Oil and Gas	10179.30	247.70	309.20		3220.31	4817.79		18774.29	36.68
Construction									
Transport & Communications		0.63		1190.23	1679.30	1931.00	1628.87	6430.04	12.56
Hotels & Tourism			300.00	435.21	357.95	288.40	97.23	1478.78	2.89
Real Estate				440.57	780.75	728.68	165.00	2115.00	4.13
Industrial Estate						10.00		10.00	0.02
Other Services			14.77	18.53	357.32	235.96	54.92	681.51	1.33
Total	**19998.9**	**4644.46**	**1419.47**	**4107.06**	**8010.53**	**9481.28**	**3521.52**	**51183.28**	**100.00**

*Till December 2016. ^Share in total FDI flows during the period 2010-11 to 2016-17. An empty cell means no FDI

Source: Directorate of Investment and Company Administration (DICA)

FDI Policy

The Myanmar government has enacted new policies which allow more foreign participation in the country by relaxing the previously strict trading rules. However, investment permits with corresponding incentives and benefits continue to be guided under the Myanmar Companies Act; Myanmar Foreign Investment Law, 2012, as well as investment permits issued under the Special Economic Zone (SEZ) Law, 2014. Through these laws, foreign investors may choose to establish a foreign branch office in Myanmar; incorporate a private limited company; apply for and secure an investment permit from the Myanmar Investment Commission (MIC), which is also known as a MIC Permit; or apply for and secure an investment permit from the relevant Myanmar SEZ Management Committee, which is also known as an SEZ Permit.

The Foreign Investment Law, enacted in 2012, vastly simplified the process for investment application and offers several tax breaks, incentives and guarantees rights and protections for foreign business ventures. Likewise, the Myanmar Investment Commission (MIC) was restructured and its members are stakeholders from the government, the private sector and academia. The MIC approves new investment proposals and provides regular market updates. Four types of FDIs are now allowed in the country:

- Full (100 per cent) investment: Foreign investors may invest without any local partners in permitted sectors.
- Joint Venture: Joint ventures may be created with foreign, local and government entities.
- Contract: Foreign investors may act under a mutually agreed upon contract.
- Other Investment Forms: These include build-operate-transfer (BOT) and build-operate-own (BOO) investments.

Myanmar's legal framework has to be consistent with international standards, which has again been revolving on a continuous basis. Some important laws, such as the Foreign Investment Law, Myanmar Companies Act and the IP regulations, are still in the pipeline. To facilitate and sustain the FDI trends, Myanmar has to revise the Companies Act on an urgent basis. Myanmar does not allow foreign companies to have stakes in existing domestic businesses, but the revision in the Companies Act is expected to allow foreign ownership in some companies. The government has fixed an upper limit of foreign stakes at 35 per cent.[22] The government may allow foreign investors to trade on the Yangon Stock Exchange (YSE).

BIAs and DTAs

As a member of ASEAN, Myanmar is also a party to various multilateral agreements that aim to develop and enhance cross-border trade and investment among ASEAN countries, such as RCEP, the ASEAN Comprehensive Investment Agreement and the agreement on the ASEAN Economic Community. Bilateral Investment Agreements (BIAs) and Double Taxation Avoidance Agreements (DTAAs) are important tools for enhancing foreign investments and restoring transparency. To further improve investor confidence, Myanmar has entered into BIAs with Japan, South Korea, the Philippines, China, Lao PDR, Vietnam, Thailand, and India. Myanmar has concluded several BIAs and DTAAs till 2016 (Table 7).

Table 7: BIAs and DTAAs

Bilateral Investment Agreement (BIA)

Country/Region	*Date of signature*	*Date of entry into force*
Philippines	17.02.1998	11.09.1998
Vietnam	15.02.2000	-
China	12.12.2001	21.05.2002
Lao PDR	05.05.2003	-
Thailand	14.03.2008	-
India	24.06.2008	08.02.2009
Kuwait	06.08.2008	-
Israel	05.10.2014	-

Double-Taxation Avoidance Agreement (DTAA)

Country/Region	*Date of entry into force*
United Kingdom	01/10/1948
Vietnam	01/04/2004
Republic of Korea	01/04/2004
Malaysia	01/04/2009
India	01/04/2009
Singapore	01/04/2010
Lao PDR	01/04/2011
Thailand	01/04/2012

- Not yet in force.
Source: Myanmar (2014)

Conclusions and Way Forward

Myanmar is a "double track" land-bridge, connecting South and Southeast Asia on one side and South and East Asia, on the other. Starting with a low base, Myanmar has a strong potential for growth. Surrounded by China, India, ASEAN and the Bay of Bengal, the country has a relatively young labour force, rich and plenty of natural resources. However, Myanmar suffers from a lack of capacity and infrastructure, which impedes Myanmar's integration with the world. Therefore, the Myanmar government should undertake structural reform programmes, prioritising trade infrastructure and capacity building. Regional integration may help Myanmar to gain higher market access and entail significant benefits. At the same time, Myanmar has to undertake policies and programmes for sustained industrial and agricultural development to attain poverty alleviation and rural development, promoting local and foreign investment, and implementing projects for all-around social development leading to improved quality of life. When trade with the bordering neighbours is vital for Myanmar's growth and development, greater economic integration with the neighbourhood will go a long way in narrowing the infrastructure gap and strengthening the country's globalisation process. Myanmar needs to aim at promoting greater cooperation and collaboration with EAS, ASEAN, SAARC, BIMSTEC, BCIM, IORA, and GMS. Myanmar's greater participation in regional integration arrangements is expected to promote further and accelerate the Asian integration process.

Launching ASEAN Economic Community (AEC) in 2015 and the GSP and GSTP benefits have improved investor sentiments on Myanmar. There is a huge scope for Myanmar to take part in value-added trade with neighbouring countries. The potential sectors of investment would be transportation, energy, information and communication technology, agriculture, horticulture, climate protection, tourism and manufacturing such as automobiles, capital goods and electronics and electrical products, and services industries such as shipping, education, tourism, etc.

The investment environment in Myanmar continues to improve, undoubtedly. However, the current FDI flow is very low. Nevertheless, FDI can be an important source of valuable technology and know-how. A supportive FDI environment is, therefore, needed for the development of physical infrastructure and global (or regional) value chains in the country. In view of Myanmar's ongoing efforts to modernise its legal framework, it seems very unlikely that this trend will continue going forward. The outlook for foreign investors seeking to expand into Myanmar is, therefore, not promising.

Myanmar should aim to achieve business-oriented joint activities for trade and investment cooperation through trade facilitation measures (e.g. WTO TFA), trade policy coordination, harmonisation of standards, harmonisation and simplification of procedures and the dissemination of information, conducting capacity-building, supporting the growth of SMEs, etc. Myanmar may consider withdrawing all import licences. To carry out these reforms, Myanmar military government may strengthen the institutions and build relations with neighbouring countries, including India. India is Myanmar's civilisational partner and can be an honest development partner. At the same time, the Myanmar government needs to restore democracy through elections.

Myanmar offers high trade and investment opportunities. Myanmar may consider promoting trade in its respective regions and also with other regions through harmonisation of non-tariff measures, trade and investment facilitation measures, etc. Besides, Myanmar should focus on strengthening trade and economic relations with the world's emerging markets, such as BRICS. Investment facilitation should be taken upfront to help build the needed infrastructure. It shall focus on strengthening physical and digital connectivity with the countries in ASEAN and the Bay of Bengal.

Myanmar is vulnerable to natural disasters. Natural disasters include a wide range of events such as earthquakes, floods, landslides, cyclones, tsunamis, heat waves, etc. In 2004, a tsunami in the Indian Ocean devastated several countries in the region, including Myanmar and cyclone Nargis in 2008 devastated Myanmar. Disasters particularly affect the poorest and most marginalised people, widening social inequalities and harming economic growth. Therefore, ignoring the disaster risk and allowing the risk to accumulate would undermine its future potential for social and economic development in Myanmar. Greater regional cooperation will help Myanmar to gain precious resources for disaster management.

Myanmar has about 2,000 km of coastline, which is dotted over a dozen of ports. It is imperative for Myanmar to safeguard coastal security, safety, conservancy and the importance of protecting the marine environment. Myanmar faces the rise of terrorism and piracy; thus, there is a need to strengthen good order at sea by adopting various best practices evident in global maritime safety and security. Therefore, collective security in terms of opposing terrorism, piracy, and the proliferation of weapons of mass destruction within or from the region would pave the way to peace and harmony in the regions. Myanmar may undertake joint efforts for immediate rescue and relief to all humans in distress in the Bay of Bengal region. It should promote policy measures to secure shipping lanes and joint projects to build maritime domain awareness. Regional cooperation certainly has an important role in strengthening Myanmar's capacity in the maritime sector.

Myanmar has the potential to become another dynamic growth centre of Asia if it restores democracy and builds a strong pool of skilled human resources, besides developing a stronger and improved connectivity with the neighbouring countries. Strengthening human resources would speed up its growth process. Myanmar has some of Asia's pioneering institutions and universities. However, to support the country's participation in international and regional forums, restoration of democracy is a must, and policy research, capacity building and training are prerequisites. At the same time, skills and technology sharing in Myanmar would promote trade and economic development. If co-manufacturing has to take place in Myanmar, the country needs to match the skill as an essential requirement.

Recent economic policy shifts are likely to have long-term effects: inhibiting potential growth, worsening macroeconomic instability, and impairing the efficient allocation of resources. Lessons from Myanmar's economic history suggest that to the extent that these trends continue, investor confidence and the business environment will weaken further, constraining Myanmar's growth potential over the long-term. The World Bank's recent forecast indicates that beyond 2022 Myanmar's growth outlook remains weak and subject to substantial risks. While the rebound is thin, Myanmar's contracting GDP indicates that the country may face crises in food and fuel, thus escalating internal conflicts further. Further expansion of trade and FDI is necessary to promote economic growth in Myanmar. For Myanmar to grow fast on the regional integration front, it has to first restore democracy, peace and political stability. Peace building and restoring democracy would help Myanmar to build a stronger partnership with India and other neighbours.

ENDNOTES

1. Refer World Bank (2022)
2. Infrastructure and growth are positively associated. Refer, for example, Straub and Terada-Hagiwara (2010)
3. Besides, several MDBs such as the ADB have temporarily put on hold sovereign project disbursements and new contracts in Myanmar effective 01 February 2021.
4. Refer, *Myanmar Economic Monitor* (World Bank, 2022)
5. According to the WTO, available at https://www.wto.org/english/tratop_e/region_e/region_e.htm Last accessed on 25 January 2023
6. Ibid
7. Refer, Myanmar's Trade Policy Review of 2021. Refer, for example, Myanmar (2021)
8. Refer, Table 2.2 of Myanmar's *Trade Policy Review*, dated 8 April 2022, reference WT/TPR/S/405/Rev.1.
9. There are also ASEAN framework agreements on the facilitation of goods in transit (AFAGIT), and the Facilitation of Inter-State Transport (AFAFIST), among others.
10. Refer, Myanmar (2021)
11. According to one estimate, once full FTA was in effect in 2017, the intra-regional trade would be scaled up to US$ 47-59 billion annually.
12. See, WTO's RTA database, available at www.wto.org
13. Guangxi Zhuang Autonomous Region of China joined the GMS programme in 2004.
14. Refer, ADB (2012b).
15. Foreign direct investment refers to direct investment equity flows in the reporting economy. It is the sum of equity capital, reinvestment of earnings, and other capital. Direct investment is a category of cross-border investment associated with a resident in one economy having control or a significant degree of influence on the management of an enterprise that is resident in another economy. Ownership of 10 per cent or more of the ordinary shares of voting stock

is the criterion for determining the existence of a direct investment relationship (World Bank, 2017).

16. Refer *Nikkei Asia* dated 19 October 2021, available at https://asia.nikkei.com/Spotlight/Myanmar-Crisis/Myanmar-FDI-drops-to-8-year-low-reflecting-post-takeover-unrest Last accessed on 25 January 2022.
17. In comparison, FDI contribution to GDP in India, China and Thailand has been an average of 2 in 2014 and 2015 (World Bank, 2017)
18. Refer, https://www.wto-ilibrary.org/content/books/9789287050953 Last accessed on 25 January 2022
19. Refer, https://www.ft.com/content/f7bda5bc-e150-11e6-8405-9e5580d6e5fb Last accessed on 25 January 2022
20. Refer, the recent commentary of Oxford Business Group, available at https://www.oxfordbusinessgroup.com/overview/letter-legal-overview-climate-foreign-investment Last accessed on 25 January 2022
21. Refer, country briefing issued by the Indian Embassy in Yangon, available at https://embassyofindiayangon.gov.in Last accessed on 25 January 2022
22. Author's own discussion with bank executives in Yangon in December 2016

REFERENCES

ADB. "Myanmar in Transition Opportunities and Challenges." Manila (2012a)

____ "GMS Strategy and Future Directions." Manila (2012b)

Ballassa, Bela. *The Theory of Economic Integration*. New York: Greenwood Press, New York, 1961

De, Prabir. "Myanmar in Regional and Subregional Initiatives", Paper presented at the Fifth Training Workshop on "Regional Cooperation and Integration in Myanmar, organised by Research and Information System for Developing Countries (RIS), New Delhi, held at Yangon on 9–11 May 2016.

De, Prabir. "Myanmar's engagement in regional integration: Status and way forward." *ARTNeT,* UNESCAP, Bangkok, Working Paper #169 (2017).

De, Prabir and Raychaudhuri, Ajitava. *Myanmar's Integration with the World: Challenges and Policy Options*. Singapore: Palgrave Macmillan, 2018

Embassy of India. "Bilateral Economic and Commercial Brief." Yangon, Myanmar (2022)

Straub, Stéphane and Terada-Hagiwara, Akiko. "Infrastructure and Growth in Developing Asia." *ADB* Economics Working Paper Series No. 231 (2010)

Viner, Jacob. "The Customs Union Issue." New York: Carnegie Endowment for International Peace, 1950

World Bank. "World Development Indicator." Washington, D.C (2017)

____ "Myanmar Economic Monitor." Washington, D.C (2022)

WTO. "Trade Policy Review." Document No. WT/TPR/S/293/Rev.1, Geneva (2014)

____ "Trade Policy Review." Document No. WT/TPR/S/405/Rev.1. Geneva (2021)

6

Infrastructure Projects and Myanmar: Progressions and Regressions with Giant Neighbours

Dr Shrabana Barua

ABSTRACT

Myanmar has been engaging with a number of states over various infrastructure projects. Among them, China took the lead in the country. Not only was China the largest investor in Myanmar until 2022, a place now taken by Singapore, but it also managed to push itself into building various infrastructures through political strings. The 'gun' bridges constructed by China in the early 1990s are a case in point. On the other hand, as Myanmar seemed to transition into a democracy in the 2000s slowly, states such as Thailand, Singapore, South Korea, India, and Japan also found space in Myanmar's infrastructure and investment sector. Despite China being on top in this so-called game of both geo-economy and geo-strategy, other states stepped in. In fact, Chinese projects faced many hurdles in the last decade when democracy seemed to thrive in Myanmar. However, the coup in 2021 reversed Myanmar's political status as a democracy. Within this context, this chapter aims to address two important questions. One, what are the various infrastructure projects over which Myanmar has engaged with other states in its neighbourhood, particularly China? Second, has the coup impacted these projects and Myanmar's relations with other states? This chapter concludes that even as other states are making a mark in Myanmar, a hitherto fertile ground for infrastructure investment, the coup has brought the ball back into the Chinese court. Therefore, dealing with Myanmar has become complicated yet unavoidable for competing countries in the region.

Introduction

Investments in the infrastructure sector and building connectivity projects have found a renewed tempo in recent times. Notwithstanding the importance of railways, telegraphs, and ports for colonial pursuits, infrastructure has re-emerged as a crucial variable in the study of geopolitical power play. This, as some argue, has been catalysed by China's vision of the Belt and Road Initiative (BRI). One can agree or disagree in this context but cannot ignore the significance of infrastructure in international relations today.

Theoretically, scholars of political economy such as A.O. Hirschman, Hans Singer, and W.W. Rostow spoke about the importance of infrastructure, such as transport, communications, irrigation, etc., as essential sectors for growth.[1] If underdeveloped states were to develop, these areas, classified as Social Overhead Capital (SOC), were to be invested in. Hirschman noted this would automatically spur growth in other sectors described as Direct Productive Activities (DPA). In the field of international relations, too, interestingly, many scholars discuss contemporary infrastructure projects and connectivity corridors under headings of 'infrastructure diplomacy',[2] noting them to be meant to influence geopolitics.[3] No doubt, countries that seek to be powerful are bound to take infrastructure investments and connectivity projects very seriously.

With much geopolitical attention now, Myanmar appears as an interesting case in Asia. It has been engaging with a number of states over various infrastructure projects. Among them, China has taken the lead in the country. Not only was China the largest investor in Myanmar for many years, but it also managed to push itself in building various infrastructures, in turn gaining influence. On the other hand, as Myanmar slowly seems to move towards democracy, states including Thailand, Singapore, India, and Japan found increasing space in Myanmar's infrastructure sector. Despite China being on top of the geopolitical game in Myanmar, particularly, as this chapter argues, by making infrastructural inroads, other states have gained some ground. Revealingly, Chinese projects faced hurdles in the last decade when democracy seemed to set in on Myanmar. However, the coup in 2021 reversed Myanmar's political status once again to military rule.

Against this backdrop, this chapter aims to address two important questions. One, how does infrastructure investment impact geopolitics in Myanmar? In answering this, it is essential to look at the various infrastructure projects over which Myanmar has been engaged with others. The cases of China and India find detailed focus within such a discussion. Second, has the coup had an impact on these projects and the relations of Myanmar with other states? This chapter concludes that focusing on infrastructure has become a must. Even as other states are making a mark in Myanmar, a hitherto fertile ground for infrastructure investment, the coup has brought the ball back into the Chinese court, albeit in a limited sense. Further, signs of progressions and regressions in terms of various infrastructure projects make it clear that dealing with Myanmar, a country so strategically located geopolitically, has become complicated, yet unavoidable for competing countries in the region.

The Myanmar Story on Infrastructure

During a speech in June 1985 in London, then British Prime Minister Margaret Thatcher said, "You might have heard a lot lately about 'infrastructure'—the new 'in word'. Some of you might even ask exactly what it is. You and I come by road and rail. But economists travel on infrastructure."[4] Today, it can be argued that not only economists but almost every person also travels by infrastructure. Largely, when China grabbed world attention by announcing the BRI in 2013, the need to enhance physical connectivity, both through land and sea, stood highlighted. The domain of infrastructure underwent a facelift over the last decade. Plans for economic corridors and connectivity projects proliferated on the world map. This multiplication of infrastructure projects and connectivity lines has translated into both competition and cooperation between states. As a result, infrastructure has become a variable that impacts geopolitics significantly.

A few months after Margaret Thatcher's speech, the then Chinese Vice Minister of Communications, Pan Qi, published an article on 2 September 1985 in the *Beijing Review.* It emphasised the need to open up the Southwest of China to facilitate its development at par with the country's eastern regions.[5] Among other things, he proposed the upgrading of roads and rail links from Yunnan through Burma, all the way up to the Indian Ocean. He encouraged the idea of an international airport in west Yunnan, which would allow easy connectivity to places including Hong Kong, Bangkok, and Singapore. In short, the idea was to build and enhance the region's infrastructure. Pan Qi's idea to develop Southwest China was in line with this theoretical framework given by scholars such as Hirschman. However, at that time, little did anybody predict the fate of Burma, a country which was economically underdeveloped and politically already under military rule. Would it manage to upgrade its infrastructure, connect to other regions, tread the path of development, or facilitate China to reach the Indian Ocean via its territory? Time was to tell.

Eyes on Myanmar

In 1988, a coup took place, the second in Burma (now Myanmar). Soon the country was internationally isolated. It was China that befriended it. China took this opportunity to make inroads into Myanmar by building roads, railways, pipelines, and ports and began to bring Pan Qi's vision to life. Through the decade of the 1990s, Beijing's growing influence in Myanmar was noted by observers around the world. In fact, China used these infrastructures to harness geopolitical gains in exchange for military hardware support. The bridges built by China in 1991-92 at the Ruili-Muse and Wanding-Kyukok borders are fitting examples. By the 2000s, it became evident that Chinese forays into Myanmar, especially marked by multiple infrastructure projects and investments in related sectors, including energy, became a concern for neighbouring countries. While Allen Booz Hamilton, an American firm, reported about the Chinese 'string of pearls' in the Indian Ocean that considered the Kyaukpyu port in Myanmar as strategic, other states in the neighbourhood became cautious.

India, in particular, felt concerned. In the mid-1990s, news about Chinese spy vessels operating from Coco Island had already created suspicions and tensions.[6] The competition between India and China was gaining pace. While Myanmar was toying with the idea of democracy through Khin Nyunt's 'seven-step roadmap to democracy' and adopted a new constitution in 2008, New Delhi's engagements with Myanmar underwent certain changes. Since India has been involved in implementing infrastructure projects in Myanmar, additionally, it has cooperated through defence diplomacy[7].

From 2011-12, under a more liberalised environment in Myanmar, infrastructure building was focused under President Thein Sein. China had overtaken Thailand as the largest investor in Myanmar. Yet, it was not a smooth ride for Beijing (as elaborated later). Additionally, with the announcement of the Special Economic Zone (SEZ) in Thilawa, Japan became a viable alternative. As it is, Japan has been involved in creating infrastructure linkages and investing in railways, funds and projects in Southeast Asia since the 20th century, not China.[8] Moreover, Myanmar was said to be the first country to accept Japan's war reparations offer in the 1940s.[9] With Japan now seeking to provide an alternative to Chinese infrastructure in the region, things are changing. These events are reminders of a geopolitical power play through infrastructure building.

Though externally, many states have begun collaboration with Myanmar over building infrastructure; infrastructural growth is not necessarily a making of them alone. Two main reasons can be identified as internal factors that catalysed infrastructure growth in Myanmar.

1. Energy sector: It is true that Myanmar reeled under economic pressure, especially due to Western sanctions throughout the 1990s and later, thus ignoring pertinent development issues within the country. The one sector

that brought Myanmar to the geopolitical forefront was energy. The oil sector thrived in the pre-World War period and was nationalised in 1963 by the Ne Win government. Gas was commercially produced in the country from 1971.[10] However, despite being an exporter of oil earlier and discovering new onshore oil and (later, offshore) gas sources in Myanmar, it had to resort to oil imports in the late 1980s. This hurt its foreign exchange leading to the eventual liberalisation of the energy sector in the 1990s. It enabled Foreign Direct Investments (FDI) and private players to come in. By 1998, a 410-km pipeline exported gas from Yadana M-5 and M-6 blocks to Thailand, built with support from the Petroleum Authority of Thailand (now PTT Public Company Limited). By 2000, a 271-km pipeline exported gas to Thailand from the Yetagun blocks.[11] Soon China, India, and South Korea entered the fray. The geopolitics of building energy infrastructure and investments thus became visible as pipelines and supporting infrastructure also to facilitate trade and commerce, came up. It peaked when Myanmar handed over the rights to buy gas production from A-1 block off the Rakhine coast to Beijing in 2005, through an unexpected deal. The off-shore block was being jointly produced through a Power Sharing Contract (PSC) by a consortium of Daewoo of South Korea (60 per cent) and ONGC (20 per cent), and GAIL (10 per cent) of India. The problem occurred due to a delay in facilitating gas transportation back to India via Bangladesh. While options have been being considered since 2005, Myanmar grew exasperated and gave the right to buy some of the produce to PetroChina. China acted swiftly by transporting the gas through a pipeline that ran from Ramree Island to Yunnan. India was left shocked. Today, the oil and gas pipelines built by China from Kyaukpyu to Kunming, where China National Petroleum Corporation (CNPC) has 51 per cent ownership in each of them, along with Myanmar Oil and Gas Enterprise (MOGE has 49 per cent), falls under the famous China-Myanmar Economic Corridor (CMEC) of the BRI. This has led to various infrastructure growth around the region.

2. Growing urbanisation: A 2017 report on 'Understanding Infrastructure Opportunities in ASEAN' by PWC (Infrastructure Series Report 1) reflects poorly on Myanmar's infrastructure build-up.[12] However, it notes that growing urbanisation is a reason that drives infrastructure spending. In this context, drawing from a United Nations Report in 2014,[13] the PWC projects that by 2050, among ASEAN states, Myanmar (and

Indonesia) would move towards fast urbanisation. From 34 per cent in 2014, urbanisation would spread to 55 per cent. This could result in growing infrastructure building and investment in Myanmar. Such aspects find obvious reflections today, mainly through projects like the New Yangon City Development plan. As evident, foreign players are deeply involved in such projects. For example, Infrastructure Asia, an infrastructure facilitation forum headed by Enterprise Singapore and Monetary Authority of Singapore, both government agencies, have assisted Myanmar with its New Yangon City Project. It has collaborated with New Yangon Development Company Limited (NYDC) to help evaluate the scope of power and natural gas supply and distribution, cyber connectivity scope and other aspects. Though Myanmar had initially signed a framework agreement with China, which declared a USD1.5 billion on the same, due to controversies, the Myanmar government called for Request For Proposal (RFP) to nine companies from states including India, France, Singapore, and Taiwan.[14]. China was not happy. This again brings to the fore the geopolitical power play revolving around the domain of infrastructure building.

China in Myanmar

Progressions: As early as 1954, the Kunming-Baoshan-Dali highway, built by China up to the border in Myanmar, was the first to be completed. Before the first coup in Burma in 1963, China had built more asphalted highways from Kunming to the Burmese border.[15] During the Ne Win era, Burma practised what Maung Maung Gyi termed as 'negative neutralism', i.e., an almost isolationist foreign policy.[16] Even then, Beijing managed to build a hydroelectric power station by end of the 1960s,[17] among smaller scattered investments.

With the end of the Ne Win era, however, China loomed large over Myanmar. As Bertil Lintner noted, Myanmar behaved very much like a 'vassal state' in the 1990s. The 'Sinicization of Burma'[18] was underway, achieved by building roads, rails, and ports in Myanmar. For instance, by 1993, China had won the contract and begun renovating the Old Burma Road with an aim to restore linkages from Yunnan to Myanmar. It completed the Myitkyina-Kambaiti part of the road in 2007[19] and the 366-km Myitkyina-Tanai part of it by 2014.[20] China not only claims this road as part of its historical southern Silk Road, but has offered to build the Myitkyina-Tanai-Pangsau pass section of the Stillwell road (in India). The Yunnan Construction Engineering Group, a Central State-Owned Enterprise

(SOE) of China, had even made progress in this regard.[21] With the revival of the Silk Road narrative, the Old Burma Road, therefore, forms an important part of China's influence through infrastructure.

During the same period, China famously built the two bridges across the Shweli River (mentioned earlier). Interestingly, it is reported that Myanmar requested a 20-ton bridge at Muse, but China insisted on it being 50 tons instead, and it persisted.[22] These were later used to deliver light infantry weapons, rocket launchers, etc., to the extent that they were locally referred to as 'gun bridges'.[23] China's bridge-building capacity and genius have been demonstrated more recently with the completion of the Nujiang river bridge in December 2019. This bridge that forms part of the Dali-Ruili railway network has the world's longest truss arch and is an important link in China's railway connectivity to Myanmar.

Progressions in China's infrastructure building in Myanmar continued. It was again in 1993 that the Myitkyina-Sadon-Sailaw-Mangmin road was inaugurated.[24]. By the mid-1990s, Bhamo in Myanmar could be reached via a 56-km road from Yinjian through Taihone-Momauk or the 104-km road from Lianghe, both built by China.[25] Mandalay was approachable via Myitkyina and Bhamo or through the road from Muse-Lashio, which forms part of NH3 and Asian Highway-14. The Asian Highway (AH) network runs through Myanmar from China.

Further, 305 km of the Golden Square highway falls in Myanmar. These infrastructure build-ups of the time indicate increased involvement of China in Myanmar's economy almost directly, also through improvement of trade (not just on the border at Ruli-Muse regarding which a trade agreement was signed in 1988, but beyond), and its politics more indirectly, through improved interactions with the *Tatmadaw*. The strategic implications of improved infrastructural presence of China in Myanmar have remained an important point of analysis for scholars since the 1990s.

In the 1990s, Chinese engineers and advisors were already inspecting matters regarding the ports at Kyaukpyu and Yangon, as well as naval bases at Haingyii.[26] In 1992, the Mregui island port was developed, while Chinese presence and assistance to upgrade some of the island ports in Myanmar, including those at Zadetkyi, Monkey Point and Kyaikkami, were creating rumours about China's intent in Myanmar. Many old ports were being renovated or new facilities built, including upgrading the Kyaukpyu port by the early 2000s.

As discussed earlier, the major focus on infrastructure in the 2000s was building the gas and oil pipelines from Kyaukpyu to Kunming (both started in 2007). Additionally, the deep-sea port at Kyaukpyu became a cherry on the cake at the time. Announced in 2007, the port is one of the most important aspects of China's infrastructure investment in Myanmar. This deep-sea port, with USD 1.3 billion of Chinese investments, on Maday Island, is also facilitated with storage capacity and designed to enable tankers of 30,000 tons to dock or unload oil to be further transferred through the pipeline.[27] Additionally, as part of the CMEC, a special economic and technology zone has been proposed at Kyaukpyu to be built by CITIC Construction Company Limited. There is also the shipping terminal and shipyard of Thilawa built by China, which is being considered for expansion (though Japan took away the limelight by building the SEZ there).

As regards railways, China has been working on three main railway projects, namely, from Kunming-Kyaukpyu, Kunming-Yangon and Kunming through Shan state up to Chiang Rai in Thailand.[28] The part on the Chinese side was being constructed in phases, in the form of the 330-km Dali-Ruili railway. Connectivity is thus being upgraded on this stretch by building railways that form part of the China-Myanmar railway corridor, mostly built by an SOE, China Railway Engineering Corporation (CREC). In 2011, an MoU was signed regarding the first line of this project from Muse-Kyaukpyu, largely in alignment with the oil and gas pipelines. Chinese projects, however, faced a few backlashes in Myanmar during the Thein Sein period. Many regressions were noted in the infrastructure sector in particular, including the halting 2014 of the railway line in this context. In 2018, a new MoU was signed to begin a feasibility study for the line from Muse to Mandalay.[29]

In 2017, Myanmar joined the BRI. The China-Myanmar Economic Corridor (CMEC) became a major part of it, which China continued to pursue even as COVID hit in 2020. However, before the BRI, already Bangladesh-China-India-Myanmar (BCIM), which evolved from the Kunming Initiative in 1999 as a Track-2 diplomatic forum, was underway. It was brought under the BRI at first. In 2019, it was left out during the Second BRI Forum. In 2020, President Xi Jinping's visit to Myanmar highlighted progressions in the infrastructure sector. Of 33 MoUs signed then, 13 were related to infrastructure. At least, since, it has not gone downhill for Beijing, even as the coup changed the situation in Myanmar.

Regressions: From 2011-12, Myanmar seemed to move in a very different direction under the military rule of Thein Sein. It was during this period that China announced the BRI and sought to put Chinese infrastructure and connectivity corridors back onto the world map. But, while China faced tough questions (and also opposition) from many quarters, Myanmar seemed to have become cautious too.

On 30 September 2011, Thein Sein announced the suspension of the Myitsone hydropower project, where China had sought to invest USD 3.6 billion in the dam. An MoU was initially signed in 2006, and the design phase began subsequently. However, reports in 2009 doubted the environmental impact of the project on the Irrawaddy river and in areas where locals resided. In particular, protests broke out in Kachin areas, demanding the project's cancellation. As of 2022, despite speculations over re-negotiation with China, the project remains in limbo. A similar situation occurred in the Letpadaung copper mine in Monywa, Sagaing. In 2010, an agreement was signed by Wanbao Mining Limited (to get 49 per cent of net profits), a subsidiary of Chinese SOE Norinco, and the Burmese government with Myanmar Economic Holdings Limited (MEHL had 51 per cent). A number of protests led to delays in construction thrice. Though production of cathode copper reached 120,000 tons by 2019, the opaqueness of operations there led to Myanmar marking them as 'suspicious'.[30]

Another regression in infrastructure building was the downsizing of the Kyaukpyu port, where China's CITIC group initially obtained an 80 per cent stake in it. The USD 7.7 billion project was, however, downsized only in 2017 to USD 1.3 billion with a 70 per cent stake for CITIC. Just a year later, the Mityikina-Tamai road which was completed by Northern Royal Company and China's Teng Myin Company in 2014, was returned to the Myanmar Ministry of Construction due to security reasons. Currently, three places of the road traversing through Kachin areas remain in a very poor state. The case of the NYCD project and China's position has already been mentioned above. By 2011 China had overtaken Thailand as the highest investor in Myanmar, a place now taken by Singapore in 2022. These developments reflect dents, if not barriers, in the relationship between Myanmar and China today.

COVID and the Coup: The coup in February 2021 came at a time when COVID-19 spread across the globe. This did not let China keep its focus away from the BRI. By September 2020, within weeks after the Japanese Foreign Minister visited Myanmar, Yang Jechi, China's top diplomat, met Daw Suu Kyi to discuss, among other things, the progress of BRI. When Suu Kyi was deposed the next year, China provided vaccine doses straight to the *Tatmadaw* (as opposed to the Indian government handing it to Red Cross in Myanmar), clearly indicating its willingness to continue with 'business-as-usual' or even impress the junta in Myanmar. It seemed to work. Myanmar proposed to include the Mee Lin Gyaing natural gas power plant project, reported to be worth USD 2.5 billion under the CMEC. Myanmar's Supreme Group is partnering with three Chinese companies (Union Resources and Engineering Company, Yunnan Energy Investment and Zhefu Holding Group) to build the 1,390 MW project in the Ayeyawady region. It is expected to be operational in 2027[31].

India in Myanmar

Progressions: India was a late entrant in Myanmar's infrastructural game. The Look East Policy (LEP) in 1991 led to an increasing focus on Myanmar. By 1993, the plan for the Tamu-Klewa-Kalemyo/Kalay road was conceived. It was inaugurated in February 2001 as the India-Myanmar friendship road. After all, the entire stretch was built by the Border Road Organization (BRO) as a gift to its neighbour, especially given that this was a major entry point between the two. Under a pact, the BRO maintained it till 2009. This also formed part of the AH network that eventually got utilised under the Tri-lateral Highway (TLH) project.

The TLH is another important infrastructure project in Myanmar. This multi-lateral initiative aims to connect Manipur's Moreh town in India with Mae Sot in Thailand via Myanmar.[32] The total cost of it is estimated at USD 140 million. In 2012, India reportedly provided USD 500 million worth of loans to Myanmar. With this, the entire cost of the THL in the country is being covered.[33] Additionally, there are two routes to reach Thailand, one via Mandalay and the other by-passing it. Part of the former aligns with the friendship road from Moreh to Tamu to Kalewa. From there onwards, the 101-km Kalewa-Yargi section has been under poor condition. India has agreed to invest USD 11 million to upgrade it into a four-lane highway.[34] At the same time, there are 69 bridges (out of a total of 70) that fall on the TLH route, which are in need of betterment. India has agreed to help. Yet, it is to be noted that the task of upgrading them is not of the BRO but of the Myanmar government.[35]

At the domestic level in India, many infrastructure development projects were rolled out in North East Region (NER) under the aegis of the new Ministry of Development for the Northeast Region (DoNER), initially established as a department in 2001. For example, the Special Accelerated Road Development Programme for North East (SARDP-NE) was conceived as a plan in the mid-2000s to improve connectivity in the NER. In doing so, it was expected to translate into better connectivity with Myanmar. Similarly, improving the railway system in the NER has been seen as a step to enhance links to Myanmar. For example, there is a proposal on laying tracks in the Jiribam-Imphal-Moreh sector, which will be linked to Mandalay as part of the larger vision of the Delhi-Hanoi rail link. The latter is a part of the multi-lateral ambition initiated by India and six other countries of the Mekong Ganga Cooperation (MGC). Under this, NER will be linked with Vietnam via Myanmar, Thailand, Malaysia and Singapore. India lent a USD 56 million Line of Credit in 2010 to Myanmar.[36]

When LEP found new vigour with the Act East Policy in 2014, India's attention in Myanmar was drawn, especially through its most ambitious project there—the Kaladan Multi-Modal Transit and Transport Project (KMTTP). Signed in 2008, the KMTTP is a government-funded plan with four main components. One is enabling a 539-km sea route transport system between Kolkata and Sittwe ports, where an integrated sea port is being constructed. Two, integrate Sittwe point to the Inland Water Terminal (IWT) at Paletwa via the Kaladan River. The 158-km stretch is being made navigable by reclaiming land and dredging. Three, through the seven barges of 300 tonnes each created, cargo will be transported via the 110-km stretch of highway to be built between Paletwa and Zorinpui in Mizoram. Four, a 10-km road from Zochawchhuah village at the Zorinpui border to Lawngtlai will connect with NH-54.[37] Though construction began in 2010, the delay in the completion of the full project remains an irritant even in 2022. A new target is set for 2023. The instability in the Arakan region is also negatively impacting on early completion of the project.

Regressions: In India-Myanmar relations, the Jawaharlal Nehru-U Nu era was marked with camaraderie, but no crucial project implementation took place. The Ne Win phase was a non-starter as well. After the 1988 coup, India was vocal in its criticism, unlike in recent times. These trends themselves are minuses in the context being discussed in this chapter. Infrastructure, therefore, did not specifically figure in this dynamic. When some progress was made since the 1990s, they were not satisfactory and lagged behind. The case of gas production from the Shwe fields given to Petrochina in 2005 has already been noted. Further, in 2008, the Governments of India and Myanmar signed an agreement to develop the Chinwin River Valley. The Tamanthith (1,200 MW) hydro-electric power project (HEP) was to be built after an investigation done by the National Hydro Power Corporation Ltd. (NHPC).[38] Despite a detailed report and feasibility study, this was scrapped in 2013. The same happened with the Shwazaye (880 MW) project. Allegedly, Myanmar delayed it under Chinese pressure.[39]

COVID-19 and the Coup: India's supply of vaccines to Myanmar has been much appreciated in recent times of turmoil in the country. To be noted is the fact that one million doses were handed over by India's Foreign Secretary, Harsh Vardhan Sringla, to the Red Cross, reflecting New Delhi's diplomatic prowess at a critical time. Unlike in the late 1980s, India has been careful in condemning the 2021 coup directly. This has been attributed to the higher stakes India has in Myanmar today, most of which are made up of infrastructure projects, especially the TLH and the KMTTP.

One case of withdrawal that caught attention in the post-coup period is the exit of the Adani group from investing in the Ahlone Terminal 2 in Yangon. In 2019, Adani port won a bid to build and operate the project after Myanmar Investment Commission granted permission. The terminal is on 54-acre land owned by the Myanmar Economic Corporation (MEC), a military-backed entity. Since MEC came under US sanctions post-coup, the Adani group and others have been asked to exit the project. It decided to comply and exit by mid-2022.

Other Players in the Picture

Myanmar has witnessed increased infrastructure investments from various foreign players. As noted, Japan has entered as a crucial player in Myanmar's infrastructure sector. Its most significant project has been the SEZ at Thilawa. Initially, the Chamber of Commerce and Industry in Myanmar and Japan External Trade Organization (JETRO) got into a joint venture (a JV company was created named Myanmar Japan Thilawa Development Limited, with a 51:49 percentage stake between Myanmar and the rest with Japan respectively) to develop it. Japanese aid flowing through the Japan International Cooperation Agency (JICA) aimed at the "development of infrastructure and systems necessary for supporting sustainable economic growth" in Myanmar. The Transport Development Plan in 2014 and the Industrial Policy Report 2016 were both made with assistance from the Japanese government.[40]

Besides, in Myanmar, Japan has increasingly sought to compete with China in the region. Before China launched the BRI, as part of Japan's foreign policy in Central Asia, Tokyo provided USD 21.91 million in Official Development Assistance (ODA) for building connectivity and related projects. Notably, Japan seemed to respond to the BRI by announcing the Partnership for Quality Infrastructure (PQI) in 2015, which was later upgraded to Enhanced PQI (EPQI). If this was not enough evidence of the growing importance of infrastructure in geopolitics, one could look at the Blue Dot Network (BDN) launched in 2019.

As a multi-lateral venture between Japan, USA and Australia, this plan acts as a screening mechanism for all infrastructure projects to bring about quality and transparency. It has been read as a response to the BRI, especially as many projects under the latter were considered as being implemented in an opaque manner, with Chinese interests as the main goal.

Singapore, too, needs to be considered an important foreign player in Myanmar. Its projects or investments in physical infrastructure may be limited, yet it has become the largest single investor in the country in recent times. It is looking at building the trunk road in the country. Further, the Singapore-Kunming Rail Network (SKRL), worth USD 23 billions, is to connect Singapore to Kunming through Myanmar, besides others areas. This was part of the 15 priority projects in the Master Plan on ASEAN Connectivity, originally (MPAC 2010), but was shifted as part of one of the strategic areas under MPAC 2025. Many cases indicate an interest in building Myanmar's infrastructure, whether directly or through financing. For instance, Singapore-based Asiatech Energy, a US firm, had signed up to finance the 230-MW cycle gas-fired power plant in Mawlamyaing, Mon state. Post-coup, however, regressions are expected in many such instances.

Conclusion

Based on the study of various infrastructure projects and the situation in Myanmar, four main conclusions can be drawn.

1. *Geopolitical importance of infrastructure:* The increasing importance of infrastructure as a variable in geopolitical power play needs to be taken seriously in general and in particular by Myanmar, a state that has yet to reach a certain level of development and growth.
2. *Numero uno China:* Despite China's regressions in the last decade vis-à-vis various projects (or perhaps given it), Beijing continues to lead in the infrastructure sector. It is true that Beijing has to push even harder now to reach out to the Indian Ocean through Myanmar and keep its BRI projects on track. The importance of maritime component in geopolitics has increased in strategic value. So has the weight of energy security. China aims to gain further strategic interests in Myanmar by securing its investments in ports and pipelines. The changed political scenario in Myanmar has raised hope in China that it will continue to thrive in the coming days, especially as many others have been discouraged and forced to exit the country amidst political turmoil.

3. *Increased competition:* Japan has the capability, and now seemingly, the will to compete with China in the infrastructure domain. India, too, has chosen not to withdraw from Myanmar despite a lag in projects and pressure to disengage with the military government. The Act East Policy places Myanmar as a crucial partner in New Delhi's foreign policy calculations. Thailand has looked more attentively at Myanmar since the coup and will not shy away from opportunities in Myanmar. Singapore has been catching up with its investments, which is expected to trickle into the infrastructure sector with time.
4. *Myanmar as a strategic player:* Given its location at the rim of Bay of Bengal, Myanmar is harnessing its strategic value. Unlike in the 1990s, Myanmar is not as vulnerable as the world may believe. True that economic aid and humanitarian assistance had to flow in, and came easily in to the country, until February 2021. Yet, domestic transitions in Myanmar have had nominal impacts on geopolitics of infrastructure.

In 2013, a McKinsey report stated that if Myanmar were to quadruple its GDP by 2030, it would need USD 650 billion in investments, of which USD 320 billion would have to be put in infrastructure projects alone. Its performance of decadal target by 2023 is yet to be studied. In 2016, the Asian Development Bank (ADB) published a report, 'Myanmar Transport Sector Policy Note: Trunk Roads' that studied the road infrastructure in Myanmar. It focussed on a '15-year modernizing agenda' and suggested that by 2030, if Myanmar is to achieve its economic needs, it would have to invest 1.5 per cent of GDP on its trunk roads.[41] These studies indicate the need for focusing on infrastructure in Myanmar in the coming years. On the other hand, at an international level, in 2017, an ADB Report titled 'Meeting Asia's Infrastructure Needs' examined Asia's infrastructure requirements up to 2030. It estimates that Asia will need USD 26 trillion to meet the current gap by then. A global perspective on the same is provided through the McKinsey Global Institute's 2016 report titled 'Bridging Global Infrastructure Gaps.'[42] Since infrastructure has emerged in such a big way as a variable in international relations at large, it would be best to seek integration at the local and international levels.

ENDNOTES

1. While propounding the theory of unbalanced growth, Hirschman explicated about the SOC and DPA sector. Rostow proposed the 'stages of economic growth' in 1962. See Kaname Akamatsu, *A Theory of Unbalanced Growth in the World Economy* (*Weltwirtschaftliches Archiv, 1961)*, 196-217

2. Eric Wicaksono, "The Art of Infrastructure Diplomacy," *The Indonesian Journal of Strategy, Policy and World Affairs-Strategic Review*, (July-September 2017), available at http://www.sr-indonesia.com/in-the-journal/view/the-art-of-infrastructure-diplomacy; Vijay Sakhuja, "China's 'infrastructure diplomacy' alive and well," *Nikkie Asian Review* 04 March 2015) available at https://asia.nikkei.com/Viewpoints-archive/Perspectives/China-s-infrastructure-diplomacy-alive-and-well, last accessed on 10 November 2022
3. See Jonathan Hillman, "Influence and Infrastructure: The Strategic Stakes of Foreign Projects," Reconnecting Asia Project, *Centre for Strategic International Studies*, Washington DC, 2019
4. Cited in Hillman, 2019.
5. Pan Qi, "Opening the Southwest: An Expert Opinion," *Beijing Review*, Vol. 28 (35) (02 September 2018): 22-23.
6. Some however argue that the news was only a rumour. See, for example, Andrew Selth, "Burma's Mythical Isles," *Australian Quarterly*, Vol. 80 No. 6 (2008): 24-28.
7. Jaideep Chanda, *Irrawaddy Imperatives: Reviewing India's Myanmar Strategy* (New Delhi: Pentagon Press, 2021)
8. Japan introduced High-Speed Railways, for instance, in the 1960s. By 2004, it popularised the Silk Road Diplomacy plan (conceived as early as in 1997) in the Caucasian and Central Asian Region.
9. "Thilawa Special Economic Zone: A Model for Growth in Myanmar," *Kubota,* available at https://www.kubota.com/global-index/myanmar/02.html, last accessed on 10 November 2022
10. Tin Maung Maung Than, "Myanmar's Energy Sector: Banking on Natural Gas," *Southeast Asian Affairs* (2005): 257-289.
11. Ibid.
12. PWC Report, "Understanding Infrastructure Opportunities in ASEAN," Infrastructure Series Report 1, 2020, available at https://www.pwc.com/sg/en/publications/assets/cpi-mas-1-infrastructure-opporuntities-in-asean-201709.pdf, last accessed on 10 November 2022
13. United Nations, "World Urbanization Prospects: The 2014 revision," 2015
14. Nan Lwin, "Nine Firms Qualify to Challenge Chinese Proposal for Myanmar's New Yangon City Project," *The Irrawaddy*, 24 November 2020, available at https://www.irrawaddy.com/news/burma/nine-firms-qualify-challenge-chinese-proposal-myanmars-new-yangon-city-project.html, last accessed on 11 November 2022
15. Bertil Lintner, "Burma and its Neighbours," *China Report*, Vol. 28(3) (1992): 233.
16. M.M. Gyi, "Foreign Policy of Burma since 1962: Negative Neutralism for Group Survival" In *Military Rule Burma since 1962: A Kaleidoscope of View*, edited by F. K. Lehman (Singapore: Maruzen Asia, 1981).
17. Bertil Lintner, 1992: 234.
18. See, for example, Swaran Singh, "The Sinicization of Myanmar and Its Implications for India," *Issues and Studies*, 33 (1) (January 1997): 116-133
19. Ruhee Neog, "Connecting South Asia: The Stilwell Road & Sub-Regional Networks," *Institute of Peace and Conflict Studies*, Issue Brief No. 188 (April 2012) available at https://www.files.ethz.ch/isn/142637/IB188-Ruhee-Stilwell.pdf, last accessed on 11 November 2022
20. Tun Lin Aung, "Damages occur in three places on Myithyina-Ledo road", *Eleven media*, 16 September 2022, available at https://elevenmyanmar.com/news/damages-occur-in-three-places-on-myitkyina-nammati-tanai-ledo-road, last accessed on 11 November 2022
21. C. Dunn, et al., "Chinese Investments in Myanmar: A Scoping Study," *Global Environment Institute,* 2016, available at http://www.geichina.org/_upload/file/book/Myanmar_Scoping_Study.pdf, last accessed on 11 November 2022
22. Lintner, 1992:252.
23. Singh, 1997:120.

24. Helen le Bail and Abel Tournier, "From Kunming to Mandalay: The New "Burma Road"-Developments Along the Sino-Myanmar Border since 1988," *Centre Asie Ifri,* (2010): 119.
25. Ibid.; also see K. Y. Myint, "New Journey on Old Roads," *Dang Economic Magazine*, Yangon, (October 1993): 71.
26. Renaud Egreteau, "India and China Vying for Influence in Burma-A New Assessment," *India Review*, Vol.7, No.1 (2008): 43; Garver JohN, *Protracted Contest: Sino-Indian Rivalry in the Twentieth Century* (Seattle: University of Washington Press, 2001), 292.
27. Dunn, et al. 2016: 37.
28. Udai Bhanu Singh and Shruti Pandalai, "Myanmar: A Need for Infrastructure Integration," In *India's Neighbourhood: Challenges in the Next Two Decades*, edited by Rumel Dahiya and Ashoka Behuria, (New Delhi: Pentagon Security International, 2012), 116.
29. "China, Myanmar sign MoU on feasibility study of Muse-Mandalay railway," *XinhuaNet*, 23 October 2018, available at http://www.xinhuanet.com/english/2018-10/23/c_137550972.htm, last accessed on 11 November 2022
30. Pei-Hua Yu, "Letpadaung Copper Mines," *The People's Map of Global China*, 23 March 2021, available at https://thepeoplesmap.net/project/letpadaung-copper-mine/, last accessed on 11 November 2022
31. "Myanmar proposes to include $2.5-bn Mee Lin Gyaing Project in early projects of China-Myanmar Economic Corridor," *Eleven media group,* 24 April 2022, available at https://elevenmyanmar.com/news/myanmar-proposes-to-include-25-bn-mee-lin-gyaing-project-in-early-projects-of-china-myanmar, last accessed on 11 November 2022
32. See ERIA report, 'The India-Myanmar-Thailand Trilateral Highway and Its Possible Eastward Extension to Lao PDR, Cambodia, and Viet Nam: Challenges and Opportunities, "Integrative Report, *Economic Research Institute for ASEAN and East Asia* (2020), available at https://www.eria.org/uploads/media/Research-Project-Report/2020-02-Trilateral-Highway-Report/Trilateral-Highway-Integrative-Report.pdf, last accessed on 11 November 2022
33. A.B. Chaudhury and Pratnashree Basu, "India-Myanmar Connectivity: Possibilities and Challenges," *Observer Research Foundation*, 2015, available at https://www.orfonline.org/wp-content/uploads/2015/12/IndiaMyanmar.pdf, last accessed on 11 November 2022
34. Ibid.
35. Ibid., 31
36. B. McCartan, "China outward bound through Myanmar," *Asia Times*, 08 January 2011, available at http://brianpmccartan.com/wp-content/uploads/2019/04/20110108-China-outward-bound-through-Myanmar.pdf, last accessed on 11 November 2022
37. For a detailed study see, Sreeradha Datta, "Kaladan Multi-Modal Transit Transport Project: Navigating Myanmar's Ethnic Conundrum," Briefing Paper, *CUTS* (2020) available at https://cuts-citee.org/pdf/briefing-paper-kaladan-multi-modal-transit-transport.pdf, last accessed on 11 November 2022
38. "Thamanti Dam," *Press Information Bureau,* Ministry of Water Resources, 26 April 2012, available at https://pib.gov.in/newsite/PrintRelease.aspx?relid=82677, last accessed on 11 November 2022
39. "India, suggests exiting out of Tamanthi hydel project to escape from China," *The Economic Times*, 26 May 2011, available at https://economictimes.indiatimes.com/news/politics-and-nation/india-suggests-exiting-out-of-tamanthi-hydel-project-to-escape-from-china-pressure/articleshow/8584615.cms?from=mdr, last accessed on 11 November 2022
40. "Selling the Silk Road Spirit: China's Belt and Road Initiative in Myanmar," *Transnational Institute,* Myanmar Policy Briefing, 22 November 2019, available at https://www.tni.org/files/publication-downloads/bri_myanmar_web_18-11-19.pdf, last accessed on 11 November 2022

41. Asian Development Bank, "Myanmar Transport Sector Policy Note: Trunk Roads," 2016, available at https://www.adb.org/sites/default/files/publication/189078/mya-trunk-roads.pdf, last accessed on 11 November 2022.
42. J. Woetzel, et al., "Bridging Global Infrastructure Gaps," *McKinsey Global Institute Report*, 2016, available at https://www.mckinsey.com/capabilities/operations/our-insights/bridging-global-infrastructure-gaps, last accessed on 11 November 2022.

7

Efforts of Poverty Eradication in Myanmar: Past and Present

Prof Chaw Chaw Sein

ABSTRACT

Poverty alleviation has been given priority in Myanmar to get rid of it from the underdeveloped to developing countries in the region. Since Myanmar gained independence in 1948, the Parliamentary democratic government initiated the Pyidawtha (Happy Land) Project to address the gap between the rich and poor. However, the project could not fulfil the needs of the Myanmar people due to political challenges. From 1974-1988, with the establishment of the Burma Socialist Programme Party, state-building and nation-building were implemented with the socialist system. Although agriculture and literacy campaigns were prioritised for farmers, the country suffered an economic failure. Finally, Myanmar was listed as a Least Developed Country (LDC) in 1987 as the administration could not pay back the debt owed to the World Bank. This led to a countrywide demonstration in 1988, widely known as the "88 Uprising". Since then, the military has held power and taken responsibility for the country until 2010.

Interestingly, rural development programmes were prioritised, focusing on 24 zones, and the poverty level dropped from 32 to 26 per cent. However, realising that decades of military administration would make it impossible to engage with the international community, the military ceded power to elected civilian rule by initiating a seven-step road map that included a national general election. In the first civilian rule (2011–2016), reform measures undertaken by President U Thein Sein and his engagement with the international community led Myanmar to escape from LDC. As a result, the poverty line has dropped by 19 per cent. The second civilian rule (2016-2020), led by the National League for Democracy (NLD), introduced the Myanmar Sustainable Development Plan (2018-2030), which included poverty alleviation as one of the plans. However, COVID-19, which reached the shores of Myanmar on 21 March 2020, has had an enormous impact on Myanmar's economy. The pandemic, together with the political transition that took place on 01 February 2021, led

Myanmar's economy to its lowest point. This chapter will investigate the major hindrance in implementing poverty eradication programmes under successive governments.

Introduction

Poverty alleviation is set as the priority sector for every underdeveloped country to narrow the development gap between rich and poor. Peace and development are intertwined, and with the belief that "without development, there can be no peace", rural development and poverty alleviation reach the top agenda of their development plans, and Myanmar is no exception. When Myanmar gained independence from the British in 1948, the Parliamentary democratic government led by Prime Minister U Nu initiated the Pyidawtha, which means "Happy Land" Plan. The plan lasted for seven years. However, it did not reach the target due to political divisions and insurgency problems. In 1962, the Revolutionary Council led by General Ne Win took power to stabilise the country, and in 1974, it introduced a new Constitution and established the Burma Socialist Programme Party (BSPP). The economy was nationalised under the administration of the BSPP. The BSPP's centrally planned socialist economy faced serious failure.

Myanmar's isolation and lack of integration into world trade networks brought Myanmar's economy to the lowest point in the region. This led to a student uprising in 1988 and the military taking power by establishing the State Law and Order Restoration Council (SLORC) and, later, the State Peace and Development Council (SPDC). Although the military has challenges like economic sanctions from the West, the SPDC continued nation-building and state-building by focusing on border area development. Fortunately, Myanmar received international assistance from the United Nations Development Programme under the project of Human Development Initiatives (HDI) for the development of rural communities. Besides UNDP, Japan continued to assist Myanmar with grass-roots engagement for community development in rural areas.

Due to the government's efforts in collaboration with international assistance, national poverty incidence fell from 32 per cent to 26 per cent between 2005 and 2010 (Living Conditions Survey in Myanmar, 2009-2010). Furthermore, Myanmar's political transition started when nationwide general elections were held in 2010 as one of the seven steps of the road map initiated by SPDC in 2003. The election results paved the way for a civilian-led administration with elected President U Thein Sein. Under his reforms, poverty is set as the top agenda item to meet the Millennium Development Goals target by 2015. However, the transitional government could not achieve the long-term plan for poverty alleviation on its own. Therefore, the Action Plan for Rural Development and Poverty Alleviation has been implemented in collaboration with entrepreneurs, NGOs, international organisations, well-wishers, local people, etc. As a result, the national poverty rate fell from 32.1 per cent to 19.4 per cent in ten years (World Bank Release).

When the National League for Democracy (NLD) won a landslide victory in the 2015 general election, the new government continued to focus on poverty alleviation by introducing the Myanmar Sustainable Development Plan (2016–2030). During the administration, international pressure for human rights issues and the impact of COVID-19 hindered the country's economy from taking off. After a successful general election was held in November 2020, the NLD won the majority vote to form a government for a second term. However, the *Tatmadaw* (Myanmar military) took over the reins of power on 01 February 2021, with the explanation of a rigged election. The military takeover of power led to Myanmar's isolation from the international community, including ASEAN. While developing countries can recover from the COVID-19 pandemic, Myanmar faces domestic and external pressures due to the military takeover of power.

Having known that the country needs to rely on its own, the military, in the name of the State Administration Council (SAC), set "agriculture and livestock" as a priority sector for food security. Against this backdrop, the first portion of this chapter explains poverty alleviation during the parliamentary democracy period. The second portion briefly gives an overview of the Burma Socialist Programme Party (BSPP) and its efforts in rural development. The third portion highlights Myanmar's continuous poverty alleviation efforts under the military administration (1988–2010). Lastly, in portion four, the post-pandemic era and Myanmar's poverty alleviation efforts have been addressed to understand the key challenges towards achieving the target. This chapter concludes by highlighting major hindrances in implementing poverty eradication programmes under successive governments.

Poverty Alleviation under Parliamentary Democracy

After a hundred years of British rule, Myanmar regained its independence in January 1948. U Nu, one of the prominent members of the thirty comrades who fought for independence, became Prime Minister during the parliamentary democracy period (1948–1958). His tenure as Prime Minister was full of nation-building and state-building hardships. This is not surprising given those newly independent countries faced difficulties due to their colonial legacy. At the domestic level, the country went through a communist and socialist divide among the elite and multi-ethnic armed rebellions. The legacy of the British's divide-and-rule policy laid the seeds for mistrust among the major and minor ethnic nationalities. The U Nu Government struggled with union disintegration while carrying out poverty alleviation. At the international level, the division of the world into two ideologies during the Cold War had a negative impact on Myanmar's politics. The success of communism in China influenced Myanmar as many politicians and the Burma Communist Party went underground. Although faced with these situations, U Nu promised with the motto of "one car, one house for every person and 800 kyats for a month". To accomplish this motto, he started a *Pyidawtha* plan which meant a peaceful, abundant and happy land (Mg Mg, *Family of Nations*, 139) that aimed to increase the economy and improve the standard of living within eight years.

In order to meet this motto, *Pyidawtha* committees were established in villages and districts. These committees were to set up their plans for more productivity and government-provided materials and funds. Some villages took part in the plan based on self-help without taking funds from the Government. In other words, the plan was implemented in the spirit of self-help (Mg Mg, *Family of Nations*). However, Dr. Ba Maw, the then President, pointed out that although it was a good plan, it went for the elite rather than the majority (Ba Maw, *Today Burma*). The plan was also supported by US aid in the form of the US Technical Assistance Programme with the agreement between the Union of Myanmar and the USA on 13 September 1950 (Mg Mg, *Family of Nations*). USD 20 million had been provided under this agreement (Ibid). As a recipient of aid from the West then, it was not an easy task as it had to deal with both domestic and international levels. At the domestic level, parliament members were pro-communist and against US aid.

Moreover, the gap between urban and rural was high due to rebellions taking root at the rural sites, and it was difficult to implement rural development plans. At the international level, Myanmar faced Kuomintang troops in Myanmar territory, and the case was brought to the United Nations. At this point, Myanmar had to receive aid to refrain from China's misunderstanding. Under a difficult situation, the *Pyidawtha* plan went on with a special emphasis on the agriculture sector. Land nationalisation and land redistribution were carried out in 1953 and 1954 in eight pilot districts. Land nationalisation faced severe criticism from foreign investors. However, distribution continued to give the landless peasants land through village land committees. Loans were provided to the peasants through agricultural banks to abolish landlordism. In 1954, the acreage of land distributed to peasants amounted to 142,737. That represented nearly half the total acreage under cultivation in the eight pilot districts. As the results met the target, they extended it to 29 districts with 635,399 acres. However, the pilot projects were hindered by communist rebels murdering village land committee members (ibid).

Myanmar's efforts to narrow the gap between the frontier and other areas through the Pyidawtha Plan could not realise the motto of U Nu. The infant parliamentary democracy after independence was muddled with political and ideological divides among the elites and nationalists. All these political factors led to significant hindrances in successfully accomplishing the plan.

The Burma Socialist Programme Party (BSPP) and Rural Development

After regaining independence, many countries in Asia, Latin America, and Africa faced difficulties forming new states. Some countries that practised democratic systems reverted to one-man rule or a one-party dominated system, and Myanmar was no exception. General Ne Win came to power in 1962 and set up the Revolutionary Council. In 1974, a new Constitution was promulgated, and the Burma Socialist Programme Party (BSPP) was established. As Myanmar is an agricultural country, he paid attention to agriculture, and three points are noteworthy under his administration.

Firstly, the farmers' prevention law was promulgated to improve the livelihoods of farmers and the cost of productivity. The law seems to prevent it, but their rice market was fixed and could not be sold beyond the state or division where they lived. Secondly, the peasant councils formed during the Revolutionary Council to become Peasant Asiayon were reformed to guide the farmers in their work. Farmers were provided with crop loans in one instalment. To achieve awareness of poverty and issues of the landless farmers, peasant seminars were held several times in which General Ne Win was present. The third point was the initiating of "Cooperative village projects". The aim of the project was to provide land to the estimated two million landless labourers in the country (Dr. Tylor, Dr. Mg Mg). These projects not seem as successful as expected because the farmers did not have the right to own their lands; the right to choose the crops they wanted to grow; the right to sell their products freely; and the right to access a free market. Finally, the agricultural sector under the government's planned economy resulted in poverty among the farmers and brought about the collapse of the socialist economy.

Even though Myanmar is large in terms of territory, population, and abundant natural resources, it was listed as the Least Developed Country in 1987 because the Socialist administration could not pay back the debt owed to the World Bank. Since then, Myanmar has been trying to graduate from LDC to improve the quality of life of the people as one of the priority areas in implementing the national development strategy. The Burmese Way to Socialism led Myanmar to be isolated from the West and limited loans were provided. Compared to the parliamentary democracy era, the socialist regime faced no political divides among the political elites when developing short- and long-term plans under a one-party system. It was indeed the failure of the planned socialist economy that led Myanmar to the list of LDC (Tylor, Dr. Mg Mg).

Rural Development as Poverty Alleviation under Military Rule (1988-2010)

As a result of the failure of socialism that led Myanmar into LDC, a student uprising broke out in 1988, widely known as the "88 Uprising". In 1988, the military detained power again by forming the State Law and Restoration Council (SLORC), later renamed the State Peace and Development Council (SPDC) in 1997. Senior-General Than Shwe chaired the Council. After more than two decades of socialist economic failure, Myanmar was seen as a failed state, and military rule led Myanmar to be isolated by the West. Taking the model of the Chinese Way to Socialism with economic reforms under Deng Xiao Peng, Myanmar tried to open its market by promulgating the Foreign Investment Law in 1989. At first, Myanmar received foreign investments from China and the West, like garments, food, and other goods. However, when political dissidents were detained, the West, including the USA and European countries, imposed tough sanctions on Myanmar. While foreign investments withdrew from Myanmar, international assistance was also suspended.

All these political incidents made Myanmar fall behind the countries in the region. With its self-help strategy at the local level, the SLORC laid down three development programmes, namely, the Border Area Development Plan, Twenty-four Special Development Zones, and an Integrated Development Plan in the 1990s. In order to effectively carry out these plans, the central committee on national races and remote area development was formed in May 1989, and the Ministry of Progress of Border Areas and National Races and Development Affairs (PBNARDA) was established in September 1992. In addition, a long-term plan was formulated to uplift the socio-economic conditions of people living in poverty. The plan included better transportation, water and sanitation, education, healthcare, and income generation in rural and remote areas.

In June 1993, the United Nations Development Programme (UNDP) started the Human Development Initiatives Programme (HDI) for grassroots development, coinciding with the SLORC's special attention to border area development. Phase by phase, UNDP-HDI was implemented from 1994 to 2010. In 2000, the UN initiated the UN Millennium Development Goals (MDGs), in which eradicating extreme poverty and hunger was set as Goal 1. As a member of the UN, Myanmar launched a poverty alleviation strategy under the term of socio-economic development plans, especially for remote areas for eradicating poverty and hunger, which are set in the UN MDGs. To meet the target of Goal 1, Myanmar believed that the government could not work alone and that international cooperation was essential.

In this regard, the government cooperated not only with the UNDP programmes but also with local non-governmental organisations (NGOs) and INGOs. The most active local NGOs are the Myanmar Women's Affairs Federation and Myanmar Maternal and Child Welfare Association, which focus on the needs of women and children in rural areas. Among the INGOs, the government actively cooperated with Save the Children, World Vision, and CARE. According to the Integrated Household Living Conditions Assessment (IHLCA) conducted in 2004-2005, the poverty rate was 32 per cent and dropped to 25.6 per cent from 2009-2010. This data shows that although Myanmar was under sanctions, the military administration opened the door for international assistance to meet MDG Goal 1.

Myanmar's Political Transition and its Poverty Alleviation Efforts

When Myanmar's political transition took place in 2011 with a new civilian-led Government, President U Thein Sein announced a policy statement emphasising the need to narrow the gap between the rich and poor. In his inauguration speech in Parliament on 30 March 2011, he highlighted the importance of a proper market economy to reduce the economic gap between the rich and the poor (The New Light of Myanmar). Consequently, the first national-level workshop on rural development and poverty alleviation was held in May 2013 with the participation of political elites, academia, responsible persons of social organisations, presidents of economic advisors, and the media. The workshop aimed to find solutions for poverty alleviation in agricultural development, with a special focus on high-yield crops, integrated farming, microfinance, and rural economic development and industrial development.

During the workshop, five strategies were set: the Rural Green Village project, the People-centred Project, the Plan for Village Development Project, Capacity Building Project, and Family Income Project (*The Mirror News*). Even though the projects seemed to be good in principle, their implementation in the villages faced weaknesses in practice. As the government could not alone accomplish the long-term plan on poverty eradication to meet the MDG target by 2015, the Action Plan for Rural Development and Poverty Alleviation was implemented in collaboration with entrepreneurs, NGOs, international organisations, well-wishers, local people, etc. As a result, the national poverty rate dropped from 32.1 per cent to 19.4 per cent in ten years. The achievement was linked to a remarkable series of reforms which led to the debt cancellation of the Paris Club members. According to a Paris Club source, the debt owed to Paris Club creditors was estimated to be USD 10.33 billion as on 01 January 2013 (Paris Club, *Cancellation of Debt*.)

The success of reforms paved the way for the next elected NLD government (2016-2020) to continue with the momentum in the efforts for poverty eradication. It released its economic policy by highlighting national reconciliation and job creation as basic considerations for the policy, which guarantees nationwide equitable development. It outlined a 12-point policy ranging from the privatisation of some state-owned enterprises to the development of infrastructure. It also included national reconciliation and job creation as basic considerations for the policy, guaranteeing nationwide equitable development, welcoming FDI, privatising some state-owned enterprises, supporting the agricultural sector, etc (The Global New Light of Myanmar).

However, these economic twelve-point policies were too vague. To systematically carry out the economic vision, in August 2018, the government released the Myanmar Sustainable Development Plan (MSDP) (2018-2030). It identifies the targets for Myanmar's development over the next ten years through three main pillars, five goals, and 28 strategies with designated project implementation programmes (MSDP, 2018). As poverty and stability are correlated especially in a transition country like Myanmar, it must effectively carry out poverty eradication in line with MSDP. The year 2020 was a challenging year for Myanmar. Countries in the world have been grappling with the outbreak of COVID-19, and Myanmar has joined the ranks. The outbreak of COVID-19 brought a huge impact on its political, security, and socio-economic sectors.

On the political front, a key national peace conference was postponed. The Union Election Commission's preparations for general elections were criticised by many political parties due to limited access to travel in the campaign areas. In the economic sector, to implement the economic recovery plan as a response to the impact of COVID-19, the Ministry of Planning and Finance on 27 April 2020 issued a comprehensive economic stimulus plan, namely, "Overcoming as One: COVID-19 Economic Relief Plan CERP", having 7 Goals, 10 Strategies, 36 Action Plans, and 76 Actions, covering a broad range of extraordinary fiscal and monetary measures, combined with a set of human-focussed and common-sense policy (The Global New Light of Myanmar). This COVID-19 Economic Relief Plan, known as CERP, is designed to meet the current exigencies Myanmar faces in ways that reaffirm the long-term strategic direction. It consists of policies and proposals to support the agricultural sector, loans for farmers, and cash for work for farmers in rural areas, which seem to be effective in contributing to poverty reduction also.

However, there is no special focus on agriculture, livestock, and fisheries, which are important for food security. CERP states that 10 per cent of the 2019-2020 government budget (32.3 trillion kyats) (The Global New Light of Myanmar) will be transferred to the COVID-19 Fund. Many economists and political activists have weighed in on the CERP and how the stimulus fund will be managed to meet the needs at the grassroots. As Myanmar has its MSDP (2018-2020), it is time for Myanmar to consider how MSDP and CERP can be applied in proposing projects and programmes from the Asia Development Bank and the World Bank to receive special projects in the outbreak of the COVID-19 pandemic.

Post-Pandemic Era and Myanmar's Poverty Alleviation Efforts

Together with the impact of COVID-19, Myanmar finally held general elections in November 2020, and the UEC announced the landslide victory of the NLD. However, the military took over power on 01 February 2021, a day before the Parliamentary session was convened to form a Cabinet, giving the reason as a rigged election. The military formed a State Administrative Council (SAC) chaired by Senior General Min Aung Hlaing, the Commander-in-Chief of Defence. A nationwide demonstration took place with several types of strikes, including civil disobedience movements (CDMs), silent strikes, sitting strikes, and night strikes under the name of "Myanmar Spring". Blaming and shaming as social punishment on social media became the anti-coup protestors' main weapon. They targeted military families, people close to the military, non-CDM government employees, and students from non-CDM families. The strikes lasted nearly a month until crowd control was resorted to by the police and finally by the military.

Anti-coup protestors led by some NLD activists formed the Committee on

Representatives of Pyidaungsu Hluttaw. They announced the formation of a National Unity Government (NUG) in April 2021, believing peaceful demonstrations could not overthrow the military institution. Since then, the NUG strategy has changed from peaceful demonstration to armed struggle ("*NUG to GUN*"). Many students, young activists, artists, and journalists went underground and joined some Ethnic Armed Organisations (EAOs) by forming the People's Defence Force (PDF). Many unexpected PDFs were also formed in central Myanmar, Sagaing and Magwe regions, where many acres of arable land are located. Some PDFs took sides with EAOs in the Kayin and Kachin states, while some went on their own. Although they have the same intention of attacking the military, they are divided on issues related to finances and command. Many villages in Chin state, Sagaing and Magwe regions were burned down. The real situation on the ground makes it difficult to evaluate who committed these atrocities, either the military or the PDF. The victims who committed the crimes were the local people and villagers, and many fled to escape this tragedy.

Facing local armed attacks and international pressure, the SAC formed the Provisional Government on 01 August 2021 under notification no. 9/2021 to effectively perform the state's power in order to save face on the international front. The five-point road map of the State Administration Council and nine objectives were set for implementation, i.e., three political affairs, three economic affairs, and three social affairs objectives. In economic affairs, the first priority is to enhance production based on agriculture and livestock through modern techniques and strengthen all-round development in other sectors of the economy (The Mirror Newspaper).

Myanmar's efforts to fight poverty have been severely hampered due to the ongoing political crisis in Myanmar. According to the World Bank, poverty is expected to have more than doubled since March 2020, with approximately 40 per cent of the population living below the poverty line by 2022 (The World Bank, Myanmar Economic Monitor). With the fragile economic recovery in the region, together with internal and external pressures, the SAC needs to meet the promises that are stated in the five-point road map and nine objectives. At the 77th anniversary of Armed Forces Day, the senior general said,

> "As our Tatmadaw is the only institution hailed from the ethnic people, it has to safeguard the lives and poverty of the people and to assist in the daily social life security of the people in all directions." (The Global New Light of Myanmar)

With this commitment, the SAC set agriculture as a priority sector and fulfilled all the needs of the agricultural sector. Agriculture has been at the heart of

Myanmar's economic growth and social development, which can contribute to poverty reduction. Seventy per cent of Myanmar's population resides in rural areas. With a population of over 50 million and nearly 30 per cent living below the poverty line, the SAC emphasised the agriculture and livestock sectors by conducting an "Ethnic Food Fair" in April 2022. Knowing that Myanmar has 33 million acres of sown acreage, farmer-oriented needs are provided, such as distributing fertilisers and loans to farmers with small interest rates. In addition, rural development projects such as "Cash for Work" in 126 villages in Myeik district were carried out for the 2022-23 financial year, including water supply, green road villages and solar-home projects.

While countries in the region like China, Korea, and India have been imposing action plans with special focus on constructing digital villages and promoting the integration of digital technologies into rural production and life, Myanmar is still cultivating with the old style of direct seed-rice cultivation, although it can reduce greenhouse gases (China Daily Newspaper, Global Edition). In addition, education is given priority as a sector to tackle poverty. In doing so, the SAC set policies to provide opportunities for those who have successfully completed KG+9 secondary education in order to get access to continuous learning and training to achieve technical and vocational qualifications.

However, as mentioned above, the young living in rural areas where arable lands are located have left their farms and have gone to the Thai border in search of jobs and to take refuge from the fighting between PDFs and the military. Some have joined PDFs to fight against the military. Due to these complications, many arable lands remain uncultivated; this remains a serious concern for Myanmar's food security and ability to carry out poverty alleviation. Without political stability, overcoming poverty alleviation is impossible. To solve these issues, the Chair of the SAC announced the year 2022 as the "Year of Peace" by inviting many Ethnic Armed Organisations (EAOs) who have and have not signed the Nation-wide Cease-fire Agreement (NCA) to the negotiation table (The Global New Light of Myanmar). Accordingly, the meeting with the EAOs individually took place in June 2022. To achieve the five-point road map, which includes a free and fair election in 2023, as well as political stability, the SAC made several announcements, including welcoming the PDFs into the legal fold and opening reception centres to receive CDM staff, students, and youth beginning 12 June 2022. Due to human rights accusations and international pressure, Myanmar struggles to fight against poverty through self-help. At this point, partnership for peace and development is crucial for Myanmar. Facing sanctions from the West, Myanmar received some funding under China's Mekong Lancang Cooperation Special Fund. The approved projects were mainly for poverty alleviation, such as agriculture and rural development.

Conclusion

Myanmar has been fighting for poverty alleviation since it gained independence in 1948 to narrow the development gap between rich and poor with different approaches under successive governments. However, why can Myanmar not get rid of poverty? This chapter concludes with some findings; while the Parliamentary administration introduced the Pyidawtha Plan, it was muddled with political and ideological divides among the elites and nationalists, which led to major hindrances in successfully accomplishing the plan. In the socialist era, although the government did not face political divides among the political elites in formulating short and long-term plans under a one-party system, the failure of the planned socialist economy led Myanmar to the list of LDCs.

In the era of military administration (1988-2010), Myanmar cooperated not only with UNDP programmes but also with local Non-Governmental Organisations (NGOs) and INGOs for rural development by focusing on 24 special zones. Although Myanmar was under tough sanctions imposed by the West, being a member of the UN, the military administration opened the door for international assistance to meet MDG Goal 1. As a result, the poverty rate dropped to 25.6 per cent in 2009-2010 from 32 per cent in 2004-2005. After a political transition in a decade (2010-2020), national poverty incidence fell to 19.4 per cent within ten years due to a series of reforms initiated by President U Thein Sein's administration by involving the international community. The cancellation of debts to Norway, Japan, and Germany of the Paris Club contributed a positive step in Myanmar's efforts to fight poverty.

The success of reforms paved the way for the next elected NLD government (2016-2020) to continue with the momentum in the efforts for poverty eradication. Although economic policies seem to be vague, plans and policies such as MSDP are one of the positive plans for all-round development of the country if they can be systematically implemented. However, COVID-19 has negatively impacted Myanmar's economy, and there have been difficulties in implementing poverty eradication even though the COVID-19 Economic Relief Plan was issued. Major political changes occurred in the post-pandemic era, and the military usurped power and formed the SAC. There have been continuous efforts made for poverty eradication with a major focus on agriculture and rural development. Myanmar's efforts to fight poverty eradication in the post-pandemic era are challenging as it faces local and international pressures. To save Myanmar as a "State" instead of a "Government" in its fight against poverty, it is necessary for the international community, including ASEAN, to understand the real situation on the ground and constructively engage. This is of utmost importance.

REFERENCES

Ba Maw, *Today Burma,* Speech delivered at Yangon City Hall, 21 December 1952.

Club De Paris, "Cancellation of the Debt of the Union of Myanmar," 28 January 2013, available at https://clubdeparis.org/en/communications/press-release/cancellation-of-the-debt-of-the-union-of-myanmar-28-01-2013, last accessed on 22 December 2022.

"Integrated Household Living Conditions Assessment 2004," *International Household Survey Network,* September 2015.

"Integrated Household Living Conditions Survey in Myanmar (2009-2010)," MDG Data Report, Yangon, *UNDP/UNOPS* (June 2011): 5.

Mg Mg, *Burma in the Family of Nations*, Amsterdam: Djambatan Ltd, International Educational Publishing House,1956.

"Myanmar Sustainable Development Plan (2018-2030)," *Ministry of Planning and Finance* (August 2019).

____ "Press Release, Poverty Declined Between 2004-05 and 2015 in Myanmar: New Joint Myanmar," *World Bank Report,* available at https://www.worldbank.org/en/news/press-release/2017/08/30/poverty-declined-between-2004-05-and-2015-in-myanmar, last accessed on 22 December 2022.

World Bank, "Myanmar Economic Monitor: Reforms Reversed," *The World Bank* (21 July 2022).

8

Current State of Healthcare in Myanmar

Win Maw, Toe Aung, Yadanar Soe, and Naing Ye Zaw

ABSTRACT

Myanmar has never been fully controlled by a central authority, with armed insurrections from both communist factions and various ethnic minority groups from the time of independence to the present. The provision of health services in Myanmar reflects the political ideologies and systems the country has experienced since its independence in 1948. Relatively low investment in the health sector by successive regimes has had a substantial impact on Myanmar's health services indicators which are ranked lowest among the regional countries in Southeast Asia. The provision of health services by the state (MoHS) evolved through four distinct political eras—the parliamentary democracy era (1948–1962), Revolutionary Council and Burma Socialist Program Party (1962–1988), State Law and Order Restoration Council (SLORC) and State Peace and Development Council (SPDC), and Quasi-civilian Government (2011–2020).

The country's recent military coup d'état on 01 February 2021, subsequent political turmoil, and civil disobedience movement by health workers significantly weakened the capacity of the MoHS to provide health services. The implementation of the ambitious National Health Plan (2017 to 2022) promulgated by the National League for Democracy-led Government to achieve Universal Health Coverage by 2030 came to a standstill. In addition, the military's targeted crackdowns on healthcare workers forced hundreds of health workers to flee to areas controlled by resistance groups or abroad. The military coup effectively derailed the National League for Democracy Government's plans for vaccination against COVID-19 due to the Civil Disobedience Movement (CDM) of health workers and the military's violent oppression of CDM health workers. Following chaos in healthcare provision and vaccination plans, the third wave of the COVID-19 pandemic with the Delta strain went uncontrolled and claimed tens of thousands of deaths. The military is unable to establish an administration in rural areas of many regions and states, and people largely rely on private healthcare providers, ethnic and community-based health organisations, and networks of CDM health workers for health services. With a dysfunctional bureaucracy, access to essential health services, including childhood immunisations, deteriorated.

Where the MoHS is unable to provide health services, ethnic and community-based health organisations (ECBHOs) fill the void in areas controlled by ethnic revolutionary organisations (EROs) and People Defence Forces, from COVID-19 vaccination to the provision of preventative and curative medical services. The provision of health services by these organisations in parallel with MoHS is not a new phenomenon. The existence of ethnic and community-based health organisations (ECBHOs) dates back to the 1988 people's uprising and earlier periods. Different EROs established their own healthcare systems in their own territories and contested regions with varying capacities. The potential for convergence or integration of these parallel health systems and ultimately for achieving Universal Health Coverage for the people of Myanmar in the medium and long term depends largely on the outcomes of the current political crisis.

Introduction

Myanmar is a Southeast Asian country located at the crossroads between China, South Asia, and Southeast Asia bordering five countries—China, India, Bangladesh, Thailand, and Laos. It has a population of 55 million people as of 2022.[1] Myanmar gained its independence from the British in 1948 and became a member of the Association of Southeast Asian Nations (ASEAN) in 1997. A long history of civil war, protracted armed conflict, and unresolved nation-building in Myanmar cast a long shadow on its health system. The health system's performance is consistently ranked among the lowest in the world. The key health indicators reflect the low health status of the people. The latest census data collected in 2014 showed the Maternal Mortality Rate (MMR) as 282 per 100,000 live births, which is well over the ASEAN's average (140 per 100,000 live births). MMR in Myanmar is significantly higher than in its neighbouring countries, such as Thailand (20) and Cambodia (161). The Infant Mortality Rate (IMR) is 62 per 1,000 live births, according to the census of the same year. Life expectancy at birth is as low as 64.7 years.[2]

This chapter discusses healthcare in Myanmar in different political eras starting from the pre-colonial period, the monarchical system of Government in Burma. In the early periods, Myanmar's healthcare system was characterised by a substantial influence of Buddhism culture and *Sanga* institutions, especially among the rural population and services. Institutionalised healthcare services for a large proportion of people in rural areas were not evident in pre-colonial and colonial periods. Limited rural healthcare services were provided after the country gained independence in 1948. The political influence on healthcare is seen in different political eras, particularly under the various military regimes in which healthcare for the general population was not prioritised as the regimes struggled to consolidate power in a survival mode.

Healthcare in the Pre-colonial and Colonial periods

Myanmar society is highly influenced by traditions in Buddhism, including healthcare. Healthcare in the pre-colonial period was run by providers trained in Buddhist traditions of Ayurveda medicine under *Sanga* institutions with minimal patronage from the state. Ayurveda doctors underwent training at specialised *Sanga* institutions for about five years, and they were honoured with the *Thama* title after the completion of training. Ayurveda practitioners with *Thama* titles could gain more advanced royal recognition of *Thamadaw* status after taking a formal exam.

The imperial state did not assume the obligation to provide health services for the general populace, and the *Thamadaw* only served the royal families and elites. Health services for rural populations were left to local healers with questionable skills and capacities with no formal training. The prevalent order of healthcare with Ayurveda doctors was deinstitutionalised and replaced with Western medical practices by the British colonial administration after the complete annexation of Burma. The existing practitioners of Ayurveda medicine lost their credibility and status and were referred to as "quacks".[3]

Under the colonial administration, healthcare was mainly focused on hospital-based medical care services, vaccination against infectious diseases, and sanitation. The health workforce was mainly staffed with foreign doctors trained in Western medicine, and native doctors constituted only a small fraction of the workforce. The healthcare services were still non-existent in rural areas, and the people remained dependent on informal practitioners and quacks.[4]

A Brief History of Healthcare in Myanmar

Myanmar has never been fully controlled by a central authority, with armed insurrections from both communist factions and various ethnic minority groups from the time of independence to the present. The provision of health services in Myanmar reflects the political ideologies and systems the country has experienced since its independence in 1948. It evolved through four distinct political eras—the parliamentary democracy era (1948–1962), Revolutionary Council and Burma Socialist Programme Party (1962–1988), State Law and Order Restoration Council (SLORC), and State Peace and Development Council (SPDC) (1988–2010), Union Solidarity and Development Party (USDP) government (2011–2015) and National League for Democracy government (NLD) (2016–2020).

Parliamentary Democracy Period (1948–1962)

Myanmar gained independence from the British on 04 January 1948. After independence, foreign health professionals were removed from the services. With limited human resources, health services in Myanmar in its immediate years of independence were in dire conditions, with virtually non-existent health services for people in rural areas and urban slums.

In 1954, the Pyidawthar Plan was developed as a long-term economic and social development plan for the country. As part of the Pyidawthar plan, a national health programme was formulated with the aims of "ensuring the full health of the people, reducing mortality including that of expectant mothers and infants, and wiping out endemic and epidemic diseases".[5]

Revolutionary Council and Burma Socialist Programme Party (BSPP) (1962–1988)

The military led by General Ne Win staged a coup in 1962, overthrew the civilian government led by Prime Minister U Nu, and formed the Revolutionary Council. As part of the nationalisation of all private sectors, the provision of health services was also nationalised, while private wards in public hospitals were abolished.

State Law and Order Restoration Council (SLORC) and State Peace and Development Council (SPDC) (1988–2010)

After the 1988 political uprising overthrew the BSPP government and another generation of military generals took power through another coup on 18 September 1988, and the State Law and Order Restoration Council (SLORC) was established. The SLORC reoriented the economy to a market-based one, and reforms in health services were introduced accordingly. A National Health Policy and a series of National Health Plans (NHPs) were formulated.

Community Cost Share schemes were introduced, and the provision of health services by private providers was allowed to address the problems of financing health services. As a result, Out of Pocket Expenditure (OOPE) for healthcare was among the highest in the world. Furthermore, the key health indicators were the lowest among the regional countries and health system performance ranked the second lowest in the world, followed by Sierra Leone (WHO, 2000).[6]

Following Cyclone Nargis in 2008, significant numbers of international humanitarian and development agencies were allowed to enter Myanmar. As part of the humanitarian responses and development interventions, a significant amount of funds and technical assistance went to the revival of the health system.

Healthcare in Transition (2011–2020)

Healthcare under the USDP Government

On 30 March 2011, the military-led SPDC transformed into a quasi-civilian government and power was handed over to a nominally new civilian government led by President Thein Sein of the Union Solidarity and Development Party (USDP). In an attempt to regain legitimacy and to open the country to the international community, Thein Sein oversaw various reform measures in the political, economic and social sectors of the country. These reform measures were welcomed by the international community, and development assistance poured into both direct health service delivery and system-strengthening efforts.

The provision of primary health services and improving health indicators to achieve the targets set in the Millennium Development Goals (MDG) were prioritised in the National Framework for Economic and Social Reform (FESR) formulated by Thein Sein-led government. The policy ground for health reforms, particularly focusing on reducing health burdens of diseases such as HIV/AIDS, Malaria and TB, was established under the umbrella of MDG. Likewise, poor performance in key healthcare indicators related to maternal and child health services was recognised by the government of Myanmar, and the service provision was then tailored to specific population groups such as mothers and children, adolescents and young people.

The Government also increased health expenditure from 1.03 per cent of general government expenditure in 2011 to 3.38 per cent in 2014-2015. To fill the financing gaps and build on the policy foundation provided by the FESR, the Ministry of Health proactively engaged with multinational development agencies such as Global Fund and the three Millennium Development Goals Fund as its strategic partner to support the implementation of the national health plan, to expand the childhood immunisation coverage and to fight against HIV/AIDS, Malaria and Tuberculosis.[7] A substantial portion of the financing for these diseases came from the contribution of international development agencies.

Healthcare under the NLD Government

The NLD changed its political direction to engage with the former Generals' Parliamentary politics and contested in the 2012 bi-elections and 2015 General Elections. The influential party declared its 15-point health commitment to universal health coverage through its 2015 election manifesto.[8] The National Health Network, which is a health branch of the National League for Democracy

(NLD), then provided a policy foundation and strategic guidance for shaping Universal Health Coverage (UHC) by the year 2030 in Myanmar. The document, namely "Programme of Health Reform: A Roadmap towards Universal Health Coverage in Myanmar (2016-2030)", was produced in 2016 and revealed as the NLD implementation plan for its health commitments that were given in the 2015 Election Manifesto.[9]

Universal Health Coverage, according to the World Health Organisation (WHO), is defined as a measure in which all individuals and members of various communities receive healthcare services that they need without suffering from financial hardship. The key elements of UHC are therefore not limited to the types and number of health services covered despite the fact that it ensures access to the full range of essential and quality healthcare services starting from "health promotion to prevention, treatment, rehabilitation, and palliative care across the life course".[10] The UHC emphasises how healthcare services are delivered, budgeted, and managed. Given this framework for UHC, the NLD reoriented the National Health Policy when they took office in 2016 after their landslide victory in the 2015 general election.

The NLD Roadmap towards UHC reiterated the existing challenges of the health system and key public health weaknesses, especially for maternal and child health, malnutrition, and the burdens of communicable diseases. Meanwhile, the health message from NLD centred on the provision of essential healthcare services aligning with the UHC targets set by the World Health Organisation and the World Bank's Monitoring Frameworks. Achievement of the UHC is operationally measured by two targets: first, the people will have access to at least 80 per cent of essential healthcare services by 2030 and second; out-of-pocket payments for healthcare services will be fully protected, at 100 per cent, for everyone by 2030.[11] The widely recognised cubic framework of UHC is suggested by the NLD's roadmap, and this defines key practical aspects for achieving universal health coverage targets. The UHC cube laid the three dimensions, such as population, services, and direct costs, and claimed to expand these three components together. These discussions provided a clear foundation for the NLD-led government to establish the first National Health Plan (2017-2021) that focussed on strengthening the health system and providing essential primary healthcare services.

The National Health Plan (2017–2021)

Building on the NLD's 2015 election manifesto and the roadmap towards UHC, the National Health Plan (NHP) was formulated by the Ministry of Health and

Sports in 2016 and officially launched in March 2017. The document provided a strategic starting point to implement UHC goals through its three-phase implementation frameworks: (a) Basic Essential Primary Health Services (2017-2021); (b) Intermediate Essential Primary Health Services (2021-2026); and (c) Comprehensive Essential Primary Health Services (2026–2031). The NHP was therefore considered the key policy document of the Ministry of Health and Sports.[12]

Key health indicators in Myanmar revealed significant health inequality between different regions, as reported by the 2014 nationwide census. For instance, the Maternal Mortality Ratio (MMR) for Chin State was 357 per 100,000 live births, while it was only 213 in Yangon Region. Given the geographic health disparities between the different regions in Myanmar, the Myanmar National Health Plan was guided by its six principles, including equity and inclusiveness. The two important priorities are geographic prioritisation and service prioritisation are observed as the strategy to provide equitable services to different ethnic regions.

The National Health Plan is unique compared to the previous national-level healthcare strategies due to its political recognition of the presence and participation of civil society institutions and Ethnic Health Organisations (EHO). The Ministry of Health and Sports developed the NHP in 2016, and there were consultation meetings and workshops with different EHOs, civil society organisations and international non-profit organisations. Clearly, the political significance of the NHP was the official recognition of the presence and participation of EHOs to design national health plans and provide healthcare services.[13]

Health Services at the Community Level

The strategic importance of implementation of the NHP was clearly seen at the township level since the Ministry of Health and Sports recognised the pivotal role of local health governance and participation of a diverse range of stakeholders, especially in conflict-affected ethnic regions to provide the basic essential primary health services. With the constant advocacy and efforts done by various civil society groups, the Ministry of Health and Sports designed a township-based health planning called "Inclusive Township Health Plan (ITHP)". The ITHP creates a wider space for decision-making over local healthcare concerns, including the budget for the local health stakeholders under the leadership of the Township Health Department.

Adding to this process, the cooperation between the Ministry of Health and Sports and different EHOs was also found in this period, particularly in providing essential healthcare services such as maternal and child health and immunisation services to the people residing in Ethnic Armed Group (EAO) controlled areas. These community-level interactions on the platform of health service delivery occurred in parallel with the national peace process[14]. However, the formal recognition of EHOs in terms of human resources for health, standardisation of quality of healthcare services and health financing was not finalised during this period (2016–2020). The military coup derailed the entire plan.

Military Coup on 01 February 2021 and Current State of Healthcare in Myanmar

The military coup of 01 February 2021 brought political turmoil and the healthcare workforce initiated a civil disobedience movement days after the coup. This has led to the weakening of the healthcare system. The military regime specifically targeted the healthcare workforce by arresting healthcare workers, issuing warrants, and raiding healthcare facilities to arrest pro-democracy health workers providing care to injured protesters. This has resulted in hundreds of healthcare workers hiding or running away from home to avoid arbitrary arrest and torture. According to humanitarian data exchange,[15] 35 health workers were killed, 360 health workers were arrested, 129 armed entries into medical facilities, and 67 occupations of medical facilities happened between February 2021 and January 2022.

COVID-19 Response

In January 2021, before the coup, Myanmar was among the first Southeast Asian countries to be able to roll out COVID-19 vaccination. Myanmar received 1.5 million doses of COVID-19 vaccines from India on 22 January 2021, and the earlier phases of the vaccination program were given on a priority basis to government officials, parliamentarians, and healthcare workers.[16]

The military coup effectively derailed the plans for vaccination against COVID-19 due to the Civil Disobedience Movement (CDM) of health workers and the military's violent oppression of CDM health workers. The health system under the military regime has been tested with the third wave COVID pandemic starting from the last week of May 2021. With minimal participation of civil society and volunteer groups in COVID-19 response activities after the coup, the daily testing capacity, volunteer workforces in quarantine centres, and medical workforces at hospitals significantly decreased when compared to the pre-coup period.

The Ministry of Health under the military regime reported 2,000 confirmed cases in the first week of July, and the number tripled within two weeks. The number of death cases was reported from 100 daily cases on 13 July 2021 to more than 300 deaths starting from 22 July 2021[17] (Htun et al., *Tropical Medicine and Health* 2022). However, independent estimates on the number of cases and death tolls were significantly higher than was reported by the regime's health department.[18]

The MOHS under the military regime has faced a human resources shortage, lack of trust from the community, and poor management practices. This has led to the collapse of the healthcare system. Citizens were relying on themselves and self-cure since there is no coordinated COVID-19 management structure. Since most of the medical staff who previously worked before the coup ran away to avoid arrest by the military regime, people treat themselves with knowledge and guidance from social media and volunteer organisations. Likewise, the shortage of critical medical supplies, including life-saving oxygen and medicines, worsened the situation and people waited on the street for many hours on a daily basis to get oxygen for their family members amidst the COVID-19 restrictions on gatherings and martial law.[19] Prices of medicines and medical products such as oxygen concentrators reached their peak resulting from a shortage of medicines.

Childhood Immunisation

Myanmar practises mandatory childhood immunisation sponsored by the state under the scheme called Expanded Programme on Immunisation (EPI). It covers various vaccines, including Polio, Diphtheria, and Measles. Immunisation programme over the last two decades (2000–2020) was characterised by a slight fluctuation of coverage but showed an overall increase for many vaccines according to recent data from the World Health Organisation and UNICEF.[20] For example, MCV1 (Measles-Containing-Vaccine first dose) coverage rose from 84 per cent in 2000 to 91 per cent in 2020. Recent updates by Community Partners International about the routine childhood vaccination after the military coup highlighted the red-alert sign for childhood vaccination at the national level in Myanmar. The report, quoting data sources from World Health Organisation, pointed out a reduction by more than half of major vaccination coverage, including tuberculosis, polio, measles, and diphtheria. In the case of Japanese Encephalitis vaccination, the coverage substantially dropped by more than 90 per cent.[21]

HIV/AIDS

The provision of services to HIV/AIDS patients was also disrupted as a result of the dysfunctional healthcare system after the coup. HIV/AIDS treatment services, especially Anti-retroviral therapy (ART), are mainly managed by the state institution, namely, the National AIDS Programme (NAP), which has the oversight responsibility for HIV/AIDS-related services. Under the supervision of NAP, non-governmental organisations and other actors provide HIV/AIDS care services, including ART.

According to *Medecins Sans Frontieres* (MSF), there were 2,929[22] missed appointments at its clinics from February to October 2021, which had a detrimental impact on the continuation of ART treatment and maintaining the health of HIV/AIDS patients. The National AIDS Programme has no longer been able to accommodate critical HIV/AIDS patients transferred from other organisations. Patients from NAP also seek access to their regular medication through other service providers such as MSF and Myanmar Positive Group (MPG).

Nutrition

With the pre-existing effects of COVID-19, loss of job, reduced income, and increased prices of basic food items, food and nutrition security are at risk. Combining the effects of the coup, Myanmar is facing the threat of a nutrition crisis. The main causes were reduction of purchasing power, changes in import rules and regulations, currency depreciation, travel restriction of aid workers, and violence caused along with the coup. According to Livelihoods and Food Security Trust Fund (LIFT),[23] only 40 per cent of people could meet their daily nutritional needs before the coup and it is estimated the nutrition needs gap will become larger because of the large displacement of people, rising food prices, and limited access to nutrition and health services.

As a result of socio-economic and political disruptions subsequent to the military coup, the critical indicators of child nutrition deteriorated. According to the United Nations Children Fund (UNICEF), the stunting rate (being too short for their age) among children under five years of age is almost 30 per cent, while the wasting rate (seriously underweight for their height) is seven per cent among the same age group. Moreover, over half of the expectant mothers are anaemic.[24]

Role of Private Healthcare Service Providers

After the collapse of the healthcare system, the role of private healthcare service providers, non-governmental organisations, ethnic health organisations and health organisations managed by People Defence Forces (PDF) in their controlled areas has become crucial. However, with the arrest of healthcare workers participating in CDM and restrictions from providing services to patients in both charitable and private hospitals, people's access to healthcare services became more limited. Some private hospitals are forced to shut down with the charge of affiliation or hiring medical workers.

Ethnic Health Organisations, Health Organisations in PDF and EAO-controlled Areas

Given the public distrust and dysfunctional healthcare system under the military regime, the scope and scale of health services provided by EHOs, ECBOs, and health organisations in EAO/PDF-controlled areas became more significant and accelerated. For example, networks of medical professionals who participated in the CDM movement fled to PDF or EAO-controlled areas. They continued to provide health services to the communities in their respective territories. PDF and EAO-affiliated health networks were also able to roll out vaccination programmes with vaccines coming from China through some EAOs based in areas that border Yunnan Province of China.[25] However, their capacity to provide more comprehensive health services is also limited due to human resources and financial shortages, and blockage of supply lines by the military regime.

The provision of health services by these organisations in parallel with MoHS is not a new phenomenon. The existence of ethnic and community-based health organisations (ECBHOs) dates back to the 1988 people's uprising and earlier periods. Different EAOs established their own healthcare system in their own territories and contested regions with varying capacities.

Conclusion

Myanmar has never been fully controlled by a central authority since its independence. When it comes to healthcare, the provision of health services is fragmented between state and non-state healthcare actors. Ethnic and other non-state organisations established their own health systems in parallel with the State's health ministry. Myanmar's healthcare system demonstrates poor performance across different political eras resulting from protracted armed conflict, relative lack of political will for health services and subsequent inability to deliver effective services, especially in rural and contested regions.

Political transition after 2011 has seen an era of health system reforms where international and national civil society and private actors can play an effective role in providing healthcare services and supporting the health system response. Ethnic Health Organisations were engaged in health policy formulation and implementation processes, especially under the NLD-led civilian government. These have resulted in noticeable improvements in service reach, coverage, and key performance indicators for health. Having said that, the recent improvements in health and strategic directions have been derailed by the military coup d'état. The health system under the military regime has performed very poorly in responding to the global pandemic and providing other health services. The prospect for the revival of the health system relies entirely on the outcomes of current political stalemates between the military and opposition groups.

ENDNOTES

1. "Myanmar Population," *World Meters*, available at https://www.worldometers.info/world-population/myanmar-population/, last accessed on 28 December 2022
2. National Census Report (2014), *UNFPA,* available at https://myanmar.unfpa.org/en/publications/union-report-volume-2-main-census-report, last accessed on 28 December 2022
3. Emily Rudland, *Political triage: health and the state in Myanmar* (Australian National University, 2003)
4. Than Tun Sein, et al., *"The Republic of the Union of Myanmar Health System Review," World Health Organization. Regional Office for the Western Pacific* (2014), available at https://apps.who.int/iris/rest/bitstreams/1246931/retrieve, last accessed on 28 December 2022
5. Ibid
6. WHO, "The World Health Report 2000," available at https://web.archive.org/web/20130117071348/http://www.who.int/whr/2000/en/whr00_en.pdf, last accessed on 28 December 2022
7. Health in Myanmar, 2014
8. National League for Democracy (NLD), "The 2015 Election Manifesto," *Burma Library,* available at https://www.burmalibrary.org/sites/burmalibrary.org/files/obl/docs21/NLD_2015_Election_Manifesto-en.pdf, last accessed on 29 December 2022
9. National Health Network of the National League for Democracy, "Program of Health Reforms: A Roadmap towards Universal Health Coverage in Myanmar (2016-2030)", March 2016, available at https://themimu.info/sites/themimu.info/files/assessment_file_attachments/programme_of_health_reforms_-_version_1_0_-_2016_03_29.pdf, last accessed on 29 December 2022.
10. World Health Organisation, "Universal Health Coverage," April 2021, available at https://www.who.int/news-room/fact-sheets/detail/universal-health-coverage-(uhc), last accessed on 29 December 2022
11. Boerma, T., Eozenou, P, Evans, D, Evans, T, Kieny, M-P, Wagstaff, A., "Monitoring Progress towards Universal Health Coverage at Country and Global Levels," *PLoS Med,* Vol 11(9) (2014)
12. Ministry of Health and Sports, "National Health Plan (2017-2021)," *Aids Data Hub*, March 2017a, available at https://www.aidsdatahub.org/sites/default/files/resource/myanmar-national-health-plan-2017-2021.pdf, last accessed on 29 December 2022
13. Ministry of Health and Sports, "National Health Plan (2017-2021)," *Aids Data Hub,* March 2017b, available at https://www.aidsdatahub.org/sites/default/files/resource/myanmar-national-health-plan-2017-2021.pdf, last accessed on 29 December 2022

14. Community Partners International, "Keeping Universal Health Coverage in Myanmar on Track," December 2020, available at https://www.cpintl.org/uploads/8/7/0/2/87020218/2020-12_cpi_synthesis_report_keeping_uhc_in_myanmar_on_track_web.pdf, last accessed on 29 December 2022
15. Insecurity Insight, "Violence Against Health Care in Myanmar Data 01 February 2021 - 31 January 2022 v. 14 February 2021, Geneva, Switzerland: Insecurity Insight (2022)
16. Physicians for Human Rights https://phr.org/our-work/resources/one-year-anniversary-of-the-myanmar-coup-detat/, last accessed on 29 December 2022
17. "Impact of containment measures on community mobility, daily confirmed cases, and mortality in the third wave of COVID-19 epidemic in Myanmar", *Tropical Medicine and Health*, available at https://tropmedhealth.biomedcentral.com/track/pdf/10.1186/s41182-022-00413-8.pdf, last accessed on 29 December 2022
18. "Myanmar's Third Wave COVID-19 Deaths Now Exceed Fatalities in First and Second Waves," *The Irrawaddy*, 26 July 2021, available at https://www.irrawaddy.com/news/burma/myanmars-third-wave-covid-19-deaths-now-exceed-fatalities-in-first-and-second-waves.html, last accessed on 29 December 2022
19. "Myanmar Suffering From Severe Shortage of Medical Oxygen as COVID-19 Cases Spike," *The Irrawaddy*, 12 July 2021, available at https://www.irrawaddy.com/news/burma/myanmar-suffering-from-severe-shortage-of-medical-oxygen-as-covid-19-cases-spike.html, last accessed on 29 December 2022
20. World Health Organisation, "Factsheet 2021 Myanmar: Expanded Programme on Immunisation", 2021, available at https://apps.who.int/iris/bitstream/handle/10665/349285/Myanmar2021_EPISheet-eng.pdf?sequence=1&isAllowed=y, last accessed on 29 December 2022
21. Community Partners International, "Myanmar's Immunization Emergency: "If we can't find more vaccines, coverage could drop to zero," July 2022, available at https://www.cpintl.org/field-notes—updates/myanmars-immunization-emergency-if-we-cant-find-more-vaccines-coverage-could-drop-to-zero, last accessed on 29 December 2022
22. "Myanmar: Political turmoil threatens HIV care," *Relief Web*, 02 December 2021, available at https://reliefweb.int/report/myanmar/myanmar-political-turmoil-threatens-hiv-care, last accessed on 29 December 2022
23. "Peri-Urban Yangon Approaches a Food and Nutrition Crisis in the Face of Loss of Livelihoods | United Nations in Myanmar," *Myanmar UN*, 19 April 2021, available at https://myanmar.un.org/en/125427-peri-urban-yangon-approaches-food-and-nutrition-crisis-face-loss-livelihoods#_ftnref1, last accessed on 29 December 2022
24. "Health and Nutrition," *UNICEF Myanmar*, available at https://www.unicef.org/myanmar/health-and-nutrition, last accessed on 29 December 2022
25. "No One Left Behind?: Covid-19 and the Struggle for Peace and Justice in Myanmar," Myanmar Policy Brief, *Transnational Institute*, 25 November 2021, available at https://www.tni.org/files/publication-downloads/bpb25_web.pdf, last accessed on 29 December 2022

9

Revisiting Gender Roles: A Rare Story of Equality and Freedom in Myanmar

Radhika Daga

ABSTRACT

This chapter explores the traditional gender roles in Myanmar while simultaneously attempting to bring out what lies beyond these essentialised roles and identities. After all, it has to be recognised that Burmese women have gained 'ambivalent' popularity by participating in every phase of uprisings, revolutions, or transitions in Myanmar. Within the realm of "The Burmese Way", the multiple identities assumed by women across ethnicities merit special attention and recognition. This chapter seeks to capture stories of participation and engagement by the women of Myanmar, sometimes as central actors, at all levels—social, economic, and political—in varied capacities over time.

The Traditional High Status of Women in Burma[1]

A weekly literary magazine, *The Burmese Review*, anonymously published an essay in 1946 in which *she* is described as the greatest asset to the land—a combination of beauty, poise, modesty and capacity—the woman of Burma.[2] The "high" status of Burmese women was long circulated in popular and scholarly discourses by natives and foreigners alike, but often in oversimplified and essentialised forms. For instance, the woman of the family was entrusted with the responsibility and progress of the Burmese *amyo* (Amjio), i.e., her race, ancestors and kin, religion, and culture. *She* would be portrayed as a proud and poised figure, dressed in her national dress who led the family as well as assisted her husband in all matters, private and professional. This description was unchallenged and unparalleled until the next few decades and caught every outsider's fancy on this land.

Sir George Scott, a late nineteenth-century British officer in Burma, recognised as an authority on the country, wrote about the "National Character," in which he attempted to outline a Burmese national identity by comparing and contrasting women in Japan and Burma: "Both are frank, and unaffected, and have a charming artlessness, but the Burmese woman is far ahead of her lord in the matter of business capacity by the way in which she rules the household without outwardly seeming to exercise any authority. The Japanese wife treats her husband as an idol, the Burmese as a comrade." (1906).

Such a conception of 'camaraderie' is inevitably predicated on the traditional norms and practices pertaining to marriage, inheritance, and ownership. In a marriage, it is symbolic of the distribution of roles and resources towards the common goal of living in harmony as a family. Another British officer, R. Grant Brown, highlighted gender equality in Burma in his writings, "Not only do sons and daughters inherit equally from their parents, but a married woman has an absolute right to dispose of as she pleases of property acquired or inherited by her either before or after marriage. She is usually a partner in her husband's business and, as such just as much right to sign for the firm as he; but she may have a business of her own, with the proceeds of which he cannot interfere. Even in matters in which she has no part, she is usually consulted before an important step is taken...." (1911).

Although there was no national family law that was applicable to all Burmese citizens, two laws the Burmese customary law, which is "unwritten", and the Buddhist Women's Special Marriage and Succession Act of 1954, were subsequently passed for both Burmese Buddhists and mixed marriages.[3] Notably, both these laws are founded in accordance with ancient Buddhist religious texts. The customary law underlines the codes for inheritance and property rights in marriage. At the same time, the succession act aims to protect Burmese Buddhist women's equal rights, particularly when they get married to a non-Buddhist. These laws were significant at the time they were passed since they evidenced Burmese cultural resistance to the imposition of non-egalitarian alien gender practices. In fact, prior to the imposition of martial law in 1988, some respected Burmese women scholars remarked that Burmese women have always enjoyed equal status, and there was no need for a women's movement in the country.[4]

Some other accepted and distinguishing practices at the core of the institution of marriage include the absence of the cognate system of Indo-China, the dowry system or patronymic names. There are no family names, and a woman always retains her maiden name even after marriage. As in other parts of Asia, polygamy was earlier an accepted practice in Burmese society, but with one important difference. A man could not marry for a second time without the consent of his first wife, and he must abide by her decision because, otherwise, she can sue for divorce and partition of the property.[5]

The right of inheritance is ensured for Burmese women through the traditional and customary laws, applicable still, which recognise them equally with men. All throughout history, they have enjoyed full inheritance rights and financial independence. These rights were further ensured by the fact that under Burmese Buddhist Law, neither a man nor a woman can write a will, and all property must be handed on according to the laws of succession. This means that during a marriage, a husband and wife are joint owners of all property acquired during their marriage.[6] There are five kinds of property in Burmese customary law with the only exception of 'private property', which is solely owned by either the husband or the wife. When parents die, the children divide the property among themselves, and then, too, sons and daughters inherit equal shares.

Existing historical evidences have recorded some cases where the inheritance of certain oil wells belonged exclusively to women; in another case, the inheritance to the headmanship of a village was through the female line. In a series of Burmese folk tales concerning wise and remarkable decisions in law, which have been collected by Dr. Htin Aung, the presiding judge in the stories was a woman called "Princess Learned-in-the-Law".[7]

Despite exercising considerable authority over family matters and occupying a privileged and independent position in society, the women accepted the inherent superiority of the men. The head of the family, "Ein Oo Nat" (Lord of the forefront of the house), was always the father. Women offered this status to their men because they felt secure in their rights and status. While the time-honoured economic and legal rights of the women instilled this sense of self-assurance in them, some studies suggest that part of the deference stems from the prevalence of Buddhism in the country. According to the Buddhist scriptures, when a new Buddha comes to the world, it will be as a man. By this virtue, men are trusted to be in exclusive possession of *hpon*, "an ineffable spiritual entity," or charisma, which causes men to be intellectually, morally, and spiritually superior to women. Notwithstanding the spiritual superiority of men, the leaders in the country have often celebrated the courage behind these choices made by women. In one of her speeches, Daw Aung San Suu Kyi exalted women's "natural" courage and willingness to sacrifice for another's greater good (within the community), while inspiring her countrymen to go beyond religious and cultural structures.[8]

The traditional high status of women was maintained and recognised throughout the colonial period. It was perceived to be deeply embedded in the indigenous culture of the people and to be protected from any foreign influence. At the time, traditional Burmese women's rights and roles also played a pivotal instrument in the nationalist agenda. In 1916, The Young Men Buddhist Association (YMBA) passed a resolution against Burmese girls marrying foreigners, which was a common and accepted practice (attributed to economic reasons) at the time of the colonial presence in the country. It was a nationalist agenda to protect the rights and the traditionally high status of Burmese women, which threatened the inter-faith, also dubbed Indo-Burmese, marriages. It was believed that this kind of arrangement led to the economic and legal disempowerment of Burmese women, particularly Buddhist women. Thereby, the façade of modernity was considered a more insidious form of foreign influence on the indigenous culture.

Although the Burmese passed laws to protect and maintain the status quo in the traditional structure under colonial rule, this was bound to change post-independence. The gender structure underwent phases of restructuring where the position of women, which was first defined by a well-structured traditional make-up, later began to be guided by a constant state of anarchy. This was rooted in the failure of the independent Burmese state to accommodate the interests and needs of a multi-ethnic society residing in a free Myanmar (then Burma). In fact, since the 1960s, the Burmese military used the same alibi of protecting the nation from corrupting foreign influences to further refashion the Burmese culture through strict control, authority and censorship later on. The "modern" Burmese masculinity, shaped through militarisation and subtle transnational exchanges, reflected a change towards sexist and xenophobic ideologies.[9]

Conceptual Framework

The above discussion makes it amply clear that a relatively high level of gender equality persisted in Burmese society, further reiterated by observers when perceived through a historical discourse. However, this relative balance was destabilised as the recently independent country underwent socio-economic changes further propelled by the state of political and civil (dis-)order. Imperatives of regional politics and existential necessities of a community by the country and deciding an equal and secure socio-economic position, gender relations in Myanmar only evolved through subsequent transitions in Myanmar.

I argue that the recurring political upheavals in independent Myanmar did not only lead to an evolution in gender relations but also contributed significantly to a more balanced and levelled relationship between men and women, especially in terms of (self) expression and participation. Society has faced continuous militarisation and experienced the longest civil war in the post-colonial world order. The consequences of the conflict and resulting political and economic turmoil, as in most cases around the world, have had the most detrimental effects on women and children. In Myanmar's case, this has manifested in reported and repeated abuses against women in the form of forced porterage, human shields, forced relocation or seizure of land and property, and extortion; women in conflict-ridden areas live and have lived in constant fear of life, arrest or persecution for political opinion or desire, ethnicity and sometimes, religion.

However, the challenges of a conflict-ridden environment have only consolidated the traditionally-anchored identity of a woman into a stabilising force moving within all sectors of life. The adaptive and aspirational inclinations have made them equal with their male counterparts in perception and sometimes even in representation. The incongruities have transformed the study of gender relations from a subject of predictability into a research topic.

Anchored in Disorder

The UN World Conference on Human Rights held in Vienna in June 1993 stated, "The human rights of women and of the girl-child are an inalienable, integral and indivisible part of universal human rights," thus, declaring that women's rights were human rights. In the case of Burma, the pursuit of women's rights, in general, is inextricably intertwined with what mainly started as the struggle for liberation for the whole population at the time of the State Law and Order Restoration Council (SLORC) in 1988. It led to mass displacement of the population, with more than eighty per cent of refugees being women and children. Refugee women, particularly those left on their own, were much more vulnerable to exploitation and deprivation of rights at every stage of flight as compared to refugee men.[10]

In many cases, women are deliberately harmed, mentally or physically, to discourage any kind of participation in anti-government movements. On 17 March 1988, Ma Ohnmar Thwe, a female student majoring in Burmese, was beaten unconscious before her arrest when the security forces entered the main campus of Rangoon University. Ma Ohnmar Thwe recalls the incident: "When I came to gain, I found myself in a room without a window. I had no idea where I was.

There were six policemen and an officer there. But they didn't ask me any questions. I was taken away to a place near a water tank. There, I was raped, first by the officer and then by the policemen. I lost consciousness again, and when I woke up, a doctor was examining me. I know that this happened to other girls also. Some of them committed suicide."[11]

Another case in point is porter's accounts from Karen State in 1991. Many female porters in the conflict-ridden Karen (now Kayin) State were conscripted by the military under the State Law and Order Restoration Council (SLORC) at the time of operation Nagha Min. They were given only boiled rice and watery bean soup to eat while there was no protection in the extreme weather conditions. Many reportedly suffered from malaria, diarrhoea and other diseases and were forced to carry heavy loads without medical treatment, according to the porters' accounts. Some escaped while others suffered. Some official laws laid down by the military for the use of civilian labour dictated otherwise. However, having a law in Myanmar does not guarantee any adherence to it.[12]

In some parts of the country, women were increasingly encouraged and sometimes necessitated to participate in the flesh trade and prostitution as a society sunk into unemployment, economic hardships and the need to survive. Families began to be lured by unscrupulous recruiters to Thailand with promises of good jobs and cash in advance, often paid to the parents, while their daughters were sold off in brothels and forced to work as prostitutes in Thailand. According to a report in 1992, there were at least 40,000 women and child prostitutes from Burma in Thailand. Meanwhile, the lack of sex education and medical facilities put them at a greater risk of contracting HIV Aids. These HIV-positive women faced other kinds of abuse when they returned to Burma. Persistent reports came regarding the SLORC executing persons with AIDS who were forcibly repatriated by Thailand to Burma. According to *The Bangkok Post* newspaper, some Burmese girls were found to have AIDS, when they were sent back to their country and were allegedly reported to have been given cyanide injections and executed.[13]

In the northern and eastern areas bordering China, reports suggested that young girls and women were duped into going to China only to be sold into a forced marriage to the growing number of Chinese men who, because there were not enough girl babies born in China, could not find wives in any other way. The limitation of resources prompted these women to assume the role of maternal self-abnegators. An estimated 7,500 women from the war-torn Kachin and northern Shan states were sold to men across borders between 2013 and 2017, a study by the John Hopkins Bloomberg School of Public Health reported.

HIV was further spread through intravenous drug use, which spiked as drug production became the pivotal unreported source of the country's political economy under the military government. Myanmar is part of the Golden Triangle drug nexus, which has recently surpassed Afghanistan (Golden Crescent region) to become the world's largest producer of synthetic drugs. The drug trade is prominent in ethnic armed groups areas that use the drug economy to purchase arms and fight the military,-especially in Northeast Burma. In the northern hills of Myanmar, they say opium is the only currency. Working in cooperation with and under the regulation of *Tatmadaw* units, the former insurgent groups are not only encouraged to increase their raw opium production but also to diversify into the manufacture of amphetamines and methamphetamines for the Thailand market.

Anecdotal data from the Palung ethnicity areas in the northern Shan areas indicated the increase in opium cultivation, which was accompanied by a decline in the local tea industry. The collapse of markets for tea and other crops drove more and more farmers to turn to opium growing or to work as labourers in opium fields, where wages were frequently paid in opium. This encouraged a growing culture of drug-taking; sometimes, the workers felt tempted to take drugs to escape their hardship. There's a common expression used by men in this region—If you don't drink alcohol, you won't go to heaven; if you don't take opium, you're not a human being. While the women suffer the burden of the men turning into addicts who stop working, put all their money into drugs and get into debt bondage. One of the local Paluang women remarked, "We used to have a poppy farm, but there were no advantages in growing opium because we didn't get any richer, and my husband became addicted to opium. He started to use drugs once we grew poppy."—this defines the state of the population. However, despite such circumstances, the women were unwilling to leave their husbands due to the systemic challenges in this area. Palaung customary law dictates divorce, if allowed, means fathers retain custody of children.[14]

Elsewhere, cases of rape and murder of women, even with no direct participation in conflicts, have increased over time. Others endured the loneliness and vulnerability of separation and bereavement. Conflict-related gender violence was majorly observed under three categories: personal security, economic security, and political and legal security. The economic hardships and deprivation compelled women to support a family alone while surrounded by violence. These women lost their homes, families and possessions and struggled for their daily survival in strange places like refugee camps. For them, the only urgent possibility was acting and working for a better political, economic, and social life.[15] This meant that women became the heads of the household and were thrust into new roles both within and outside the private domain.

Degrees of Influence and Power

It is worth noting that since its inception, the women in the country have played an active role in political movements and decision-making. The position of power and influence has never been unknown or squandered by these leaders. Some have played a central role in their times and are repeatedly mentioned as role models for the younger generation who aspire to be a part of the change. In pre-historical times, Queen Shin Saw Bu from the Pegu kingdom (15 C) succeeded to the throne, and Queen Supayalat, the queen of the last Burmese king of the Konbaung dynasty (19 C), was known to have exercised great power over her husband and hence over state matters.[16] During the period of transition from colonial occupation, some periodicals focusing on women's issues stressed the exalted role of these queens to inspire further participation.

Some relevant Burmese women's organisations based on patriotism, such as the Wunthanu Konmari Association, Burmese Women Union, the Burmese Women National Council, the Burmese Women Association and Darna Thukha were established as early as 1919 under British colonial rule. They later became involved in the struggle for independence. Under the banner of the General Council of Buddhist Association (GCBA), these organisations joined hands and worked with the other male-dominated political organisations in the country. They played an active role until the first military government[17] under Ne Win banned all organisations and associations, including the women's organisations which led to a hiatus in the activities of most of them.

Back in 1920, the time when the Rangoon University Act was passed, many female university students actively participated in the strike. The strike was spearheaded by Daw Mya Sein, a scholar, author, teacher, wife and mother. The daughter of a distinguished jurist and scholar, she was chosen to represent Burmese women at a special Burma Round Table Conference in London in 1931, and later, on the eve of the Second World War, to lead a delegation to China.[18] The role of women's organisations would later decline, but no one could deny the role these women's organisations played during the anti-colonialism and pro-independence periods. Despite the fact that the women's organisations in that era were short-lived, by the end of it, the social and political struggle of Burmese women was in progress, and those organisations raised political awareness among Burmese women.

Post-independence, during the period of the U Nu government, there was only one woman Minister. She was Mrs. Ba Maung Chein, who worked as Minister for the Karen State from 1952 to 1953. She was the first and only woman who had taken a ministerial position in Burmese history. After a long spell, in 1974, nine women were elected in the first Pyithu Hullaw (national assembly) under the new constitution, and in the next four years, 13 women representatives were included in the second assembly. Finally, in 1988, when Burmese society virtually exploded against the military, Daw Aung San Suu Kyi, daughter of the late Burmese national hero, General Aung San, put Myanmar on the world map. She assumed the most prominent role during the struggle for democracy. At that time, she was joined by many women from all walks of life and all classes, such as merchants, labourers and even Buddhist nuns, who came out on the streets and called for the restoration of people's power. Her first public appearance was at a public gathering at Shwe Dagon Pagoda on 26 August 1988. About 500,000 people attended the gathering and expressed their support for her. The demonstration came to an end when the military staged a coup and suppressed the peaceful demonstrators with violence. Thousands of demonstrators, including women and school girls, were killed during the uprising.[19] In 1991, Aung San Suu Kyi was awarded the Nobel Peace Prize for her non-violent struggle for democracy and human rights. At the time of the announcement, she was under house arrest.

Social Status Defined by Religion

In this country, the social status of women can be gauged by how a woman is respected and protected within Burmese society, particularly under the Buddhist epistemologies. Buddhism remains a common space on which the social mores, ethical system, and spiritual values are based. As noted previously, the Dhammathats, the ancient Buddhist texts, is a major source of customary law which dictates communities in Burma today as it did in the pre-colonial era. These codes remain significant for issues related to marriage, inheritance, and property rights. The Buddhist Women's Special Marriage and Succession Act of 1940 protected Burmese Buddhist women's equal rights when they married non-Buddhist men.

However, it is sometimes debated that the Burmese (Theravadan) Buddhist institutions entail an apparent sexism which categorises Buddhist nuns (called Thilashin) as less enlightened than men and hence ineligible to enter the highest ranks of the sacred Buddhist order called the Sangha. Most Burmese think the pink-robed nuns' major role is to serve the community of maroon-clad Buddhist monks. Scholars argue that, at a deeper level, this is based on the Buddhist ideology that suggests that woman has to endure all of the *aweinikaì dokkhaì ngaÌ-baì* (five aspects of female suffering). These are (1) menstruation, (2) pregnancy, (3) childbirth, (4) separation from her parents, and (5) having to attend to her husband.

Secondly, in Theravada Buddhism, the renunciation of home life is considered essential in the path of spiritual development or to reach the final goal of Nibbana. Gradually, eight special rules (*garu-dhamma*) were laid down for nuns who wanted to be accepted into monastic life. This structure was used as a means to allow the exploration of feminist possibilities of Buddhist life, signalled as "a culturally approved alternative lifestyle" in the *gyaung*, a choice often taken by women in South and Southeast Asia to find an escape from the monotony of a materialistic life.[20] Separately, all religious institutions in the country admit young children, both boys and girls, for a rudimentary level of education. Textbooks on social rules and how to respect women are also published and circulated through these institutions.

Fighters, Activists and Creators

The traditional order of gender equality was not disturbed until years passed by in the absence of modern industrialised organisations and the imposition of greater censorship in various aspects of life.[21] Here what must be highlighted is how institutionalised representation can shape gender dynamics within the broader social and cultural paradigms. In fact, some anthropologists suggest that the existing form of patriarchal repression has its roots in the period before independence, as even reflected by female authors of those times.

"*Not of Hate*" by author-cum-activist Ma Ma Lay, originally published in 1955, looked into the future of male domination and voice through a fictional love story between two native Burmese. The man was an Anglophilic, who was increasingly influenced by masculine discourses dictated by the Englishmen and looked down on his wife's preferences which were still rooted in the original Burmese culture. Ma Ma Lay and Wendy Law-Yone are two critically acclaimed authors credited with influential work in journalism and academia. Burmese women's writings at various historical moments in the twentieth-century map the rhetorical tactics which flexibly negotiate between nation, gender, and culture through their synthesis of competing discourses. Another author-cum-activist from Kayin, Zoya Phan, was forced to go into exile at the age of 14. She writes in her literary account '*Undaunted*': "I don't want you to feel sorry for me, I want you to feel angry, and I want you to do something about it.... I told the audience, I don't want your heart; I want you to take action. I say the same to you now. So few people know what is going on in my country, but you do now. Will you do something about it or just pick up another book".

Many other examples abound, calling attention to "problems of uneven visibility and representation" of gender, particularly by the non-Burmese minorities. Having gone overseas, these women straddled modernity and tradition, gained knowledge of local cultures with scholarly study of other forms of resistance, and critiqued the hegemonies of globalisation and corrupt Burmese managerialism.[22] After the nationwide protests of August 1988, writing and art perceived as anti-government social commentary was either banned from publication or, if a work was already printed and bound, the Press Scrutiny Board (PSB) could require publishers to "ink over" controversial passages with silver paint, to cover offensive text with opaque tape, to rip out whole pages or to glue pages together.[23]

Sao Nang Hearn Kham (Mahadevi), a Shan woman and wife of the first Burmese President Sao Shwe Theik (1948-52), was recognised for her political activities. She was elected as a Member of Parliament from Theini (North), Shan State, in 1956 until the caretaker Government took over two years later. She was in England when the military staged a coup and arrested her husband on 2 March 1962. She returned to Burma after her husband died in custody and fled to Thailand in 1963, where she founded the Shan State Army (SSA), which was joined by the Shan State Independence Army and the Shan National United Front. Based in the Shan State, she led the armed struggle movement fighting against the military regime. For her work against the military regime in armed struggle, she has been recognised as the most prominent woman leader from the Shan State in Burmese history.[24]

Women participated in all the major uprisings against the one-party dictatorship system under the BSPP including the South East Asian Games demonstration (1969), U Thant's funeral riots (1974), worker demonstration (1974), uprising commemorating the centenary of Thakin Ko Daw Hmaing (1976) and 8-8-88 uprising and bore the consequences of the breakdowns by the security forces. In the 1988 uprising, millions of women came out on the streets and joined in the demonstrations. Many women were also arrested and incarcerated in the sinister Insein prison,[25] among others across the country. Naykyi Ba Swe and Nayye Ba Swe, both daughters of Burmese former Prime Minister, U Ba Swe, were arrested on 11 June 1975 and sentenced to five years imprisonment with hard labour for their involvement in the 1975 demonstration. They emerged again in the political arena in the 1990 elections as candidates. Other prominent names include Nan Khin Htwe Myint and Ma Hla Myaing who, among other demonstrators, served anywhere between three to nine years in imprisonment and later entered politics.[26]

As the fight for democracy continues in the country after the 2021 putsch, women activists, social workers and voices have multiplied with the support of the male members of society. They are actively standing up against violence and repression faced by all their fellow countrymen. Moreover, this time women are formally training to fight against the armed soldiers under the various People's Defence Forces (PDF) that have emerged across Myanmar. The last words of a 19-year-old woman activist, killed during the demonstrations, were, "I'm afraid, but we will fight for our freedom" and "we won't run." These words are emblematic of the spirit of the entire generation fighting for freedom and democracy right now. The young activist Angel, whose real name was Ma Kyal Sin, was shot dead on 3 March 2021, one of the deadliest days since the coup was declared on 1 February 2021.[27]

'The good things that must never die'

Daw Khin Kyi, mother of three, lost her middle child in an accident just a few years after her husband's assassination. Despite life's tragedies, she devoted her life to propagating qualities and traditions central to Burmese life—politeness, gentleness and the habit of mutual sharing. One of the leading Burmese personalities in her own right, she was also the widow of Aung San, the father of the nation. She has been honoured by her own and three foreign governments. She erected institutions and welfare centres and stressed the *good things common that must never die*. She also established Operation Keep Fit, a successful movement for the physical education and conditioning of women. Through this programme, world-class women champions in sports have been produced in the country. She encouraged the inherent qualities and traditions of Burmese life and insisted that they never change. She always spoke about the togetherness of the people of this land.[28]

This inspires an outsider to acknowledge the collectivist nature of Myanmar's society and culture, which in turn gives shape to its original non-hierarchal structure. Gender relations, particularly, were defined by the separate qualities of men and women instead of categorisation into better or worse, higher or lower. This kind of life philosophy, in contrast with the Western world, is unique to

Asia and more to Myanmar. However, with changing life scenarios, women have developed the ability to straddle between masculinity (authority) and femininity (appeal) and play a more cohesive role in the welfare of society.

Moreover, society, in its most vulnerable state today, is accepting these multiple hats donned by women to fight the necessary evils and even contribute to the growth of the community. Women have significantly upscaled their participation in various degrees of agency, in both political and economic activities, to be able to augment their strength and rid themselves of poverty and fear. The only caveat in this natural order is the traditional Burmese concepts pertaining to power which are seen through personal attributes rather than attributes of systems. This has been a constant since independence. Although this demands deep structural changes, it will be crucial for the next phase of evolution, which the country together is aspiring for.

ENDNOTES

1. Chie Ikeya, "The 'Traditional' High Status of Women in Burma: A Historical Reconsideration," *Journal of Burma Studies*, NUS Press Pte Ltd, Volume 10, (2005/2006): 51-81
2. Helen G. Trager, *We the Burmese* (New York: Frederick A. Praeger, 1969), 21-25.
3. Aye Kyaw, "Status Of Women In Family Law In Burma And Indonesia," *Crossroads*: An Interdisciplinary Journal of Southeast Asian Studies, Northern Illinois University Centre for Southeast Asian Studies, Vol. 4, No. 1, Special Burma Studies Issue (Fall 1988): 100-120
4. H. J. Muller, "Women in Urban Burma," *Women's Studies International Forum*, 17(6), (1994): 609–620.
5. Daw Mya Sein, "The Women of Burma: A tradition of hard work and independence," *The Atlantic*, 1958, available at https://www.theatlantic.com/magazine/archive/1958/02/the-women-of-burma/306822/, last accessed on 25 November 2022
6. Ibid.
7. Ibid.
8. Tamara C Ho., *Romancing Human Rights: Gender, Intimacy, and Power Between Burma and the West* (University of Hawai'i Press, 2005), 128-129.
9. Tamara C Ho., *Romancing Human Rights: Gender, Intimacy, and Power Between Burma and the West* (University of Hawai'i Press, 2005), 69
10. "Burma and the Role of Burmese Women," *Burma Library*, 1995, available at https://www.burmalibrary. org/reg.burma/archives/199510/msg00070.html, last accessed on 22 December 2022.
11. Ibid.
12. Ibid.
13. Ibid.
14. "Poisoned Flowers: The Impacts of Spiralling Drug Addiction on Palaung Women in Burma," A report by *The Palaung Women's Organisation*, 2006.
15. This is not to negate that the armed conflict took its toll of men who joined combatant forces, and who were arrested and tortured, disappeared or were killed in action.
16. Josef Silverstein, *Aung San Suu Kyi: Is She Burma's Woman of Destiny in Freedom from Fear and Other Writings*, (ed.) Michael Aris (New York: Viking Penguin, 1991).

17. The reign of Burma Socialist Programme Party (BSPP) from 1964-1988.
18. "Burma and the Role of Burmese Women," *Burma Library,* 1995, Available at: https://www.burmalibrary.org/reg.burma/archives/199510/msg00070.html, last accessed on 22 December 2022.
19. Ibid.
20. Ingrid Jordt, Bhikkhuni Thilashin, and Mae-Chii, "Women who renounce the world in Burma, Thailand and the Classical Pali Buddhist Texts", *Crossroads*: An Interdisciplinary Journal of Southeast Asian Studies, Vol. 4, No. 1, Special Burma Studies Issue (Fall 1988): 31-39
21. Muller, "Women in Urban Burma," Women's Studies International Forum, 17(6) (1994): 609–620.
22. Tamara C Ho., *Romancing Human Rights: Gender, Intimacy, and Power Between Burma and the West (*University of Hawai'i Press, 2005): 159-162.
23. Anna Allot, *Inked Over, Ripped Out: Burmese Storytellers and the Censors* (New York: PEN American Centre, 1993): 16.
24. "Burma and the Role of Burmese Women," *Burma Library,* 1995, Available at: https://www.burmalibrary.org/reg.burma/archives/199510/msg00070.html, last accessed on 22 December 2022.
25. A penitentiary built by the former British colonial power in the 19th century.
26. Ibid.
27. Sandi Sidhu, Helen Regan, Ivan Watson and Salai TZ., She was shot dead, her body dug up and her grave filled with cement. But her fight is not over, CNN (13 March 2021), available at https://edition.cnn.com/2021/03/12/asia/myanmar-protester-angel-democracy-martyr-intl-hnk/index.html, last accessed on 22 December 2022.
28. Helen G Trager, We the Burmese (New York: Frederick A. Praeger, 1969), 162-63.

SECTION THREE

Security Issues

10

Buddhism, Constitutionalism, and the Status of Ethnic Minorities in Myanmar

Dr Nazia Khan

ABSTRACT

The Constitution defines a nation, and Myanmar has struggled both with constitutional making and democratisation. Since independence, Buddhism, which is practised by the majority, has held a special position within the Constitution. It has been established by the three constitutions adopted since independence, which were in the years 1947, 1974, and 2008. The 2008 constitution was hailed as a roadmap for Myanmar's democracy, further establishing the military's authority over the country. Being an ethnically diverse nation, Myanmar has also faced insurgency from various ethnic groups. It identifies 135 ethnic groups within the country, which excludes the Rohingyas. Myanmar citizenship is based on indigeneity—defined as residents in the country before 1823. This chapter seeks to trace constitutionalism, Buddhism, and the status of minorities in Myanmar regarding the policies of the state and constitutional provisions. The total population of Myanmar is 56.6 million, out of which 88 per cent comprise Theravada Buddhists, six per cent are Christians, and four per cent are Muslims. The 2014 census excluded Rohingyas, but the NGOs and the government estimated 1.1 million Rohingyas before October 2016. Ethnicity and religion are related to each other in Myanmar; in a way, Theravada Buddhism is the dominant religion among the Bamar majority and the Shan, Rakhine, and Mon ethnic groups. The ethnic groups of Kachin, Chin, and Naga follow Christianity. The ethnic community of Rohingya and Kaman follow Islam. In analysing the status of minorities, this study will reflect on the historical as well as the current dispositions of state and minority relations. It proposes to answer the following questions: What are the constitutional rights of minorities? What rights do minorities enjoy in relation to the Bamar Buddhist majority? How is the state and minorities' relation defined in Myanmar?

Introduction

This chapter explores the relationship between Buddhism, Constitution, and minorities within Myanmar. Myanmar, formerly known as Burma, gained Independence in 1948 and established parliamentary democracy. However, the coup in 1962 brought the country under military rule, which still continues barring a decade (2022-2021) of democratic transition. This failed to strengthen the relationship between the ethnic races and the state, which has led to the creation of Ethnic Armed Organisations (EAOs). This chapter addresses the gap in scholarship in this area. It will add to the knowledge of how minorities interact with or distance themselves from the state in a Buddhist majority state. Myanmar society has been majoritarian in character and has held Buddhism to be the prominent religion of the country.

According to the Constitution of Myanmar, Part 1 Section 3 (2008: 5), "State is where multi-national races collectively reside." The military-state is divided administratively into seven regions and seven states, which are: Kachin, Kayah, Chin, Kayin, Mon, Rakhine, and the Shan States, and Sagaing, Taninthayi, Bago, Magway, Mandalay, Yangon, and Ayeyawady regions. The ethnic composition of Myanmar is Bamar 68 per cent, Shan 9 per cent, Karen 7 per cent, Rakhine 4 per cent, Chinese 3 per cent, Mon 2 per cent, Indian 2 per cent, and others 5 per cent (Maizland, 2021). The majority of Burmese ethnicity is predominantly Buddhist and lives in the central plains and valleys. The other ethnic groups live in the rugged hills and mountains surrounding the central lowlands (Kramer, 2015). The ethnic states comprise 60 per cent of Myanmar's territory, and the majority ethnic population of each state is reflected in its name. The majority Burman population inhabits the seven regions. The region and states are not mono-ethnic and cannot be seen as representing an entire ethnic group. (Kramer, 2015: 357-358).

The National people who constitute Myanmar are the national races. The country recognises 135 ethnic races dominated by Burmese ethnicity. The non-recognition in the national race automatically leads to exclusion from nationality. The ethnic minorities which predominantly reside in the borderlands have, since independence, struggled with marginalisation, lack of socio-economic development, and lack of representation in the political system of the country. The major form of conflict between the state and the ethnic minorities is the form of governance. Myanmar has always practised a centralised form of governance with an emphasis on a united Union. On the other hand, the ethnic minorities residing on the country's periphery have advocated for a federal form of governance.

The military hold over the governance of the country under the democratic transition (2011-2021) was through a constitutional body, the National Defence and Security Council (NDSC), which was an eleven-member committee dominated by them. The 2008 Constitution established the prominent role of the military in the country. There was also a reservation of twenty-five per cent of the legislative seats. The military also held one of the two vice-president positions and permanent control of three key ministries: Defence, Border, and Home Affairs (Curtis, 2021). And so, Crouch (2019) refers to the country as a military-state, which she describes as "the co-existence of civilian and military authorities". Since 1962, the military has held dominance over the governance of the country. So, even though Myanmar was transitioning into a democracy, the hold of the military over the country was strong. Aung San Suu Kyi-led National League for Democracy (NLD) won the elections in 2015 and 2020 and had augmented faith in a multi-party democratic government.

Besides, a military coup carried out by General Min Aung Hlaing in February 2021 has again reversed this path. The coup attempt by the military was opposed by people known as the Spring Revolution. Several ministers, including State Counsellor Aung San Suu Kyi, were arrested on election fraud and corruption charges. The government in exile has formed a National Unity Government (NUG) along with the other elected members of the legislature. It has its own army, known as a People's Defence Force (PDF), to counter the military forces.

Buddhism versus Ethnic Diversity

In a pluralistic society, it is important that the state treats every minority equally and does not institutionalise discrimination. The Constitution of Myanmar, Part 8, Section 361 (2008), "recognises the special position of Buddhism as the faith professed by the great majority of the citizens of the Union". At the same time, it recognises other religions, including Hinduism, Islam, Christianity, and Animism, as existing ones. The Constitutions of 1948 and 1974 maintained the same position on religion. According to Than (1988),

> *In a nation where ethnic diversity also manifests itself in a multitude of religious beliefs, it would seem that Buddhism has been amalgamated with nationalistic sentiments in the quest for a Burmese identity under colonial hegemony and in subsequent struggles for self-determination and political emancipation.* (Sarkisyanz, 1965; Maung Htin Aung, 1967; Bechert, 1972)

The Constitution of Myanmar (2008: in Part 34) states, "Every citizen is equally entitled to freedom of conscience and the right to freely profess and practice religion subject to public order, morality or health and to the other provisions of this Constitution." Symbolically the Constitution has used provisions to ensure equality of ethnicity and religion. However, by maintaining different kinds of citizenship, it has categorised citizens on the basis of their ethnicity.

Myanmar is an ethnocratic state which holds Buddhist identity and Burmese culture in high regard. The Sangha has also played a crucial role in the politics of Myanmar. Under Prime Minister U Nu (1948-1962), the Sangha and Buddhism played a key role. However, the military-junta role tried to restrict the role of the Sangha to religious duties. A State Sangha Maha Nayaka Committee was formed in 1980 to consolidate the control of the state over the *Sangha*. However, this did not stop the monks from participating against the unjust economic policies and pro-democratic movements, so they participated in the 8888 Uprising and were at the forefront of the 2007 Saffron Revolution. So, the national culture of Myanmar is synonymous with the majority culture.

Situating Minorities in the Constitution

The concept of citizenship in Myanmar is based on the idea of indigeneity and ethnicity. The 1982 Citizenship law restricts citizenship by introducing three tiers of acquiring it, "citizen by birth or descent, associate citizen, and naturalised citizen. Only members present in Myanmar prior to 1823 are eligible for citizenship by birth (ICJ, 2020)" The Rohingya community was excluded as an ethnic community in Myanmar due to this law. The Constitution of 2008 only re-established this fact as "a person whose parents are from one of the official national races and were born in Myanmar, or a person who had already been granted citizenship at the time the Constitution came into force" (Crouch, 2019).

An amendment was introduced in 2013 to the Political Parties Registration Law by the chairperson, Aye Maung, of the Rakhine National Development Party (RNDP) in Amyotha Hluttaw.[1] The Bill, which was passed as an amendment in 2014, "proposed to remove the right of naturalised and associate citizens, as well as temporary registration card holders (white cards) to be members of a political party or to vote" (Crouch, 2019). The Rohingya community, who are white card holders, were exempted from taking part in elections or voting in the 2015 elections, further marginalising them.

One of the prominent debates over the inclusion of ethnic races, as was promised in the Panglong Agreement, was a federal structure. The Agreement was signed in 1947 between Aung San and Kachin; Chin and Shan people and drawn on similar lines of providing full autonomy within the Union. However,

Aung San was assassinated before the Constitution of Burma in 1947 came into force in September. The current Constitution emphasises that citizens have the duty to uphold, "non-disintegration of the Union, non-disintegration of national solidarity and perpetuation of sovereignty". This clearly overrules any chances of federalism for the ethnic States.

As the demand for ethnic communities has not been addressed, it has resulted in the rising of ethnically armed organisations. Due to the conflict, there are Internally Displaced Persons (IDPs) in the Kachin, northern Shan states, Kayah, Karen, and Mon states. The Rakhine region has already faced violence and attacks on Rohingyas who are excluded, which not only created IDPs but led to an exodus of one million Rohingyas to neighbouring countries. The Arakan Army has also become active in the Rakhine region post-coup.

The Constitution of Myanmar has provided self-administered areas to six ethnic groups with geographically concentrated populations, which include: Danu, Kokang, Palaung, Pao Wa, and ethnic groups in Shan State and the Naga in the Sagaing region (ICJ, 2020). The parliaments in the state and region have a few seats reserved for the ethnic groups who are not in the self-administered area but fulfil the criteria of minimum population. This is a complex situation as this often leads to the formulation of exaggerated figures by some communities to gain favour.

Barriers to an Inclusive Society

The most crucial factor acting as a barrier to an inclusive society in Myanmar is the military's authoritarian rule. It has controlled the country since 1962 and has constituted the state in a way that has led to divisions within society. Firstly, the democratic transition and liberalisation of 2011 brought out a positive change within the socio-political economy of Myanmar. However, the position of the military junta in relation to the Rohingyas and the conflict which ensued brought the country again into the limelight. The conflict of 2012 and the ethnic cleansing, and the exodus of Rohingyas in 2017 led to a case of genocide against Rohingyas in the International Court of Justice (ICJ). On the other hand, the reconciliation process with EAOs was also underway. The military worked towards disarming them by bringing them on the same platform through the Nationwide Ceasefire Agreement (NCA) and was somewhat successful in it. This process has again been stalled due to an attempted military coup. The military has always maintained its stranglehold and devised laws to strengthen the unitary structure of the state.

Secondly is the failure of the 2008 Constitution to establish an inclusive and federal democratic Union. The 2008 Constitution, unlike the earlier constitution, should have removed the discriminatory citizenry practice. It should also have addressed the federal structure of the state instead of reiterating the unitary structure. It did not amend the error of the past constitution. Since the military carried out a coup in February 2021, the exiled members of the National League for Democracy (NLD) have initiated military and political alliances with ethnic armed groups. They have formed National Unity Government (NUG) which even recognised the atrocities that Rohingyas underwent in these years. They took out their position statement on the most persecuted ethnic community stating they would repeal the 1982 Citizenship Law. They further stated they would initiate the process in order to "grant International Criminal Court jurisdiction over crimes committed within Myanmar against the Rohingyas and other communities".[2] The parallel government of NUG has also "sought to build political and military alliances with ethnic armed groups. They have made a number of important concessions, including appointing an ethnically diverse cabinet, repealing the military-drafted 2008 Constitution, and announcing plans for a new federal charter" (ICG, 2022). So, it has emerged as a credible opposition to the military junta, and failure to address these issues might make things strenuous for the military state.

Thirdly, the 21st Century Panglong Conference (21CPC) did not propose a fresh take on the issue of armed conflict in the country. However, no fruitful conclusion could be arrived at over issues of federalism, security, and economy in the three dialogues that ensued. The ethnic conflict in Myanmar is linked to the armed conflict, so it is crucial to address this issue. According to Kramer (2015), "inequitable distribution of resources between the Burman centre of the country and the resource-rich ethnic periphery is one of the key drivers of ethnic conflict in Myanmar." The government did initiate peace talks with major ethnic armed opposition groups after 2011. The important factor in the peace talks is also the protection of land rights of ethnic communities as well as resolving the continuing civil war. Nearly eight ethnic armed groups signed the Nationwide Ceasefire Agreement (NCA) in 2015, and the conflict was confined to the Shan, Kachin, and Rakhine States. The two important groups, the Karen National Union and the Restoration Council of Shan State refused to be signatories to the peace process, and since 2018 the peace process was stalled. In the wake of the 2021 military coup, it has become more difficult to tackle the ethnic armed groups along with the anti-regime protestors.

Fourthly is the systematic discrimination that few ethnic minorities have undergone due to the 1982 Citizenship law and the various restrictions on movement, marriages, education, jobs, and childbearing. The Rohingya ethnic community has been termed as illegal Bengali migrants by the state and excluded from grant of citizenship. Some groups of Chinese and Indian descent have also been left out of the national races. There are approximately one million Rohingya refugees residing in Bangladesh, and the Myanmar government has made little or no effort towards the repatriation of its own citizens.

Lastly, Myanmar is such a diverse country, and the way it has undergone a political, social, and economic transformation over the years has further complicated the relations between the communities. The 1962 military and the Burmese Road to Socialism under Ne Win isolated Myanmar and made it a least-developed country. The military junta's lack of political command in resolving the country's issues through dialogue has halted the nation's progress.

Conclusion

This chapter attempted to bring into focus the issue of ethnic minorities in Myanmar, which is a crucial factor in the politics of Myanmar. The issue with minorities has existed since Myanmar gained independence. In the absence of democracy and the continuation of military-junta rule, a political solution to the crisis has been delayed. By analysing the relationship between the state and minorities, this chapter wants to address the root cause of the problem. The military-junta rule has failed to bring peace and reconciliation with ethnic groups. However, it is also important to note that military rule came as a response to the armed conflict, which is still ongoing owing to the complex structure and multi-ethnic composition of the population.

The unitary form of governance has clearly overlooked the federal structure and the development of the ethnic periphery of the country, which is embroiled in the insurgency. The democratic transition did open a path towards peace and reconciliation between the military and Ethnic Armed Organisations. The military coup in 2021 has become more challenging for the military as the NUG has also formed its People's Defence Force (PDF) against the *Tatmadaw*. The only way forward for the military to end the civil war is to bring together the three parties—the military, NUG, and the EAOs—and amend the constitution to give the ethnic groups their rights. The NUG has recognised the need to give representation as well as prepare a federal charter for these suppressed groups.

ENDNOTES

1. Amyotha Hluttaw is the upper house of the tricameral legislature of the Republic of the Union of Myanmar. The Basic Principle of the Constitution distributes legislative power between the Pyidaungsu Hluttaw, the Pyithu Hluttaw, and the Amyotha Hluttaw (Constitution of Myanmar, 2008, s 12). Crouch (2019) considers that the three houses function as co-operative centralism in the military-state and each has a distinctive role to play in the legislative functions.
2. "NUG releases statement recognising Rohingyas' right to citizenship, *Myanmar Now*, Available at: https://www.myanmar-now.org/en/news/nug-releases-statement-recognising-rohingyas-right-to-citizenship?page=2#:~:text=In%20its%20place%2C%20it%20said,principles%2C%E2%80%9D%20 the%20 statement%20added, last accessed on 21 December 2022

REFERENCES

Crouch, M. "*Ethnic Rights and Constitutional Change: The Constitutional Recognition of Ethnic Nationalities in Myanmar/Burma.*" (*Forthcoming),* A. Harding (ed.), Constitutional Reform and Legal Change in Myanmar, *UNSW Law Research Paper*, (2015-11)

Devi, K. S. "Myanmar under the military rule 1962-1988," *International Research Journal of Social Sciences*, 3(10) (2014): 46-50

International Crisis Group. "Identity Crisis: Ethnicity and Conflict in Myanmar," *ICJ (*2020) Belgium.

International Crisis Group. "Myanmar Coup Shakes U its Ethnic Conflicts," *ICJ* (2022) Belgium.

Kramer, T. "Ethnic conflict and land rights in Myanmar," *Social Research*, 82 (2) (2015): 355-374.

[Online:web] URL: https://www.britannica.com/place/Myanmar/Government-and-society.

[Online:web] URL: https://www.cia.gov/the-world-factbook/countries/burma/#people-and-society

[Online:web] URL: https://www.cfr.org/backgrounder/myanmar-history-coup-military-rule-ethnic-conflict-rohingya

Trager, F.N. "The failure of U Nu and the return of the armed forces in Burma," *The Review of Politics*, 25(3) (1963): 309-328.

Walton, M. J. "Ethnicity, conflict, and history in Burma: The myths of Panglong," *Asian Survey*, 48(6) (2008): 889-910.

11

Assessing the Civil-Military Responses toward the Rohingya Community

Sreeparna Banerjee

ABSTRACT

The United Nations has long considered the Rohingyas to be one of the most persecuted minorities in the world. Deprived of citizenship under the 1982 Citizenship law has effectively curtailed their basic rights towards free movement, occupation, health, and education. Since the 1970s, dogmatic policies adopted by the military regime have been instrumental in making hundreds of thousands of Muslim Rohingyas flee to neighbouring nations, for instance, Bangladesh, Malaysia, Indonesia, Thailand and India. After the democratic transition in 2015, there were hopes that democratic reforms would lead to more comprehensive social developments and human rights protection. However, this failed to change the ground situation due to the complex civil-military relations. The exodus in 2017 led close to a million to travel to neighbouring Bangladesh, and they have been there living there since. While many remedies have been forwarded by the international community and different scholars, however, without an understanding of the long-term military and political goals of Myanmar, it is difficult to look beyond current problems and anticipate future challenges or solutions.

Against this backdrop, this chapter attempts to consolidate the challenges of finding sustainable solutions for the Rohingya community by assessing the military and civilian policies toward them. This chapter is divided into four sections; the first part examines the Rohingya people's experience historically by providing a brief history of these people since Myanmar gained independence. The second section analyses the policies implemented by the military Government for five decades of its rule towards these people. The next section examines the policies of the civilian Government. The fourth section addresses human rights abuses and responses by other international organisations. The final section concludes with the challenges on the way forward.

History of the Rohingyas

The Rohingyas are ethnic Muslim minorities living in the Buthidaung and Maungdaw townships of Rakhine State, earlier known as the Arakan State, which is on the western coast of Myanmar, then known as Burma. They have been alleged to be "illegal Bengalis" who have migrated from the Chittagong Hill Tracks. If one tracks the history of the Rohingyas, it is quite disputed. While Rohingya historians claim indigenous status traceable for more than 1,000 years, others trace it back to only the 1950s when Bengali Muslim intellectuals began to call themselves Rohingya (a term which did not exist before 1950). They were descendants of immigrants from the Chittagong District of East Bengal who had migrated to Arakan after it was ceded to the British at the end of the first Anglo-Burmese War (1824–26). However, there were Muslim settlers in Arakan long before 1826. The earliest such settlers were the Bengali retinues of King Min Saw Mon, the founder of the Mrauk-U Dynasty (1430–1784). They were allowed to settle in Mrauk-U after the King regained his throne with military assistance from the Sultan of Bengal.[1] Historians claim that in the 17th century, the Arakan region was filled with enslaved Muslims who used to work in agricultural lands. Arakan was conquered by the Burmese in 1784, who ruled it until 1824. During this period, many Arakanese fled to British Bengal.

As a result, Arakan was scarcely populated when the Britishers captured Burma in 1826 and required manual labour to produce rice to meet the world's demands. The Britishers encouraged Bengali Muslims to migrate as agriculturalists into the fertile valleys of Arakan to reinstate former high-yield paddy fields. At the time, there was no international boundary between Bengal and Arakan, and no restrictions were imposed on movement between the two territories. Thus, the pull factors forced Muslim Bengalis to travel for better opportunities. This opened economic development in the region. Regular shipping lines opened between Akyab (now Sittwe) and Chittagong, and thus Akyab became one of the major rice-exporting cities in the world. During this period, the British introduced Zamindary System, which favoured Bengali Muslims in Arakan. As a result, many Chittagonians made Arakan their home, and after a century of colonial rule, they became the numerically dominant social group in the region.[2]

After the withdrawal of the British from Burma in 1942, ethnic violence between Arakan Buddhists and Muslim Chittagonians broke out. According to some historians, the underlying cause for the violence was the discriminatory Zamindary System.[3] In 1946, initially, Arakan Muslims formed the Muslim Liberation Organisation (MLO). They sent a delegation to Karachi to discuss a proposal with the leaders of the Muslim League to incorporate some of Arakan State's northern townships into East Pakistan. This proposal was, however, ignored. In 1948, after subsequent demands for recognition made to the newly independent Government of Burma were also ignored, the MLO, renamed the Mujahid Party, destroyed Arakan villages in the north of Maungdaw.[4]

In 1951, the Mujahid Party demanded that Northern Arakan become a Muslim State as an equal constituent of the Union of Burma. This demand was not acceded to, and subsequent uprisings threw the entire region into turmoil for a decade. In 1962, a military coup resulted in Burma becoming a one-party military state, and the Mujahid movement was driven underground. They did not acknowledge this group of Muslims who started calling themselves Rohingyas, meaning "inhabitant of Rohang", which was the early Muslim name for Arakan. In 1982, the military Government passed the Citizenship Act that recognised only ethnic groups that had lived in Burma before 1824 when the First Anglo-Burmese War began. This legislation was designed to deny citizenship rights to Rohingya Muslims, most of whom had arrived in Myanmar after 1824. In this way, the Rohingyas became officially stateless.[5]

Military's Policies toward Rohingyas

The military Government since 1948 wanted to subdue ethnic movements that various ethnic groups carried out after Myanmar gained independence. These ethnic groups mostly demanded autonomy and recognition, to which the democratic leaders were unable to respond with appropriate policies or actions. Thus, the Prime Minister voluntarily acceded the state powers to the military general to stabilise the situation. The primary focus of the military government once in power was to bring stability to the land, and they did so successfully through force and censure. When the democratic government was due to come back to power, the military leaders staged a coup in response to the belief that the democratic government would not be able to control the state fittingly. Many scholars on regime change have opined that, in most cases, military leaders never define themselves as the permanent rulers of the country. Instead, they claim, as did Myanmar's generals, about briefly assuming power to save the country from instability. The sentiment is that when the country is stable, the military will leave its temporary stint of ruling the nation and return to its previous military duties. However, in the case of Myanmar, the temporary stint has become permanent.

With respect to the Rohingyas, the growing demand for a separate state meant instability, which was not possible for the present government. Thus, they were focussed on subduing this movement. Therefore, the first step applied by the military Government to make these people powerless was passing the 1982 Citizenship Act. This act provided legal means to strip these people of their citizenship and the rights associated with it. The then military regime carried out two major operations, namely, Naga Min (King Dragon) in 1978 and Pyi Thaya in 1991. Both operations were aimed at ousting illegal immigrants from Myanmar soil. In both cases, the hapless people voyaged across the region to escape the violence of the armed forces. The Bangladesh Government has continued to provide a safe haven in Cox's Bazar district to the displaced people fleeing military operations in the latter's homeland.

(a) Operation Naga Min

Shortly after General Ne Win and his Myanmar Socialist Programme Party (BSPP) grabbed power in 1962 through a coup, the military regime started banning social and political institutions established by the Rohingya community. In 1977, Myanmar immigration and military authorities conducted what they called Operation Naga Min with the aim of keeping a record of the citizens, which automatically made way for the marking of foreigners who do not belong to the land.[6] This led to eviction, detention, and bloodshed that forced more than two hundred thousand to cross over to Bangladesh. This act, the Myanmar authorities claimed, signified the Rohingyas' illegal status in Myanmar.

While the Bangladesh Government initially provided proper conditions for the people, thirteen camps were established with the UN's help to accommodate and attend to the immediate needs of the said people. Almost immediately upon the Rohingyas' arrival, the Bangladesh Government engaged its Myanmar counterpart in a discussion on their repatriation. At first, the Myanmar Government did not concede; however, pressure from the UN forced them to come to terms with the situation and take back the Rohingyas. Thus, many Rohingyas were forced to go back to Myanmar. Interestingly, while the policies have been made for repatriation, it was not ensured that the conditions would improve once they were back. Incidentally, this led to the second exodus in 1991.

(b) Operation Pyi Thaya

In 1991-92, Than Shwe, the then military leader of the State Law and Order Restoration Council (SLORC), launched Operation Pyi Thaya, or 'Clean and Beautiful Nation'. This operation took place as a response to the military expansion of the Rohingya Solidarity Organisation (RSO). Similar to Operation Nagamin in 1978, the Government's official explanation for the operation was to expel so-called "foreigners" from the area and capture RSO insurgents. The resulting violence resulted in 200,000 to 250,000 civilians being displaced. Most of them fled to neighbouring Bangladesh.

In December 1991, *Tatmadaw* soldiers crossed the border and accidentally fired on a Bangladeshi military outpost, causing a brief strain in Bangladesh–Myanmar relations. The Bangladesh Government, as usual, sought repatriation from Myanmar. However, in this case, it was believed that many displaced people were sent back without consent. Thus, UNHCR set up mechanisms to monitor the completion of the process. Initially, the UNHCR representatives were not permitted to travel within the Rakhine State without prior clearance from the Myanmar Government. The latter also failed to provide a firm commitment that it would recognise the rights of the Rohingyas to Myanmar citizenship. Thus, the conditions for Rohingyas remained filled with challenges once they came back without any reassurances.

(c) 2012 Attacks

The next major attack on the Rohingyas was conducted in 2012 when lethal sectarian violence occurred between the Buddhists and the Muslim Rohingyas. The violence was the outcome of sexual violation and the killing of a Hindu girl, which aggravated the situation since it was thought without much evidence that a few Rohingya boys/men were the culprits. In retaliation, ten Rohingyas were assassinated in front of the police while the latter did nothing to stop the act. This was followed by major violence and destruction in both communities that led to the intervention of the military generals who initiated targeted brutality on the Rohingya community.[7] Around 167 people were killed, and nearly two hundred thousand were displaced, of which a few fled to neighbouring countries.

Consequently, in the 2014 census, the people who were identified as Rohingyas were not reckoned with. The white cards that were provided to the Rohingyas as an ID for voting were relinquished right before the 2015 elections.[8] The Population Control Healthcare law was passed in 2015 to limit Rohingya birth rates.[9] Thus, the 2012 incident opened the door for a long-standing strategy to deal with the Rohingya community.

Civilian Government Policies towards Rohingyas

Much of the political landscape started shifting while the violence inflicted on the Rohingyas continued to more or less remain the same. In 2011, Myanmar, in a guided manner, changed from a military regime to a semi-military regime under the leadership of Thein Sein. He was looked upon as an agent of change. Many reforms took place in the process, for instance, freedom of expression, press, the release of political prisoners, changes in political laws, and liberalisation of the economy. It was finally hoped that Myanmar could turn into a democratic system soon.

The release of Aung San Suu Kyi from house arrest was a major development. The coming of the National League of Democracy (NLD) party to power, especially Aung San Suu Kyi as the State Counsellor, imparted a lot of hope that the Rohingya issue may now be dealt with in a humane manner and may be resolved by introducing national policies that integrate the needs of this community. She is a recipient of the Nobel Peace Prize for her commitment to peace and stability. Ironically, the change to the democratic government did not lead to the dissipation of the Rohingya issue but rather the intensification of it.

The Myanmar military's campaign against the Rohingya population was sparked by a 25 August 2017 attack by militants belonging to the armed group, the Rakhine Rohingya Salvation Army (ARSA). Thirty police posts and an army base were targeted and damaged. In retaliation, the junta not only attacked the bases of the ethnic militant group but particularly targeted Rohingya civilians spread across the entire region. This included mass burning, killings, rape, and other abuses, which have caused more than 700,000 Rohingyas to flee to neighbouring Bangladesh. Nearly 284 villages were completely destroyed.

There have been justifications for the acts by the military and the NLD Government, who tried to portray this infliction of violence on the displaced communities as an internal matter. The State Counsellor's office put out a statement implying that the people who fled to Bangladesh were responsible for the violent attacks on the army posts.[10] In another statement, General Min Aung Hlaing emphasised the need for the rehabilitation of villages of their citizens, implying that if the Rohingyas did return since they are not a part of the national race, they might not be given a chance to live in their previous space.[11]

The Rohingya issue has been a major catastrophe. It was expected that the NLD party and Aung San Suu Kyi would intervene to voice their support against the inhuman treatment meted out against the stateless people. The silence and fumbling on the part of the ex-State Counsellor jolted the national and international community. The concern of international spectators was that the ex-State Counsellor shielded the military's action and called the situation an internal matter despite millions crossing the border to live in neighbouring nations.[12]

The press was censured for reporting on the issue. Such actions created ramifications over the image of Suu Kyi, resulting in the taking away of several accolades by various countries who had honoured her for her peace-driven thoughts and actions. She held on to her statement and protected the junta in the International Court of Justice (ICJ) in 2019, calling the entire issue an internal matter and articulated that no genocide had taken place.

International Responses

For decades, Myanmar has been an isolated nation for its personally selected policies since 1962. Post-2011, as the military turned into a semi-military Government and gradually released some of its political control, the country's interactions have grown dramatically with its neighbouring nations and the world. Sanctions imposed following the military misconduct during the 1988 revolts and 1991 elections by the European Union and the USA were pulled back after the elections in 2012. This move was made in recognition of the advancement of democracy in Myanmar. However, the 2017 exodus brought the human rights abuses of the Rohingyas to the fore. Thus, Western countries placed sanctions to push Myanmar to take back the displaced people and supposedly build a conducive environment. The neighbouring nations, however, adopted a constructive approach. For instance, China and India, by engaging with the nation, created further opportunities to make the Rakhine State more developed so that the displaced people could return to a proper environment. China also shielded the nation from further sanctions in the UNSC.

The UN has described the 2017 exodus as a textbook example of ethnic cleansing.[13] It has been further stated that the acts, for instance, forcibly putting them in camps where conditions are brutal, supporting anti-Rohingya campaigns by political parties that allow discrimination and hatred to grow and spread, controlling their birth or marriage rates, targeted killings and rape and torture of Rohingya population that forced more than one million to escape to another nation may establish the intent of the Government to target this group specifically and thus resemble genocide.[14]

This was important since the genocide case was brought up in the International Court of Justice (ICJ) by Gambia in 2019. The State Counsellor was present to defend 'the honour of her nation' by constantly shielding the act as a legitimate counter-insurgency operation. However, in a noteworthy verdict, the ICJ on January 2020 ordered the Myanmar Government to safeguard its Rohingya population and not inflict harm on them or erase the evidence of any harm caused. An appeal was made again after the coup in Myanmar by the military generals; however, in July 2022, the court disregarded the reservation that the junta was not involved in steering genocide acts on the Rohingyas. This opens the scope for the further exhibition of fact-based evidence that will prove the breach of the 1948 Genocide Convention in the subsequent hearings. While this ruling does not bring new restrictions on the military regime, it generates the required weight on the current regime. It is significant that the Biden Administration, through its own independent fact-based evidence team, has declared the decades-long suppression of Rohingyas as 'genocide'.[15]

Major Challenges to a Way Forward

(a) Constitution of Myanmar

After the 1962 coup, the Government of General Ne Win adopted the second Constitution of Myanmar on 03 January 1974. This Constitution defined Myanmar as a socialist democracy but also demarcates seven ethnic minority states (Rakhine, Chin, Kachin, Shan, Karenni, Karen and Mon) and seven predominantly ethnic Myanmar divisions (Tenasserim, Rangoon, Irrawaddy, Pegu, Magwe, Mandalay and Sagaing). Critics describe this demarcation and division as a major reason for conflict between the majority and minority, directly impacting the Rohingya. This Constitution states that to gain Myanmar citizenship, one must be a person born of parents who are both nationals of Myanmar or have been vested with citizenship according to existing laws (Article 145).[16]

The 1974 Constitution did not directly deny citizenship to the Rohingyas. Still, it removed the provision of the 1947 Constitution that permitted the Rohingyas to gain citizenship on the basis that either they had a grandparent from an "indigenous race" or lived in British Myanmar prior to 1942. These two measures also resulted in denying the Rohingyas any specific status collectively as one of the nation's indigenous ethnic groups. Thus, the effect of the 1974 Constitution are subtler than a straightforward taking away of citizenship of a group. As the Rohingyas were mentioned in the Parliamentary list of ethnic groups, most of them would not have formalised their citizenship status. If they had formalised their status, they could have come under Article 145, which states that a citizen is one born of parents both of whom are nationals of the Socialist Republic of the Union of Myanmar or who are vested with citizenship according to existing laws on the date this Constitution comes into force.

This is an important step in the process of dispossession, owing to two technicalities of law: (i) it deprives the Rohingyas of their group status; and (ii) it asks them to prove that both of their parents are nationals of Myanmar rather than proving that their grandparents were so. Thus, a distinction is drawn between those persons who became citizens more than a generation back and those who did not. Furthermore, the realities of the socio-political status of the Rohingyas were not conducive to them complying with the constitutional requirement since many of them would not have any information that they were required to do something to be recognised as citizens of the state.[17]

2008 Constitution

In the 2008 Constitution, to be a citizen, one has to prove either that one was born of parents "both of whom" are nationals of the Republic of the Union of Myanmar or that one is already a citizen according to the law on the day this Constitution comes into force (art 345).[18] This is a dramatic narrowing down of the grounds on which citizenship could be claimed compared to the past constitutions. For example, a Rohingya is now required to prove that their parents are citizens or that they are already citizens. However, most Rohingya are not able to meet these requirements, as the majority of their parents do not hold any documents to show that they are nationals of the Republic.

The far-reaching impact of these changes in the 2008 Constitution became evident to the Rohingyas in the Myanmar national election of 2015 when the Union Election Commission (UEC) rejected 88 candidates without giving specific reasons. More than a third of them were Muslims, 28 were from Rakhine state, and so were probably ethnic Rohingyas. One of them was U Shwe Maung, a sitting MP, who is an ethnic Rohingya and was planning to stand as an independent candidate for this election. Some newspaper commentaries gave reasons that included failing to meet a minimum age requirement, ties to "unlawful associations" and residency requirement shortcomings.

The Pyithu Hluttaw Election Law, 2010, states that a candidate must have lived in Myanmar for the last ten years and be a citizen born to parents who are citizens. The Constitution of 2008, within the meaning of Article 120(b), also states that the candidate has to be a citizen who was born to both parents who are citizens. Therefore, the assertion is that the Rohingyas were not considered eligible for candidature on this basis. However, in contrast, the argument is made, for example, by the HRW that the action of the UEC was fundamentally flawed for two reasons: firstly, the Rohingya had run in prior elections without issue, and secondly, their families had lived in Myanmar for generations. However, holding appropriate documents is an essential part that has been destroyed or absent or not recognised by the military regime.

(b) The Inability of the Democratic Regime

The Senate majority leader, Mitch McConnell of Kentucky, points out that "publicly condemning Suu Kyi is simply not constructive". He noted that under Myanmar's Constitution, she is barred from the Presidency and her civilian Government has no authority over the military. Thus, her position is an exceedingly difficult one. Balancing civil-military relations thus continues to be her focus in order to continue holding the reins of the nation.

The 2008 Constitution ensures the transfer of partial powers to any new leadership. It maintains military dominance irrespective of whoever is in charge at that time. The 2008 Constitution was always contentious. The NLD landslide in 2015 enabled the formation of an NLD-led, but still military-controlled Government, and a period of—at least partially elected—civilian rule. In return, however, the NLD had to accept that any further constitutional advances would take place within the confines of the 2008 Constitution, meaning that amendments would have to be made in accordance with the process set out by the 2008 Constitution. As this would require a 75 per cent majority in Parliament, with 25 per cent of the seats in the legislature reserved for the military, any further constitutional change would have had to be agreed upon between the NLD and the military.

However, it was never in the NLD government's interest to help the cause of the Rohingyas. After coming to power, the government never introduced any policy to amalgamate them into their society so that they need not upset the Buddhist nationalists. Incidentally, recognising the Rohingyas might threaten the civilian government's power-sharing agreement with the military. The focus always remained to appease the military regime in order to facilitate the normal functioning of the democratic government.

(c) Shortcomings of Regional Blocs and Powers

The Western and neighbouring countries have been unable to forward proper solutions to address the issue. Most of the proposals have been regarding the sanctions and arms embargo but no stringent action has been taken on the nation to bring the people back. Any major decisions in this regard have been shielded by heavy-weight allies, for instance, China and Russia. The regional and sub-regional blocs, ASEAN and BIMSTEC, have also been unable to formulate solutions to address the issue. ASEAN has been criticised for not pushing Myanmar enough to facilitate the repatriation process. While ASEAN did send a team to conduct a preliminary need assessment, the report was however criticised for not undertaking the Rohingya point of view. The ASEAN team also went with Myanmar officials to persuade displaced people surviving in Bangladesh camps to return. However, the team could not assure them of either citizenship or protection once back in Myanmar. Thus, the second repatriation attempt remained unsuccessful.

There is not much pressure from countries of the region on Myanmar to resolve the Rohingya problem. Only Malaysia, and to a lesser extent, Indonesia, have pushed for a diplomatic solution to the crisis. Thailand, Vietnam, and even the Philippines have been supporting Myanmar. All that is expected of ASEAN is that it does something about the boatloads of Rohingyas travelling by sea. Separately, there is also an UN-backed regional forum, the Bali Process, started in Bali, Indonesia, in 2002, which seeks to raise awareness of human trafficking. Indonesia, which currently co-chairs the Bali Process along with Singapore, has agreed to provide humanitarian assistance to nearly 100 displaced Rohingyas stranded off the northern coast of Aceh. However, more is required if proper solutions are to be forwarded for the betterment of the community. The coup in 2021 has further created fewer opportunities to open discussions on the matter. The focus of the bloc is so that Myanmar adheres to the Five-Point Consensus that is supposed to kick-start the resolution of the current political crisis; this is currently failing.

On the five-year mark of the exodus of Rohingyas, the embassies of 13 countries and the European Union in Bangladesh have vowed to put continuous pressure on the Myanmar Government to create solutions for the Rohingyas.[19] During the visit of Ms. Heyzer, the UN Special Envoy of the Secretary-General to Myanmar, she stated that the responsibility for the fate of the displaced people and their return exclusively lies on Myanmar. In this regard, there is a need to design inclusive and comprehensive policies to ensure the well-being of the people. In this process, it is important to involve the Rohingyas to ensure that the policies benefit the community and are not meant from the majority perspective.

The shadow Government of Myanmar, called the National Unity Government (NUG), comprising ex-NLD leaders, has promised to provide the Rohingyas with citizenship, equal legal opportunities, and warranting dignified repatriation if and when they come to power. However, the current situation lacks any mechanism to deal with the ongoing crisis.[20] Lack of political will, and inclusive policies are instrumental to the decades-long problem of the Rohingyas. Changes in this direction may bring about some proper resolution to the Rohingya issue.

Conclusion

While the Rohingyas continue to live in anguish it is both the civilian and military government policies that have escalated the issue. The growing hate and Buddhist centralisation have never been addressed by either regime and neither has anyone been held accountable for the crimes committed against these people. Moreover, secular behaviour has never been encouraged. By not taking justifiable and accurate actions to safeguard the rights of the marginalised population, the state has become the perpetrator of violence. The statements from international nations and organisations have also been ignored despite the pitiable situation of these people. The international community must continue to raise its voice against the inhuman situation of the Rohingyas. The ICJ verdict and the subsequent hearings will hold the key towards this end. An arms embargo pushed to this end will also be fruitful.

Sub-regional and regional organisations must play a more substantial role in maintaining their relevance in regional political dynamics. It is well known that most of the countries in the South and Southeast Asian region where the Rohingyas have fled post-violence in Myanmar are not a party to the 1951 Convention or its 1967 Protocol; thus, the status of refugee rights and protection is denied to them. Even the migration and subsequent crimes associated with it are addressed through a security lens, but a sturdy legal apparatus is required for those seeking opportunity and safety through migration.

Also, for countries hosting the Rohingyas, especially Bangladesh, funding is essential for the setting up of proper mechanisms and continued implementation. Unfortunately, the widespread trend of humanitarian funding falls short of meeting the needs and demands required to comprehensively provide for people facing protracted displacement since the focus remains mostly on short-term funding rather than long-term. As the crisis lingers, the level of assistance contributed to humanitarian appeals continues to dwindle. According to the JRP report of 2022, USD 881 million is required for the proper functioning of different sectors like health, WASH, protection, education, and nutrition, to name a few. Still, so far, only 49 per cent has been funded. Without the much-required support, most of the activities will remain half-hearted. The Rohingya crisis is a lesson for regional and sub-regional institutions to be prepared and equipped with better policies and proper mechanisms to deal with such a large-scale movement of people. The situation needs close monitoring if better regional cooperation is to lead to improved protection for its displaced or stateless people. A refugee-and-asylum policy that includes guidance for action to be taken when a member-state's internal issues cause people to flee to neighbouring states needs to be framed. Such a policy agreed to by all ASEAN or BIMSTEC members will help build proper mechanisms to address such situations appropriately and inclusively. Thus, comprehensive solutions are still required to deal effectively with the crisis.

ENDNOTES

1. M. Yegar, "*The Muslims of Burma: A study of a minority group*" (Harrassowitz, Wiesbaden 1972).
2. Ibid.
3. Ibid.
4. Ibid.
5. E. Abdelkader, "The Rohingya Muslims in Myanmar: Past, present and future", *Oregon Review of International Law*, 15, (2013): 393-412
6. "Myanmar's Brutal Campaign Against the Rohingya", *Congressional Research Service,* 26 September 2017, available at https://www.congress.gov/115/meeting/house/106434/witnesses/HHRG-115-FA05-Wstate-MartinM-20170927.pdf, last accessed on 26 December 2022
7. Sreeparna Banerjee, "Decade-long detention: Rohingyas in Myanmar camps", *Observer Research Foundation,* 01 July 2022, available at https://www.orfonline.org/expert-speak/decade-long-detention-rohingyas-in-myanmar-camps/, last accessed on 26 December 2022.
8. "Myanmar's Brutal Campaign Against the Rohingya", *Congressional Research Service,* 26 September 2017, available at https://www.congress.gov/115/meeting/house/106434/witnesses/HHRG-115-FA05-Wstate-MartinM-20170927.pdf, last accessed on 26 December 2022
9. Kieran Guilbert "Myanmar population control law threatens minorities: rights group", *Reuters*, 22 April 2015, available at https://www.reuters.com/article/us-myanmar-law-minorities-idUSKBN0ND1XI20150422, last accessed on 26 December 2022
10. "Thousands of Rohingya refugees continue to flee violence", *UNHCR,* 04 July 2018, available at https://www.ohchr.org/en/statements/2018/07/thousands-rohingya-refugees-continue-flee-violence, last accessed on 26 December 2022
11. Ibid.
12. Hannah Beech, "What Happened to Myanmar's Human-Rights Icon," *The New Yorker*, 25 September 2017, available at https://www.newyorker.com/magazine/2017/10/02/what-happened-to-myanmars-human-rights-icon, last accessed on 26 December 2022
13. Andrew J. Burchett and Amna Q. Rana, "The International Community's Inaction Amidst the Rohingya's Suffering", *Towson University Journal of International Affairs*, Vol. LI, No. 1 (2017) available at https://cpb-us-w2.wpmucdn.com/wp.towson.edu/dist/b/55/files/2018/06/Fall-2017-Rohingya-Article-24zw9fl-1yee0uw.pdf, last accessed on 26 December 2022
14. Ibid.

15. "Application of the Convention on the Prevention And Punishment of the Crime of Genocide (The Gambia v. Myanmar)", 22 July 2022, available at https://www.icj-cij.org/public/files/case-related/178/178-20220722-JUD-01-00-EN.pdf, last accessed on 26 December 2022.
16. The Constitution of the Union of Myanmar (1974), available at http://www.myanmar-law-library.org/IMG/pdf/constitution_de_1974.pdf, last accessed on 26 December 2022.
17. Parashar and Alam, "The National Laws of Myanmar: Making of Statelessness for the Rohingya", *IOM*, 2018, available at https://www.researchgate.net/publication/328815015_The_National_ Laws_of_Myanmar_Making_of_Statelessness_for_the_Rohingya#:~:text=The%20earlier %20constitutions%20, last accessed on 26 December 2022
18. "Myanmar's Constitution of 2008", available at https://www.constituteproject.org/constitution/Myanmar_2008.pdf?lang=en, last accessed on 26 December 2022
19. "Int'l community vows to pressure Myanmar over Rohingya crisis", *Daily Sabah*, 26 August 2022, available at https://www.dailysabah.com/world/europe/intl-community-vows-to-pressure-myanmar-over-rohingya-crisis, last accessed on 26 December 2022
20. Sreeparna Banerjee, "5 years in exile: What lies ahead for the displaced Rohingyas," *Observer Research Foundation*, 03 September 2022, available at https://www.orfonline.org/expert-speak/5-years-in-exile-what-lies-ahead-for-the-displaced-rohingyas/, last accessed on 26 December 2022

12

Climate Change as Threat Multiplier: The Case of Myanmar

P K Khup Hangzo

ABSTRACT

Myanmar is one of the most vulnerable countries in the world to the worsening impact of climate change, extreme weather events in particular. Considered the day-to-day "face" of climate change, extreme weather events such as storms, floods, etc., have exacted a severe human and socio-economic toll on the country. In fact, from 2000 to 2019, Myanmar was the second most-affected country in the world in terms of extreme weather events. As the world gets warmer, extreme weather events are projected to become more frequent and more severe. Thus, climate change has become a threat multiplier for Myanmar as it could increase state fragility, imperil the well-being and security of its people, exacerbate existing grievances, and fuel social unrest and event conflicts.

In the face of this challenge, the country's adaptation efforts have been slow to materialise as they are hampered by a number of factors, including political instability and violent conflicts. This article assesses Myanmar's vulnerability to climate change and its potential implications for the country. It argues that effective adaptation to the impact of climate change is critical as it could help reduce the risk of future conflicts in Myanmar. Conversely, this chapter also argues that the failure to adapt to the worsening impacts of climate change could exacerbate existing grievances and fuel social unrest and even violent conflicts in the country.

Introduction

Myanmar is one of the most vulnerable countries in the world to climate change. Its impacts have already been felt by the country through an increase in the prevalence of drought events, an increase in intensity and frequency of cyclones/

strong winds, rainfall variability including erratic and record-breaking intense rainfall events, an increase in the occurrence of flooding and storm surges, and an increase in extremely high temperatures (The Republic of the Union of Myanmar, 2012a). Projections indicated that the country's climate would "shift dramatically" in the coming decades, having a lasting and significant impact on the country's ecosystems and, in turn, on human health, agriculture, food security, infrastructure, local livelihoods, and the larger economy (Horton et al., 2017).

Myanmar, however, has been less able to cope with the impact of climate change because its ability to adapt has been significantly weakened by decades of conflict and political instability. Following the democratic reforms that began in the late 2000s, Myanmar has formulated several policies to bolster its ability to address climate change and adapt to its impacts. However, those efforts have been upended by the 01 February 2021 coup. This chapter argues that climate change could interact with Myanmar's security situation in dangerous and unpredictable ways. Although climate change may not necessarily be a direct cause of conflict, it may indirectly increase the risk of conflict by exacerbating existing social, economic, and environmental factors. Climate change, therefore, is a threat multiplier, and it could increasingly become a major factor in Myanmar's conflicts and instability.

Assessing Myanmar's Vulnerability to Climate Change

The impacts of climate change are now being felt across many parts of the world. Not only have the frequency and intensity of extreme weather events (heat waves, droughts, extreme rainfall, flooding, cyclones, etc.) increased, but the rate of melting of sea ice and glaciers and global sea level rise has also accelerated. Limiting the increase in global average temperature to 1.5°C by the end of 2100 is seen as key to minimising the impact of climate change. That critical threshold, however, is now dangerously close to being breached. Global temperatures already reached 1.1°C in 2021 (WMO, 2022a). At the current rate of greenhouse gas emissions, the 1.5°C threshold could be breached by 2035 (Ravilious, 2022), and the average global temperature could reach at least 2.5°C by 2100 (CAT, 2023). That would prove devastating for the world. While every country in the world is vulnerable to climate change, some countries are more vulnerable than others as they have a lesser ability to cope and adapt to its impacts. Myanmar offers a case in point.

According to Horton et al. (2017), Myanmar has "already experienced climate change over recent decades." They observed in a 2017 report titled *Assessing Climate Risk in Myanmar: Technical Report* that during 1981-2010, the country's national average daily temperatures increased by about 0.25°C per decade and daily maximum temperatures by 0.4°C. They projected the average annual temperature to rise by 0.7-1.1°C during 2011-2040 and by 1.3-2.7°C during 2041-2070. As a result, Myanmar could experience anywhere from four to 17 days of extreme heat each month compared to about one day of extreme heat per month during 1981–2010. The Eastern and Northern hilly regions could see the most dramatic warming, with the hot season average temperatures projected to rise by up to 3°C. Annual total rainfall also increased during 1981-2010, with coastal regions recording more rainfall than inland areas. Projections indicated that annual total rainfall will increase by one per cent to 11 per cent by 2011-2040 and six per cent to 23 per cent by 2041-2070 compared to the 1980 to 2006 baseline. Meanwhile, along the entire coast of Myanmar, sea levels are projected to rise between 5 centimetres (cm) to 13 cm in the 2020s, between 20 cm to 41 cm in the 2050s, and between 37 cm to 83 cm in the 2080s, respectively.

Even at the current level of global warming, Myanmar has already been highly exposed to a number of extreme weather events, including extreme temperatures, droughts, cyclones, floods, extreme rainfall, etc. These extreme weather events are considered to be one of the clearest indicators and most visible consequences of climate change. As such, they are deemed to be the "showcase of climate variability" (Cattiaux and Ribes, 2018) and "the day-to-day "face" of climate change" (WMO, 2022b). In all, half of Myanmar's population lives in a "multi-hazard" region (Kapoor et al., 2021). It is therefore not surprising that Myanmar was ranked the second-most affected country in the world by extreme weather events from 2000 to 2019 in the *Global Climate Risk Index 2021* (Eckstein, Kunzel, and Schafer, 2022). The index was published by German-Watch, a Germany-based independent development and environmental NGO, and it analyses the extent to which countries and regions have been affected by extreme weather events. It further observed that from 2000 to 2019, Myanmar recorded 57 extreme weather events, including Cyclone Nargis, that struck the country's Ayeyarwady delta in 2008. The cyclone was the worst natural disaster ever recorded in Myanmar, and it led to the death of over 140,000 people. At least 2.4 million people were severely affected, and over a million people were left homeless. The cyclone also caused USD 10 billion worth of economic damage (Besset, Anthony, Dussouillez, and Goichot, 2017).

Table 1: Projections for Mean Annual and Seasonal Temperature Change above the Baseline Across Myanmar

	Model baseline (1980 to 2006)	*Warming by 2011-2040*	*Warming by 2041-2070*
Annual	23.6°C	0.7-1.1°C	1.3-2.7°C
Hot Season	25.1°C	0.8-1.2°C	1.4-2.9°C
Wet Season	25.1°C	0.6-1.1°C	1.1-2.4°C
Cool Season	20.5°C	0.7-1.2°C	1.3-2.8°C

Source: Horton et al, 2016.

Climate Change Governance in Myanmar

Myanmar has made significant progress in its efforts to address climate change in recent years. Much of the country's policies were put in place during the country's democratic transition that began around 2010. That year, Myanmar held a general election, the first since the 1990s. That election was won by the military-backed Union Solidarity and Development Party (USDP), and it marked Myanmar's transition from military rule to civilian democracy. The following year, in 2011, Myanmar's military government, the State Peace and Development Council (SPDC), was officially dissolved, and Thein Sein, a former military general, was sworn in as President of a nominally civilian government.

Alongside the historic democratic transition, Myanmar has also accelerated its climate change mitigation and adaptation efforts and the country submitted its National Adaptation Programme of Action (NAPA), a work programme to address climate change, to the United Nations Framework Convention on Climate Change (UNFCCC) in 2012. Myanmar's NAPA identified 32 priority activities for effective climate change adaptation for eight main sectors/themes, namely, agriculture, early warning systems, forests, public health, water resources, coastal zones, energy and industry, and biodiversity (The Republic of the Union of Myanmar, 2012b). Following this, Myanmar was eligible to access funding under the Least Developed Countries Fund (LDCF) mechanism. LDFC was established at the 2001 United Nations Climate Change Conference or COP7 in Marrakech, Morocco, to meet the adaptation needs of Least Developed Countries (LDCs). Specifically, it financed the preparation and implementation of NAPAs. LDCF, in turn, is managed by the Global Environment Facility (GEF), a multilateral environmental fund that was established on the eve of the 1992 Rio Earth Summit in Brazil.

Then, in 2015, Myanmar submitted its Intended Nationally Determined

Contribution (INDC), a climate action plan to cut emissions and adapt to climate impacts, to the UNFCCC. That has since been converted into a Nationally Determined Contribution (NDC). Myanmar's NDC envisaged a reduction in the country's total emissions by 414.75 million carbon dioxide equivalent (tCO_2e) by 2030 (The Republic of the Union of Myanmar, 2021). It aimed to achieve this by increasing the total share of renewable energy (solar and wind) to 53.5 per cent, i.e., from 2,000 megawatts (MW) to 3,070 MW, and decreasing the share of coal by 73.5 per cent, i.e., from 7,940 MW to 2,120 MW, respectively. The country also subsequently signed the Paris Agreement on 22 April 2016 and ratified it on 19 September 2017. The Paris Agreement is a legally binding international treaty on climate change. Its goal is to limit global warming to well below 2°C, preferably to 1.5°C, compared to pre-industrial levels by 2100. The agreement was adopted by 196 parties at the 2015 United Nations Climate Change Conference or COP 21 in Paris, France, on 12 December 2015 and entered into force on 4 November 2016.

To further mainstream climate change into its development agenda, Myanmar launched the *Myanmar Climate Change Policy* in 2018. It sets out a vision for the country that is a "...climate-resilient, low carbon society that is sustainable, prosperous and inclusive, for the wellbeing of present and future generations" (The Republic of the Union of Myanmar, 2019a). As a first step towards implementing this policy, Myanmar adopted the *Myanmar Climate Change Strategy* and the *Myanmar Climate Change Master Plan,* which are to be implemented between 2018 and 2030, respectively. The *Myanmar Climate Change Strategy* envisaged that by 2030, Myanmar would have "achieved climate resilience and pursued a low-carbon growth pathway to support inclusive and sustainable development" (The Republic of the Union of Myanmar, 2019b). The *Myanmar Climate Change Master Plan,* on the other hand, promises actions across sectors such as agriculture, fisheries and livestock; environment and natural resources; energy, transport and industry; cities, towns and human settlements; climate hazards and health; and education, science and technology (The Republic of the Union of Myanmar, 2019c). Another indication of the progress made by Myanmar in its climate change mitigation and adaptation efforts is the rise of civil societies and climate activism in the country. They are mostly engaged in a range of climate change-related work, including advocacy, weather and air quality monitoring, reforestation, and the promotion of sustainable agriculture practices and sustainable waste management (Derville et al. 2020). Though global movements have inspired them, Myanmar activists are motivated by local concerns about climate action.

Unravelling Myanmar's Climate Change Mitigation and Adaptation Efforts

The 01 February 2021 coup and the subsequent escalation of violence between state security forces and the anti-junta coalition have gradually derailed Myanmar's recent progress on climate change mitigation and adaptation. One environmental lawyer who has worked in the country opined that the military coup was "very much a crime against the environment, as much as a crime against human rights" (Win, 2021). He also observed that governments and United Nations agencies faced a "huge amount of risk" in how they dealt with the coup because it was "illegal" and "unconstitutional" and therefore "they just can't lawfully work with the military."

The United Nations has since suspended a number of climate projects that require working with Myanmar's military government, and other international donors have also followed suit. For example, GEF, the multilateral environmental fund that finances climate change mitigation and adaptation efforts, has halted its operations in Myanmar, fearing too much political and social risk to operate in the country. GEF has 39 projects in the country in sectors including agriculture, forestry, fisheries and aquaculture, biodiversity, renewable energy, and health (GEF 2022). These projects are carried out by various United Nations agencies such as the Food and Agriculture Organisation (FAO), the United Nations Development Programme (UNDP) and the United Nations Environment Programme (UNEP) as well as organisations like the International Union for Conservation of Nature (IUCN), and the Asian Development Bank (ADB). Given that even before the coup, "fragile" countries like Myanmar had one of the world's lowest climate finance per capita, it is only 1/80 or 1.25 per cent of that to "non-fragile" countries (UNDP, 2021), the withdrawal of international donors and organisations from the country will have severe implications on its climate change mitigation and adaptation efforts.

Myanmar's growing isolation from the international climate change negotiation process following the coup could further deal a major blow to its climate change mitigation and adaptation efforts. For example, the United Kingdom, host of the 2021 UN Climate Change Conference (COP26) that was held in Glasgow from 31 October to 12 November 2021, left Armed Forces Chief Min Aung Hlaing off the guest list and the event organiser, the UNFCCC, disinvited Myanmar military government representatives (Liu and Wallace, 2021). Although Chit Win, the military-appointed chief diplomat in London, did manage to register temporarily on the event page with three associates, they were denied entry and were subsequently taken off the system. Still, in his written remarks submitted to COP26, the military-appointed Natural Resources and Environmental Conservation Minister, Khin Maung Yi, pledged to achieve 50 per cent net emissions reductions by 2030 "if adequate international assistance is received." He also reiterated that Myanmar would increase its share of renewable energy targets from 2,000 MW to 3,070 MW by 2030. That is now highly unlikely to be achieved, given the current circumstances.

In addition, Myanmar's natural environment risks becoming more degraded, fragile, and vulnerable to climate change due to the increased exploitation of natural resources. The country's GDP contracted by 18.4 per cent in 2021 due to the COVID-19 pandemic and political instability (ADB, 2022). Projections indicated that it would continue to contract by 0.3 per cent in 2022 on continued political instability and the worsening security situation. Not surprisingly, the military junta has increasingly relied on revenue from natural resources to support their operations and their ongoing campaign to retain power. Forest Trends, the Washington, DC-based environmental group, reported in March 2022 that Myanmar had accelerated the timber trade since the coup, and it exported more than USD 190 million worth of timber between February and November 2021 (Forest Trends, 2022). Much of this export went to China, India, and Thailand.

Mining activities, rare earth elements in particular, have also intensified, especially in Kachin State, although it is illegal under Myanmar's laws. Rare earth elements are a set of seventeen metallic elements, and they are essential for high-tech devices such as smartphones and green technologies such as rechargeable batteries for electric and hybrid cars and permanent magnets for wind turbines. China is a major importer of Myanmar's rare earth elements. Global Witness, a London-based NGO that investigates and campaigns to prevent resource-related conflict, corruption, and environmental and human rights abuses, reported in August 2022 that China's import of rare earth elements from Myanmar has increased from a paltry USD 1.5 million in 2014 to USD 780 million in 2021 (Global Witness, 2022). According to a report by *Global Times*, a Chinese government mouthpiece, Myanmar accounted for 74.39 per cent of all rare earth elements imported by China in 2020 (Zhang and Li, 2021). One region in Kachin State, the Kachin Special Region 1, has now become the world's single largest source of supply for rare earth elements. This region, which straddles the China-Myanmar border, is a semi-autonomous territory and is run by militias that are affiliated with the military junta.

Jade mining has also seen an uptick following the coup. Myanmar produces about 70 per cent of the world's jade stone, and the estimated value of jade production in the country in 2014 was about USD 31 billion or 48 per cent of its official GDP for that year (Global Witness, 2015). The vast majority, 80 per cent, was smuggled to China, where it is highly sought after. Global Witness warned in a report that was published in June 2021 that the military coup could turn the jade industry into a "slush fund" for the military and a source of political patronage to prop up the military regime unless sanctions and other forms of punitive measures are taken (Global Witness, 2021).

Prospect for the Climate-Conflict Nexus in Myanmar

The idea that climate change could cause conflict has been around for many years now. The relationship between climate change and deadly conflict, however, is complex and context-specific. For example, while some countries manage a given impact of climate change well, others do not, and that makes conflict more likely. The general conclusion, therefore, is that climate change is not the sole or even the primary driving force behind violence and conflict. A landmark 2007 CNA Corporation report titled *National Security and the Threat of Climate Change* argued that "climate change acts as a threat multiplier for instability in some of the most volatile regions of the world" (The CNA Corporation, 2007). Since the publication of that report, the notion that climate change may indirectly increase the risk of conflict by exacerbating existing social, economic, and environmental factors have become mainstream.

The United States Department of Defence (DoD), in its 2014 Quadrennial Defence Review also called the effects of climate change as "threat multipliers that will aggravate stressors…such as poverty, environmental degradation, political instability, and social tensions—conditions that can enable terrorist activity and other forms of violence" (DoD, 2014). More recently, a report by the Stockholm International Peace Research Institute (Black et al., 2022) warned that the "environmental crisis" is increasing risks to security and peace worldwide, notably in countries that are already fragile (SIPRI 2022).

Experts have often pointed to the conflict in Darfur in Sudan as evidence that the effects of climate change are threat multipliers and additional causative factors of conflicts. Darfur has for many years witnessed a deadly conflict between herders and farmers. Long periods of drought resulted in the loss of both farmland and grazing land in the region. As a result of the failure of their grazing lands, the nomads migrated southwards in search of water and herding grounds. That, in turn, led to confrontations with the farming tribes occupying those lands. Experts worry that the same dynamic could play out in Myanmar. The country lacked the political stability and social infrastructures to cope with the types of stressors that could be brought on by climate change, including livelihood insecurity. That could become a major factor in Myanmar's instability and conflict in the coming years. While there is no conclusive proof that climate change could have played a role in the current upheaval, some experts have nonetheless alluded to it. For example, Naruemon Thabchumpon, Professor of cross-border migration at Bangkok's Chulalongkorn University, opined that, "When we look at the intensifying conflict, the first region that started fighting against the military is the dry zone region of Sagaing. The conflict map bears this out; there is a clear relationship between climate crisis, economic concerns, and areas experiencing recent political instability" (Duncan, 2022).

The Central Dry Zone encompasses parts of Sagaing, Mandalay, and Magway regions. It is home to an estimated 12 million people and accounts for 35 per cent of Myanmar's grain cropping (Herridge et al., 2019). As such, it is widely considered to be the country's agricultural heartland. The Central Dry Zone, however, is highly vulnerable to the impact of climate change, extreme temperatures in particular, and it has witnessed record-breaking temperatures over the past several years. Notably, twenty-two of the region's cities registered recorded high temperatures in 2020, with the riverine market town of Chauk in central Magway registering a staggering 47.5°C (Duncan, 2022). That led to unprecedented crop failures throughout the region. *The Guardian*, a British newspaper, quoted one farmer as saying in its 21 June 2022 report that "Our farmland, which was previously 100 per cent productive, saw output levels drop to between 60 and 40 per cent per acre." That has prompted people to migrate from the region in increasing numbers. According to a 2013 survey, only 6 per cent of dry zone inhabitants planned on migrating overseas (MMN and AMC, 2013).

However, owing to a combination of factors such as crop failure, a post-coup collapse in trade, and the plummeting value of Myanmar's currency, the kyat, that number has surged to unprecedented levels in recent years. Thus, climate change has already induced livelihood insecurity in the Central Dry Zone. Given this context, it is not surprising that the people of Magway were among the first to mount a resistance to the military government following the 1 February 2022 coup. As Myanmar is projected to face an increase in average temperatures as well as changing rainfall patterns and sea-level rise over the coming years, climatic distress could play an increasingly major role in the country's conflicts.

Conclusion

Myanmar is already exposed to a multitude of extreme weather events, including extreme temperatures, droughts, cyclones, flood, storm surges, and extreme rainfall. As the world gets warmer, their frequency and intensity will increase. Yet, the country has limited climate change mitigation and adaptation capacity due to years of political instability and conflicts. As a result, communities in Myanmar are among the least prepared and the least able to adapt to the impact of climate change. The unprecedented democratic reforms of the last ten years or so have presented Myanmar with an opportunity to address climate change comprehensively, and much has been achieved towards that end. However, the 1 February 2021 military coup has thrown reversed the progress achieved over those years. The suspension of funding and operations by the United Nations and other international donors, coupled with the growing exploitation of natural resources, has made the country much more vulnerable to climate change.

Critically, Myanmar's reduced capacity to deal with the impact of climate change could become a major factor in the country's conflicts. This is because climate change matters to the issue of peace and security. Although the relationship between climate change and conflict is complex and context-specific, it is undeniable that climate change is a threat multiplier. There is a danger that climate change could intersect with other factors, and that could lead to the heightened risk of violence and conflicts in Myanmar. It is, therefore, imperative that climate change mitigation and adaptation remain a strategic priority of the country's powers that be.

REFERENCES

Asian Development Bank. "Asian Development Outlook 2020: Mobilizing Taxes for Development." Manila, April 2022. available at https://www.adb.org/sites/default/files/publication/784041/ado2022.pdf, last accessed on 27 December 2022.

Black, R. et al. "Environment of Peace: Security in a New Era of Risk." *Stockholm International Peace Research Institute*, (2022) Stockholm, available at https://sipri.org/sites/default/files/2022-05/environment_of_peace_security_in_a_new_era_of_risk_0.pdf, last accessed on 27 December 2022.

Besset, Manon; Edward J. Anthony; Philippe Dussouillez, and Marc Goichot. "The impact of Cyclone Nargis on the Ayeyarwady (Irrawaddy) River delta shoreline and near shore zone (Myanmar): Towards degraded delta resilience?" *Comptes Rendus Geoscience*, Volume 349, Issues 6-7 (October–November 2017), 238-247.

Climate Action Tracker (CAT). "Temperatures." Last updated on 9 November 2021, available at https://climateactiontracker.org/global/temperatures/, last accessed on 27 December 2022.

Cattiaux, Julien and Aurélien Ribes. 2018. "Defining Single Extreme Weather Events in a Climate Perspective." *Bulletin of the American Meteorological Society*, Volume 99, Issue 8 (01 August 2018), 1557-1568. https://journals.ametsoc.org/view/journals/bams/99/8/bams-d-17-

0281.1.xml, last accessed on 27 December 2022.

Department of Defence (DOD). "2014 Quadrennial Defence Review." United States of America (USA), 04 March 2014, available at https://www.acq.osd.mil/ncbdp/docs/2014_Quadrennial_Defense_Review.pdf, last accessed on 27 December 2022.

Duncan, Kiana. "Coup, Covid, climate: the triple threat chasing citizens from Myanmar's rice bowl." *The Guardian*, 21 July 2022, available at https://www.theguardian.com/world/2022/jul/21/coup-covid-climate-the-triple-threat-chasing-citizens-from-myanmars-rice-bowl, last accessed on 27 December 2022.

Derville, Thomas et al. "Climate Activism: Assessing Civil Society Engagement in Myanmar." ActionAid. December 2020, available at https://myanmar.actionaid.org/sites/myanmar/files/publications/Climate%20Activism%20A%20civil%20society%20engagement%20assessment%20in%20Myanmar_Eng.pdf, last accessed on 27 December 2022.

Eckstein, David; Vera Kunzel, and Laura Schafer. "Global Climate Risk Index 2021: Who Suffers Most From Extreme Weather Events? Weather-Related Loss Events in 2019 and 2000-2019." Briefing Paper (2022) German Watch, available at https://www.germanwatch.org/sites/default/files/Global%20Climate%20Risk%20Index%202021_2.pdf, last accessed on 27 December 2022.

Forest Trends. "Myanmar's Timber Trade One Year Since the Coup: The Impact of International Sanctions." Report. Forest Policy Trade and Finance Initiative. March 2022. available at https://www.forest-trends.org/wp-content/uploads/2022/03/Forest-Trends_Myanmars-Timber-Trade-One-Year-Since-the-Coup.pdf, last accessed on 27 December 2022.

Global Environment Facility (GEF). 2022. "Country-At-A-Glance." https://www.thegef.org/projects-operations/country-profiles/myanmar

Global Witness. "Myanmar's poisoned mountains." 9 August 2022, available at https://www.globalwitness.org/en/campaigns/natural-resource-governance/myanmars-poisoned-mountains/, last accessed on 27 December 2022.

Global Witness. "Jade & Conflict: Myanmar's Big Secret." Report. June 2021, available at https://www.globalwitness.org/en/campaigns/natural-resource-governance/jade-and-conflict-myanmars-vicious-circle/, last accessed on 27 December 2022.

Global Witness. "Jade: Myanmar's Vicious Circle." Report. 23 October 2015, available at https://www.globalwitness.org/en/campaigns/oil-gas-and-mining/myanmarjade/, last accessed on 27 December 2022.

Herridge, David F. et al. "The cropping systems of the Central Dry Zone of Myanmar: productivity 2 constraints and possible solutions." *Agricultural Systems,* Volume 169 (February 2019), 31-40, available at https://www.sciencedirect.com/science/article/abs/pii/S0308521X18305778, last accessed on 27 December 2022.

Horton, R. et al. "Assessing Climate Risk in Myanmar." New York, USA: Centre for Climate Systems Research at Columbia University, WWF-US and WWF-Myanmar, (2016) available at https://unhabitat.org/sites/default/files/2019/10/assessing-climate-risk-in-myanmar_technical-report.pdf, last accessed on 27 December 2022.

Kapoor, Aditi et al. *Climate Change Impacts on Health and Livelihoods.* Red Cross Red Crescent Climate Centre. April 2021, available at https://www.climatecentre.org/wp-content/uploads/RCRC_IFRC-Country-assessments-MYANMAR_corrected.pdf, last accessed on 27 December 2022.

Liu, John and Rory Wallace. "Climate danger grows in 'vulnerable' Myanmar after military coup." *Al Jazeera*, 01 December 2021, available at https://www.aljazeera.com/news/2021/12/1/myanmar-climate, last accessed on 27 December 2022.

Mekong Migration Network (MMN) and Asian Migrant Centre (AMC). "Climate Change and Migration: Exploring the Impacts of Climate Change on People's Livelihoods and Migration in the Greater Mekong Sub-region (GMS)." 05 June 2013, available at http://

www.mekongmigration.org/wp-content/uploads/2019/03/CC-M-Report-Final-1.pdf, last accessed on 27 December 2022.

National University of Singapore (NUS). "Over 60 per cent of Myanmar's mangroves deforested in the last 20 years." *NUS News*, 03 March 2020, available at https://news.nus.edu.sg/over-60-per-cent-of-myanmars-mangroves-deforested-in-the-last-20-years/, last accessed on 27 December 2022.

Ravilious, Kate. "When will the world reach 1.5C of global heating?" *The Guardian*, 05 April 2022, available at https://www.theguardian.com/environment/2022/apr/05/when-will-world-reach-global-heating-limit-ipcc-climate-crisis, last accessed on 27 December 2022.

The Republic of the Union of Myanmar. "Nationally Determined Contribution." July 2021, available at https://unfccc.int/sites/default/files/NDC/2022-06/Myanmar%20Updated %20%20 NDC%20July%202021.pdf, last accessed on 27 December 2022.

The Republic of the Union of Myanmar. 2019a. "The Myanmar Climate Change Policy (2019)." available at https://unhabitat.org.mm/wp-content/uploads/2019/06/MCCP_2019.pdf, last accessed on 27 December 2022.

____ 2019b. "Myanmar Climate Change Master Plan (2018-2030)." available at https://myanmar.un.org/sites/default/files/2019-11/Myanmar%20Climate%20Change%20master %20plan.pdf, last accessed on 27 December 2022.

____ 2019c. "Myanmar Climate Change Master Plan (2018–2030)." available at https://unhabitat.org/sites/default/files/2019/10/mccmp_eng_ready-to-print_27-may-2019.pdf, last accessed on 27 December 2022.

____ 2012a. "Myanmar's National Adaptation Programme of Action (NAPA) to Climate Change." available at https://unfccc.int/resource/docs/napa/mmr01.pdf, last accessed on 27 December 2022.

_____ 2012b. "Myanmar's National Adaptation Programme of Action (NAPA) to Climate Change." available at https://unfccc.int/resource/docs/napa/mmr01.pdf, last accessed on 27 December 2022.

The CNA Corporation. "National Security and the Threat of Climate Change." CNA Corporation. CNA-MAB. National Security and the Threat of Climate Change. CNA Corporation (Alexandria, Virginia). 2007.

United Nations Development Programme (UNDP). "Climate Finance for Sustaining Peace." New York, 2021, available at https://climatepromise.undp.org/sites/default/files/research_report_document/UNDP-Climate-Finance-for-Sustaining-Peace-V2.pdf, last accessed on 27 December 2022.

World Meteorological Organization (WMO). "Four key climate change indicators break records in 2021." Press Release No. 18052022, 18 May 2022, available at https://public.wmo.int/en/media/press-release/four-key-climate-change-indicators-break-records-2021, last accessed on 27 December 2022.

World Meteorological Organization (WMO). "WMO update: 50:50 chance of global temperature temporarily reaching 1.5°C threshold in next five years." Press release. No. 09052022, 09 May 2022, available at https://public.wmo.int/en/media/press-release/wmo-update-5050-chance-of-global-temperature-temporarily-reaching-15%C2%B0c-threshold, last accessed on 27 December 2022.

Win, Thin Lei. "UN suspends climate work with Myanmar government following military coup." *Climate Home News*, 3 March 2021, available at https://www.climatechangenews.com/2021/03/03/un-suspends-climate-work-myanmar-government-following-military-coup/, last accessed on 27 December 2022.

Zhang, Hongpei and Li Xuanmin. "Myanmar rare earths heading toward China encounter shipment obstacles amid upheaval." *Global Times*, 21 March 2021, available at https://www.globaltimes.cn/page/202103/1218983.shtml, last accessed on 27 December 2022.

13

Consistent Challenge of Narcotic Substances in Myanmar

Anurag Sharma

ABSTRACT

Narco-trafficking is one of the 'Non-Traditional Security (NTS)' threats that hover over the South Asian/Southeast Asian region. The huge profit margins, nearly hundreds of per cent, have made the narcotic business the most lucrative means of generating illicit money to finance terrorist activities in the region. The nexus between drug cartels and insurgents/terrorists have proven to be a symbolic relationship to support the established routes for the trafficking of arms and drugs. Myanmar is the second-largest opium poppy grower in the world, wherein Shan State remains the centre of opium activities with around 83 per cent of poppy cultivation, and the remainder 17 per cent is in Kachin State (UNODC, 2022).

Myanmar's opium industry generates significant profits both inside and outside the country. Opium production significantly contributes to Myanmar's Gross Domestic Product (GDP), with around 25 per cent of the world's opium production. The latest findings place the value of opium in Myanmar at USD 0.5-1.1 billion. At the same time, heroin from Myanmar contributes significantly to the regional drug market, with over three million heroin users consuming approximately USD 10 billion of drugs each year (UNODC, 2022).

This chapter elaborates on the menace of narcotics and the challenge it poses to India-Myanmar relations. On 30 June 2022, the Tengnoupal battalion of Assam Rifles foiled a cross-border narcotics smuggling operation and seized 228 grams of WIY (World is Yours) tablets worth ₹ 10 lahks in the Khudengthabi area in Chandel district in Manipur. Likewise, on 02 July 2022, Assam Rifles personnel foiled narcotics smuggling of one lakh WIY tablets worth ₹ 5 crores at New Sangjong village in Chandel district in Manipur. Several incidents of narcotic consignment seizures, mainly in Manipur and Mizoram, among other North-East Indian States, support the theory of linkages between illicit drug trafficking and funding of insurgency in North-East India. In conclusion, this chapter highlights the measures implemented by India, jointly with Myanmar, to counter narco-trafficking and strengthen their bilateral relationship.

Introduction

Being one of the largest country in South-East Asia, Myanmar has an estimated population of 57 million as of 2022.[1] Along with the credit of being one of the largest country in South-East Asia, Myanmar is the world's second-largest opium poppy grower, after Afghanistan, producing nearly 25 per cent of the world's opium and has been the leading supplier of narcotic substances, including opium, to most of the South-East and East Asia countries. The history of opium production in Myanmar goes back to the Konbaung kingdom in 1750 when it was practised on a modest scale in Lower Burma, mainly for the consumption of foreign visitors or travellers.[2]

With the massive production of opium, Myanmar forms an imaginary Golden Triangle region, having Lao People's Democratic Republic (hereafter Laos) and the Kingdom of Thailand (hereafter Thailand) as its other member countries. However, Laos and Thailand managed to reduce the production and illicit trade of opium. In the case of Myanmar, the 2021 military coup and COVID-19, *aka* Wuhan virus/coronavirus pandemic, have adversely affected the socio-economic situation furthering the rise of opium cultivation in Myanmar. The political turmoil caused by the military coup in 2021 has been a gift for the narcotics-trafficking syndicates in Myanmar.

Based on anonymity, an official of the United Nations Office on Drugs and Crime (UNODC) stated that there had been a rise in the manufacturing of drugs and opium cultivation in Myanmar, notably in the Golden Triangle, as well as drug trafficking in South-East Asia and other regions.[3] According to a UNODC report cited by Reuters, law enforcement agencies in Laos, Thailand, and Myanmar seized 4.4 tonnes of crystal methamphetamine and at least 90 million methamphetamine tablets in January 2022, nearly a year after a military coup; the majority of the seized drugs were produced in the isolated border regions of the Shan State.[4]

Even before the military coup of 2021, the worrying scenario of opium cultivation and drug production in Myanmar was present. The trafficking of meth and other synthetic narcotics from Myanmar's Shan State was a problem for South and South-East Asia countries. Law-enforcement agencies from South-East Asian countries announced the seizure of 82.5 tonnes in 2017, around 127 tonnes in 2018, and a record 139 tonnes of methamphetamine in 2019.[5] In 2020, the number of drugs seized increased even more, setting a new high of 170 tonnes.[6] Following the February 2021 military coup, Aung San Suu Kyi, a former Myanmar state counsellor, and other National League for Democracy (NLD) leaders were detained. This tragic event was then followed by violent crackdowns on pro-democracy protesters and the collapse of the formal economy amid strikes, acts of civil disobedience, and growing violent opposition to junta rule.

The "Golden Triangle"

South Asia and South-East Asia consist of two imaginaries but the most prominent psychotropic substances producing geographical areas in the world—the Golden Crescent and the Golden Triangle. Along with Golden Crescent comprising Afghanistan, Iran, and Pakistan in the West, the Golden Triangle has been one of the largest opium-producing regions in the world, comprising three South-East Asian nations—Myanmar, Laos, and Thailand. The term 'Golden Triangle' was coined by the US Central Intelligence Agency (CIA)'s operative, referring to the area of approximately 950,000 sq. km., overlapping adjacent mountains of these three nations. The mountain region is a major producer of opium poppy, also known as *Papaver somniferum*.

Image 1: The "Golden Triangle"

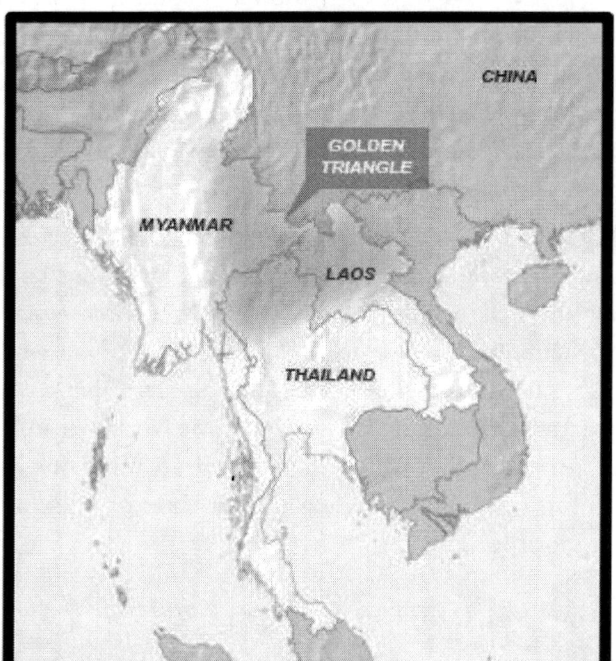

Source: Wikimedia Commons/VOA.

The Golden Triangle was the primary supplier of heroin, a narcotic substance derived from opium. Since the 1950s, Afghanistan has been leading the ranks of the largest opium producers in the world, followed by Myanmar. The demand for the majority of opium production in the South-East Asia region is supplied by Myanmar and, to some extent, by Laos. There are several estimated data about the amount of opium cultivation in Myanmar, especially in the Shan State; however, it will be difficult to confirm the reliability of those estimates. These estimates open several questions, such as why farmers are involved in opium production, how they manage to sell their opium production, and how much they earn from it.

Historically, the expansion of the Chinese Communist Party (CCP) and growing power in China also significantly impacted the cultivation of opium and the formation of the Golden Triangle. In the early 1950s, the CCP handed the opium cultivation monopoly to the KMT army in Burma's Shan State. The KMT or Kuomintang in Burma was Chinese troops who fled from CCP-controlled China to Burma after their defeat during the Chinese Civil War (1927-1949). At that time, Burma was a nation with a weak government post-independence. The Kuomintang took advantage of the situation and controlled the border area for enhancing opium production. KMT troops began charging heavy taxes on opium farmers; as a result, the farmers increased the production of opium to meet the demands. As per an estimate, the annual opium cultivation increased nearly twenty-fold, from 30 tons at the time of Burma's independence in 1948 to 600 tons in the mid-1950s.[7]

For several years, the Golden Triangle has remained a centre for the cultivation and production of more solid and lucrative narcotic substances, primarily methamphetamine, making the trijunction the world's largest producer and exporter of synthetic drugs.[8] Due to decades of political unrest and violence, most of Myanmar's borders are now lawless, leaving them open to exploitation by producers and cartels of illegal drugs. For long, the Myanmar military has been involved in an armed conflict with ethnic armed organisations because opium production, processing, and distribution in that country are strongly linked to ethnic armed minority groups.[9]

Thriving Business of Drugs in Myanmar

The conflict or insurgencies in Myanmar has become routine since its independence in 1948. These conflicts mainly comprise ethnic armed groups fighting with Myanmar's forces—the *Tatmadaw*—demanding self-determination. From 1948 to the present, the country witnessed six significant phases of conflict and military coups, including post-independence insurgencies (1948-1962), the Ne Win period (1962-1988), the "8888" Uprising, the State Peace and Development Council (SPDC) rule (1988-2011), the election of a democratic government (2011-2021), and finally, the 2021 military coup with the resurgence of violence in the country. By the 1970s and late 1980s, Myanmar had become a significant producer of processed heroin for export and trafficking through Thailand to Hong Kong, with additional destinations in North America and Australia.

The Golden Triangle was born from the convergence of opium cultivation and drug processing in Shan State, Western Laos, and northern Thailand. During the 1970s and 1980s, the opium and heroin trade witnessed a competition for dominance among drug kingpins, starting with the Kuomintang, then the ethnic Kokang warlord,—Lo Hsing-Han, and later with the Sino-Shan rebel leader and local militia commander, Khun Sa.[10] However, after the surrender of Khun Sa to the Burmese/Myanmar authorities in the mid-1990s and the collapse of Khun Sa's Mong Tai Army (MTA),[11] the Thailand trafficking route (part of the Golden Triangle) faced challenges due to disruption.

Among the Golden Triangle's areas, the Wa area in the North-East of Shan State in Myanmar has emerged as the most extensive opium-producing area in the world, with a trade estimated to be worth tens of billions of dollars per year. Significant parts of the Shan State are controlled by armed ethnic groups, not the Myanmar military or police.[12] Therefore, few people only may have access to the area. In April-May 2020, authorities in Myanmar declared Asia's biggest-ever counter-drug operation and seizure of around 193 million methamphetamine pills, hundreds of kilograms of heroin-laced crystal methamphetamine, and over 162,000 litres and 35.5 tonnes of drug precursors, as well as sophisticated machinery for making drugs.[13] As mentioned earlier, the Shan State of Myanmar contributed significantly to Myanmar's opium poppy cultivation at 83 per cent of the national total.

The *Myanmar Opium Survey: Cultivation, Production and Implications,* a report prepared by the United Nations Office of Drugs and Crime (UNODC), collected and analysed the data related to opium cultivation before the military coup in February 2021. According to the analysed information, there was a two per cent increase in cultivated area from 29,500 hectares (ha) to 30,200 ha, as well as a four per cent increase in yield to 423 metric tonnes (MT).[14] "The data reflected scenarios prior to the military coup, i.e., 01 February 2021, but it must be viewed in the context of Myanmar's ongoing economic crisis and a shrinking economy, as well as the instability faced by farmers engaged in opium cultivation, where opium earnings are traditional and primarily crisis proof employer," said the UNODC Regional Representative, Jeremy Douglas.

Image 2: Opium Cultivation (in hectares) in Myanmar from 1996-2021

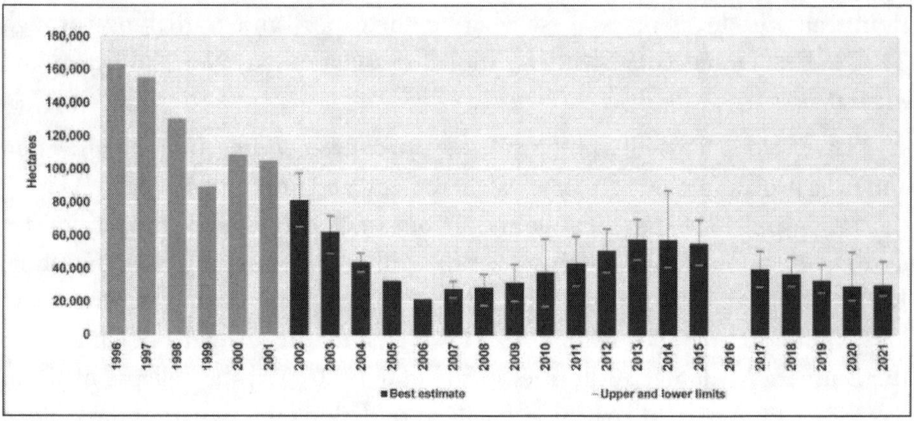

Source: UNODC.

Image 2, *Opium Cultivation in Myanmar* shows the production of opium from 1996 to the estimated figures for 2021. As highlighted in the image, Myanmar decided to become an 'opium-free' country by 2014,[15] decreasing opium cultivation from around 160,000 ha in 1996 to around 90,000 ha in 1999. Opium cultivation experienced a significant fall from 1996 to 2006. The government's strategy of initially subordinating counter-narcotics while establishing stable ceasefires with the majority of ethnic armed groups actively involved in the economy generated by opium production was the reason for the decline rate from 1996 to 2006. The combined change in the dynamics of the regional and global drug markets resulted in a significant decrease in illicit opium cultivation and, as a result, the opium economy in Myanmar. However, from 2006 to 2014, the production increased, reaching 60,000 ha in 2014 as opposed to 21,000 ha in 2006. The growing heroin demand across Asia helped to fuel opium cultivation. estimates have fluctuated between 2011 and 2021, which may be the consequence of a government attempt to outlaw opium growing as part of political reform after a long period of the military rule until 2011.

Although opium cultivation is a significant factor, Myanmar is one of the world's largest methamphetamine, also known as meth, producers. Because of its border sharing with India and China—two major chemical-producing nations in South and South-East Asia, respectively, the trafficking or supply of methamphetamine from Myanmar is one of the challenges for other South Asian and South-East Asian countries such as India and Bangladesh, where the market of narcotic psychotropic substances is expanding. According to estimated data from the United Nations Office of Drugs and Crime (UNODC), a record quantity of methamphetamine, approximately 172 tons, was seized in East and South-East Asia in 2021, with over a billion methamphetamine tablets. Methamphetamine/crystalline methamphetamine seizures on a minor scale were made in 2021, including 1.5 kg in October 2021 and three seizures of 01 kg each in November 2021. As of April 2022, more than 5.6 million methamphetamine tablets and over 33.6 kilograms of crystalline methamphetamine were taken into custody.[16]

Along with a strong impact on the country's social, economic, and political sphere, the military coup of February 2021 significantly impacted opium production and drug trade/trafficking. Referring to the rise in opium cultivation, Richard Horsey, a senior adviser of Myanmar issues at the International Crisis Group (ICG), said that "the military coup has been a win-win for the drug cartels. 'Super-labs' producing ice (crystal meth) have gone into overdrive irrespective whether they are run by pro-military militias or anti-military armed groups."[17] The UNODC's most recent report, *Myanmar Opium Survey 2022: Cultivation, Production and Implications*, examined production statistics post-military coup in 2021. According to the data, in 2022,[18] the potential yield of opium increased by 88 per cent while the cultivated area increased by 33 per cent (approximately 40,100 hectares) compared to the previous year. The increase in opium yield and cultivation indicates that Myanmar's opium-based economy has grown significantly. The Shan state saw the highest rise in cultivated hectares, with an increase of 10,000 hectares (around 39 per cent) compared to the statistics from 2021. The data also highlighted significant increases being reported in North and South Shan (57 per cent and 50 per cent, respectively), Chin (14 per cent), East Shan (11 per cent), and Kayah (6 per cent). Merely an increase of three per cent was observed in Kachin State, which is considered to have significant stability in cultivation.

Myanmar's post-coup situation of civil conflict and economic crisis weakened the country's drug enforcement capacity and gave drug cartels a free hand. The coup diverted the attention of law enforcement agencies attention away from their respective anti-drug operations, creating an ideal environment for drug cartels or organisations to thrive in gaps where the authorities did not have an easy approach.[19] Along with other factors that have contributed to the proliferation of drug production over time, elements of the military regime are deeply involved in and make monitoring the production and trade of narcotic substances within and outside Myanmar difficult.

Impact of Narcotics on Socio-economic Spheres

Drug abuse facilitated by the narcotic trade affects public health and safety immensely and threatens the smooth activities of the society. Drug abuse not only affects the health of the abuser, but also affects the society in which an individual sustains her/his livelihood. Although there is a lack of official statistics on drug abuse in Shan State, an estimate suggests that approximately 20 per cent of the region's youth are using drugs, and some reports also state that children are trafficked for work in Thailand to support their parents' drug habits.[20] Women in Myanmar consume drugs for a variety of reasons, including a kind of leisure, to help them do challenging work or to forget painful or upsetting events. Although many cases of female drug users are not troublesome, they suffer social and economic problems, such as being criminalised. One of the cases in which a woman briefly highlighted various aspects related to the use of drugs is highlighted below:

> "*There are five to six women drug users in my village; some mothers are also using it. Most of them are daily wage workers. When the husband uses drugs, the wife also starts using. They use drugs together with their friends. Some women started using because their families did not take care of them. There are instances that the woman has sexual relations with the man to get the drugs for free. The community avoids drug users. So, they then use more drugs and finally, their mental situation becomes abnormal.*" (**Female youth *leader, Lamine Town, Mon State)***[21]

Although there is a paucity of official and accurate data on drug usage among women in Myanmar, there are signs which highlight that it is significantly less common than it is among men. Children are victims of the emotional and socio-economic harms brought on by their parents' imprisonment due to drug abuse.

In the agricultural sector, opium cultivation offers job opportunities to migrant workers and small-scale farmers with minimal agricultural training and education. Additionally, processing the opium plant to make drugs for the illicit market provides laboratory operators, wholesale and retail distributors, and drug peddlers with the most accessible mode of earning income.[22]

When it comes to nations like Myanmar, where illegal opium cultivation and unemployment are high; these employment prospects may substantially impact some economic sectors. Although it has been stated that illicit opium cultivation and trade provide employment opportunities and contribute to the economy in the short term, there is a lack of evidence to support the phenomenon. There are no indicators available to support the claim that the expansion of illicit opium cultivation has resulted in long-term economic improvement and contributed to broader development indicators at the national level.

Several international organisations concluded after analysing some data that countries involved in illicit opium cultivation have experienced a drop in economic growth over time. While opium production in Myanmar rose ten-fold in the 1980s, the country's GDP growth was simultaneously the lowest in the area. Contrarily, opium cultivation decreased by 30 per cent in the 1990s as GDP growth rates grew noticeably.[23] This study may not be a definitive example showing how the drop in overall economic growth is related to rising illicit drug production. Opium cultivation, however, can be regarded as one of the many diverse elements that affect Myanmar's economy. Due to the nation's corrupt leadership and administrative structure, political and economic instability may increase opium production and drug trafficking.

The connection between narcotic substances' production and conflict is well-known. The narcotic trade often becomes the primary income source to fuel insurgencies as these groups require money to acquire arms and ammunition, furthering logistic support. In return, these drug networks or cartels require protection, creating a symbiotic relationship between the cartels and the insurgent groups. In addition to the previously mentioned terrorism and organised crime, the destabilisation of the government and administrative system allowed the illegal drug cartels to finance and influence the country's political establishment.

Table 1: Yearly approved/permitted amount of Foreign Investment in Myanmar

Timeline	*2018-2019*	*2019-2020*	*2020-2021*	*2021-2022*
Amount (in USD million)	4,158.5	4,881	3,791.4	647.1

Source: DICA (dica.gov.mm).

In Table 1, the figures highlight the trend of foreign investment (permitted or approved) in Myanmar. According to the compilation provided by Myanmar's Directorate of Investment and Company Administration (DICA), foreign investment in Myanmar rose by USD 722.5 million from USD 4,158.5 million during 2018-2020. Political and public safety in Myanmar is in a precarious position due to the current political unpredictability, which may or may not lead to a return to normalcy. The international sanctions and other related factors will also harm foreign investments, thus limiting the possibility of a prosperous economic environment in Myanmar. In such situations, Myanmar has seen a decline in the revenue it receives in foreign currencies, which is used to bolster its economy.

Concerns for India

Myanmar remains a top priority for India due to its strategic and security issues and proximity to North-East India. India and Myanmar share a significantly long border of approximately 1,643 km, with the Indian States—Arunachal Pradesh (520 km), Nagaland (215 km), Manipur (398 km) and Mizoram (510 km), and from Kachin State, Sagaing Region and Chin State in Myanmar. The long and porous border with Myanmar provides an entry point for drugs such as Ya Ba and heroin. Consignments of heroin and ATS (Amphetamine Type Stimulant) produced in the Golden Triangle, mainly Myanmar, are trafficked into India through the neighbouring States of Mizoram, Manipur, and Nagaland from Bhamo, Lashio, and Mandalay. Myanmar-originated heroin and methamphetamine enter India through two entry points—Moreh in Manipur and Champai in Mizoram.[24]

A few reports also suggested that opium cultivated in Manipur and Mizoram along the border area with Myanmar is also transported to different areas of the Golden Triangle[25] and processed in the labs controlled by rogue elements of the Myanmar military and other organisations. The end-product in the form of heroin is sent back to India. "It is a profitable venture, and the bulk of the produce [cultivated opium] transported to the laboratories [in Myanmar] located at a distance not far from the India-Myanmar border. Moreover, some of these facilities have the "unspoken" support of rogue elements of the Myanmar military and insurgents as it means extra income for them," said an official based on anonymity.[26]

Concerns have also been raised about the trafficking of Yaba pills from Myanmar to Bangladesh via India. The Rohingya crisis in Myanmar significantly aided the drug trade, particularly the trafficking of Yaba pills. According to estimates, drug peddlers and local gangs are using the Rohingya refugee camps in Bangladesh's Cox Bazaar to smuggle Yaba pills into the country. As they lack a source of income, the Rohingyas are more likely to be recruited by drug peddlers or smugglers.[27] For India, countering narcotics trafficking across the border remains a severe challenge due to the porous border, the size of the country and the established pharmaceutical industry. Several incidents of narcotic substance seizure, including Yaba tablets, along the India-Myanmar border areas have been reported.

In May 2022, 44.5 kilograms of Yaba tablets worth ₹ 9 crore were seized from the Tengnoupal district of Manipur[28] and at least 1.26 kilogram of 'brown sugar'/ heroin packed in soap cases worth ₹ 2.52 crore in July 2022 were seized from a militant of the Kanglei Yawol Kanna Lup (KYKL) group in Imphal East district of Manipur.[29] The evolution of technology, as well as the desire of drug peddlers to expand their business model through the use of bitcoins, complicates matters for Indian law enforcement agencies. The anonymity feature of the dark web makes it challenging for law enforcement to identify and track the trail of drugs and money flow in the form of bitcoins. In 2021, Indian law enforcement officers arrested a Bengaluru-based hacker for obtaining narcotic substances through the dark web. He used to hack into bitcoin exchanges and poker websites to pay for drugs, and when he was apprehended, police seized ₹ 9 crore from him.[30]

Way Forward for Myanmar: Steps to Counter Drug Challenge

As per the reports of the United Nations Office on Drugs and Crime (UNODC), until 1998, Laos had been the third-largest opium producer country in the world, but due to stringent policies and commitment to eradication efforts, the Government of Laos managed to reduce opium cultivation to marginal levels.[31] Similarly, the coordinated efforts between the Royal Family, the Government and Non-Governmental Organisations (NGOs) have almost entirely eradicated the narcotic trade in opium. As per the strategy to counter the narcotic substance problem, opium cultivation was replaced with other crops. The collaborative efforts of all stakeholders in Thailand focussed on educating people about the menace of drugs, establishing strong law enforcement measures and building upon an alternative income channel in fruit production. As a result, Thailand has become one of the leading examples of Alternative Livelihood Development (ALD).

In the case of Myanmar, the drug trade has fuelled a political economy that is detrimental to stability and security. The armed ethnic groups controlling the narcotics production and cultivation areas are least interested in disarming. Officials were bought off by organised crime groups in exchange for security and assistance and turned a blind eye to the drug trade. Because the military in Myanmar has control over militias and other paramilitary organisations and makes money off the drug trade, it will also be less motivated to combat the problem of drug trafficking.[32]

Opium Replacement: An Alternative to Counter-Opium Production

As the term suggests, opium replacement refers to replacing or substituting opium poppy crops with non-narcotic alternatives, subject to environmental conditions. The concept was first implemented in Thailand, one of the nations of the Golden Triangle. The UN, under the Sustainable Development Goals (SDG) Good Practices framework, identified these projects as "Sustainable Alternative Livelihoods (SAL)". The Sustainability Alternative Livelihoods (SAL) project was launched in the Golden Triangle in the late 1980s. Through the project's efforts to address poverty and unemployment, the opium cultivation region was converted into a reforested area. According to data from 2019, a total of 10,617 people in 29 villages of the Doi Tung area covered by the project's operations included provided healthcare, education, and alternative livelihood options for opium addicts. In order to continue the sustainable development programme for local employment and climate change adaptation and mitigation measures, the project is currently extending the contract with Thailand's Department of Forestry until 2051, as the original contract to use the land expired in 2021.[33] Along with other measures mentioned, the respective governments must bring in the social security umbrella to protect the unemployed, who are vulnerable to taking up forced jobs, including narco-trafficking.

ENDNOTES

1. "Population-Burma", *The World Factbook—Central Intelligence Agency,* available at https://www.cia.gov/the-world-factbook/countries/burma/summaries, last accessed on 02 November 2022
2. Helen James, *Security and Sustainable Development in Myanmar/Burma* (London: Routledge, 2006), pg. 94.
3. Wongcha-um, Panu and Tom Allard, "Drug trafficking surging in year since Myanmar coup", *Reuters,* 02 February 2022, available at https://www.reuters.com/world/asia-pacific/drug-trafficking-surging-year-since-myanmar-coup-2022-02-01/, last accessed on 02 November 2022.
4. Ibid.
5. "Asian drug lords likely producing precursor chemicals in Golden Triangle", *Reuters,* 12 February 2021, available at https://www.reuters.com/article/us-asia-drugs-idUSKBN2AC0KF, last accessed on 02 November 2022
6. Sebastian Strangio, "Laos seizes record meth haul amid regional production boom", *The Diplomat,* 16 July 2021, available at https://thediplomat.com/2021/07/laos-seizes-record-meth-haul-amid-regional-production-boom/, last accessed on 02 November 2022
7. Bertil Lintner, "Heroin and Highland Insurgency in the Golden Triangle". In *War on Drugs: Studies in the failure of US narcotics policy,* edited by Alferd W. McCOy and Alan A. (Colorado: Routledge, 1993), 288; Andrew Marshall, "An overview of the Kuomintang in Burma (1950-1961)", *Boot Camp and Military Fitness Institute,* 29 September 2021, available at https://bootcampmilitaryfitnessinstitute.com/2021/09/29/an-overview-of-the-kuomintang-in-burma-1950-1961/, last accessed on 01 November 2022
8. "Fire and Ice: Conflict and Drugs in Myanmar's Shan State", *International Crisis Group,* Report No. 299, 08 January 2019, available at https://icg-prod.s3.amazonaws.com/299-fire-

and-ice.pdf, last accessed on 02 November 2022

9. Grant Peck, "1B meth pills: East, Southeast Asia drug industry hits ominous peak", *The Diplomat,* 30 May 2022, available at https://thediplomat.com/2022/05/1b-meth-pills-east-southeast-asia-drug-industry-hits-ominous-peak/, last accessed on 02 November 2022
10. "Fire and Ice: conflict and drugs in Myanmar's Shan State", *Crisis Group,* 08 January 2019, available at https://www.crisisgroup.org/asia/south-east-asia/myanmar/299-fire-and-ice-conflict-and-drugs-myanmars-shan-state, last accessed on 09 December 2022
11. Chin, Ko-lin and Sheldon X Zhang, "The Chinese Connection: Cross-border Drug Trafficking between Myanmar and China", *US Department of Justice,* April 2007, available at https://www.ojp.gov/pdffiles1/nij/grants/218254.pdf, last accessed on 09 December 2022
12. "Myanmar's Shan State becoming world's biggest meth producer", *CTN News,* 05 July 2019, available at https://www.chiangraitimes.com/asean/myanmars-shan-state-becoming-worlds-biggest-meth-producer/, last accessed on 02 November 2022
13. Tom Allard, "Huge fentanyl haul seized in Asia's biggest-ever drugs bust", *Reuters,* 18 May 2020, available at https://www.reuters.com/article/myanmar-drugs-exclusive-idINKBN22 U0PH, last accessed on 02 November 2022
14. "UNODC Report- signs of increased opium production in Myanmar", *UNODC Regional Office for Southeast Asia and the Pacific,* 08 April 2022, available at https://www.unodc.org/roseap/en/myanmar/2022/04/myanmar-opium-survey-report/story.html, last accessed on 02 November 2022
15. Todd Pitman, "UN says Myanmar opium production on rise," *The Seattle Times,* 31 October 2012, available at https://www.seattletimes.com/nation-world/un-says-myanmar-opium-production-on-rise/, last accessed on 02 November 2022
16. Border Guard Bangladesh official Facebook account, October, November, and December 2021, and April 2022, available at https://www.facebook.com/permalink.php?story_fbid=1455533771486097&id=241407426232077; https://www.facebook.com/permalink. php?story_fbid=1489042204801920&id=241407426232077; https://www.facebook.com/permalink.php?story_fbid=1491689214537219&id=241407426232077; https://www.facebook.com/permalink.php?story_fbid=1492928444413296&id=241407426232077; https://www.facebook.com/BorderGuardBangladeshNews/posts/363118152512946
17. Vijitra Duangdee, "Meth 'Super Labs' said to thrive in Myanmar Coup Chaos, Spilling Drugs Across Mekong", *Voice of America,* 09 September 2021, available at https://www.voanews.com/a/meth-super-labs-said-to-thrive-in-myanmar-coup-chaos-spilling-drugs-across-mekong/6219494.html, last accessed on 11 February 2023.
18. "Myanmar Opium Survey 2022: Cultivation, Production, and Implications", *United Nations Office on Drugs and Crime,* 27 January 2023, available at https://www.unodc.org/roseap/uploads/documents/Publications/2023/Myanmar_Opium_Survey_2022.pdf , last accessed on 11 February 2023
19. John Reed, "How Myanmar's coup fuelled a rise in the illegal drugs trade", *The Irish Times,* 24 August 2021, available at https://www.irishtimes.com/news/world/asia-pacific/how-myanmar-s-coup-fuelled-a-rise-in-the-illegal-drugs-trade-1.4653998, last accessed on 11 February 2023.
20. "Poverty, drugs, and violence against women: breaking the chain in Myanmar", *United Nations Population Fund (UNFPA),* 15 January 2016, available at https://asiapacific.unfpa.org/en/news/poverty-drugs-and-violence-against-women-breaking-chain-myanmar, last accessed on 10 December 2022.
21. Dania Putri et al. "Women and Drugs in Myanmar", *Transnational Institute,* February 2022, available at https://www.tni.org/files/publication-downloads/primer_womenanddrugs _ hires.pdf , Last, accessed on 11 December 2022.

22. Stepanova, Ekaterina. "Addressing drugs and conflicts in Myanmar: who will support alternative development?", *SIPRI,* June 2009, available at https://www.sipri.org/sites/default/files/files/misc/SIPRIPB0906.pdf, last accessed on 02 November 2022
23. "Illicit drugs and economic development", *International Narcotics Control Board,* 2002, available at https://www.incb.org/documents/Publications/AnnualReports/AR2002/AR_02_Chapter_I.pdf, last accessed on 02 November 2022
24. Pushpita Das, "Security Challenges and the Management of the India-Myanmar Border", *Strategic Analysis,* Vol. 42, No.6 (2018), pp. 578-94, available at https://www.tandfonline.com/doi/pdf/10.1080/09700161.2018.1557932, last accessed on 02 November 2022
25. Ibid.
26. Rajeev Bhattacharya, "Narcotics from Myanmar still flowing into India's Northeast despite crackdown", *The Irrawaddy,* 09 March 2022, available at https://www.irrawaddy.com/opinion/guest-column/narcotics-from-myanmar-still-flowing-into-indias-northeast-despite-crackdown.html, last accessed on 02 November 2022
27. Michael Van Ginkel, "Rohingya refugees smuggle drugs for insurgents in Myanmar", *New Security Beat,* 25 May 2020, available at https://www.newsecuritybeat.org/2020/05/rohingya-refugees-smuggle-drugs-insurgents-myanmar/, last accessed on 02 November 2022
28. Saroj Kumar K. Sharma, "Rs 9 crore seized from two peddlers in Manipur", *The Times of India,* 25 May 2022, available at https://timesofindia.indiatimes.com/city/imphal/9crore-drugs-seized-from-two-peddlers-in-manipur/articleshow/91776020.cms, last accessed on 02 November 2022
29. Vangamla K S. Salle, "Manipur: Insurgent, drug peddler arrested in separate ops", *East Mojo,* 14 July 2022, available at https://www.eastmojo.com/manipur/2022/07/14/manipur-insurgent-drug-peddler-arrested-in-separate-ops/, last accessed on 02 November 2022
30. "Dark web, drugs, and bitcoins send Bengaluru police into a tizzy", *Hindustan Times,* 22 February 2021, available at https://www.hindustantimes.com/cities/bengaluru-news/dark-web-drugs-and-bitcoins-send-bengaluru-police-into-a-tizzy-101613964407423.html, last accessed on 02 November 2022
31. "Lao People's Democratic Republic", *United Nations Office on Drugs and Crime,* available at https://www.unodc.org/unodc/en/alternative-development/laos.html, last accessed on 02 November 2022
32. "Fire and ice: conflict and drugs in Myanmar's Shan State", *International Crisis Group,* Report No. 299, 08 January 2019, available at https://www.crisisgroup.org/asia/south-east-asia/myanmar/299-fire-and-ice-conflict-and-drugs-myanmars-shan-state, last accessed on 02 November 2022
33. "Sustainable Alternative Livelihood Development: Doi Tung Development Project, Thailand", *United Nations Department of Economic and Social Affairs,* available at https://sdgs.un.org/partnerships/sustainable-alternative-livelihood-development-doi-tung-development-project-thailand, last accessed on 02 November 2022

SECTION FOUR

Myanmar's Relations with Major Partners

14

China's Regional Quest: Relations with Myanmar

Prof Srikanth Kondapalli

ABSTRACT

China's relations with Myanmar are undergoing major transformations in light of Beijing's quest to become a regional and global leader. Overwhelmed by its priority projects of the Belt and Road Initiative and access to the Indian Ocean Region through an economic corridor but with strategic implications, China has been assiduously building its relations with Myanmar. Despite major political changes in Myanmar—such as the Rohingya crisis and the more recent military coup and repression since February 2021—China has been pushing through its agenda in the region as well as in Myanmar in order to become the dominant power. This chapter explores the efforts made by China to become the dominant power in Myanmar, reflected initially in economic, trade and investment arenas but extended into the political and security domains as well. It is argued here that before and after the February 2021 coup, China provided the much-needed shield to the military junta in the international and regional domain by opposing the sanctions and providing sustenance to the regime. However, such assistance is made with the objective of expanding China's interests in the region.

Introduction

China's relations with Myanmar are undergoing major transformations in light of Beijing's quest to become a regional and global leader as ordained by the 19th communist party congress in 2017. Although they trace their relations back to the 9th century Pyu kingdom, bilateral relations are complex in nature given Myanmar's non-aligned status and policy disruptions in China.[1] Historical differences exist with Mao Zedong alluding to the relations of tributary states with Myanmar in 1954 or the four wars waged in the 17th century during the Konbaung dynasty. Foremost, apart from stability in its South-Western regions, China has prioritised resource exploitation and the Belt and Road Initiative (BRI) since 2013. Prior to this, on 27 May 2011, both signed a "comprehensive strategic cooperative partnership" agreement. Myanmar plays a significant role in these two with abundant timber and minerals; besides, the BRI appeared in Myanmar as the China-Myanmar Economic Corridor (CMEC) after the Bangladesh-China-India-Myanmar (Kunming) Initiative took a long time to fructify. However, Myanmar also demands diplomatic and political attention from China, given the civil war, the February 2021 military coup and dislodging of the democratic forces led by Aug San Su Kyi and others.[2]

While China's relations with the military junta were consolidated with the Tiananmen Square incident in Beijing in 1989 and the military coup in 1988 in Myanmar, the recent period provided new challenges and opportunities for China. For instance, the recent attacks on Chinese businesses across the country did affect the bilateral relations as with the Rohingya crisis.[3] However, in the backdrop of the spread of the pandemic, the Russian invasion of Ukraine, and the strengthening of the Indo-Pacific and the QUAD recently, China is getting closer to Myanmar in several areas.[4] In fact, during the visit of Myanmar Foreign Minister Wunna Maung Lwin to Beijing in April 2022, China's foreign minister Wang Yi stated that "No matter how the situation changes, China will support Myanmar in safeguarding its sovereignty, independence and territorial integrity, and in exploring a development path suited to its national conditions".[5]

China is keen to strengthen its relations with Myanmar/Burma which is the second largest country in Southeast Asia (after Indonesia) and is also part of the ten-member Association of Southeast Asian Nations (ASEAN) grouping since 1997, although the ASEAN was established in 1967 with focus on the Treaty of Amity and Cooperation and nuclear-weapon-free zone tenets.[6] In 2014, Myanmar chaired the ASEAN and played a significant role.[7] In the post-coup period, when the ASEAN was reluctant to allow Myanmar into its deliberations, China approached the Southeast Asian countries to resolve issues amicably. As a non-contestant in the South China Sea islands sovereignty dispute, Myanmar could take sides with China, besides its role in countering the USA or other "extra-regional" powers in the region. These are very useful in pushing China's influence in the region.

Bilateral Relations

However, while multilateral institutions are important for China, it is at the bilateral level that it has invested heavily in Myanmar as with the other countries. Myanmar's geographical location has attracted China enormously since the reform programme was begun in the late 1970s. Myanmar straddles South and South-East Asia with important sea lanes of communications in the Bay of Bengal connecting to the Andaman, Gulf of Thailand, and the Straits of Malacca with over 2,000 kilometres of coastline. China has ambitions to bypass the Straits of the Malacca through the Kra Isthmus project and overcome its "Malacca dilemma" of importing energy resources securely.[8] China's "*qiaotou*" [bridgehead] strategy of connecting to the Indian Ocean could be realised by cooperating with Myanmar.

An energy pipeline was constructed from China's South-Western province of Yunnan to the coast of the Bay of Bengal with an estimated investment of about USD 2 billion. Today, significant transportation of energy resources is done through this pipeline, providing much-needed support to the South-Western regions of China, besides earning revenues for Myanmar.

Territorial dispute resolution in 1960 created a modicum of stability in the border areas, which was crucial for the latter-day infrastructure connectivity projects. China and Myanmar share a 2,192-km long border that was resolved in 1960 under the Chinese "mutual understanding" principle. China almost recognised the British Indian McMahon Line here as Burma was toying with the idea of joining the US-led Southeast Asian Treaty Organisation (SEATO), which was detrimental to border stability with China. China consolidated this gesture through frequent political visits, such as the nine visits made by the then premier, Zhou En-lai, and Burmese leader U Ne Win's 12 visits. However, anti-Chinese riots broke out in 1967 in Rangoon (Yangon) that resulted in a setback to the bilateral relations, even though such riots happened across major Southeast Asian countries, given the Chinese penchant to expand communist insurgencies across the region. Subsequently, China's leader Deng Xiaoping promised to rope in the Burma Communist Party cadres operating in Yunnan Province.[9] Border stability again was a consideration when China cobbled up relations with the military junta that displaced the democratically-elected government in 1988. However, ethnic conflict flared up in the border areas, with the Kokang uprising as one of the major disturbances.

For instance, in 2009, Myanmar troops in Shan state clashed with Kokang ethnic armed forces, that not only triggered refugee flow into Yunnan but also created business losses.[10] China was involved in this incident actively by creating a neutral zone along the borders for peace talks between the stakeholders at Ruili. Also, the Kachin Independence Army's umbrage at the military junta had a spill-over effect on China, with more than 50,000 refugees landing at Dehong prefecture of Yunnan province. China had set up several refugee camps in Yunnan province. Anti-Chinese sentiments in the border areas were to create demographic stress levels in these areas. While the peak of diplomatic and political relations could be said to have been reached between 1988 to 2007, and despite the loss of opportunities to reshape Myanmar's political spectrum since 2011,[11] subsequently, readjustments have taken place since February 2021 coup in Myanmar.[12] It was reported that China had been sending feelers into Shan and other states to cobble up with the junta leaders.

Despite the problems at the borders, China had stepped up its diplomatic relations with Myanmar. Premier Li Peng visited it in 1994, Vice President Hu Jintao in 2000 and President Jiang Zemin in December 2001. President Xi Jinping visited Myanmar in January 2020, about the time the pandemic was spreading from Wuhan in late 2019. This was his last visit abroad till he visited the Samarkand Shanghai Cooperation Organisation summit meeting in September 2022.[13] President Xi's visit marked the 70th anniversary of the establishment of diplomatic relations between China and Myanmar; he was also the first Chinese leader in 19 years to visit Myanmar.[14] Jiang Zemin was the last Chinese President to visit Myanmar when he signed several economic and border agreements in 2001. According to Chinese Vice Foreign Minister Luo Zhaohui, the visit was to strengthen relations, deepen BRI cooperation and to "materialise" the China-Myanmar Economic Corridor (CMEC), i.e., the Myanmar component of the BRI. Nearly 33 agreements were signed on the occasion. However, Myanmar ministers soon expressed concern about possible debt accumulation given the nature of investments proposed at Kyaukphyu and other ports.[15]

Economic and Trade Relations

In the economic sphere, China's footprint in Myanmar is gaining traction, although it also has its own share of ups and downs.[16] China's bilateral trade includes the import of commodities and export of finished goods and services (specifically in the 4G/5G telecom sectors), grants, loans, aid or investments and in other forms. The overall bilateral trade hovered around USD 10 billion, with commodities predominating the composition of trade. Significantly China's exports to Myanmar increased consistently at around 12 per cent on average in the last quarter century, specifically in manufactured goods. Guangdong and Yunnan provinces dominated in terms of exports to Myanmar.

In 1996, bilateral trade was USD 265 million; in 2005, it reached USD 5 billion; and in 2015, it increased to USD 11 billion, with China's exports constituting about USD 5.6 billion. By 2011, China became Myanmar's biggest trading partner, with political implications. Border connectivity through Muse, Lweje, Chinshwehaw, Kambalti, and other border ports, complementarities and monetary settlement resulted in high trade growth. In 2020, China exported to Myanmar over USD 11 billion, with broadcasting equipment, heavy synthetic cotton fabrics, and light rubberised knitted fabrics taking the lion's share.[17] Significantly, smuggling is quite rampant in the border areas of Yunnan with Myanmar. For instance, Myanmar exported jade worth USD 6 to 9 billion in 2011. In 2013, -2 million cubic metres of logs were shipped through Ruili, and between 2000 and 2014, China imported over 11 million m^3 of logs from Myanmar, worth USD 2.7 billion.[18] This is in addition to over 3,000 tonnes of rice smuggled into Yunnan every day.

China's investments in Myanmar are increasing, although it has faced several hiccups. By 2015, China had invested USD 15 billion in 115 projects. However, due to the continuing political turmoil in Myanmar and environmental protests and other reasons, China's investments were reduced from USD 12 billion in 2008-2011 to USD 407 million in 2012-13. The investment decline resulted in setbacks to the construction of Myitsone Dam in 2011 (with a planned allocation of over USD 3.6 billion; the dam was to produce about 6,000 MW of electricity, even though it displaced over 15,000 people in the region). Indeed, in May 2011, President Thein Sein wrote to Parliament that the dam project had led to the displacement of people and created environmental issues downstream.

China's investments also went into Letpadaung Copper Mine and Sino-Myanmar oil and gas pipelines. The 771-km crude oil pipeline that began in 2009 and was operationalised in 2017 had nearly USD 2 billion in investments. It connects Madè Island in Myanmar with Ruili in Yunnan province. Another parallel gas pipeline connects Ramree Island of Myanmar with Ruili and is 793 kilometres in Myanmar. These are some of the four such energy pipelines China initiated in recent times, with the others including the Kazakhstan-China crude oil pipeline, the Central Asia-China gas pipeline, and the Russia-China crude oil and natural gas pipelines.[19] After the coup, in May 2021, the junta approved a Chinese-funded, Chinese-majority stake-owned USD 2.5 billion gas-fired project at Ayeyarwady Region[20] Overall, 26 Chinese multinational corporations were involved in more than 62 hydropower, oil and gas, and mining projects in Myanmar.

With Myanmar joining the BRI at its first summit meeting in 2017 and duly acknowledged by President Xi Jinping, bilateral relations should have flowered.[21] However, the ground reality in Myanmar and political differences in its domestic sphere has been stalling the spectacular implementation of BRI projects.[22] The BRI includes the restructured Bangladesh-China-India-Myanmar Economic Corridor,[23] China-Indochina Peninsula Economic Corridor, and other connectivity projects. China's Foreign Minister Wang Yi, during his visit to Myanmar in 2018, had proposed the construction of the China-Myanmar Economic Corridor (CMEC),[24] resembling the China-Pakistan Economic Corridor (CPEC), both intended to connect the interior of China with the Indian Ocean through the Arabian Sea and the Bay of Bengal. The CMEC includes two special economic zones at Yangon and Kyaukphyu, with a deep-sea port at the latter place.[25]

To further strengthen economic relations and to counter the sanctions following the military coup, China and Myanmar have begun trading in local currencies. Earlier, in January 2019, China's renminbi was included in Myanmar's official settlement currency. In June 2021, Myanmar's central bank began accepting Yuan accounts, and by December of the same year, Myanmar accepted China's currency for border trade transactions.[26]

Apart from the infrastructure projects, Myanmar had expressed interest in the "digital silk road", "health silk road", and other extended aspects of the BRI. In the light of the spread of the pandemic that affected Myanmar extensively, China shipped vaccines, although there were reservations about the high price and ineffectiveness of those vaccines. In the telecommunications field, however, even though many Western countries have taken countermeasures against Huawei 4G/5G networks due to hidden devices or lack of transparency and surveillance concerns, Myanmar has evinced keen interest. Its Ministry of Transport and Communications concluded an agreement in 2018 with Huawei for the deployment of 5G telecommunications across the country. China's Alibaba also began providing e-commerce services in Myanmar.

Arms Transfer

One of the major areas of cooperation between China and Myanmar has been in arms transfers from Beijing since the late 1980s. In fact, while there is no evidence to suggest any arms transfer from China to Myanmar till the 1980s, once the symbiotic relationship emerged coinciding with the Tiananmen Square incident in 1989 and the military coup in Yangon in 1988, there was a sudden spurt in such transfers. According to the SIPRI arms transfers database, China transferred over USD three billion worth of arms to Myanmar between 1989 and 2021.[27] These include the Anawrahta corvette licence-produced in Myanmar, Aung Zeya frigates licence-produced in Myanmar, patrol craft, Type 035 submarines, C-801, C-802 and Haiying anti-ship missiles, T-59, T-63, T-69, T-85 tanks, T-85, ZFB-05 armoured personnel carriers, F-6, F-7 M, JF-17, A5G Fantan fighter aircraft, K-8 trainers, Y-8, Y-12 transport aircraft, CH-3 armed drones and others. In late 2022, Myanmar acquired six Mountain Eagle fighter aircraft (Guizhou JL-9). China's arms transfers have emboldened the military junta and opened up international and regional space for both.[28]

Conclusion

China provided crucial support to the military junta that ruled over Myanmar except in a brief democratic interregnum. It provided aid and loans to the junta at a time when the latter was under international approbation. It blocked crucial human rights violations and genocide charges at the UN Security Council China, thus providing international space for the junta. However, both the unbridled ambitions of China to dominate Myanmar space and domestic turmoil in Myanmar created different outcomes. The political transition in Myanmar has brought about a turbulent phase in the China-Myanmar relationship, as with the outside world.

As a result, China started working toward enhancing its time-tested tactics of mutual trust, strategic communication, and people-to-people exchanges. The protests on several Chinese-funded projects in Myanmar affected the investment environment marking a new era in economic and political relations. Meanwhile, the people-centred development model adopted by Myanmar forced some of the cooperation projects for revision while others got delayed. Nevertheless, Myanmar has approved a few Chinese-funded projects during this period. Most significantly, in late 2018, both began the China-Myanmar Economic Corridor as a mega project. In 2014, China began the China-Pakistan Economic Corridor. With these two corridors, China intends to enter the Indian Ocean Region through a two-pronged approach to secure its energy interests and also to counter India and QUAD maritime initiatives.

In the regional security aspects, China had come to the rescue of beleaguered Myanmar during the Rohingya crisis. China has refused to condemn the government in Myanmar over the Rohingya crisis and claimed foreign intervention does not work. The international community has widely condemned the military response to Rohingya militants, which has seen over 700,000 refugees flee from Myanmar to neighbouring Bangladesh. China said it supports the country's efforts in "safeguarding peace and stability". China had defended Myanmar in the UN Security Council as well. China's Foreign Minister Wang Yi suggested a three-stage path for Myanmar and Bangladesh to work out the Rohingya crisis, i.e., ensuring a ceasefire and restoring stability, and talks between the two countries to create a workable solution for repatriation and poverty alleviation as a sustainable solution. However, no concrete proposals are coming from China, nor is there an offer to accommodate refugees or contribute to humanitarian relief and to their welfare.

China and Myanmar have expanded security and military engagement to strengthen the comprehensive strategic cooperative partnership. Military cooperation continues to expand in personnel training and maritime exercises. China remains a major exporter of arms to Myanmar with submarine and fighter aircraft sales. On border areas management and peace process in Myanmar, both sides cooperate in cracking down on illegal trade and other non-traditional security threats. The outbreak of the first conflict between the Myanmar Army and the Kokang armed group in August 2009 in northern Myanmar caused the loss of lives and properties in China. China's close ties with some of the ethnic armed groups and the illegal trade along the China-Myanmar border have been the focus of Myanmar's engagement with China in the peace process. Addressing these issues remains the core element of China's constructive role in Myanmar's ethnic peace process.

The construction of the Kyaukphyu deep sea port, Kyaukphyu SEZ, CMEC projects, Muse-Kyaukphyu railway and Irrawaddy (Ayeyarwady) River land-river transport project. The construction of the Kyaukphyu deep-sea port and Kyaukphyu SEZ has been mired in controversy over the sharing of stakes, land compensation, and environmental and social impact assessment. However, China is persuading Myanmar to start the construction of the CMEC. International pressure on Myanmar over the Rohingya issue and conflict in northern Myanmar could be instrumental in China's efforts to construct the economic corridor under the framework of the BRI. China has proposed strengthening the military relationship to safeguard the "common security and development interests" of the two countries.

Under the leadership of Xi Jinping, China is re-evaluating its policies towards Myanmar to consolidate its economic and strategic interests and expand regional influence under the framework of BRI projects, even though some influential

Myanmar leaders expressed concerns about the emerging dependence on China as well as debt diplomacy. Nevertheless, in the immediate aftermath of the February 2021 coup, China readjusted its policies towards Myanmar with initial remarks of a "cabinet reshuffle" to provide active space for Myanmar in the ASEAN as well as at the bilateral level. Moreover, it was reported that China is also actively intervening in the ethnic components of Myanmar with the intention of securing its interests first among the Kokang and then that of the junta. However, with the Sri Lankan financial meltdown in 2022, Myanmar leaders have become more cautious in their approach towards China, even though the restrictions on Chinese investments are being lifted gradually.

ENDNOTES

1. Tin Maung Maung Than, "Myanmar: Myanmar-ness and realism in historical perspective", in Ken Booth and Russel Trood (eds.) *Strategic Cultures in the Asia-Pacific Region* (New York: St Martin's Press, 1999)
2. In November 2010, soon after her release, Aung San Suu Kyi said she did not consider China as a threat and that it is an important neighbour.
3. Jaesoo Park "Myanmar's Foreign Strategy Toward China Since Rohingya Crisis: Changes, Outlook and Implications" *Journal of Liberty and International Affairs,* Vol. 6, No. 1 (2020)
4. See Jason Tower, "Ukraine Crisis Prompts China to Swing Behind Myanmar's Junta," *Unites States Institute of Peace,* 13 April 2022 available at https://www.usip.org/publications/2022/04/ukraine-crisis-prompts-china-swing-behind-myanmars-junta, last accessed on 23 January 2023
5. Wang cited in "China to back military-ruled Myanmar regardless of the situation," *AP News,* 02 April 2022, available at https://apnews.com/article/wang-yi-aung-san-suu-kyi-china-myanmar-diplomacy-d68de69436c1462f647f6475b6315c92, last accessed on 23 January 2023
6. S.D. Muni, "China's Strategic Engagement with the New ASEAN, An Exploratory Study of China's post-Cold War Political, Strategic and Economic Relations with Myanmar, Laos, Cambodia and Vietnam," *Institute of Defence and Strategic Studies*, IDSS Monograph No. 2 (Singapore: Institute of Defence and Strategic Studies, 2002)
7. Yang Razali Kassim, "Myanmar's China Policy Shift: Preparing for ASEAN Chair?" *RSIS Commentaries,* 14 March 2012
8. Malik, J. Mohan, "Myanmar's Role in China's Maritime Silk Road Initiative" *Journal of Contemporary China*, Issue 111, Volume 27 (2018): pp. 362-78
9. For the early diplomatic history of China-Myanmar relations, see Fan Hongwei and Charles Kraus, "Reassessing China-Myanmar Relations during the Cold War," *CWIHP dossier* No. 49, available at https://www.wilsoncenter.org/publication/reassessing-china-myanmar-relations-during-the-cold-war, last accessed on 23 January 2023
10. Ian Storey, "Emerging Fault Lines in Sino–Burmese Relations: The Kokang Incident," *The Jamestown Foundation, China Brief,* Vol. 9, Issue 18 (2009)
11. Sun Yun, "China's Strategic Misjudgement on Myanmar", *Journal of Current Southeast Asian Affairs, No 31 (1)* (2012): 73-96
12. Joshua Kurlantzik, "China's Support for Myanmar Further Shows the World Dividing into Autocracy versus Democracy," *Council on Foreign Relations,* 04 April 2022, available at https:/

/www.cfr.org/blog/chinas-support-myanmar-further-shows-world-dividing-autocracy-versus-democracy, last accessed on 23 January 2023

13. See "Full text of Xi's signed article on Myanmar's newspapers" 16 January 2020, available at http://www.china.org.cn/world/2020-01/16/content_75619897.htm, last accessed on 23 January 2023.
14. Earlier Xi visited Myanmar as Vice President in 2009, available at https://www.irrawaddy.com/news/burma/busy-schedule-awaits-chinese-president-xi-2-day-visit-myanmar.html, last accessed on 23 January 2023
15. See Yuichi Nitta and Thurein Hla Htway, "Myanmar will ask China to downsize project, minister says $10bn port investment should be 'as lean as possible' to avoid debt trap," *Nikkei Asian Review*, 04 July 2018, available at https://asia.nikkei.com/Politics/Myanmar-will-ask-China-to-downsize-project-minister-says, last accessed on 23 January 2023; Jason Koutsoukis, "China's $7.3 Billion Myanmar Port 'crazy' Suu Kyi Adviser Says," *Bloomberg News*, 23 March 2018, available at https://www.bloomberg.com/news/articles/2018-05-25/china-s-7-5-billion-myanmar-port-crazy-suu-kyi-adviser-says, last accessed on 23 January 2023; "China's Belt and Road dreams under pressure," *The ASEAN Post*, 11 April 2019, available at https://theaseanpost.com/article/chinas-belt-and-road-dreams-under-pressure, last accessed on 23 January 2023
16. Poon Kim Shee, "The Political Economy of China-Myanmar Relations: Strategic and Economic Dimensions" Ritsumeikan Annual Review of International Studies, 2002. ISSN 1347-8214. Vol.1, pp. 33-53; Andrzej Bolesta, "Myanmar-China peculiar relationship: Trade, investment and the model of development" *Journal of International Studies,* 11(2), 23-36
17. See "China-Myanmar", available at https://oec.world/en/profile/bilateral-country/chn/partner/mmr, last accessed on 23 January 2023
18. "Domestic issues blamed on Chinese failure to block illegal timber trade." 09 November 2014, available at http://www.elevenmyanmar.com/index.php?option=com_content&view=article&id=8060:domestic-issues-blamed-on-chinese-failure-to-block-illegal-timber-trade&catid=44:national&Itemid=384, last accessed on 23 January 2023
"A Disharmonious Trade: China and the Continued Destruction of Burma's Northern Frontier Forests." *Global Witness*, London, 20019 available at http://www.globalwitness.org/library/disharmonious-trade-china-and-continued-destruction-burmas-northern-frontier-forests, last accessed on 23 January 2023
19. Dawei Liu, Kensuke Yamaguchi, and Hisashi Yoshikawa, "Understanding the motivations behind the Myanmar-China energy pipeline: Multiple streams and energy politics in China" *Energy Policy,* 107 (2017) pp. 403–412
20. "Junta approves $2.5 bn power plant project backed by Chinese companies" *Myanmar Now,* 14 May 2021, available at https://myanmar-now.org/en/news/junta-approves-25bn-power-plant-project-backed-by-chinese-companies, last accessed on 23 January 2023 Three Chinese companies including Union Resources and Engineering Company, Yunnan Energy Investment and Zhefu Holding Group hold the majority shares in this project.
21. Mi Mi Gyi, "The Belt and Road Initiative" (BRI) and Its Implication on Myanmar" *Mandalay University of Foreign Languages Research Journal*, 2019, Vol. 10, No. 1
22. For Xi Jinping's speech at the 1st summit of the BRI, available at http://www.xinhuanet.com/english/2017-05/14/c_136282982.htm. Also see Bertil Litner, "Myanmar A Perfect fit on China's Belt and Road. Four Priority BRI Projects in Myanmar promise to make China a balance of power tilting Indian Ocean force," *Asia Times*, 27 January 2020, available at http://asiatimes.com/2020/01/myanmar-a-perfect-fit-on-chinas-belt-and-road/, last accessed on 23 January 2023
23. Shahidul Islam, Wuyi Wang and Laping Sheng, "The Construction of Bangladesh–China–

India-Myanmar Economic Corridor: Current Situation, Problem, and Countermeasures", *Asian Journal of Social Science Studies*; Vol. 7, No. 4, 2022

24. Zhao Hong and Yang Mu, "China-Myanmar Economic Corridor: Opportunities and Challenges," *EAI Background Brief*, No. 670, 27 October 2011, available at http://www.eai.nus.edu.sg/BB670.pdf, last accessed on 23 January 2023
25. "Myanmar scales back China-funded Kyauk Pyu port project in Rakhine state due to debt Concerns", *South China Morning Post*, Reuters, 02 August 2018
26. This is based on Li Xuanmin, "Myanmar accepts yuan as official settlement currency for border trade with China", *Global Times*, 15 December 2021 available at https://www.globaltimes.cn/page/202112/1241577.shtml#:~:text=Myanmar%20has%20accepted%20 the%20 Chinese,the%20matter%20told%20the%20Global, last accessed on 23 January 2023
27. See SIPRI, Arms Transfers Database at < https://armstrade.sipri.org/armstrade/page/trade_register.php> Also see *Xinhua News*, "China, Myanmar to enhance military ties," English.news.cn, 28 November 2011, available at http://news.xinhuanet.com/english2010/china/2011-11/28/c_131275049.html, last accessed on 23 January 2023.
28. Cici Ernasari and Anak Agung Banyu Perwita, "Sino-Myanmar Defence Cooperation and China's Efforts to Bolster its Sphere of Influence in The Indian Ocean (2013-2017)", *Jurnal Pertahanan,* Vol. 4, No. 3 (2018), pp.120-135

15

Russia's Strategic Interests in Myanmar

Amb P S Raghavan and Cchavi Vasisht

ABSTRACT

Russia and Myanmar established diplomatic relations on 18 February 1948, immediately after Myanmar became independent. By 1951, the two countries sent their ambassadors to each other's countries. Though the two countries do not share geographical and social proximity, they have enhanced defence and strategic closeness in recent years. Their economic relations also received attention, especially post-2010, when Myanmar opened its borders for economic cooperation. In this chapter, the attempt is to identify how both countries serve each other's interests. Myanmar is Russia's gateway to the Indo-Pacific and to increase Russia's clout since its decline in 1989. The objective is also to challenge Western domination in the region. On the other hand, because of three military coups, Myanmar was isolated by the Western sanctions and found a resort in its neighbouring partners. Moreover, the over-dependency on China and China's tacit support to Ethnic Armed Organisations has created fear in the minds of the Myanmar military. Therefore, Myanmar, in recent years, has diversified its partners and reached out to Russia as a strategic partner. A similar strategy was adopted since Independence, as Myanmar had been balancing relations between China and the Soviet Union. Further, the relations have become necessary since the 2021 coup, which has been discussed in detail in this chapter.

Introduction

In pre-Independent Myanmar, Russia provided both the ideology as well as funding for the Burmese revolutionary freedom movement. Aung San, the founder of the Communist Party of Burma (1939), borrowed Stalin's views on socialism (as stated in Josef Silverstein in *The Political Legacy of Aung San*). Even after he left the Communist Party, he followed the path to socialism and founded the Burma Revolutionary Party. Earlier, Aung San had asked for Japan's help to overthrow

Britain. However, after the Japanese invasion of Burma, he followed the Burmese-adopted model of socialism (primarily inspired by the Soviet Union). According to the historian Maung Khin, "A newly independent Burma stayed close to the Soviet Union, but that was also largely because it held grievances against the Japanese". Burma also refused to attend the 1951 San Francisco Peace Treaty negotiations, which set final WW II settlements with Japan. The signatories to the treaty called on the Soviet Union to return the Southern Kurils and the southern half of Sakhalin Island to Japan. By boycotting the conference, Burma (India and Yugoslavia) were the only countries that recognised Soviet sovereignty over the territories.

Post-Independence, Myanmar adopted an independent and non-aligned policy, but an inclination towards the Soviets was visible. In 1971, Myanmar changed its policy to an independent and active one. The domestic and international scenarios helped shape closer ties between the two countries. Post the disintegration of the Soviet Union, the relations between the two countries hit a low. Nevertheless, since the 2000s, both countries have strengthened economic, defence and diplomatic ties. However, post the 2021 coup, Russia is actively supporting the military in defence procurement as well as diplomatically in the international arena. Russia has refused to condemn the military actions and argued that the Myanmar military could only guarantee unity and peace. On the other hand, Myanmar has supported Russia's actions in Ukraine. The following section explains how political relations have developed between the two countries since Myanmar's Independence.

Political Relations between Russia and Myanmar

Since Independence, the relations between the two countries have been guided by domestic and international situations. Domestically, surplus rice in Myanmar had to be exported to other countries. That is why in 1954, two delegations led by the Minister of Agriculture and Cabinet officials visited Russia (September and December). During the same year, China helped negotiate a barter system with Burma to buy rice in which 20 per cent of the purchase would be paid in goods from the Soviet Union and East European countries. Following this, the Soviet Union concluded a three-year trade agreement with Burma, further extended by five years. The Soviet Union agreed to buy 150,000 to 200,000 tons of rice from Burma in exchange for the supply of industrial goods, machinery and technical services. However, challenges were reported in this barter trade regarding the overpricing of goods, delays in deliveries and delivery of goods which were not useful to Burmese economic development.

Internationally, there was estrangement with the USA over the Chinese nationalist forces in Burma and the efforts of Chinese Prime Minister Chou En-lai to get the two countries together. The two countries have supported each other on regional and international issues. For instance, the communiqué signed in 1955 reiterated the similar views of the two countries on the success of the Bandung Conference, the easing of Soviet-Yugoslavia relations, and support for China's seat at the United Nations. The two countries also expressed their support against conventional arms and the prohibition of nuclear weapons. The following year in October 1955, Burmese President U Nu visited the Soviet Union for the first time and reiterated his support for the mutual coexistence of the two countries. To further discuss the issues, in December 1955, Russian Prime Minister Nikolai Bulganin and Communist Party Secretary Nikita Khrushchev, came to Myanmar. The visit was used to criticise the West and expand its domain of influence. Table 1 lists important official visits from each side:

Table 1: High-Level State Visits by Myanmar Officials to Russia

Year	*Visits by*	*Outcomes*
October 1955	President U Nu	Joint Communiqué was issued reiterating support for mutual coexistence. Both Prime Ministers supported the policy of non-interference and non-participation in any bloc and upheld the five principles of Peaceful Coexistence.
September, 1965	General Ne Win	Exchanged views with Soviet leaders, Prime Minister Alexis Kosygin, Soviet Communist Party First Secretary and others. Joint Communiqué was issued highlighting the peaceful coexistence of the two countries, denounced imperialism and upheld the principles of Afro-Asian cooperation under the second Bandung Conference (Similar to the first Communique).
April 2006	Vice Senior General Maung Aye, the Vice Chairman of the State Peace and Development Council of Myanmar	MoU between chambers of commerce and industry was signed. This led to cooperation between sectors of education and the training of scientists. (first visit after four decades).
June 2013	Min Aung Hlaing's first visit to Russia	Met Defence Minister Sergei Shoigu.
November 2014	Min Aung Hlaing	Stopover at Moscow and met at the airport with Lt. Gen. Alexander Fomin, Russia's director of military-technical cooperation.
June 2017	Min Aung Hlaing	He met Defence Minister Shoigu and visited the Black Sea Fleet at Sevastopol in Crimea.
August 2018	Min Aung Hlaing, accompanied by a	Participated in the "Army 2018 International Military Technical Forum" and National Security Week events;

Year	Visits by	Outcomes
	prominent nationalist monk, Sitagu Sayadaw	Met Defence Minister Shoigu.
April 2019	Min Aung Hlaing	Attended the 8th Moscow Conference on International Security; Met Defence Minister Shoigu.
June 2020	Min Aung Hlaing	Attended Russia's victory day parade and met Deputy Defence Minister Alexander Fomin, who awarded him honorary medals for strengthening military cooperation with Russia.

Table 2: High-Level State Visits by Russian Officials to Myanmar

Year	Visits by	Outcomes
December 1955	Prime Minister Nikolai Bulganin and Communist Party Secretary Nikita Khrushchev	Joint statement similar to Moscow Communique (1955). Also, details of the Soviet Burmese Economic Agreement were announced. The visit was also used to criticise the West and expand its domain of influence.
March-April 1956	First Deputy Premier Anastas Mikoyan	Announcements about the construction of buildings, such as hospitals, industrial exhibitions and cultural centres. In return, Burma offered goods produced in the country along with rice.
February 1960	Prime Minister Nikita Khrushchev	Promoted cultural and scientific exchange and reiterated support for each other's policies, such as disarmament. The Soviet side also supported Burma's neutralist foreign policy.
July 1962	First Deputy Premier Anastas Mikoyan	Discussions with Brigadier Aung Gyi, a prominent figure in Revolutionary Council. Further, it decided to set up a fertiliser plant
April 1963	Soviet Defence Minister Marshal Radion Yakovlevich Malinoski	In his address, he stated that Burma was a close ally in its fight against anti-colonialism.
September 1965	Anastasia Mikoyan	The visit aimed to denounce the USA and its interference in the region, especially Vietnam. However, the Burmese side maintained its neutral stand.
October 1971	President Nikolai Podgorny	Held talks with General Ne Win on international situations, especially in South East Asia and the need to strengthen economic and technical relations. During the visit, he also proposed the "Asian Collective Security System".
November 2020	Defence Minister Sergei Shoigu held a video conference with the Myanmar military chief, General Min Aung Hlaing	He stated that Russia was ready to expand cooperation with Myanmar, including joint work in the framework of the "ADMM-Plus" expert working group on countering terrorism. Min Aung Hlaing was also awarded the title of "Honorary Professor of the Military University" by the Ministry of Defence of Russia and a medal "For distinction".
January 2021	Defence Minister Sergei Shoigu	Agreed to supply Pantsir-S1 surface-to-air missile systems, Orlan-10E surveillance drones and radar equipment.

It is important to note that as the domestic situation changed in Burma and the U Nu Government was taken over by Ne Win in 1962, the Soviet Union took some time to recognise it. This delayed recognition was due to the change in Ne Win's approach to scientific socialism, which gave less importance to the significance of Marxism-Leninism. This recognition was followed by a visit by the Soviet First Deputy Premier, Anastasia Mikoyan, in 1962. The relations got a further push with the Sino-Soviet conflict in 1967. Also, China's Red Guard Diplomacy and the Cultural Revolution led by China pushed Burma toward the Soviets. The Soviets used the opportunity and gave their full economic and military support in the ensuing rift between China and Burma[1]. However, the breakdown of the Soviet Union pushed relations to the lowest level as Russia focused on its domestic transition.

Since 2000, Russia has maintained a non-interference policy in the country and used its United Nations Security Council (UNSC) veto to help Myanmar. As a result, the focus of the relations became economic and defence ties, including nuclear cooperation, as discussed below. Post the military coup in 2021, diplomatic relations have been strengthened as both countries have been supporting and recognising each other's actions. This has been further explained in the strategic section of their relations. Here, a look at the number of visits since the military coup will be relevant (Table 3).

Table 3: Visits Post-2021 Military Coup

Year	*Visits by*	*Outcomes*
March 2021	Russian Deputy Defence Minister Alexander Fomin visited Myanmar	Attended Myanmar's Armed Forces Day. During the parade, several Russian pilots demonstrated fighter jets that the military purchased. Fomin stated that Russia "adheres to a strategic line to intensify relations between the two countries". In September 2021, Myanmar's Vice Senior General, Soe Win, visited Russia to attend the International Army Games, an annual Russian military sports event organised by Russia's Ministry of Defence.
June 2021	Min Aung Hlaing visited Russia	Attended the 9th Moscow Conference on International Security, and was awarded an honorary professorship by the Russian Military University. He also met Defence Minister Shoigu. Later, a Myanmar military delegation travelled to Russia to learn about Pantsir production techniques, accompanied by Aung Hlaing and Air Force Chief Maung Maung Kiaw. Held talks with Nikolai Patrushev, the Secretary of Russia's Security Council, to strengthen defence ties.

Year	*Visits by*	*Outcomes*
September 2021	Myanmar's Vice Senior General, Soe Win, visited Russia	To attend the International Army Games, an annual Russian military sports event organised by Russia's Ministry of Defence.
March 2022	Myanmar delegation of Senior Police Officers led by Union Minister for Home Affairs, Lt-Gen Soe Htut, visited Russia	To attend the EXPOTECXNOSTRAZH-2022, International Advanced Technology Exhibition on Community and National Security. At the meeting with Mr Yalcubov Evgenig, Director for Special Commissions of ROSOBORONEXPORT, Myanmar officials discussed forms of technology and products that can systematically implement security and use of advanced information technology in combating violence and drug and gang crimes. They also discussed matters related to enhancing cooperation with the Ministry of Home Affairs.
July 2022	Min Aung Hlaing visited Russia	Though it claimed to be a "private" visit, he met Deputy Defence Minister Fomin
August 2022	Russian Foreign Minister Sergei Lavrov visited Myanmar	Met the military-appointed foreign minister, Wunna Maung Lwin, and Senior Gen. Min Aung Hlaing. Lavrov described Myanmar as a "friendly and longstanding partner" and said that the two nations "have a very solid foundation for building up cooperation in a wide range of areas." Discussed at the third meeting of the Russian-Myanmar Intergovernmental Commission on Trade and Economic Cooperation scheduled for the second half of 2022. A Plan for Consultations for 2022-2024 was signed between the ministries of foreign affairs of Russia and the Republic of the Union of Myanmar.
September 2022	Min Aung Hlaing visited Russia	To attend the Eurasian Economic Union meeting (The third visit since the coup but the first time he met Putin).

An analysis of these visits depicts that there were more high-level visits from the Myanmar side *vis-a-vis* the Russian side. Especially since 2010, Min Hlaing has visited Russia nine times and met Defence ministers and partners. On the other hand, the Russian side visits are dominated by minister-level officials or secretaries. It was only in September 2022 that Russian President Putin met Min Hlaing for the first time on the sidelines of the Eastern Eurasian Forum in Russia (however, nothing substantial was discussed).[2] Earlier, when Aung San Suu Kyi was in power as State Counsellor, Putin met her on the sidelines of the second Belt and Road Forum for International Cooperation. Further, the focus of relations has been enhancing defence ties; for instance, in December 2021, USD 96 million worth of classified defence-related goods were delivered to Myanmar.

Moreover, under an agreement signed in 1999, the two countries have exchanged regular consultations between the Ministries of Foreign Affairs. Along with this, many high-level officials visited each other's countries. Russian officials, such as the Chairman of the Supreme Court of the Russian Federation, Mr Vyachslav Lebedev (2006), and the Secretary of the Security Council of the Russian Federation, N. P. Patrushev (2014), visited Myanmar. Similarly, Myanmar officials, such as the Speaker of Pyithu Hluttaw, Thura U Shwe Mann (2011), visited Russia.

Myanmar-Russia Economic Cooperation

Russia and Myanmar's economic relations date back to Myanmar's independence. From buying Myanmar's surplus rice to selling oil in the present times, the two countries have strengthened their economic ties. The trade between the two countries has not been significant, but it serves each other's interests. As discussed earlier, during the 1950s, the Soviet Union and Myanmar entered into a barter exchange agreement. The Soviet-Burmese Economic Agreement was signed in December 1955. Myanmar agreed to send rice and other goods of Burmese origin, and the Soviet Union agreed to send agricultural and industrial goods and machinery. Following the agreement, Russia has helped Myanmar to develop economic and social infrastructure, such as the General Hospital in Tanggyi, the Rangoon Institute of Technology, and the cultural and sports centre. Further, infrastructure deals were signed in 1958; the Soviet Union offered 4-7 million roubles at a 2.5 per cent interest rate to build dams and send an expert team on agricultural projects. Following the 1962 coup, the second economic cooperation agreement was signed in which the Soviets decided to provide 3.5 million roubles to build a dam.

Since the democratic transition in Myanmar, the country has established economic relations with important partners. Russian Prime Minister Dmitry Medvedev attended the East Asia Summit in 2014 in Myanmar and emphasised its shift in establishing economic and strategic cooperation between Russia and the Indo-Pacific region. In 2014, an intergovernmental commission for trade and economic cooperation was established between Russia and ASEAN. In pursuance of its objectives, the Russia-ASEAN summit was held in Sochi, Russia, in 2016. The first Business-to-Business Dialogue was held in September 2021.

Discussions are also underway on the signing of the Russia-Myanmar Economic Cooperation Development Strategy (Draft) and establishing industrial zones in Myanmar during the 25th St. Petersburg International Economic Forum (2022). The preparatory meeting for the third Russian–Myanmar

Intergovernmental Commission for Trade and Economic Cooperation meeting was held in August 2022. Myanmar and Russia looked at the possibility of using Russian Mir payment cards in Myanmar. The two sides also discussed ways to decrease dependency on US dollars and concluded an agreement on a barter system for exchanging fertiliser and oil in 2022. However, trade relations between the two countries have not been significant though many Russian companies are working with military-based companies in Myanmar. For instance, the Russian government enterprise, *Tyazhpromexport,* established a plant in Shan State to produce cast iron. Table 4 depicts the total trade between Russia and Myanmar since 2014:

Table 4: Total trade between Russia and Myanmar (2013-2020)

Year	*Total Trade Russia-Myanmar (million USD)*
2014	83
2015	130
2016	258
2017	217
2018	344
2019	388
2020	371
Total	1.9 billion

Source: Ru-Sat Russia-Myanmar Export and Import https://en.ru-stat.com/date-Y2013-2020/RU/export/MM).

The bilateral trade gained momentum in 2014, and by 2020 Russian trade with Myanmar had grown threefold, from less than USD 114 million in 2013 to over USD 371 million in 2020. In 2021, trade went up by 20 per cent to USD 430 million, and it has increased another 50 per cent in the first five months of this year (over 2021). Within this, 35 per cent falls under the category of hidden partition, machinery and mechanical appliances (16.2 per cent), textile and textile articles (16.2 per cent), optical, photographic, medical, and musical instruments (9.6 per cent), vegetable products (5.3 per cent) and mineral products (4.2 per cent) and so on.[3] Despite efforts, the bilateral trade between Russia and Myanmar remains low compared to China and Thailand, the two biggest trading partners.

Furthermore, bilateral trade and investments have been promoted via organising dialogues between Myanmar's Ministry of Investment and Foreign Economic Relations and the Eurasian Economic Commission. Another dialogue was organised between Myanmar and the Eurasian Economic Union (EAEU) to promote bilateral trade and investment. During the discussion, the Union Minister called for the revival of the economy in the post-COVID-19 period and cooperation in the sectors of agriculture and livestock, fertiliser production, cooking oil, electric power and energy, and basic infrastructure. The two also discussed reforms to increase export volumes to EUEA member-countries and importing fertilisers, oil and gas and farming machines to Myanmar.[4]

The two sectors that have received special focus in forging closer economic relations are the tourism and energy sectors. A delegation from the Eurasian Economic Commission led by the deputy director of the International Relations Department of the Ministry of Transport of Russia visited Myanmar for a workshop on "Tourism and Institutions". Myanmar resumed international flights in April 2022 and signed an MoU on Government-Private Tourism Cooperation and Bilateral Tourism Development to facilitate the visit of Russian tourists to Myanmar. During the Eurasian Economic Summit in September 2022, efforts were made to promote tourism, and negotiations were underway to open direct flights between the two countries. Finally, in November 2022, civil aviation authorities agreed to commence direct flights from Vladivostok, Novosibirsk, and Krasnoyarsk to Yangon with Myanmar Airways International from 2023. The two sides also discussed assistance for opening Russian language courses and hospitality training for human resource development in Myanmar.[5]

Within the energy sector, Russia's Bashneft operates the EP-4 oil field and has recently sought to expand cooperation in oil and gas exploration. The field already has the presence of China, India, France, Britain and the USA. Due to European Union sanctions till 2012, Gazprom International (based in the Netherlands) could not enter Myanmar. However, after the 2012 lifting of sanctions, the company has invested in joint projects. According to a June 2022 report, a Myanmar military delegation met with the Russian Minister of Energy, Shulginov Nikolay, on the sidelines of the International Economic Forum to discuss energy cooperation in St. Petersburg. The two sides discussed prospects for Russian oil drilling in Myanmar and the export of oil and petroleum products. They also explored the means through which the two countries could exchange their currencies, and Myanmar could buy fuel from Russia.[6] In September 2022, both countries agreed to use the barter system for Myanmar's fertiliser imports from Russia while its fuel oil purchases from the country would be paid in roubles.

In addition, Russia reached out to Myanmar in times of crisis. Since Myanmar is mainly affected by floods during the monsoon season, in 2015, Russia's Emergencies Ministry decided to help Myanmar build an early warning system and supply it with equipment needed for clean-up operations. Russia also provided humanitarian aid, including food and tents.[7] Russia has also been supporting

Myanmar in its fight against COVID-19 by supplying two million COVID-19 vaccines.[8]

Nuclear Energy

A specific focus of relations has been enhancing cooperation in the nuclear field. In 2000, Myanmar approached Russia to set up a nuclear research centre, and negotiations began to establish a 10-megawatt light water pool-type research reactor and an isotope laboratory for peaceful purposes. Following the negotiations, in 2007, the two countries signed an agreement to form a nuclear research centre, train around 300-350 specialists in Myanmar, have the nuclear waste treatment and burial facilities, a medical isotope production laboratory and a silicon doping system. Earlier, the centre was to be established in five years. However, it got delayed due to inadequate resources and international scenarios. In June 2015, Russia and Myanmar signed a preliminary agreement.

Finally, in September 2022, on the sidelines of the Eastern Economic Forum, Russia, Russian state-owned nuclear corporation Rosatom signed an agreement on a roadmap to further atomic energy cooperation, including the possible implementation of a modular reactor project in Myanmar.[9] In November 2022, Myanmar's Science and technology minister Dr. Myo Thein Kyaw, signed a deal at the nuclear technology centre in St. Petersburg with Rosatom to establish a similar institution in Yangon during the Myanmar military delegation's visit to attend the Transport Week and other international forums in Moscow.[10]

Myanmar-Russia Defence Relations

The Soviet Union has repeatedly emphasised the close cooperation between the two countries, and since Burma's independence, the Soviets have claimed to be Burma's close ally. In 1963, Soviet Defence Minister Marshall Radion Yakovlevich Malinoski visited Burma and claimed that Burma was a close ally in its fight against anti-colonialism. Since 1995, Russia and Myanmar have pushed for greater military-technical cooperation. As a result, Russia has provided a significant quantity of military equipment to Myanmar, which is listed below. According to the SIPRI (Stockholm International Peace Research Institute) Arms Trade Database, Russia has delivered 2,000 Igla-1 MANPADS (Man-Portable Air Defence System), S-125 Pechora-2M mobile air defence systems, 10 Mi-24P/Mi-35P attack helicopters, 14 MiG-29 fighter aircraft, 6 MiG-29S fighter aircraft, 12 Mi-2 light helicopters, 6 Yak-130 combat trainer aircraft, BRDM-2MS 4×4 reconnaissance armoured vehicles, and Pantsir-S1 mobile air defence missile/

cannon system. The data shows that between 2011 and 2020, Russia sold weapons worth 649 million Euros to Myanmar. In December 2021, the delivery of USD 96 million worth of classified defence-related goods was recorded.[11]

In February 2022, Thomas Andrews, U.N. Human Rights Council, identified Russia as one of three states to have supplied weapons to Myanmar, in addition to China and Serbia. According to an analysis done by ISEAS-Yusof Ishak Institute, between 2000 and 2019, Myanmar purchased USD 1.44 billion from Russia. Justice for Myanmar (JFM) has reported that 19 Russian arms suppliers have provided the Myanmar military with equipment. For instance, Russia's state-run defence conglomerate, Rostec, and its conglomerates have supplied the Myanmar military with equipment such as parts for combat helicopters, fighter jets and surface-to-air missiles. The JSC Tactical Missiles Corporation of Russia is another major supplier of air force technology to Myanmar's military. Post the coup in November 2021, a delegation from JSC Rosoboronexport met Senior General Min Aung Hlaing and Commander-in-Chief (Navy) Admiral Moe Aung and explored views on enhancing naval cooperation between the Myanmar Navy and JSC Rosoboronexport.[12]

It is crucial to understand that Myanmar's defence budget is approximately USD 2.5 billion per year, of which only about USD 500 million is allocated for defence procurement. This amount is just a small proportion of the actual cost of Russian arms. For instance, Sukhoi Su-30 fighter jets have an estimated list price of USD 47 million each, which is just nearly a tenth of its entire budget. There are concerns that since the military cannot buy all of its military equipment from Russia in dollars, there is a probability that the purchases are made in exchange for raw materials, including gemstones and timber. The given arrangement supports the current circumstances as both countries face international sanctions. As a result of Russia's actions in Ukraine, the West-sanctioned seven major Russian banks and excluded them from the SWIFT messaging transfer system.[13]

The two countries displayed stronger ties as the senior leaders attended each other's celebrations. In 2021, right after the military coup in February, Myanmar's Armed Forces Day celebrations were honoured by Russian Deputy Defence Minister Alexander Fomin. During the parade, several Russian pilots demonstrated fighter jets that the military had purchased. The details of the visits and the outcomes post the military coup are stated in the first section of the chapter. Moreover, since the 1990s, more than 7,000 Myanmar military officers and military-connected scientists have studied in Russia. The officers and scientists have enrolled at the Omsk Armour Engineering Institute, the Nizhniy Novgorod

Command Academy, the Air Force Engineering Academy, the Kazan Military Command Academy and many more. Some of the Myanmar soldiers even served as cadets with the Russian Air Force to ensure better training on Moscow-made equipment used by the Myanmar Air Force.

Myanmar-Russia Strategic Relations

The erstwhile Soviet Union was one of the major powers in Southeast Asia but lost influence with its disintegration in 1991. Under President Vladimir Putin, Russia is slowly rebuilding many of those frayed ties with regional autocracies and democracies alike, primarily through arms deals. Bertil Lintner sees Russia as geopolitically resurgent, telegraphing its presence in Southeast Asia, as it lost all its allies since the collapse in 1991. Under Putin's rule, Russia is emerging as a key negotiator in various conflicts in Asia and increasing its economic and strategic presence. It is also essential for Russia to set an example as it strives to disrupt Western efforts to promote democracy and Western rule-based order in Asia.[14]

Russia became an ASEAN Dialogue Partner in 1999 and had been enhancing economic and defence ties since then. Annual dialogues are conducted; in May 2022, the 18th ASEAN-Russia Senior Officials' Meeting (ARSOM) was held, and Myanmar Representative U Chan Aye attended it. In August 2022, the Russia-ASEAN Foreign Ministers' meeting was held, which adopted the Comprehensive Plan of Action (CPA) to implement the ASEAN and Russian Federation strategic partnership (2021–2025). As a result, Russia-ASEAN trade recorded substantial growth in 2021, exceeding USD 20 billion (though the ninth-largest trade partner). Furthermore, Russia's foreign direct investment flows into ASEAN registered a value of USD 45 million in 2019, making Russia the ninth largest investor in ASEAN.

Defence ties have also gained importance as Russia is Southeast Asia's leading arms supplier, selling around USD 10.7 billion of defence equipment to the region between 2000 and 2019, according to SIPRI. Vietnam is the leading importer (Russia has provided almost 80 per cent of Vietnam's military equipment since 2000). Between 2015 and 2021, Russia sold USD 247 million worth of arms to Myanmar, USD 105 million worth to Laos, and USD 47 million worth to Thailand. However, since 2014, arms sales have decreased in Southeast Asian countries (Ian Storey, Singapore's ISEAS-Yusof Ishak Institute). Russia and ASEAN also conducted their first naval exercises in Indonesia in December 2021.

Currently, Myanmar and Russia face international isolation and condemnation for their acts. However, they continue to support each other. Russia, along with

China, blocked the UN Security Council from imposing sanctions against Myanmar's military. In June 2021, the United Nations General Assembly adopted a resolution with an immediate demand to end the military's violence against its civilians and called for a halt to weapons exports to Myanmar. Similarly, in May 2022, Russia, along with China, blocked the UNSC Resolution on the Myanmar crisis. The draft statement authored by the United Kingdom's delegation expressed its concern at the violence and serious humanitarian situation in Myanmar and misgivings about the "limited progress" on the implementation of ASEAN's Five-Point Consensus peace plan.

Furthermore, the visits between the two countries are marked by significant defence cooperation. While Senior General Ming Aung Hlaing has visited Russia thrice since the coup, there are other top military generals, including Gen Soe Win, the deputy Commander-in-Chief of the armed forces, and air force chief General Maung Maung Kyaw, who has also visited Russia. The Myanmar military also came to Russia's defence after the invasion of Ukraine, describing the attack as an "appropriate action". The military spokesman, Major General Zaw Min Tun, stated that the action was to consolidate Russian sovereignty, and it reckoned with the belief that Russia is a force to ensure the balance of power in the world.

David Mathieson, an independent analyst on Myanmar, explains the reason for Myanmar's military interest in strengthening its relations with Russia. He argues that Myanmar aims to diversify its list of defence partners in which China is the regime's largest arms supplier and distance itself from China. Mathieson notes that the reason could also be the selling of "substandard" Chinese equipment. Furthermore, after the 1988 coup, Myanmar was dubbed a Chinese "client state".[15] The military is also suspicious of China's intentions as China continues to supply weapons to ethnic armed groups such as the United Wa State Army. It is predicted that due to the conflict between Russia and Ukraine, there could be a slow transfer of weapons from both countries, especially Russia. In such a situation, there is a probability that Myanmar would again fall back on China.[16] Despite these differences, Myanmar and China share close economic and strategic ties, which are discussed in another chapter.

Nevertheless, there are differences in the approaches of Russia and China towards Myanmar. The Russians have engaged just with the military. At the same time, China maintains cordial relationships with ethnic armed organisations, primarily the United Wa State Army, as well as the Myanmar military and government. China's policy is to lure Myanmar's military and government with business, trade and support at the UNSC and simultaneously use the UWSA and its armed rebel allies against the military and government. Therefore, Myanmar's military is wary of Chinese interests and suspicious of their motives. Senior General Min Aung Hlaing, on his trip to Russia, complained about the interference by a "foreign state" via supporting ethnic minorities on Myanmar's northern border.[17] While China plays its power games in Myanmar to enhance China's strategic interests in Myanmar, Russia is a relatively problem-free ally.

Moreover, Russia offers effective air combat systems to the military, which are being used by the military in present times against the opposition forces. On a visit to Russia in September 2022, Min Hlaing personally inspected the production and testing of the planes at the Irkutsk Aviation Plant. Under the contract signed in 2018, Russia had to deliver six Sukhoi SU 30SM fighter jets. Two jets were delivered in March 2022, and the remaining four will likely be delivered soon. The Russian-made helicopter gunships are used in the war against the Kachin Independence Army and the Karen National Union. China's capabilities, on the other hand, are mostly confined to land and sea domains.

Russia has also become diplomatically important as Bangladesh approached Russia to use its good offices with Myanmar's military to address the Rohingya crisis. Bangladesh Foreign Minister A. K. Abdul Momen approached Russia's Foreign Minister, Sergey Lavrov, to launch a 'trilateral initiative' with Myanmar at a meeting in Tashkent on the sidelines of the international conference on connectivity. Previously, Russia and China supported the "Human Rights Situation of Rohingya Muslims and other Minorities in Myanmar" resolution at the UN.[18]

Conclusion

To conclude, the year 2023 will mark the 75th year of diplomatic relations between the two countries. Ties between the two countries have strengthened since Myanmar's independence, given the domestic and international circumstances. The two countries have continued with regular visits by high-level defence officials to enhance defence relations and strategic ties. Russia provides army training and university scholarships to the soldiers and, most importantly, sells arms to the Myanmar military, which faces international isolation. Military cooperation also balances Myanmar's increasing dependence on China, as China is the main supplier of arms.

The relations have become especially pronounced since the military took over the country in 2021. "Facing stronger international sanctions and diplomatic isolation, the two countries are actively exploring ways to strengthen their security and economic ties," the ICG briefing stated. Russia served as a key security partner to the military, sold more than USD 2.3 billion of weapons, and supported the military's establishment of a new coast guard and port of call. Even though economic relations have not been the bedrock of their relations, the two countries strive to strengthen defence and strategic relations in present times. Gleb A. Ivashensov argues that for Russia, Myanmar is an "important present and perspective partner". He defines Myanmar's importance in terms of its geographic location, size, natural resources as well as membership in ASEAN.

ENDNOTES

1. Briefly, China and Burma had amicable relations till the 1960s, though boundary issues were raised more often. The diplomatic ties between Myanmar and China were restored post-1970s. This gap of around 20 years gave space for the Soviets.
2. "Myanmar Junta Leader to Meet Putin in Russia", *The Irrawaddy*, 06 September 2022, available at https://www.irrawaddy.com/news/burma/myanmar-junta-leader-to-meet-putin-in-russia.html, last accessed on 23 November 2022
3. Ru Stat, "Trade between Russia and Myanmar", available at https://en.ru-stat.com/date-Y2013-2020/RU/trade/MM, last accessed on 23 November 2022
4. "Myanmar, EAEU discuss bilateral economic relations", *Myanmar National Portal*, 25 March 2022, available at https://myanmar.gov.mm/news-media/news/latest-news/-/asset_publisher/idasset354/content/myanmar-eaeu-discuss-bilateral-economic-relations, last accessed on 23 November 2022
5. "MoHT Union Minister attends workshop on "Tourism and Institutions", receives Eurasian Economic Commission delegation", *Myanmar National Portal*, 26 March 2022, available at https://myanmar.gov.mm/news-media/news/latest-news/-/asset_publisher/idasset354/content/moht-union-minister-attends-workshop-on-tourism-and-institutions-receives-eurasian-economic-commission-delegation, last accessed on 23 November 2022.
6. "Myanmar Junta Leader Min Aung Hlaing visits Russia", *RFA*, 12 July 2022, available at https://www.rfa.org/english/news/myanmar/junta-russia-07122022165512.html, last accessed on 23 November 2022
7. "Russia to Help Myanmar tackle Natural Disasters after Devastating Floods," *Sputnik*, 14 October 2015, available at https://sputniknews.com/20151014/Russia-Myanmar-Disasters-1028491808.html, last accessed on 23 November 2022
8. "Myanmar General Says Russia will Supply 2 mn Vaccines as Outbreak Worsens", *Reuters*, 09 July 2021, available at https://www.reuters.com/world/asia-pacific/myanmar-general-says-russia-will-supply-2-mln-vaccines-outbreak-worsens-2021-07-09/, last accessed on 23 November 2022
9. "Myanmar Regime, Russia Sign Nuclear Cooperation 'Roadmap'", *The Irrawaddy*, 07 September 2022, available at https://www.irrawaddy.com/news/burma/myanmar-regime-russia-sign-nuclear-cooperation-roadmap.html, last accessed on 23 November 2022
10. "Russia agrees to establish Yangon flights and Nuclear Energy Hub in Myanmar", *The Irrawaddy*, 21 November 2022, available at https://www.irrawaddy.com/news/burma/russia-agrees-to-establish-yangon-flights-and-nuclear-energy-hub-in-myanmar.html, last accessed on 23 November 2022
11. "Russia to deliver Pantsir missile to Myanmar", *Rising BD*, 25 August 2021, available at https://www.risingbd.com/english/international/news/81883, last accessed on 23 November 2022

12. "Commander-in-Chief (Navy) meets JSC "Rosoboronexport" officials", *Myanmar National Portal*, 16 November 2021, available at https://myanmar.gov.mm/news-media/news/latest-news/-/asset_publisher/idasset354/content/commander-in-chief-navy-meets-jsc-rosoboronexport-officials, last accessed on 23 November 2022;
"State Administration Council Chairman Senior General Min Aung Hlaing receives Chairman of Russian-Myanmar Military Technological Cooperation Joint Commission Deputy Director of FSMTC of Russia", *Myanmar National Portal*, 13 November 2021, available at https://myanmar.gov.mm/news-media/news/latest-news/-/asset_publisher/idasset354/content/state-administration-council-chairman-senior-general-min-aung-hlaing-receives-chairman-of-russian-myanmar-military-technological-cooperation-joint-com, last accessed on 23 November 2022
13. "Junta Watch: Myanmar Military 'Not Worried' as World Shuns Main Supplier Russia", *The Irrawaddy*, 05 March 2022, Available at: https://www.irrawaddy.com/news/burma/junta-watch-myanmar-military-not-worried-as-world-shuns-main-supplier-russia.html, last accessed on 23 November 2022
14. "Myanmar opens a strategic gateway for Moscow," *MENAFN*, 07 May 2021, available at https://menafn.com/1102392104/Myanmar-opens-a-strategic-gateway-for-Moscow, last accessed on 23 November 2022
15. "'Stronger together': Myanmar, Russia parade military relationship", *Al Jazeera*, 27 March 2022, available at https://www.aljazeera.com/news/2022/3/27/holdstronger-togethermyanmar russiaparademilitary-relationship, last accessed on 23 November 2022
16. Patrick Dupont, "Is the Ukraine War Boosting China's Influence in Myanmar", *The Diplomat*, 27 April 2022, available at https://thediplomat.com/2022/04/is-the-ukraine-war-boosting-chinas-influence-in-myanmar/, last accessed on 23 November 2022
17. "Moscow sells warplanes to Burmese generals", *Asia News*, 26 July 2021, available at http://www.asianews.it/news-en/Moscow-sells-warplanes-to-Burmese-generals-53724.html, last accessed on 23 November 2022
18. "Bangladesh urges Russia to mediate in Rohingya crisis after China-led efforts fail", *The Economic Times*, 25 July 2021, available at https://economictimes.indiatimes.com/news/international/world-news/bangladesh-urges-russia-to-mediate-in-rohingya-crisis-after-china-led-efforts-fail/articleshow/84722357.cms, last accessed on 23 November 2022

REFERENCES

ASEAN. "The 18th ASEAN-Russia Senior Officials' Meeting convened on 23 May 2022 via video conference." 23 May 2022. available at https://asean.org/the-18th-asean-russia-senior-officials-meeting-was-convened-on-23-may-2022-via-videoconference/, last accessed on 23 November 2022

____ "Co-Chairs' Statement of the Special ASEAN-Russia Foreign Ministers' Meeting". 06 July 2021. available at https://asean.org/wp-content/uploads/AMS-Consolidated-Input-Draft-Co-Chairs-Statement-of-the-SARFMM-FINAL-1.pdf, last accessed on 23 November 2022

____ "ASEAN Russia Economic Relations." available at https://asean.org/our-communities/economic-community/asean-russia-economic-relations/, last accessed on 23 November 2022

Holmes, Robert A. "Burma's Foreign Policy Toward China Since 1962." *Pacific Affairs* 45. no. 2 (1972), 240–254

International Crisis Group. "Coming to Terms with Myanmar's Russia Embrace." Briefing 173/Asia 04 August 2022. available at https://icg-prod.s3.amazonaws.com/b173-myanmar-russia-embrace.pdf, last accessed on 23 November 2022

Ivashentsov, Gleb. "Myanmar Spiral." *RIAC*. 24 June 2021. available at https://russiancouncil.ru/

analytics-and-comments/comments/myanmanskaya-spiral/?sphrase_id=86863991, last accessed on 23 November 2022

Kamalakaran, Ajay. "How Russia supported Burma's independence struggle." *Russia Beyond.* 05 April 2016. available at https://www.rbth.com/arts/history/2016/04/05/how-russia-supported-burmas-independence-struggle_581631, last accessed on 23 November 2022

Ministry of Foreign Affairs of the Republic of the Union of Myanmar. *Foreign Policy*. available at https://www.mofa.gov.mm/sample-page-3/foreign-policy/, last accessed on 23 November 2022

Ministry of Foreign Affairs of Russian Federations. "Press release on Foreign Minister Sergey Lavrov's visit to the Republic of the Union of Myanmar." 03 August 2022. available at https://mid.ru/en/foreign_policy/news/1824850/, last accessed on 23 November 2022

____ "Foreign Minister Sergey Lavrov's remarks and answers to media questions following talks with Foreign Minister of the Republic of the Union of Myanmar Wunna Maung Lwin." Nay Pyi Taw. 03 August 2022. available at https://mid.ru/en/foreign_policy/news/1824868/, last accessed on 23 November 2022

____ "Foreign Minister Sergey Lavrov's statement and answers to media questions following ASEAN ministerial meetings." Phnom Penh. 05 August 2022. available at https://mid.ru/en/foreign_policy/news/1825270/, last accessed on 23 November 2022

____ "Russia's position at the seventy-seventh session of The UN General Assembly (Talking points)." 10 August 2022. available at https://mid.ru/en/foreign_policy/en/foreign_policy/un/1825729/, last accessed on 23 November 2022

President of Russia. "Meeting with Myanmar's State Counsellor Aung San Suu Kyi." 26 April 2019. available at http://en.kremlin.ru/events/president/transcripts/60390/photos, last accessed on 23 November 2022

"Russia's Policy in Myanmar and in South East Asia". *Peace Nexus Foundation.* March 2022. available at https://peacenexus.org/wp-content/uploads/2022/04/V2-Report-Russian-Policy-in-Myanmar-and-SouthEast-Asia-1.pdf, last accessed on 23 November 2022

Tun, Thaung Tun. "Myanmar Russia Relations in a Changing World: Growing ties based on Strategic Partnership and Economic Prospects." (eds.) Victor Sumsky, Mark Hong and Amy Lugg, "ASEAN-Russia Foundations and Future Prospects." ISEAS–Yusof Ishak Institute. 2012

Wezeman, Seimon T. "Arms Flows to South East Asia." *SIPRI.* December 2019. available at https://www.sipri.org/sites/default/files/2019-12/1912_arms_flows_to_south_east_asia_wezeman.pdf, last accessed on 23 November 2022

16

Japan-Myanmar Relations: Navigating through a Perilous Path

Prof Rajaram Panda

ABSTRACT

The Japan-Myanmar relationship is too complex an issue for experts and analysts to come to a common viewpoint on any aspect of Myanmar. Unlike history that clouds Japan's relations with its immediate neighbours such as South Korea and China, Myanmar does not suffer from any such legacies though there are some parallels. For most of the period of military rule in Myanmar, Japan has successfully engaged with Myanmar diplomatically, economically, culturally, politically, and in defence cooperation, despite international criticism of some of its policies. Japan has navigated through the turbulent waters diplomatically and overcome international opprobrium over its stance in some of its policies on Myanmar. The economic content is strong, if not robust. Defence cooperation has been non-controversial until recently. Cultural cooperation remains time-tested. The geo-strategic dimension has its own space. Overall, Japan-Myanmar relations cannot be seen as a zero-sum game, as relations in all spheres have remained mutually beneficial. Japan-Myanmar relations can be an ideal case to test the realistic theory of international politics in which all other considerations are subsumed over national interests. Opinions will differ, however, if this is a win-win situation for both.

Introduction

The Japan-Myanmar relationship is one of the most complex and contentious ones driven by geopolitical compulsions and Japan's policy of engagement with the ASEAN bloc. Even before Japan entered into the phase of "lost decades" following the period of high growth in the '60s and '70s, Japan's economic foray into the neighbouring countries concentrated on relocating its labour-intensive industries to overseas bases. Japan, while shifting focus on high-tech and knowledge-intensive industries in the 'flying geese' pattern of economic development, led to the emergence of the Four Tigers.

The success of this model of economic development soon embraced other smaller Asian countries, with Japan remaining the leader. As a result, Myanmar, despite a military government, soon fell into place as economic rent started to benefit the people and the country. Against this broad background, it need not be missed that China, too, pursued the path of economic development under authoritarian control and scored a considerable success, leading to competition in the economic field. These phenomena soon assumed a strategic dimension for increased space. With a military dictatorship in place, Myanmar emerged as the new theatre for competition between Japan and China for an economic and strategic foothold.

In this vortex of evolving strategic competition, India found itself in a tricky situation as Myanmar's role in executing India's Act East Policy emerged crucial. For engaging with the ASEAN bloc to further its Act East Policy, Myanmar became extremely important as the only gateway to the ASEAN. Therefore, India was compelled to continue engaging with the military government. In this narrative, India and Japan are on the same page. This aspect is, however, outside the purview of this chapter.

Evolution of Japan-Myanmar Relations

Owing to wartime legacies, Myanmar occupies a special space in Japan's relations with Asia. This has contributed to an element of warmth in the bilateral ties. Japan has navigated its foreign policy carefully by building a "special relationship" even after the removal of Myanmar's long-term strongman, Ne Win. This relationship has been crafted by economic means by liberal disbursement of Official Development Assistance (ODA) and technical assistance that has benefited the people.

The subsequent emerging trends in the region have made Japan-Myanmar relations one of the most critical relationships in Asia as broader geo-political and strategic shifts make compelling ground to stay engaged. This dimension assumes greater salience as strategic competition between Japan and China over expanding influence in Myanmar is intensified.[1]

Myanmar finds itself in a position where it has to make critical choices while protecting its national interests. With an export-oriented economy, Japan's foreign policy priority is to deepen ties economically with most countries in the world, sometimes compromising some of its cherished value-based principles to achieve larger goals. No wonder the economic content remains the fulcrum of the Japan-Myanmar relationship. Over the years, this component has only strengthened and given a strategic heft.

Symbolically if one analyses for comparison purposes, the population size of Japan is around 126 million, and Myanmar is around 54.45 million. However, in terms of age groups, Japan is an ageing society with over 60,000 centenarians and the number is increasing every year and a declining birth rate; the median average age in Myanmar is 28.2 years, with a total life expectancy of approximately 68.2 years.

If one compares the symbolism attached to the flags, Japan's national flag is a rectangular white banner bearing a crimson-red circle at its centre, embodying the country's sobriquet, the Land of the Rising Sun. The sun plays a vital role in Japanese mythology and religion as the Emperor is believed to be the direct descendent of the Sun goddess, Amaterasu. This belief gives legitimacy to the institution of the Emperor, endowing the divine appointment to remain as the head of the state. The flag's design, therefore, reflects the sun's importance to Japan. As regards the flag of Myanmar, the yellow colour symbolises national unity, the green colour represents peace and a rich natural environment, and the red represents courage and determination. The white star in the middle represents the country's geographical and ethnic unity.

In terms of geographical size, Myanmar is about 1.8 times the size of Japan. As a multi-ethnic country with 138 ethnic minorities, almost 90 per cent of the people are Buddhist. Myanmar became a colony of Great Britain in 1886, but as the de-colonisation movement gathered speed, the colonial masters were on retreat. Myanmar sought Japan's help to fight the British and succeeded in freeing itself from the British colonial yoke in 1943 but soon fell victim to Japanese rule. Myanmar finally got its freedom in 1948.

During most post-independence periods, the military continued to rule the country. Willy-nilly, the world continued to engage with the military. After several military coups in 1989, Aung San Suu Kyi, the leader of the National League for Democracy (NLD) and daughter of General Aung San, was placed under house arrest. The military changed the country's name to the Union of Myanmar, and the capital was shifted from Rangoon to Naypyidaw. In 2010, the NLD, led by Aung San Suu Kyi, emerged as a legitimate political party and in 2011, Thein Sein took office as President. This heralded a new democratic process and ended military rule. As it transpired soon, this was short-lived as the military staged a coup and regained power.

Establishment of Diplomatic Relations

Diplomatic relations were established between the two countries in 1954. A defeated Japan in World War II with its economy in ruins, Myanmar was the first Asian country to come to Japan's rescue by providing food aid when Japan faced food shortages after its defeat. A grateful Japan did not forget this gesture and felt it obligatory to return the favour by liberal economic assistance and through receiving a large number of students from Myanmar who chose Japan as the destination for their studies.[2]

Starting with a low key, it gathered momentum from 2002 onwards when high-level officials' visits from each other countries commenced. Such visits started with a visit by Japan's Minister for Foreign Affairs, Yoriko Kawaguchi, in October 2002; Foreign Minister Koichiro Gemba, in December 2011; Deputy Prime Minister and Minister of Finance, Taro Aso, in January 2013; Prime Minister, Abe Shinzo, in May 2013, and Minister of Foreign Affairs Fumio Kishida (present Prime Minister) in March 2014. Prime Minister Abe and Deputy Prime Minister Aso repeated visits in November 2014 and September 2015, respectively. Foreign Minister Kishida visited for a second time in May 2016. There have also been other high-level visits by political leaders from Japan, demonstrating Japan's interest in engaging with this strategically located country.

Similarly, high-level leaders from Myanmar have reciprocated by visiting Japan. Among the important leaders are Prime Minister General Khin Nyunt in December 2003; Prime Minister U Thein Sein in November 2009; President U Thein Sein in April 2012; and State Counsellor Daw Aung San Suu Kyi in October 2018. There were other visits in between.[3]

Japan's Role as a Peace-broker in Rakhine Crisis

Even before the troubled and impoverished Rakhine State plunged into armed conflict due to the Rohingya crisis, Japan did not shy away from responding to Myanmar Government's plan to boost economic development in the state so that the lives of the impoverished people are uplifted. Myanmar was seeking foreign investment, and Japan was a willing partner. Japan was the first responder to the slogan that "Rakhine is open for business to the world". The Japanese government agency, Japan International Cooperation Agency (JICA) and the Japan External

Trade Organisation (JETRO) readily acted as co-organisers of the Rakhine Investment Fair on 21-23 February 2019.[4]

Indeed, since 2017, Japan has been brokering in the Rohingya repatriation process with the Myanmar government to seek solutions to the problems in Rakhine State. In October 2018, when Myanmar's State Counsellor, Daw Aung San Suu Kyi, visited Japan, she praised Japan's understanding and help. However, there is a strategic dimension to Japan's proactive stance on Rakhine State. Its strategic location helps the Chinese-owned pipeline to carry natural gas and oil from the Bay of Bengal across Myanmar to Kunming in China's Yunnan Province since 2010. China took advantage of the manner the Myanmar government handled the Rohingya crisis in Rakhine State and inked a framework agreement for the Kyaukphyu Deep Sea Port in November 2018. This gives China access to the Bay of Bengal and enhances its regional connectivity as part of Beijing's Belt and Road Initiative (BRI). By remaining engaged economically, Japan wishes to check the Chinese influence there.

In November 2019, Japan sent a Special Envoy, Yohei Sasakawa, for a round of shuttle diplomacy between Rakhine State and Naypyitaw. Just before the elections were held on 08 November 2019, Sasakawa met State Counsellor Aung San Suu Kyi and the military commander-in-chief, Senior General Min Aung Hlaing and urged that the election in Rakhine State, be also held. It had been suspended due to clashes between the Myanmar military and the Arakan Army. Though General Min Aung Hlaing and Sasakawa had developed good bonding, and the latter was willing to listen to Sasakawa's advice,[5] it soon transpired that the General had a hidden agenda when months later, he launched the coup and unseated the democratically elected government.

Japan-Myanmar Defence Cooperation

Despite a prolonged period of military rule in Myanmar, Japan has maintained close defence cooperation with Myanmar. Japan has welcomed military cadets from Myanmar to receive training at the Japanese Defence Academy, a Defence Ministry facility, since 2015 under Article 100-2 of the Self-Defence Act. This permits the training and education of foreign nationals in Defence Ministry facilities, including the academy, with the approval of the defence minister. The programme is operated under "strict civilian control" and cultivates a "relationship" between SDF personnel and students, thereby contributing to mutual understanding between Japan and cadets' countries.

Even after the coup in February 2021, Japan continued to host eight cadets. Through this programme, the cadets participate in an extensive curriculum of academic and military training, including combat and arms training. The Human Rights Watch criticised this Japanese policy to train Myanmar's Armed Forces, who under the leadership of the *Tatmadaw*, committed crimes against humanity. It demanded that the Japanese government should suspend the programme immediately.[6]

Economic Cooperation

The Japan-Burma (now Myanmar) Peace Treaty and Agreement on Reparations and Economic Cooperation, signed in 1954, laid the foundation of the economic relations between the two countries. Since then, economic ties have strengthened in all forms, such as ODA, trade and investment, collaboration in projects, etc. Japan is the sixth largest investor in Myanmar, the third-largest importer of Myanmar's products, established the Thilawa SEZ, and working on the Y complex and Bago projects.[7] At the same time, since the 1990s, Japan has rejected the sanctions regime and tried to cooperate in different areas especially humanitarian support not just during COVID-19 times but also during floods.

Bilateral trade between the two countries is smooth, though not huge. The merchandise trade from Myanmar to Japan consists of clothing, shoes, beans, electrical appliances, and shrimp and from Japan to Myanmar, transportation equipment, machinery and appliances, and chemical equipment. Following the experiment with democracy, albeit brief, as the military returned, consumption increased and the country registered moderate economic growth. Japan and other countries looking to do business saw Myanmar as Asia's last frontier. Internet penetration improved. More people could afford cell phones. So, the communication networks improved, contributing to success in business.

Soon, Japanese electronic products, which had already gained world popularity in terms of quality and competitiveness, emerged as popular brands. Products such as Panasonic, Hitachi, Sony, and Canon, and cosmetics brands such as Kanebo and Shiseido, also became household names. An industrial park was opened in September 2015, and a special economic zone was created where, out of 49 companies, 25 or 50 per cent of the total were Japanese, which entered to do business. Though a multi-ethnic country, Myanmar showed enthusiasm to welcome foreign companies with which it can do business for the benefit of the country and its people.

Amid international condemnation, the Japanese government was forced to halt new non-humanitarian ODA projects earlier in 2021 but allowed the existing projects to continue. The Japanese Diet passed a resolution in June 2021 condemning the coup and called for a swift restoration of the democratic political system. However, Japan continues its support, not just during the COVID-19 pandemic but also during floods.

Change in Scenario following the Return of the junta

The favourable roadmap that had opened for expanding business received a rude shock when the *Tatmadaw* staged a coup d'état on 01 February 2021, deposing the democratically elected members of the NLD. The military detained the country's civilian leader Aung San Suu Kyi, and numerous other top Government figures. Since then, thousands have been killed, some executed, and civilian leaders have been charged on the grounds of election irregularities and put in prison for varying periods. Thus, the power-sharing arrangement between the military and the elected civilian representatives since the 2015 elections ended abruptly.

Suu Kyi was celebrated as an international democracy icon. She was put up for 15 years under house arrest due to a decades-long struggle against military rule. Finally, she was released in 2010 and participated in the country's elections. The NLD was the first civilian representative to form a democratic government in a power-sharing arrangement with the military after 50 years of the military regime.[8]

Despite this apparent transition to the democratic process, the military did not appear to cede power. The newly-drafted Constitution in 2008 ensured that the military continues to hold the upper hand even in a democratic process. Besides retaining control over the home and defence ministries, the military retained the veto power on any attempt to amend the Constitution. The military-drafted a Constitution that barred Suu Kyi from becoming President. When the ethnic civil wars started over the issue of Rohingyas, Suu Kyi came under fire for failing to speak out against atrocities committed by the military against the Rohingya Muslims in the western Rakhine state.

When elections were held in November 2020, Suu Kyi won another term in the election. The military-backed Union Solidarity and Development Party (USDP) scored dismally. The military decided to assert its losing ground by accusing the NLD of irregularities in the elections. This triggered the coup and prompted international condemnation. Following this, power was transferred to the Commander-in-Chief, Senior General Min Aung Hlaing.

Suu Kyi is 77 years old. She has been in prison since the coup, with a total prison term of 33 years in different cases. In the latest of the charges, she was given six years in jail for corruption in mid-October 2022. Other charges include violating the official secrets act, electoral fraud, and illegally possessing walkie-talkies. She has been charged with accepting bribes from a businessman, Maung Weik, who offered Suu Kyi USD 550,000 over several years, which she denied.[9] Given her old age, it is extremely unlikely that she would ever play any political role in Myanmar politics. She could face a maximum of 190 years in jail if found guilty in all the cases, including fraud allegations surrounding the 2020 elections. She has been kept in solitary confinement in the capital of Naypyidaw.

Many countries, including the USA, urged the junta to immediately relinquish power, release activists and officials, lift all telecommunications restrictions and refrain from violence against civilians. Human rights activists say Suu Kyi's treatment amounts to a show trial and the junta wants to silence her for good. US President Joe Biden threatened to review sanctions. Other countries, including Canada, India, Japan, the UK, New Zealand, and Australia released statements calling for de-escalation and release of those detained.

Impact of the Coup on Japan's Myanmar Policy

As it transpires, the military is going to stay for the unforeseeable future. There are entrenched business interests of the military, which it is keen to guard and would not allow to be interfered with if a civilian government is in power. Three factors seemed to have influenced the political situation in Myanmar: rebels, the armed forces, and the international community.

The rebel group, the National Unity Government's armed wing, and the People's Defence Forces have fought against the junta. Similarly, the Karenni Army promised to fight against the military junta and create a federal union involving other ethnic groups across the country. There is also an economic dimension as to why the rebel groups want a share of the cake, as the areas inhabited by the minority ethnic groups are rich in natural resource deposits, and they do not want the junta to take control of this precious asset.[10]

As regards the international community, the West is aghast at the turn of events in Myanmar and used both "carrot and stick" to make the junta see reason but with little success. Cambodia, as the ASEAN Chair, has also tried its bit but with little hope. Both India and Japan have strong strategic considerations and have engaged with the junta in the past. It enjoys China's support because of Beijing's geopolitical considerations. Beijing did not even call the overthrow of a democratically government a coup but preferred to use the term as a "major cabinet reshuffle". Beijing has often bailed out the junta at the UN and used its veto power on the issue of sanctions.

Though the developments in Myanmar represent both danger and opportunity for Japan's foreign policy, the leverages it enjoys are limited. Yet, Japan was not deterred from condemning the *Tatmadaw*'s coup. Though Yoshihide Suga, who succeeded Abe Shinzo, chose a tougher stance on the junta, Abe was criticised for allegedly contributing to the exacerbation of the Rohingya crisis because of geopolitical interests. As a maritime nation, the bulk of its cargo passes from the Gulf through the Strait of Malacca and the South China Sea and Japan is highly dependent on imports of energy resources through this route. Any geopolitical instability could jeopardise Japan's economic interests hugely. Japan has remained an important partner in Myanmar's economic lifeline. Japan's disbursement of the ODA money through its disbursement agency, the Japan International Cooperation Agency (JICA), constituted almost 50 per cent of the total ODA received by Myanmar between 1970 and 1988, despite the fact that the military regime was under a prolonged period of economic sanctions.

Keeping human security and regional stability as its main foreign policy tool, Japan is seen as a role model in forming and maintaining Asia's liberal order. This is demonstrated by its effort to resurrect the Trans-Pacific Partnership by rechristening it as the Comprehensive and Progressive Agreement for Trans-Pacific Partnership (CPTPP) after the Trump Administration pulled out from the TPP.

Sometimes Japan has used the principle of engaging with repressive regimes through multilateral institutions so that it is not seen to be aligning with a state violating democratic values. When it is benign, it has engaged unilaterally, as the case of ODA or humanitarian assistance would show. Such a policy strategy somewhat suits Japan's foreign policy interests. As a member of the QUAD, Japan, in cooperation with the other three members, finds the QUAD forum as an important tool for engaging with Myanmar. Japan does exercise some leverage through the QUAD to influence the *Tatmadaw*. During the COVID-19 pandemic, Japan played a vital role in vaccine distribution as deficiencies were seen in vaccines from China and Russia reaching on time.

Emergency Humanitarian Assistance

Like other countries in the world, the people of Myanmar were also affected by the COVID-19 pandemic that swept the world for two long years. The danger is still not over and thus requires utmost precaution. Since the coup in February

2021, armed clashes continued between the *Tatmadaw* and the citizens and Ethnic Armed Organisations who continued to resist the military regime. Thousands of people were displaced and faced acute food shortages and daily necessities.

Against this background, politics took a backseat in Japan's diplomacy, and Japan decided on 01 April 2022 to provide an Emergency Grant Aid of USD 8.3 million for humanitarian assistance for the people.[11] This Emergency Aid was delivered directly to the people of Myanmar through the offices of the United Nations Children's Fund (UNICEF), the World Food Programme (WFP) and the United Nations High Commissioner for Refugees (UNHCR), benefitting about 165,000 people.

The UN issued a dismal outlook for Myanmar and said an estimated 14.4 million people, or about a quarter of the country's population, would require humanitarian aid such as food and medical supplies in 2022. The UN Office for the Coordination of Humanitarian Affairs said food prices and other key household commodities surged after the coup. The situation worsened further due to the prolonged period of the pandemic. As a democratic nation that has always stood for human values, Japan was ready to assist the people of Myanmar when they needed help the most.

Impact of the Coup on Japanese Business

However, businesses were circumspect and were not overtly enthusiastic about the government's political considerations to stay engaged and started to review their operations in Myanmar. Japanese energy conglomerate Eneos Holdings announced in May 2022 that it would withdraw from a gas project in coup-hit Myanmar.[12] It came days after its Thai and Malaysian partners announced they would pull out.

This is, however, part of the business story. According to a Japan External Trade Organisation (JETRO) report, about 70 per cent of Japanese companies investing in Myanmar are not deterred by the coup and prefer to not only stay put but also expand their operations despite the negative impact on business as a fallout of the coup.[13] The JETRO survey said 52.3 per cent will maintain current levels of operations in Myanmar and 13.5 per cent will expand them, 27.5 per cent will scale back their business and 6.7 per cent will withdraw from the country or move their operations to a third country.[14]

As of June 2021, nearly 433 Japanese companies had invested in Myanmar. A total of 63.6 per cent felt their operating profits would fall from the preceding year. Only 27.8 per cent felt they would retain their profit level. The main concern of the business entities was the deteriorating business environment propelled by the unstable political situation and uncertainty about the country's future. The suspension of new official development assistance (ODA) following the military coup dented the confidence of several construction companies. Tokyo has been the top ODA contributor to Myanmar. In fiscal 2019, its ODA to Myanmar amounted to 189.3 billion yen (USD 1.8 billion).

The United Nations observed on 31 December 2021 that Myanmar's political and security situation would remain volatile for the following year and beyond. The Japanese companies took note of this and started to rethink whether their operations could be scaled down, if not suspended or closed. The fourth wave of COVID-19 and the emergence of new variants further dampened the mood of Japanese companies as the perceived risk remained high. The cautious approach of the Japanese companies was also influenced by the projection of the International Monetary Fund (IMF) in October 2021 that Myanmar's economy would shrink a whopping 17.9 per cent in 2021. The IMF also projected that Myanmar's gross domestic product would contract by 0.1 per cent in 2022.

Japan under Flak

The international community accused Japan of failing to use its leverage over the *Tatmadaw*, even though it had plenty. Overlooking Japan's limitations, the international community accused Japan of failing to pursue non-military R2P or 'Responsibility to Protect' options.[15] Though the Japanese Foreign Ministry condemned the shooting of the civilian protestors and joined the global community in condemning human rights violations in Myanmar, Japan did not join the USA, Britain and the EU, which placed economic sanctions on individuals and groups involved in the military coup. Japan suspended the new ODA as a measure against the coup but did not place explicit sanctions against the Myanmar military. Australia suspended its defence cooperation programme with Myanmar.

The global community overlooked and failed to appreciate Japan's strategic vulnerability that if it had joined the Western bandwagon in imposing sanctions, the *Tatmadaw* might have been drawn closer to China. India faces a similar dilemma; therefore, even before the coup, both India and Japan have engaged with the military in the past.

The ASEAN grouping has proved to be ineffective in persuading the *Tatmadaw* to end military rule and restore democracy. Unfortunately, the joint statement issued at the special ASEAN summit on Myanmar in Jakarta on 24 April 2021,[16] though it called for the cessation of the violence and atrocities against civilians, it is not legally binding as it is against the ASEAN Charter, which prevents a member of the group to interfere in the internal affairs of another member-state.

Since the ASEAN statement was not legally binding, the R2P option remained a choice for international intervention to adopt. The R2P principle was affirmed at the 2005 high-level UN World Summit. According to this, a sovereign state is responsible to protect its own civilian population, but if the country has no will or ability to protect its people, the international community through the UN has the responsibility to protect civilians from genocide, war crimes, ethnic cleansing, and crimes against humanity.

Since the R2P concept is incongruous with the "principle of non-interference" in the domestic affairs of other countries, China and Russia opposed any international intervention in the Myanmar crisis. The ASEAN member-states cite the ASEAN Charter to hide behind the non-interference principle. The junta in Myanmar is aware of such facts and does not feel deterred from consolidating its power further, even if it means killing more people. The protesters' demand to the international community to invoke the R2P doctrine has evoked a docile response.

Does R2P entail the use of force or military intervention? The short answer is 'NO'. Any military intervention from outside, or even if authorised by the UN, is bound to exacerbate the situation in Myanmar further.[17] Instead, four non-military tools of R2P could possibly be pursued: diplomatic rebuke through a resolution; targeted sanctions, arms embargo; and judicial action through a referral to the International Criminal Court. The truism is that a military determined to maintain power may not find any of the four reprisals biting and thus ineffective. Thousands of Myanmarese in Japan appealed to the Japanese government to save their people from the Junta's atrocities but yielded little outcome. However, these protests raised awareness before the global community.

Japan's virtual non-action in the affairs of Myanmar, as perceived by the outside world, dented its image. Because of Japan's unique relationship with the *Tatmadaw*, it was expected that Japan could emerge as an effective negotiator to break the impasse in Myanmar. The people inside and outside Myanmar were disappointed that it did not happen.[18] The official statement of Japan criticising the coup came too late compared to other countries. Though the USA, Singapore, South Korea and other countries issued statements directly condemning the military, the government of Suga Yoshihide did not even open its mouth, though new ODA money was halted.

Despite the assurance of Japan's ambassador to Myanmar, Maruyama Ichiro, to convey the protestors' concerns to the Japanese government, the protestors remained unconvinced, and the sense of distrust in Japan only increased. Japan's stance was seen as ambiguous. Indeed, Japan's appeasement policy towards the Myanmar junta was always driven by geopolitics and disregard for human rights and, therefore always remained a toxic friendship.[19]

Execution of Democracy Activists and Japan's Reaction

When the military junta executed four democracy activists[20] on 25 July 2022, accused of helping to carry out "terrorist acts", it sparked widespread condemnation and outrage.[21] Around this time, 2,100 were killed, 8,000 were detained and put in custody, one million were displaced, and 140 persons were sentenced to death. There was also news that 382 children were either killed or maimed.

This was the first execution since 1976. The last judicial execution to be carried out in Myanmar is generally believed to have been of another pro-democracy activist, student leader Salai Tin Maung Oo, in 1976 under a previous military government led by Dictator Ne Win. In 2014, during the period of democratic reform, the sentences of prisoners on death row were commuted to life imprisonment. The execution in 1976 was by hanging, but there is no information on how the four democracy activists were executed this time. There was worldwide condemnation, but the junta defended its action and remained unmoved. China, often seen as soft towards the military regime, was too shocked. However, China was not expected to use its leverage even this time. India, too has its strategic vulnerabilities. That limits its role.

How did Japan react to the executions? Like other countries, Japan, too, was shocked. In a statement issued on 25 July 2022, Foreign Minister Hayashi Yoshimasa deplored the actions by the Myanmar military and warned that this act of the junta would further harden public sentiment and isolate Myanmar from the international community.[22] Expressing Japan's deepest condolences, Yoshimasa promised support to the efforts of the ASEAN and Cambodia in particular as the then ASEAN Chair and strongly urged the Myanmar military to faithfully work towards the peaceful resolution of the situation by taking concrete actions to (a) immediately stop the violence, (b) release those who are detained, and (c) swiftly restore Myanmar's democratic political system and swiftly implement ASEAN's "Five-Point Consensus".

The following day, Yoshimasa released a joint statement on this issue and opposition leaders, together with the High Representative on behalf of the

European Union, the Foreign Ministers of Australia, Canada, New Zealand, Norway, South Korea, England and the USA. The joint statement said the executions by the military were "reprehensive acts of violence that further exemplify the regime's disregard for human rights and the rule of law".[23] The joint statement underlined the obligation of the military junta to fulfil its obligations under the ASEAN's Five-Point Consensus to seek peace through dialogue and not indulge in further violence. In a statement issued on 28 July 2022, the Foreign Ministers of G-7 countries—Canada, France, Germany, Italy, Japan, Britain, the USA and the High Representative of the European Union—also strongly condemned the executions of the pro-democracy activists by the military junta.[24]

Did any of these condemnations affect the thinking of the *Tatmadaw*? From the reactions of the junta, it transpired that it dismissed such condemnation with disdain. It is possible that it is aware of the strategic relevance of the country in the geo-strategic calculation of major players and that it has been using this as leverage to carve out its own space to maintain an iron grip on power in the country. This also explains the audacity of the junta to punish the pro-democracy activists without any fair trial and, thus, show contempt for the unwavering democratic aspirations of the people of Myanmar.

Japan and Invitation to Myanmar for Abe's State Funeral

Japanese diplomacy faced another hiccup when the Kishida government extended an invitation to Myanmar to the state funeral of the slain former Prime Minister Abe Shinzo on 27 September 2022. As per diplomatic protocol, Japan was to extend invitations to those countries with which it maintains diplomatic relations. Taiwan was an exception because of its special status. By inviting Myanmar's Ambassador to Japan to the event to offer tribute, Japan was seen to be legitimising the *Tatmadaw*.

Concluding Observations

From the discussion, it transpires that politics in the Indo-Pacific, Myanmar included, is being driven by geo-strategic considerations. Nations in the region willy-nilly are bound to compromise certain values in the larger interests of national and regional security. Myanmar is a test case in this narrative. Though Japan, India and other countries in the world disapprove of the conduct of the military junta, there is little they can do except making some cosmetic statements of disapproval and appeal to the conscience of the junta to respect and honour human lives and their dignity. Japan is caught in this vortex of great power politics and therefore continues to remain engaged in Myanmar.

ENDNOTES

1. Ryan Hartley, "The Evolution of Japan-Myanmar Relations since 1988", in James D. J. Brown and Jeff Kingston, (eds.), *Japan's Foreign Relations in Asia* (Routledge, 2018), pp. 291-311.
2. Taka, "Relations between Japan and Myanmar (Burma), Asia's last frontier", *The Hidanotaka*, 08 January 2021, available at https://hidanotaka.com/relations-between-japan-and-myanmarburma/, last accessed on 27 October 2022
3. Ministry of Foreign Affairs, "Japan Myanmar Relations," available at https://www.mofa.go.jp/region/asia-paci/myanmar/data.html
4. Nan Lwin, "Japan to Take Leading Role in Pushing FDI in Rakhine", *The Irrawaddy*, 08 February 2019, available at https://www.irrawaddy.com/news/japan-take-leading-role-pushing-fdi-rakhine.html, last accessed on 27 October 2022
5. "Japan's Stepped-up Negotiating Role a Welcome Development in Myanmar", *The Irrawaddy*, 03 December 2020, available at https://www.irrawaddy.com/opinion/analysis/japans-stepped-negotiating-role-welcome-development-myanmar.html, last accessed on 27 October 2022
6. Human Rights Watch, "Tatmadaw Cadets Receive Training at Japanese Defence Academy", available at https://www.hrw.org/news/2021/12/21/japan-cut-defense-ties-myanmar-military, last accessed on 27 October 2022
7. For background, see David Steinberg, "Japanese Economic Assistance To Burma: Aid in the "Tarenagashi" Manner?", *An Interdisciplinary Journal of Southeast Asian Studies*, vol. 4 (1990): pp. 51-107
8. Jessie Yeung, "Myanmar's military has detained leader Aung San Suu Kyi in a coup. Here's what you need to know", *Edition,* 10 March 2021, available at https://edition.cnn.com/2021/02/01/asia/myanmar-military-coup-explainer-intl-hnk-scli/index.html, last accessed on 27 October 2022
9. "Suu Kyi to spend 6 more years in jail for corruption", *The South Asia Times*, 13 October 2022, available at https://thesouthasiantimes.info/suu-kyi-to-spend-6-more-years-in-jail-for-corruption/#:~:text=Suu%20Kyi%20to%20spend%206%20more%20years%20in, corruption%2C%20according%20t, last accessed on 27 October 2022
10. Luke Austin, "Trouble at the mill: Japan-Myanmar relations and implications of the coup for Japanese foreign policy", *HS Centre*, 18 September 2021, available at http://www.hscentre.org/asia-and-pacific/trouble-mill-japan-myanmar-relations-implications-coup-japanese-foreign-policy/, last accessed on 27 October 2022.
11. Ministry of Foreign Affairs, "Emergency Grant Aid for humanitarian assistance to the populations affected by the coup in Myanmar", 1 April 2022, available at https://www.mofa.go.jp/press/release/press1e_000280.html, last accessed on 27 October 2022
12. "Japan's Eneos withdraws from Myanmar gas project", *The Japan Times*, 2 May 2022, available at https://www.japantimes.co.jp/news/2022/05/02/business/corporate-business/eneos-myanmar-project/, last accessed on 27 October 2022
13. The JETRO conducted a survey in August-September 2021 to judge the mood of the Japanese companies, to which 180 companies responded. "70% of Japan firms keep, expand business in Myanmar even after coup", *Kyodo News*, 10 January 2022, available at https://english.kyodonews.net/news/2022/01/7e3de89004f5-70-of-japan-firms-keep-expand-business-in-myanmar-even-after-coup.html, last accessed on 27 October 2022
14. "Business Sentiment Survey Report: Perception of ASEAN businesses Towards Japan 2022", *Jetro,* 09 December 2021, available at https://www.jetro.go.jp/ext_images/en/reports/survey/pdf/202208.pdf, last accessed on 27 October 2022
15. Daisuke Akimoto, "Japan's ambivalent diplomacy in Myanmar", *The Diplomat*, 13 May 2021, available at https://thediplomat.com/2021/05/japans-ambivalent-diplomacy-in-myanmar/, last accessed on 27 October 2022

16. ASEAN, "Chairman's Statement on the ASEAN Leaders' Meeting," 24 April 2021, available at https://asean.org/wp-content/uploads/Chairmans-Statement-on-ALM-Five-Point-Consensus-24-April-2021-FINAL-a-1.pdf#:~:text=The%20ASEAN%20Leaders%E2%80%99%20 Meeting%20was%
17. See, "R2P and the UN", available at https://www.un.org/en/chronicle/article/r2p-and-un
18. Keiho Sasamori, "Japan's Myanmar Missteps Are Damaging Its Image", *The Diplomat*, 10 March 2021, available at https://thediplomat.com/2021/03/japans-myanmar-missteps-are-damaging-its-image/
19. Yuzuki Nagakoshi, "Japan and Myanmar's Toxic Friendship", *The Diplomat*, 15 January 2020, available at https://thediplomat.com/2020/01/japan-and-myanmars-toxic-friendship/
20. The four executed were prominent members of the democratic opposition – democracy activist Kyaw Min Yu (known as "Ko Jimmy"), former Member of Parliament Phyo Zeyar Thaw, as well as Aung Thura Zaw and Hla Myo Aung.
21. Rajaram Panda, "Executions in Myanmar Disturbing News for the Region and the World", *VIF*, 04 August 2022, available at https://www.vifindia.org/article/2022/august/04/executions-in-myanmar-disturbing-news-for-the-region-and-the-world
22. Ministry of Foreign Affairs, "Regarding Executions of Myanmar Citizens including Pro-democracy Activists (Statement by Foreign Minister Hayashi Yoshimasa)", 25 July 2022, available at https://www.mofa.go.jp/press/release/press1e_000312.html, last accessed on 27 October 2022
23. Ministry of Foreign Affairs, "Joint Statement on Execution of Pro-Democracy and Opposition Leaders in Myanmar", 26 July 2022, available at https://www.mofa.go.jp/press/release/press1e_000312.html, last accessed on 27 October 2022
24. Ministry of Foreign Affairs, "G7 Foreign Ministers' Statement on the executions by the military junta in Myanmar", 28 July 2022, available at https://www.mofa.go.jp/press/release/press4e_003153.html, last accessed on 27 October 2022

17

Myanmar-ASEAN Relations: An Overview

Brig Vinod Anand

ABSTRACT

Myanmar was admitted as a member of the Association of South East Asian Nations in July 1997. ASEAN itself had been formed thirty years earlier, in 1967, as an endeavour to reduce outside interference in the region and promote regional integration. These countries were keen to exploit the complementarities of their economies besides finding common ground on security challenges. Myanmar's rich resource-based economy was seen as complementary to support the growth of the region as a whole. There was also a belief that Burma's entry into ASEAN would pressure it to improve its human rights record. With the formation of the 2008 Constitution, Myanmar's democratic transition started. However, the 2021 military takeover has raised concerns over this transition. It has also raised concerns about ASEAN's role and credibility in these conflicting times. This chapter explores the relationship between Myanmar and ASEAN from 1997 to 2012, the role of Myanmar as ASEAN chair and the scenario post the 2021-military coup.

Introduction

Myanmar was admitted as a member of the Association of South East Asian Nations in July 1997 despite serious objections from the USA and Western countries due to the lack of democracy there. ASEAN itself had been formed thirty years earlier, in 1967, as an endeavour to reduce outside interference in the region and promote regional integration. These countries did not wish to be influenced by the West and were also wary of communist China. They were also keen to exploit the complementarities of their economies besides finding common ground on security challenges. Myanmar's rich resource-based economy was seen as complementary to support the growth of the region as a whole.

There was also a belief that Burma's entry into ASEAN would pressure it to improve its human rights record. The military administration that had taken over the reins of power in August 1988 called itself Burma's State Law and Order Restoration Council, which changed its name to State Peace and Development Council in late 1997 after getting admission to ASEAN. Since 1988, the military government had been placed under broad sanctions by the USA, and the West and diplomatic engagement and contacts had been reduced; all these actions were aimed at encouraging Burma to move towards a democratic polity.

Sanctions against Myanmar were imposed by the European Union in 1991 when the military refused to recognise the results of the May 1990 elections, and Aung San Suu Kyi, leader of the National League for Democracy (NLD), had been under house arrest since 1989. ASEAN, in general, had been uncomfortable with the EU and other actors that had been vociferously critical of the military Junta's undemocratic practices and human rights. ASEAN members were more in favour of constructive engagement of the Myanmar military government, which would 'eventually contribute to more sustainable achievements in all fields'. ASEAN's emphasis continued to be on adhering to the principle of non-interference and achieving its objectives through diplomacy and enhanced economic engagement with Myanmar. It is also worth noting that ASEAN had not gone about making its membership conditional to carrying out any internal political reforms by the prospective member country.

Looking Back: Period 1997-2012

The period between 1997 and 2012 saw several changes in the political and economic scenarios both at the internal and regional levels of the ASEAN member-countries and the organisation, which led to changed attitudes towards Myanmar and to some subtle dilution in the principle of non-interference. The Asian financial crisis of 1997-98 also led to the ASEAN questioning its ability to deal with such a crisis and its worth and value as a regional entity. Indonesia, Thailand, and Malaysia were most affected by the crisis. In fact, President Suharto of Indonesia had to resign due to popular unrest created by the collapse of the economy, which also led to the democratisation of Indonesian politics.

Three countries, in particular, Thailand, Indonesia and the Philippines, expressed concerns about the policy of non-interference and called for 'flexible engagement' to enable ASEAN to deal with the regional crisis caused by a domestic situation. Earlier, only good governance and not necessarily democratic polity were the basic criteria amongst the ASEAN members, but gradually and increasingly, human rights also started finding a degree of resonance.

The ASEAN's Hanoi Plan of Action of December 1998, among many diverse areas of regional cooperation on finance, economy, trade and security cooperation, also included its intention of exchanging information in the area of human rights with a view to protect all human rights and promote fundamental freedoms as per the UN Charter, the Universal Declaration of Human Rights and the Vienna Declaration and Programme of Action.

Within Myanmar's military government, there was some movement towards increasing its engagement with the international community and changing its attitude towards Aung San Suu Kyi and her political party, the NLD. In May 2002, she was released by the government, and the Myanmar military stated that "*Today marks a new page for the people of Myanmar [Burma] and the international community. We shall re-commit ourselves to allowing all of our citizens to participate freely in the life of our political process while giving priority to national unity, peace, and stability of the country as well as the region.*"

However, she was again in prison in May 2003 after an attack engineered by a pro-government group on her convoy resulted in her NLD guard's death. Evidently, this incident did not go down well with the ASEAN. In their Joint Communiqué of Foreign Ministers meeting on 16-17 June 2003, they referred to the incident of 30 May 2003 and '*urged Myanmar to resume its efforts of national reconciliation and dialogue among all parties concerned leading to a peaceful transition to democracy*'.

This was the first time that ASEAN had talked about democracy in Myanmar. It also encouraged Myanmar to remove restrictions placed on Aung San Suu Kyi and NLD members. It expressed its continued support for the efforts of the UNSG Special Representative (Tan Sri Razali Ismail of Malaysia). This was the beginning of democracy, and the treatment meted out to political leaders, especially Suu Kyi, became contentious issues in the evolving ASEAN-Myanmar relationship. Ensuring a smooth transition to democracy was also mentioned, for instance, in the subsequent Joint Communiqué of 2004.

Further, Myanmar missed its turn to become Chair of the ASEAN in 2006 because the military government said it needed to 'devote attention to the ongoing national reconciliation and democratic process'. In any case, a number of ASEAN countries were opposed to Myanmar taking over the Chairmanship. The ASEAN members' view was that the 'road map towards democracy' of Myanmar's military regime had not made much progress.

Member countries like Indonesia, Singapore, Malaysia, and the Philippines had their own interpretations of the shortcomings of the SPDC. The military junta had resorted to the brutal suppression of anti-government protests in September 2007, which invited further criticism of the SPDC; these protests were also termed as the 'saffron revolution'. Nevertheless, the grouping spurned attempts by the USA and Western countries to take stronger action, like throwing Myanmar out of the ASEAN.

In May 2008, the military regime conducted a referendum for drafting Myanmar's Constitution, which was said to have been passed with 92 per cent of votes in its favour. The Constitution was drafted later and came into force in January 2011; this Constitution was quasi-democratic in nature that worked in favour of the military regime. Meanwhile, Suu Kyi remained under arrest for some reason or the other on various pretexts.

At the 14th ASEAN Summit held in Feb-March 2009, the ASEAN asked Gen Thein Sen to brief them on the situation in Myanmar. He apprised the ASEAN leaders about implementing the seven-step roadmap to democracy. ASEAN also advised the General to hasten the multi-party political process, including the release of political detainees leading to general elections in 2010. While the NLD had opposed the 2008 constitution, it participated in the 2012 bye-election for 46 seats achieving a landslide victory. The ASEAN saw these developments as significant steps undertaken by Myanmar and its inclination to march towards democracy.

It is also worth noting that the visit of President Barack Obama to Myanmar in November 2012 was in recognition of the fact that political and economic reforms were underway. Though there could also have been geopolitical reasons, as in November 2011, the Obama Administration announced its 'pivot to Asia Pacific' policy. Restricting the influence of China in Myanmar was another factor that was taken into account by the USA and Western actors. Further, European countries like France, Germany, and UK were also keen to participate in Myanmar's opening up in economic arenas. The visit also opened up space for civil rights groups, NGOs, and activists. Moreover, the Myanmar military was invited to send observers to joint USA-Thailand Cobra Gold military exercises in 2013.

Myanmar as ASEAN Chair

In 2014, Myanmar became the Chair of ASEAN and conducted hundreds of meetings and summits of ASEAN and its partners, showcasing its organisational capacities. During the ASEAN Chairman's statement by Gen Thein Sein, he reaffirmed the "*pledge to strengthen democracy, enhance good governance and the rule of law and to promote and protect human rights and fundamental freedoms*". Further, India's Prime Minister Modi also visited Myanmar in 2014 to attend the ASEAN-India Summit and East Asia Summit; besides meeting Government leaders, he also met Aung San Suu Kyi. Thus, the ASEAN-Myanmar relationship seemed to have turned a corner, with Myanmar leadership expressing its will to usher in more political and economic reforms.

In November 2015, Myanmar elections were conducted under the military-drafted Constitution, wherein Aung San Suu Kyi's NLD party won the elections with a landslide victory. Though Suu Kyi could not become President because of certain restrictions imposed by the previous government and included in the Constitution, she continued to exercise her authority in the party and the government. The new civilian government took over the reins of power in February 2016.

This was also the time when the ASEAN-Myanmar relationship continued to be strengthened with the hope of further political and economic reforms. A "Business Outlook Survey" undertaken by the US Chambers of Commerce named Myanmar as one of the three most popular countries for investment and economic expansion besides Indonesia and Vietnam. With further liberalisation of the economy, investments in Myanmar were expected to double by 2020.

The bonhomie between Myanmar and ASEAN lasted till about August 2017, when the human rights situation deteriorated in Rakhine because of widespread reprisals by the *tatmadaw* against the Rohingya community and their consequent flight to Bangladesh as refugees. Though Myanmar and Bangladesh had reached an agreement for the return of the displaced persons in November 2017, not much substantive action was taken by Myanmar in the succeeding years. In the joint communiqués of the ASEAN Foreign Ministers of 2018, 2019, and 2020, the paras regarding the need for the Myanmar government to address the situation arising out of the Rohingya situation continued to get longer with ASEAN urging the Nay Pi Taw to create conditions for the return of displaced persons from Bangladesh as also to make progress on national reconciliation with other ethnic minorities.

However, the response from the Myanmar government was not satisfactory. Both Suu Kyi and Myanmar were unable to take any effective measures to ensure the safe return and resettlement of the Rohingyas in Rakhine State. In December 2019, ASEAN, on its part, sent its representatives from ASEAN Humanitarian Assistance along with Myanmar government representatives to Cox Bazar refugee camp in Bangladesh to assess the delivery of humanitarian assistance and return of the displaced persons. As is well known, the Rohingyas have not been able to return.

Scenario Post Military Coup of February 2021

In the general elections of Myanmar held in November 2020, the NLD led by Aung San Suu Kyi won with a massive majority; however, before the new government could be installed, the military, headed by its Senior General Min Aung Hlaing, overthrew the civilian government on 01 February 2021 and took over the reins of power. This action was condemned by the international community and ASEAN as well. In April 2021, the ASEAN's Chairman (Sultan of Brunei Darussalam), in a Special Summit held in Jakarta, declared that a 'Five Points Consensus'[1] had been arrived at to address the challenges arising out of the situation in Myanmar.

Gen Min Aung Hlaing also attended the Summit but conveyed that his attendance in no way means that his administration in Myanmar has been recognised. President Joko Widodo of Indonesia told Gen Hlaing that violence must be stopped and democracy and stability in Myanmar must be restored. Similarly, Malaysian Prime Minister Muhyiddin Yassin termed the situation deplorable and asked for political detainees to be released[2].

The main features of the consensus were; first, violence should be stopped immediately, and all parties should exercise utmost restraint. Second, dialogue amongst all parties should be commenced to find a peaceful solution. Third, a Special Envoy appointed by ASEAN will be tasked to facilitate the dialogue process and mediation. Fourth, humanitarian assistance will be provided through ASEAN's AHA, and lastly, ASEAN's Special Envoy will visit Myanmar and meet all the parties concerned.

However, Myanmar's military regime has not been receptive to giving a practical shape to the Consensus. It has created many obstacles in stymieing the mission and task of the Special Envoy. It is also worth noting that neither any military representative of the Myanmar regime nor General Min Aung Hlaing was invited to a number of ASEAN-related summits held in October 2021 through Myanmar was asked to send a non-political representative for various summits. Some analysts saw this as a reaction to not allowing ASEAN's Special Envoy to meet Aung San Suu Kyi. This was also viewed as some sort of censure to Myanmar's State Administration Council, i.e., the military junta. The general refrain of the summit meetings was to urge Myanmar to cooperate with the ASEAN's Special Envoy and fully implement ASEAN leaders' Five Point Consensus (FPC).

In October 2021, Cambodia became Chair of ASEAN and the country's Foreign Minister, Prak Sokhonn, was appointed ASEAN's Special Envoy to Myanmar. Cambodian Prime Minister Hun Sen visited Myanmar in January 2022 despite criticism from ASEAN leaders, the international community, and protests by Myanmar's opposition groups and activists.[3] Such a visit was viewed as giving legitimacy to the military regime of Myanmar. Hun Sen justified his visit by saying that the visit would help ASEAN's peace plan to be realised.

However, after the visit, he told the Indonesian President that there was hardly any progress on the Five Point Consensus. He was also not able to have a meeting with Suu Kyi, who had been detained by the military authorities since the coup and had been awarded 26 years of imprisonment based on several trumped-up charges. Thus, Hun Sen's visit to Myanmar did little to help advance the ASEAN's FPC objectives.

Later, in March and June-July 2022, Cambodian Foreign Minister Prak Sokhonn, designated as ASEAN's Special Envoy, carried out two visits to Myanmar, concentrating on stopping violence, dialogue between the parties and humanitarian assistance; these were his three priorities out of the five laid down in the FPC. He met many stakeholders, including General Min Aung Hliang, the Foreign Minister, Myanmar's Task Force on ASEAN Humanitarian Assistance, as also representatives of seven Ethnic Armed Organisations and seven political parties who won seats in the November 2020 elections.

However, he was not allowed to meet either Suu Kyi or elected political party representatives. Evidently, in the absence of discussions with a major stakeholder, the efforts to achieve peace and reconciliation lacked credibility. Meanwhile, Myanmar's violence and civil strife continued to increase, with EAOs and PDFs putting up stiff resistance to the *Tatmadaw*. There were also reports that the Myanmar military's forces were weakening due to desertions and increasingly popular opposition to authoritarian rule.

ASEAN Chairman Hun Sen issued a statement on 25 July 2022 denouncing the execution of four activists in Myanmar despite his requests to the military regime to reconsider the matter and stated that it was a setback to the process and a 'gross lack of will to support the efforts'.[4] The fact that this execution took place a few days before the forthcoming ASEAN's Foreign Ministers 55th meeting in August 2022 showed the little regard the military junta had for the ASEAN as an organisation as also a lack of any serious commitment to the FPC.

During the above-mentioned meeting, the ASEAN Foreign Ministers discussed developments in Myanmar and observed that despite the visits of Prime Minister Hun Sen and Mr. Prak Sokohonn, ASEAN's Special Envoy to Myanmar, limited and little progress had been made on the FPC and they were deeply disappointed with Nay Pi Taw authorities' ineffective implementation of FPC.[5] Further, a Special Meeting of the ASEAN Foreign Ministers was held by Cambodia at the ASEAN Secretariat in Jakarta on 27 October 2022 to address the implementation of FPC; a non-political representative from Myanmar was invited, but there was no positive response. Nevertheless, there were reports that the Special Envoy of ASEAN was planning to visit Myanmar once more in the last quarter of 2022 to find a modus vivendi with the military junta to make progress on FPC. However, the visit did not fructify due to the uncooperative and truculent behaviour of the military regime. The ASEAN leaders' summit held in November 2022 was also unable to come out with any concrete agenda on resolving Myanmar situation except for making some anodyne statement on the Myanmar issue (which formed part of the Chairman's statements of the 40th and 41st ASEAN Summits held at Phnom Penh).[6]

Concluding Observations

Myanmar military, since its independence from British colonial rule in January 1948, has considered itself to be the guarantor of Myanmar's national unity due to many prevalent ethnic, social and political divisions in the country. Historically, it views itself as an army with political experience and not as a 'mercenary' army; it emerged as a powerful institution in the '40s and '50s after dealing with various separatist and communist insurgencies. After Myanmar's political crisis in October 1958, it interfered in the political process multiple times.

Though after the 2015 elections in Myanmar and the installation of the Suu Kyi-led NLD government in March 2016, it was hoped that the military would gradually advance on the path of democracy, including possibly amending the military-dominated constitution. However, the military coup of February 2021 has put brakes on the prospects of further liberalisation of democracy, and it is difficult to visualise when it is restored in Myanmar even though General Hlaing has promised elections in 2023.

In so far as the ASEAN-Myanmar relationship is concerned, it commenced with Myanmar being admitted to ASEAN in July 1997 despite the reservations of the USA and Western countries due to its lack of democracy and its disregard for human rights. While ASEAN wanted to adhere to its much-avowed principle of mutual non-interference in internal affairs and not be critical of internal political processes, it became increasingly difficult to stick to such principles as time passed and the UN and the international community became more vocal on human rights violations and abuses by the Myanmar military. On the part of ASEAN as a grouping, it was keen to integrate Myanmar because of several geopolitical changes occurring in the region with China and other outside powers like the USA and EU jockeying for power influence.

The continued disregard of the ASEAN FPC by the Myanmar military regime also puts a question mark on the credibility and cohesiveness of ASEAN as a regional grouping. There is also a view among the international community that as per the UN Charter/Resolutions, the 'Responsibility to Protect' (R2P) clause could become applicable to Myanmar's situation if the human rights situation continues to worsen and violence escalates further. However, it is felt that it might create more problems than solve, with instability likely to intensify further. The UN Special Rapporteur for Myanmar, in its October 2022 report, has recounted that the military has killed thousands and displaced nearly a million people; over 12,000 political prisoners have been tortured, and an unknown number have died in custody.

Lastly, the ASEAN needs to continue with its efforts to mediate with all the parties involved in the Myanmar peace and reconciliation process, including the National Unity Government (NUG). General Hlaing has promised to hold elections in August 2023; will he stick to his promise is another question? ASEAN also needs to take stock of its relationship with Myanmar if the situation does not stabilise by then. Would ASEAN be ready to take much more assertive action against the Myanmar military regime if it does not make progress on the Five-Point Consensus?

ENDTNOTES

1. ASEAN, "Chairman's Statement on the ASEAN Leaders' meeting," 24 April 2021, available at https://asean.org/wp-content/uploads/Chairmans-Statement-on-ALM-Five-Point-Consensus-24-April-2021-FINAL-a-1.pdf, last accessed on 31 October 2022.
2. "Will ASEAN's actions match its tough talk on Myanmar?" *The Japan Times*, 01 May 2021, available at https://www.japantimes.co.jp/opinion/2021/05/01/editorials/myanmar-asean-human-rights-democracy/, last accessed on 31 October 2022
3. "Cambodian PM Hun Sen's visit with Myanmar military chief sparks protests", *The Guardian*, 08 January 2022, available at https://www.theguardian.com/world/2022/jan/08/cambodian-pm-hun-sens-visit-with-myanmar-military-chief-sparks-protests, last accessed on 31 October 2022
4. ASEAN Cambodia, "Joint communiqué of the 55th ASEAN foreign ministers' meeting", 03 August 2022, available at https://asean.org/wp-content/uploads/2022/07/final-2-Eng-

Chairmans-statement-on-execution.pdf, last accessed on 31 October 2022

5. ASEAN Cambodia, ASEAN Chairman's Statement on the Execution of Four Opposition Activists in Myanmar, 25 July 2022, available at https://asean.org/wp-content/uploads/2022/08/Joint_Communique-of-the-55th-AMM-FINAL.pdf, last accessed on 31 October 2022
6. ASEAN Cambodia, "CHAIRMAN'S STATEMENT OF THE 40TH and 41ST ASEAN SUMMITS," 11 November 2022, available at https://asean.org/wp-content/uploads/2022/11/01-Chairmans-Statement-of-the-40th-and-41st-ASEAN-Summits-2.pdf, last accessed on 31 October 2022

SECTION FIVE

India-Myanmar Relations

18

Bilateral Ties through Various Political Changes in Myanmar[1]

Amb V S Seshadri

ABSTRACT

Myanmar gained independence on 04 January 1948, less than five months after India. For both countries, it is now the completion of 75 years of freedom. During the colonial period, till a decade before its independence, Myanmar, then called Burma, was a province of the British Empire in India. It was ruled from Delhi up to 1937 when it was made into a separate entity directly administered by London. While that factor did not bring closer ties between the two independent neighbours, their relations have travelled a long way in subsequent years. These have, however, not been without their ups and downs from time to time. These unsteady trends have shown up more due to political changes, even as India's national interests needed to be factored in. In retrospect, the decade of 2010, when Myanmar showed greater promise of a transition to democracy, perhaps witnessed the most fruitful relations between the two countries. However, it is not clear how the decade of the 2020s decade will work out, considering the difficult times Myanmar is presently going through.

The Initial Years After Independence

Two important factors defined the relationship during the initial years after independence when both countries were fledgling democracies. One was the warm friendship between the two Prime Ministers, Jawaharlal Nehru and U Nu, that contributed to close consultations and frequent exchange of visits. The second, a restraining factor, at least at the popular level, was the treatment meted out to Indians in Burma who had been brought in by the British in various capacities during the colonial period and who were seen by the Burmans as foreigners notwithstanding that several of them had become residents for a generation or more. From the 1930s onwards, measures taken towards discriminating against Indians resulted in waves of them returning to their homeland and resettling.

The Ne Win years

The military takeover by General Ne Win in 1962 and his harsh and quixotic rule for the next 26 years, marked by what was billed as the 'Burmese way to socialism' saw the country also withdrawing into a shell internationally, espousing its own version of neutrality and quitting the non-aligned movement. Poor economic policies led to the intrinsically resource-rich country ending up weak economically. Indian and Burmese leaders did exchange some visits, and the two countries also signed the land border agreement in 1967 and the maritime border agreement in 1986. However, beyond that, there were no notable outcomes. The decision by General Ne Win early during his rule to nationalise enterprises in 1963 also dealt a severe blow to several Indian businesses still left in the country and led to another round of exodus.

Prime Minister Rajiv Gandhi did undertake an official visit to Myanmar in December 1987, and it was reported that the discussions centred on the expansion and consolidation of friendly relations between the two countries. However, the reality was apparently different, with General Ne Win displaying a very negative approach to India's proposals.[2] There was also discontent brewing against the Ne Win administration, with the country's economic decline further exacerbated by a thoughtless demonetisation with new currency denominations divisible by nine for astrological reasons.

Aung San Suu Kyi Enters the Scene and the Struggle for Democracy

The democracy movement led by students and Aung San Suu Kyi (ASSK) in 1988 did initially appear to offer change and hope. Democratically held elections in 1990 resulted in a resounding win for the National League for Democracy (NLD) led by ASSK. Even before the new government could take office, the military intervened in what eventually became two more decades of military rule led eventually by General Than Shwe, who took over in 1992. Initially, India took a fairly strong line supporting the democracy movement when several of the movement's leaders, including ASSK, had been put under house arrest. This led to a cooling off of ties with the military regime. However, this policy underestimated the durability of the regime, and soon a correction was needed.

The Start of Engagement with the Myanmar Military Regime

Two further elements entered India's calculus at this stage. China, which had hitherto had a difficult relationship with Myanmar, began to develop cosier ties with the regime helping with arms supplies and facilitating truce arrangements between the Myanmar military and certain rebel ethnic groups of Myanmar near the China border. Secondly, the need to tackle some of India's own ethnic rebel groups that had been taking shelter across the border in Myanmar, which also drew support from China, acquired greater focus. Security imperatives required India to enhance its engagement with Myanmar. They thus began a two-track approach from 1994 onwards that focussed on engaging with the ruling dispensation on the one hand while also showing some support for democratic forces and its leaders. As the military regime lengthened and Myanmar's dependence on China appeared to grow, India's engagement track acquired greater importance.

Bilateral Relations Gain Focus

India's economic and technical cooperation programme received an impetus during this period. The Tamu-Kalay/Kalewa India-Myanmar Friendship Road in Myanmar across Manipur state was constructed by India as grant assistance and inaugurated in 2002. Institutes for imparting English language skills, entrepreneurship development, industrial skills training and computer education were set up. Plans were also made to construct the Kaladan River-cum-road transit transport corridor project that would provide an alternative route for supplies to reach from Kolkata to Mizoram through the Sittwe port in Myanmar. Similarly, the trilateral highway that would extend the friendship road further to link up to Mandalay and then further to Thailand was also conceived during this period, with feasibility reports prepared. Further, Indian companies, ONGC and GAIL, were permitted to acquire a share in the Shwe gas project off the Myanmar coast.

Matters also appeared to acquire more salience on the political front with exchanges of visits by President Abdul Kalam to Myanmar in 2006 and by Senior General Than Shwe in 2004, apart from visits at other levels. Dialogues and visits also got featured at the military level. Even as the Myanmar military regime still remained substantially isolated globally, engagement with India must have helped. From Myanmar's perspective, a degree of balance vis-a-vis China was also important, even as it depended on the Chinese veto at the UN Security Council to escape condemnatory actions, particularly after the 'saffron uprising' in 2008.

Elections in Myanmar Offered Hopes of Transition to Democracy

There was welcome relief worldwide when Senior General Than Shwe decided to hang up his boots, and elections were held in the year 2010 in a controlled manner under a new constitution adopted in 2008 that was intended to usher in a 'disciplined democracy' with the military having a 25 per cent reservation of parliamentary seats. The NLD led by ASSK, who was still under house arrest, did not participate in these elections, which were won by the newly-formed Union Social Development Party (USDP), comprised mostly of retired Generals and other senior military officers who had shed their military uniforms and had become civilian candidates just before the elections. While there was much scepticism about the results and widespread criticism internationally about the elections, India took a more constructive stance. It hoped that it would mark a transition towards a return to democracy. ASSK was also released soon after the elections, and former Prime Minister Thein Sein, a general in Than Shwe's regime, became the new President of the country beginning in April 2011.

The Country Opened up under President Thein Sein

The five years of Thein Sein's government saw the government opening up on several fronts. These included the release of political prisoners, greater media freedom, ushering in economic reforms and launching a peace process with the ethnic rebel groups. ASSK could return to political activity, and the NLD soon sprang to life and decided to participate in the bye-elections held for 40-odd seats in April 2012. The elections conducted then, which were widely witnessed by the international media and election observers, including from India, were mostly free and fair, and the NLD candidates, including ASSK herself, won handsomely in virtually every contested constituency. Myanmar suddenly became a sought-after nation with many Western countries with no resident diplomatic representation, opening embassies or others upgrading them. ASSK was also permitted to travel to global capitals, where she received warmth, accolades, and awards. Foreign investors began to make a beeline. Soon economic indicators began ticking up with expert predictions that Myanmar could leave behind its Least Developed Country (LDC) status and emerge with a middle-income profile. The only country that received some setbacks in its relations during this period was China which had to contend with the unilateral suspension of the mega Myitsone hydroelectric project by the Thein Sein administration on environmental grounds.

Bilateral Relations Begin to Show Greater Promise

Relations with India, too, prospered on various fronts. The state visits by President Thein Sein in October 2011 and by PM Dr. Manmohan Singh in May 2012, the latter by a Prime Minister of India to Myanmar after 25 years, significantly contributed to this regard. ASSK also visited India in November 2012 and delivered the Jawaharlal Nehru Memorial lecture. These were in addition to exchanges and visits of several other delegations, including Chiefs of the Armed Forces, Speakers of national assemblies and Cabinet Ministers. India supported and encouraged the path-breaking reform measures taken by Myanmar towards greater democratisation and national reconciliation. Bilaterally, a host of new initiatives were taken apart from reinforcing ongoing ones in many areas, including connectivity, power and energy, trade and investment, development cooperation projects, defence supplies, culture and people-to-people relations. India also extended a line of credit for US$ 500 m to Myanmar for development-related projects.[3]

A similar politically conducive environment prevailed for promoting bilateral relations during the subsequent five-year period of the NLD government that was *de facto* headed by ASSK even as she was designated as the State Councillor. She was accorded a state visit to India in October 2016, which took place just a couple of months after the then Myanmar President Htin Kyaw's visit. PM Modi also returned the visit the following year when he was warmly welcomed. The Western world, however, began to distance itself again from Myanmar during this period, principally because of the manner of treatment of the Rohingya people in Myanmar, which resulted in hundreds of thousands of Rohingyas fleeing as refugees to Bangladesh. ASSK appeared to go along with the Myanmar military involved in these actions. She did constitute an Advisory Commission on Rakhine state led by former UN Secretary-General Kofi Annan, who came up with several recommendations, but these were eventually ignored. When Gambia took the matter to the International Court of Justice, ASSK led the Myanmar delegation to defend the country. Besides, international efforts to repatriate these refugees from Bangladesh to Myanmar made little progress.

India's Response to the Rohingya Issue

India's response to these developments was, however, unlike that of the Western countries. With several Rohingya refugees also making their way to India, India's response, as it evolved over this entire period, was fourfold.[4] India condemned the initial terrorist actions of the Arakan Rohingya Salvation Army (ARSA) group resulting in the loss of life of some Myanmar security forces. It also expressed its deep concern about the situation in Rakhine State and the outflow of refugees. It further urged that the situation in Rakhine State be handled with restraint and maturity, focussing on the welfare of the civilian populations alongside those of the security forces. Secondly, India took a tough stance on the entry and stay of Rohingya refugees in India, and there were pronouncements that they would be returned to where they had come from. Third, India extended some relief assistance for Rohingya refugees in Bangladesh under 'Operation Insaniyat' to support the latter's humanitarian efforts. Fourth, India did try to use its engagement with Myanmar to persuade the country to take the refugees back quietly. It announced some measures for the development of the Rakhine region in Myanmar, including the construction of prefabricated housing to meet the needs of the returning people.

India had to keep in view two aspects. Firstly, it was getting assistance from the Myanmar military in dealing with the Indian ethnic rebels taking shelter in Myanmar. Secondly, the Chinese were back into enhancing engagement with Myanmar and were developing closer ties with the NLD government. Suu Kyi made several visits to China during this period, and President Xi Jin Ping also visited Myanmar in January 2020. China strove hard to get the China-Myanmar Economic Corridor proposals pushed through during this period and to consolidate its participation in the Kyaukphyu port-related projects. The Kyaukphyu port was connected through cross-country pipelines to the Yunnan province of China for transporting natural gas and crude secured from the Gulf and other sources.

PM Modi's Visits Help Strengthen Relations and Further

India's overall engagement with Myanmar, therefore, continued to expand during the NLD government, which in fact, got reflected in the joint statement released after PM Narendra Modi's state visit to the country in September 2017, again covering a whole range of areas from security-related issues to trade and investment, power and infrastructure, technical cooperation and culture.[5] In comparison with India's exports at the beginning of the decade in 2011-12, when they were USD 545 m, they doubled to USD 1.2 bn in 2018-19. They also diversified to include pharmaceuticals, buffalo meat, cotton yarn, machinery, electrical machinery, vehicles including tractors and parts, certain steel items and soya bean meal.

The number of Indian companies that had set up offices in Myanmar also grew, including some of India's large business groups. An India-Myanmar Chamber of Commerce was established in 2017. The CII also got active and hosted an Enterprise India show in Yangon in December 2018. With India's assistance, the Myanmar Institute of Information Technology, a full-fledged university, set up as a centre for excellence in Mandalay and started its undergraduate and postgraduate programmes. An advanced centre for agricultural research offering Master's and doctoral research programmes set up in Yezin in Myanmar under the bilateral development cooperation programme was inaugurated by President Ramnath Kovind when he visited Myanmar in December 2018.

It was also unique that in early October 2020, despite the COVID precautions in both countries, India's Foreign Secretary Harsh Shringla and the Chief of the Indian Army, General M.M. Naravane, jointly visited Myanmar, which included calls on ASSK and other senior functionaries. Considering the flurry of visits that took place from China during that year and the increasing rebel activities of the Arakan Army in Myanmar, apart from COVID-related health emergencies at that time, it was perhaps an effort to indicate India's support towards Myanmar's security and autonomous development at a time when there were jockeying pressures for strategic projects. It could also have been aimed at showing India's support and encouragement to Myanmar at a time when it was heading for elections that were to be held in November 2020.

The Military Takeover once again Ushered in Uncertainty

All these have, however, changed somewhat with the Myanmar military taking over the reins of power once again on 01 February 2021, based on allegedly fraudulent elections, just as the newly-elected members of the Myanmar Parliament were to take the oath and form a new government led by the NLD after it won the General Elections held in November 2020. The Chief of the Armed Forces, Senior General Min Aung Hlaing (MAH), has also declared himself the Prime Minister and is administering the country through a State Administration Council (SAC) set up by him.

Meanwhile, the opposition set up a shadow National Unity Government (NUG) comprising 27 ministers in May 2021, drawn from not only the NLD but also some of the ethnic groups. The NUG came up with its idea of a federal constitution and a federal army. Since September 2021, the NUG has also declared a 'peoples' defensive war' against the regime. All this has again taken the country backwards, with the military now facing armed resistance from civilians-turned-activists, with some going underground or joining local militias termed 'peoples defence forces'. Deaths from violence continue to mount, with the toll now reportedly exceeding 2,000 and a huge number under house arrest or detention. ASSK herself and the ousted President Win Myint, apart from various other senior figures in the NLD and their supporters, have been facing multiple charges and legal proceedings with harsh sentences being handed down.

It is unclear if the armed resistance supported by the NUG (of which the NLD is a part) would have obtained the approval of ASSK, under arrest, for straying away from peaceful means. In her Jawaharlal Nehru Memorial lecture in 2012, she said, 'Our movement for democracy is firmly rooted in the principle of non-violence that Gandhi made into an effective political force even against the most powerful opponents. His influence on my political thinking is widely recognised.[6] It is also unclear whether the armed resistance mounted by the people's defence forces and certain ethnic groups to the military takeover (the military is termed *Tatmadaw* in Myanmar) would lead to any comedown by the latter. The well-armed *Tatmadaw* has fought only internal wars with some or the other ethnic armed groups, reaching, at best tactical, a temporary truce with some of them. The *tatmadaw* has been taught to think it is they who have held the country together. At the entrance to the Defence Services Academy in Pyin Loo Win, which provides training to the officer corps, the academy's signboard says, 'The triumphant elite of the future'.

The dilemma confronting Myanmar also comes out starkly if the different visions, aspirations and apprehensions are discerned from the speeches of ASSK and Gen. MAH at the inaugural session of the fourth round of the Union Peace Conference involving the ethnic armed organisations (EAOs) held in August 2020, just a couple of months before the general elections in November 2020. In her speech, ASSK reportedly,[7] stated that peace-building was not only about stopping shooting and bombing but was also about rejecting the logic of the current "bad political culture" in which 'might make right' and people must rely on arms to be recognised or succeed. She added that it was necessary to end the attitude that had led to this bad political tradition that taking up arms was the effective way of achieving one's goals.

MAH rejected that the armed military was solely responsible for the armed conflict and reportedly blamed the government and ethnic armed organisations (EAOs) for the failure of the peace process. He also criticised the National League for Democracy-led government for mediating between the *Tatmadaw* and the EAOs, saying the government was acting as if it were a neutral peacemaker. He further clarified, "The EAOs have opposed the Union and successive governments. If one studies history objectively, it can be seen that the *Tatmadaw* has protected the Union and successive governments". Tellingly, he added (and this was just a few months before the military takeover) that "based on its experience, the *Tatmadaw* is taking measures to prevent what should not happen from happening and to pave the way for what should happen to happen."

India's Stance on the Takeover and its Support for the ASEAN Initiative

While India has refrained from sharply criticising the military takeover, it has expressed its interest in Myanmar's return to democracy at the earliest, the release of detainees and prisoners, the resolution of issues through dialogue and the complete cessation of all violence. India has also fully backed the ASEAN initiative, put together in a Five-Point Consensus (ASEAN-FPC), towards cessation of violence and making progress through dialogue among all parties involved. While the ASEAN is making efforts, including its unprecedented decision to suspend Myanmar military representation in ASEAN-related meetings conducted at political levels, there is not much evidence that the military is willing to allow the ASEAN initiative involving dialogue with all, including ASSK, to move forward. Rather the execution of four political activists, including a former lawmaker, on the grounds of 'aiding terrorism' in July 2022 had given disturbing signals and invited wide criticism, including from the ASEAN, which has termed it 'highly reprehensible.' India too, has noted the development with deep concern.

ASEAN's growing concern was also evident in the statements of some of its member countries at the recent UNGA general debate in September 2022. The Cambodian PM Hun Sen, speaking in the UNGA also as ASEAN chair for the year, termed the situation in Myanmar as worrisome with its direct implications on the security and stability of the region but added that the crisis was complex with deep-rooted causes.[8] The Malaysian Prime Minister, Dato Ismail Sabri Yaakob, also conveyed that Myanmar's situation remained a grave concern. He further stated that Malaysia fully supported the work of the ASEAN Chair's Special Envoy on Myanmar but added that Malaysia remained concerned that the authorities there had yet to allow ASEAN's Special Envoy to visit the country to expedite the implementation of the 'Five-Point Consensus'. Malaysia has also become the first country from ASEAN to receive NUG representatives. Its Foreign Minister, Saifuddin Abdullah, met the NUG Foreign Minister, Daw Zin Mar Aung, in May this year and also held discussions with a group of NUG representatives on the sidelines of the UNGA session.[9]

The Foreign Minister of Indonesia, Retno Marsudi (his country will be ASEAN chair in 2023), also expressed her deep concern at the Myanmar military's lack of commitment to implement the ASEAN-FPC and stated that ASEAN must move forward and not be taken hostage by the situation there.[10] She further stated that the support of the international community, in particular the neighbouring countries of Myanmar, was very important to bring back democracy in Myanmar.

The Possible Future Course of Events

It is far from clear how the situation will develop in the coming months. Three possibilities exist. One could be that the ASEAN, assisted by the international community, manages to foster a dialogue between the military and the NUG elements and helps chart a way forward. This may seem far-fetched at this stage, particularly because of the wide chasm between the military and the NUG, which are both adopting fight-to-win strategies and a complete lack of mutual trust. The military could also be emboldened to hold out with the support it is receiving from Russia (Russian FM Lavrov was in Myanmar on 04 August 2022) and the increasing engagement seen with the regime by China, whose FM, Wang Yi, was also in Myanmar in July. However, if the rest of ASEAN remains reasonably united at this stage in pressurising Myanmar, it could have an influence.

Second, the military regime may carry out its plan for conducting an election in August 2023 through the Election Commission constituted by it. It can well be expected that NLD, which is being continually discredited by the military, will be kept out of the elections. The NUG parties, including the NLD, have in any case, made clear their opposition to such new elections demanding that the Parliament that was annulled in 2020/2021 be restored. The NLD also issued a statement on 27 September 2022 stating that it would not accept any work programme of the State Administration Council set up by the military, including the election process.[11] However, such elections, if proceeded with by the military, could be an attempt to enable the military-backed USDP to win a majority of seats, as happened in 2010. In that case, Min Aung Hlaing could be elected President, but whether he can succeed in re-enacting a Thein Sein-type era towards greater openness, peace and development is far from certain. The third possibility is, of course, the continuation of military rule over an extended period citing the emergency situation in the country and the security threats from ethnic armed groups. That would mark a repeat of the Than Shwe or Ne Win era of substantial international isolation, with economic development taking a back seat.

Myanmar has experienced each foregoing possibility in some form or the other in recent history. But none of them may come about or be sustained this time easily. All this remains a cause for concern for India since it has already faced a spillover impact in the form of civilians fleeing the Chin state of Myanmar to cross over to Mizoram. Indian rebels sheltering in Myanmar could also use the disturbances to their advantage, as seen in the killings of Col. Tripathi of Assam Rifles and his family in Manipur's Chrachandpur district in November 2021. India's development projects like the Kaladan project or the trilateral highway stand little chance of making headway if the unrest prevails.

For India, there is much at stake for peace and stability to return to Myanmar. Notwithstanding its consistent support for an inclusive and democratic process to evolve and strengthen in Myanmar, it will have to continue to calibrate its level of engagement with whatever the ruling dispensation in the country considers India's own national interests. The continued scope and depth of bilateral relations will accordingly get determined. All the same, it will be important for India to be closely engaged with and be supportive of ASEAN's efforts in finding a resolution to the current difficult situation if the same is possible.

ENDNOTES

1. This essay is an expanded and updated version of an article 'India Myanmar relations over the years' written by the author which appeared in the September 2022 edition of *The Book Review*.
2. See page 97 of the book '*India-Myanmar relations: Changing Contours*' by Rajiv Bhatia, Routledge Publishers, 2016
3. The joint statement issued at the conclusion of PM Dr. Man Mohan Singh's visit, available at https://www.mea.gov.in/bilateral-documents.htm?dtl/19893/Joint+Statement+by+India+and+Myanmar+on+the+State+visit+of+Prime+Minister+of+India+to+Myanmar, last accessed on 21 November 2022
4. K Yhome, "Examining India's Stand on Rohingya Crisis," *Observor Research Foundation*, 11 July 2018, available at https://www.orfonline.org/research/examining-indias-stance-on-the-rohingya-crisis/, last accessed on 21 November 2022
5. The outcome of the visit is covered in the joint statement, available at https://mea.gov.in/bilateral-documents.htm?dtl/28924/indiamyanmar+joint+statement+issued+on+the+occasion+of+the+state+visit+of+prime+minister+of+india+to+myanmar+september+57+2017, last accessed on 21 November 2022
6. The text of ASSK Jawaharlal Nehru Memorial lecture, available at https://www.mea.gov.in/Speeches-Statements.htm?dtl/20812/Jawaharlal+Nehru+Memorial+Lecture+2012+quot Discovery+of+Nehruquot+by+Aung+San+Suu+Kyi, last accessed on 21 November 2022
7. See, "Military Chief Blames Ethnic Armies, Govt for Myanmar's Protracted Peace Process, *The Irrawaddy*, 20 August 2022, available at https://www.irrawaddy.com/news/burma/military-chief-blames-ethnic-armies-govt-myanmars-protracted-peace-process.html, last accessed on 21 November 2022; See also "Myanmar's Aung San Suu Kyi, Army Chief Trade Blame Over Stalled Peace Process," *The Irrawaddy*, 19 August 2020, available at https://www.rfa.org/english/news/myanmar/peace-process-08192020202512.html, last accessed on 21 November 2022.

8. See, "Statement by Samdech Techo Hun Sen at the 77th Session of the United Nations General Assembly," *Office of Council of Ministers*, 24 September 2022, available at https://pressocm.gov.kh/en/archives/75971, last accessed on 28 November 2022
9. See, "Malaysian Foreign Minister Meets With Myanmar's Parallel Civilian Govt," *The Irrawaddy*, 27 September 2022, available at https://www.irrawaddy.com/news/burma/malaysian-foreign-minister-meets-with-myanmars-parallel-civilian-govt.html, last accessed on 28 November 2022
10. See, "Statement By Minister For Foreign Affairs Of The Republic Of Indonesia At The General Debate Of The 77th Session Of The Un General Assembly New York", *Portal Kementerian Luar Negeri Republik Indonesia*, 26 September 2022, available at https://kemlu.go.id/portal/en/read/4018/pidato/statement-by-minister-for-foreign-affairs-of-the-republic-of-indonesia-at-the-general-debate-of-the-77th-session-of-the-un-general-assembly-new-york-26-september-2022, last accessed on 28 November 2022
11. See, "NLD announces all procedures of SAC including election are unacceptable, *Eleven Myanmar*, 28 September 2022, available at https://elevenmyanmar.com/news/nld-announces-all-procedures-of-sac-including-election-are-unacceptable, last accessed on 28 November 2022

19

An Entangled Web: Some Aspects of India's Relations with Myanmar

Amb Pankaj Saran

ABSTRACT

In the public eye, India's relations with Myanmar have not attracted the level of interest that relationships with our other neighbours have received. Myanmar attracts attention only in times of crisis. Notwithstanding its relatively low profile, the relationship is multi-layered and complex, impacting almost every aspect of India's national welfare, interest and security. In the modern era, both India and Myanmar were under colonial rule and, therefore, hostage to the domestic and foreign policy priorities of others. This chapter will highlight the key factors that have shaped and influenced India's relations with Myanmar since its independence and how they remain relevant today. Despite challenges and limitations, India and Myanmar have made persistent efforts to understand each other and reach a strategic compact that addresses their mutual needs. This chapter examines the main issues involved to understand how and why this relationship is unique and asserts that it contains important lessons for India's overall neighbourhood policy.

Introduction

India's most consequential relationships are those with its immediate neighbours. This is not surprising given our historical, cultural, and geographical linkages with each of them. The Indian subcontinent is a common civilisational space. At the same time, each of our neighbours has unique characteristics that are essential for us to understand. It is for good reason that the Government of India is pursuing a "Neighbourhood First Policy". In fact, every country that has multiple land or maritime neighbours accords high priority to its periphery. We see this in the case of the USA, China, and Russia. It is also true that these countries have a mixed record of "success" in dealing with their neighbours. India is no exception. The Indian subcontinent is unique because it consists of countries whose modern-day origins can be traced to a common legacy of colonial rule.

Myanmar is an exceptionally interesting case study of relations between two sovereign States which were once part of the same colonial empire. Both countries gained their independence within a year of each other in 1947 and 1948 but took very different paths thereafter. Their historical experiences leading up to and soon after their independence played a significant part in shaping their worldviews. So have their other well-known attributes of size, location and ethnic features. This chapter attempts to bring out some of the striking features of a relationship that is entangled at multiple levels and the lessons these hold for India's relations with the rest of its neighbourhood. It suggests that India has successfully protected and promoted its interests in Myanmar in the face of existing realities, internal challenges, and external factors beyond its control. Nevertheless, the relationship has not been an easy one to navigate.

Pillars of India's Policy

Any discussion on Myanmar cannot but begin with its geographical location. In some ways, it is as strategically significant as Pakistan's location on the western side of the subcontinent. One of India's primary goals has been to establish connectivity with and through Myanmar to connect itself to South-East Asia as well as to the Bay of Bengal. Accordingly, a large amount of financial resources have been allocated during the last few decades to building connectivity by road, rail, inland waterways, and sea. Some of the iconic projects include the Kaladan Multimodal Transit Transport Project, the India-Myanmar-Thailand Trilateral Highway, the upgradation of key roads between the North-East and Myanmar as well as within Myanmar, such as the Tamu-Kalewa-Kalemyo road and the Rhi-Tiddim Road.

In addition, the focus on building a proper border trade infrastructure is critical to connectivity and people-to-people links. India and Myanmar signed a border trade agreement in 1994 and have two operational border trade points, viz., Moreh-Tamu and Zowkhatar-Rhi. A third border trade point is proposed to be opened at Avakhung Pansat/Somrai. In addition, attention has also been paid to establishing connectivity for power, oil, and gas.

The focus on connectivity is dictated by two major considerations—to integrate the north-eastern states of India with the rest of India's economy, and to create routes that are natural gateways for India's eastward access to the rest of

Southeast Asia, notably Thailand, Laos and even Vietnam and Cambodia. The drivers of India's policies towards Myanmar are rooted firmly in meeting domestic goals. Myanmar has the potential to be a force multiplier in boosting the economies of the North Eastern States.

The second consideration that has guided India's policy has been preserving our security interests in a turbulent part of the country. The Northeast is a complex mosaic of tribes and overlapping ethnicities within and across the border with Myanmar. Myanmar's own complexity with competing ethnic and religious identities and a federative structure have historically been a source of instability with serious cross-border implications. The fact that the Chin, Sagaing, and Kachin regions border the Indian States of Arunachal Pradesh, Nagaland, Manipur, and Mizoram makes them vulnerable to insurgencies, drug and weapons trafficking, smuggling and a host of other illegal activities. Over time, a common thread of Indian policy has been to find ways to shield the Northeast from instability in Myanmar.

It was, therefore, most appropriate for India to be represented by Shri Ajit Doval, the Indian National Security Adviser, at the signing of the Nationwide Ceasefire Agreement between eight ethnic armed groups and the Government of Myanmar in October 2015. Not without coincidence, the Nagaland Peace Accord was signed between the Government of India and the National Socialist Council of Nagaland a few months earlier, in August 2015. It is similarly understandable that the Indian Army maintains regular channels of communication with the *tatmadaw*, and security agencies on both sides cooperate with each other. India's defence cooperation with Myanmar has been growing steadily. India-Myanmar defence engagement was further strengthened with the signing of a MoU on Defence Cooperation in 2019. It is also axiomatic that relations between India and Myanmar have done well when bilateral security cooperation has been effective and robust.

The third pillar of Indian policy has been to be a partner in Myanmar's economic development by engaging in a trade and development partnership that is mutually beneficial. Indian strategy has been to strengthen Myanmar's institutions and human capital, create employment opportunities in industry and agriculture, and expand the boundaries of its economic well-being. Giving Myanmar access to the rapidly growing Indian economy is a strategic objective. Some major schemes and projects have focussed on improving border infrastructure, converting trade corridors into development corridors, trade facilitation, credit lines and training.

Development cooperation is a prominent feature in India's comprehensive bilateral cooperation with Myanmar. India has set up major connectivity infrastructure and established long-term, sustainable and relevant institutions for capacity building and human resource development in areas such as agricultural research and education, IT and skill development. These initiatives are grant funded, though India also extends concessional finance for projects ranging from transport and communications to agriculture, farm mechanisation, and highway development. The total portfolio of projects involving Indian assistance is valued at approximately USD 1.75 billion, of which projects worth nearly USD 1 billion are grant-funded.

A relatively new dimension of India's approach to Myanmar has been to expand cooperation in the maritime domain in the Bay of Bengal and Andaman Sea to address common challenges such as human trafficking, smuggling of weapons and drugs, piracy, illegal fishing, terrorism and transnational crime, HADR, pollution and protection of the sea lines of communication. The Andaman and Nicobar Islands are separated from the Myanmar coastline by the narrow Coco Channel. The Coco Islands are about twenty nautical miles north of the Andaman Islands, while the Andaman and Nicobar Islands are about eighty miles from the Ayeyarwady Delta in Myanmar. This area is, therefore, of critical interest from the security point of view for India. In 1986, India and Myanmar signed an agreement on the delimitation of the maritime boundary in the Andaman Sea, in the Coco Channel and the Bay of Bengal. However, some aspects of the maritime boundary involving Myanmar, Bangladesh and India are still unresolved. In September 2017, the two countries signed agreements on maritime security and cooperation, including one on information-sharing with regard to white shipping. Subsequently, in 2020, the two countries signed a coastal shipping agreement.

A crucial fourth pillar of policy has been to function as the first responder during natural disasters. India offered large-scale assistance during the tsunami in 2004 and the Nargis cyclone in 2008 when Operation Sahayata was launched. Assistance during natural disasters in the neighbourhood has become one of the most prominent symbols of India's Neighbourhood First Policy. Such assistance has been seen, particularly during the tsunami in 2004, the earthquake in POK in 2005, the cyclone in Bangladesh in 1991 and the earthquake in Nepal in 2015. India's emergency aid and response to the neighbours scaled new heights during the COVID-19 pandemic in 2020-2021.

The Benefits of Multilateralism

Myanmar is the bridge between the Indian subcontinent and South-East Asia. Myanmar is an Observer State in SAARC and a full member of ASEAN. India has always supported Myanmar's desire to join SAARC because it would be yet another way to integrate Myanmar with the region and break its international isolation. Unfortunately, this never happened; meanwhile, the efficacy of SAARC waned. In 1997, Myanmar joined India and five other countries to form the BIMSTEC grouping. Myanmar attended the grouping's five Summits, the last of which it attended at the Foreign Minister level in 2022.

In 2000, India and five other countries, including Myanmar, established the Mekong-Ganga Cooperation initiative, again with the objective of building upon the natural geographical and cultural links between them. India, therefore, has sought to deal with Myanmar through bilateral channels and multilateral bodies. This is another pillar of Indian policy towards Myanmar, which overcomes the historical anachronism of Myanmar choosing not to become a member of the British Commonwealth after independence. All these initiatives indicate how the Neighbourhood First Policy and Act East policies of the Government of India have been successfully merged in the case of Myanmar.

The Policy Dilemmas

India has historically faced three principal dilemmas in its dealings with Myanmar. First is the dilemma between interests and values. Second is the dilemma of dealing with Myanmar's relations with outside powers and its other neighbours, primarily China. Third, the dilemma of reconciling the local realities of the border regions with national interests is seen in Delhi.

In general, India has pursued a policy guided more by its national interests than values. This is hardly surprising, as this is what would be expected by any country in the given situation. Nevertheless, this has often pitted us against the West and has required us to be the voice of moderation and balance when extreme positions, including the imposition of sanctions, have been taken. The challenges in framing Indian policy lie in the structural factors that characterise Myanmar's society and polity, which have shaped its governance models since independence. The net result of these has been that the Myanmar military has, in one form or the other, ruled the country for most of the period ever since General Ne Win's takeover in 1962. However, in the early 2000s, India was a consistent advocate of allowing Myanmar to pursue its gradual process of democratic reform, despite the Western policy to apply maximum pressure on Myanmar.

The Indian approach was vindicated by developments inside Myanmar through the framing of a new Constitution in 2008, a period of political reform between 2011 and 2015 and the holding of general elections in Myanmar in 2015. In later years, India worked closely with the elected government and the NLD led by Aung San Suu Kyi. As a result, India's policy was characterised by engagement rather than sanctions and the isolation of Myanmar. To this end, India worked closely with the ASEAN consensus on Myanmar. Over time, India has been able to keep its channels open to civil society, political groups, the Buddhist clergy, students, as well as with the military leadership.

The ouster of the government led by Aung San Suu Kyi in 2021 and her imprisonment, as well as the major internal disturbances and killings of students and civilian protestors, have posed a major challenge to Indian foreign policy, as they have to the ASEAN countries. In fact, there are rare divisions among the ASEAN countries on how to respond to these latest developments. The West has imposed significant sanctions against the military leadership, members of their families, military holding companies, state-owned enterprises, and sectors like timber. As in previous such cases, India has not joined these sanctions.

This is a reflection of the geopolitical realities that India faces in its dealings with Myanmar, but it does not mean that India condones the actions taken by the military or has sacrificed its belief in the principles of democracy and human rights. There are many cases around the world where the West has engaged with and interacted with authoritarian regimes due to geopolitical compulsions, including in the case of Egypt, Pakistan, and Afghanistan. India's response was, however, much sharper in July 2022 when the military junta executed four political prisoners. Apart from issuing a statement expressing deep concern, India also joined the consensus resolution adopted by the UN Security Council in July 2022, condemning the executions.

The second challenge that India faces is the relationship between Myanmar and China. There are non-benign aspects of this relationship which impinge on India's core security interests and necessitate a response. The matter has been a subject of discussion between the two countries, and India's views are well-known to Myanmar's leaders. China has exploited Myanmar's weaknesses and vulnerabilities, including Western pressure on it, to entrench itself in Myanmar through projects such as the China-Myanmar Economic Corridor, domination of the country's fragile economy, rapacious exploitation of Myanmar's natural and mineral resources and investments in dual-use infrastructure in Myanmar's ports and defence supplies. Chinese investments in Myanmar's port infrastructure are aimed with an eye at gaining access to the Indian Ocean. Additionally, China has exploited weak central control in Myanmar and ethnic conflicts to instigate cross-border ethnic violence in the North-East. It has backed groups such as the Arakan Army to sabotage Indian projects in the country.

There is, however, growing awareness in Myanmar about the heavy China hand. The case of strong opposition to the Chinese-funded Myitsone dam in Kachin State, close to China, is well known. Not so well known is that the Myanmar authorities drastically cut back on the scope of the Chinese-funded Kyaukphyu port project because its original scope had no relationship to the needs of the Myanmar economy. More recently, in 2021, Chinese-funded factories in Yangon were torched after the February 2021 military takeover, and there were persistent rumours about Chinese secret flights and assistance to quell the protests and help the Army with the use of social media and internet technologies. In the last few years, the *tatmadaw* has sought to reduce its dependence on Chinese weaponry and other supplies. There is also mutual suspicion about the activities of certain Ethnic Armed Organisations along the Myanmar-China border.

Apart from China, Pakistan has been active among the Muslim population of Myanmar. There is evidence of the involvement of the ISI among Rohingya organisations, such as the Rohingya Solidarity Organisation and the Arakan Rohingya Salvation Army, to promote radicalisation and terrorism. Terror groups such as the Lashkar-e-Taiba and its front, the Falah-e-Insaniyat, have been involved in using the Rohingya issue to target India and Bangladesh.

The West naturally looks upon India as a fellow democracy to join their efforts in pushing for democratic reforms, free and fair elections and respect for human rights in Myanmar. They see India as the upholder of values which are different from China's. India, as a country bordering Myanmar, and as a society which has its own tribal population and ethnic diversity, has remained in regular dialogue with different Western countries to make them more aware of the peculiarities of the local realities. This has not always met with success, but the West has high regard for India's role and understanding of the complexities of Myanmar.

The third main challenge to India comes from the geography and demography of the Indo-Myanmar border in the four states of Mizoram, Manipur, Nagaland, and Arunachal Pradesh. These border areas are defined by the close ethnic, linguistic, and religious links between their peoples and the tradition of free movement and border trade between them. Therefore, it is incumbent upon Delhi to safeguard its international borders while, at the same time, being aware of the local realities. A recent challenge in this regard was the entry of Chin refugees into Mizoram after the military takeover in February 2021, which exemplified the strong links on both sides of the border. In addition, the flow of narcotics remains a major factor in perpetuating the nexus between arms smuggling, human trafficking, and insurgent activity.

The Case of the Rohingyas

The Rohingya exodus in 2017 has resulted in more than one million refugees being present in Bangladesh. India is faced with the challenge not only of preventing their flow into India through Bangladesh, which is of utmost importance but also of managing the tensions and mutual acrimony between Myanmar and Bangladesh. Given the fragility of the ethnic and cultural balance in the Northeast and its highly limited resources, India is not in a position to take in the Rohingya refugees. Instead, it has advocated a peaceful resolution of the problem through bilateral dialogue between Myanmar and Bangladesh. This has not made much headway, but as a friend and partner of both countries, India has given both sides substantial humanitarian and economic assistance to alleviate the burden on their limited resources, prevent further cross-border flows, and facilitate the return of existing refugees voluntarily and with dignity.

The Organisation of Islamic Countries (OIC) and the European Union (EU) have particularly been active in agitating against the matter at the international level. Apart from such actions, it is important that these countries also contribute by facilitating third-country resettlement in their countries since most of them are signatories to the 1951 UN Refugee Convention. This is what many of them had done during the Southern Bhutanese/Bhupali refugee problem between Nepal and Bhutan in the mid-2000s and the case of Syrian and Afghan refugees.

Conclusion and Lessons

Myanmar has been and remains a challenge for Indian foreign and security planners. North-East India can only be as secure as the borders are with Myanmar, and indeed, with another eastern neighbour—Bangladesh. However, despite a sizeable Indian diaspora and the critical strategic aspects involved, Myanmar does not feature high in mainstream Indian strategic discourse. This is unfortunate. Yet, Myanmar is a country that matters immensely to India. Therefore, it needs to be demystified and understood much better. For this, the Indian media, academia, cultural and business community must contribute by being more interested and invested in understanding Myanmar and its people.

The management of our relations with Myanmar contains essential lessons for our overall policies in the neighbourhood. Contrariwise, there are many common strands in our approach to our neighbours, which are equally applicable to Myanmar. First, at an institutional level, policymaking has to be multi-disciplinary and holistic in nature. Only in this way can the complexities of our interactions with our neighbours be addressed. Secondly, integration of our economy with those of our neighbours, except Pakistan, which can wait till the circumstances are right, through the means of trade, investment, physical connectivity, and movement of people are among the most enduring methods of promoting stability and peace in the sub-continent. The projected growth of the Indian economy in the next few decades will continue to open increasingly more significant opportunities for spreading prosperity among our neighbours. They will be the immediate beneficiaries of India's rise.

Third, India's national security interests have to remain a non-negotiable determinant of the scope and pace of our relations with each of our neighbours, which must be known to them. Our neighbours should be cautious of being used by external powers as pawns in their expansionist designs and attempts to create problems for India. Hostile actions of any sort against India from a neighbouring country's territory will have consequences, while a cooperative security architecture will open doors for newer and more beneficial relationships.

REFERENCES

Chanda, Jaideep. *Irrawaddy Imperatives: Reviewing India's Myanmar Strategy.* New Delhi: Pentagon Press, 2021

Embassy of India, Yangon, available at https://embassyofindiayangon.gov.in/, last accessed on 27 October 2022

Ministry of External Affairs. "India and Neighbours, Myanmar." available at https://mea.gov.in/myanmar-in.html, last accessed on 27 November 2022

____ "India-Myanmar Bilateral Brief." available at https://mea.gov.in/Portal/ForeignRelation/Bilateral_Brief_myr_2020_Jan.pdf, last accessed on 27 November 2022

____ "MEA Annual Report, 2021-2022." available at https://www.mea.gov.in/Uploads/PublicationDocs/34894_MEA_Annual_Report_English.pdf, last accessed on 27 November 2022

Vivekananda International Foundation. "Talking Points: India-Myanmar." available at https://www.vifindia.org/2022/june/28/talking-points#8, last accessed on 27 November 2022

Banerjee, Sreeparna. "The Enduring Challenges to Democratic Transition in Myanmar." Observer Research Foundation, 09 May 2022. available at https://www.orfonline.org/research/enduring-challenges-to-democratic-transition-in-myanmar/, last accessed on 27 November 2022

US Department of State. "Burma Sanctions." available at https://www.state.gov/burma-sanctions/, last accessed on 27 November 2022

20

Changing Dynamics of India-Myanmar Relations

Amb Preet Mallik

ABSTRACT

The SLORC took over the executive power of the state in 1988 and renamed the country Myanmar which was a consolidation of two factors that came into play, particularly after the Ne Win takeover of the country. First, there shall be no challenge to preserving the unity and the nation's integrity. Second, the land hitherto known as Burma was the land of the majority of the Bamar, and as such, it was renamed Myanmar, which effectively made it the Land of the Bamar people. This development, in effect, went a long way in reflecting the distrust that has remained a permanent factor in the relations between the Bamar majority and the ethnic minorities, who, in geographical terms, occupy the sensitive frontier areas of Myanmar. If anything, the 2008 Constitution, which was forced through by the military and brought into play a limited democracy to govern the nation, only served to keep the gap between the two demographic entities alive, with distrust remaining the defining aspect of the relations, with insurgency remaining a live issue.

The history behind the making of the Constitutions of Burma (Myanmar) throws light on the complexities that have governed the whole issue of peace and governance that the country has faced from 1948 onwards, as it threw off its colonial yoke to become the Independent Union of Burma. Perhaps, nothing reflects the attitude of the armed forces towards a democratically ruled Myanmar, as the reference to the Constitution adopted in 1947, contained in the Preamble to the 2008 Constitution, "In order to gain independence speedily, the Constitution was hastily drafted, and it was adopted by the Constituent Assembly... However, as the democratic system could not be materialised, the new Constitution of the Socialist Republic of the Union of Myanmar was drafted...."

This chapter aims to project how peace is at a premium because of the role played by the armed forces, from the commencing of the nationalist movement to an extent consolidated during the Japanese occupation of Burma, and how the internal factors came to ensure it since Independence. The role of the Armed Forces and the powerful presence they occupy in the country's governance and to what extent the problems with the ethnic minorities have contributed to the prevalence of a disrupted country and the fallout of these internal developments on Myanmar's neighbouring countries. Here one element of a defining nature is reflected in Article 20(e) of the 2008 Constitution, which states, "The Defence Services is mainly responsible for safeguarding the non-disintegration of the Union, the non-disintegration of national solidarity and the perpetuation of sovereignty." This is the factor that allegedly came into play as Ne Win carried out a coup against the democratically elected government, headed by U Nu and the subsequent discarding of the 1947 Constitution as it did contain a provision that an ethnic group had the right to secede from the Union, after ten years, since the adoption of the Constitution.

What is a significant development since the coup by General Min Hlaing is how the Bamar youth has now joined hands with the ethnic groups to act against the overtaking of the limited democracy by the Armed Forces. With the consolidation of the internal democratic forces around an agenda for the restoration of democracy and the establishment of a Federal State with full autonomy, all of which have been the long-term demand of the Ethnic Groups that the Aung Sang promised and led to the Panglong Convention. This could be considered the first but critical step towards restoring the trust between the two demographics; that is the only way peace can be brought about in Myanmar. Here, of course the most important factor shall be to what extent the political class and the united view of the Bamar youth with the ethnic minority groups can negotiate a working settlement with the leadership of the armed forces and gain their agreement to the drafting of a new constitution.

Finally, how China has exploited the situation created by the distrust between the majority and the minority from the very inception of Myanmar as an independent country. While in the case of India, there has generally been a sympathetic relationship with Myanmar, India's relations with Myanmar have to take ground realities into account here. One factor that would serve several factors in India's interests would be a deeply planned relationship with a socio-economic content with all frontier areas of Myanmar that border India. This has to be a long-term goal once a political settlement is achieved. From a strategic point of view, a civil war situation in Myanmar is not in India's interest as it would complicate issues along our borders with Myanmar. Here the most sensitive areas from our point of view, given the present circumstances, are the Sagaing and Chin States.

Introduction

The armed forces of Myanmar, known as the *tatmadaw*, once again reduced the nation to a military dictatorship with its current Senior General Min Hlaing, carrying out a coup against the elected government led by the head of the NLD, Aung San Suu Kyi. On every occasion that the people of Myanmar are given a choice, they have overwhelmingly endorsed democracy as a form of governance. In equal measure, the *tatmadaw* leadership has trampled on the wishes of its people and imposed authoritarian rule. What has been the measure of misery that the people of Myanmar have had to face, the world has largely shut its eyes to what is happening in that strategically located country that sits on the crossroads connecting South Asia to Southeast Asia and the Asian behemoth, the People's Republic of China.

India has a large land and maritime border with Myanmar. It has long-standing security concerns arising out of the insurgencies that prevail in the North-east of India, where the insurgents not only have secured shelter on the territory of Myanmar but have also been exploited by China both directly and indirectly through the agency of the Myanmar tribal groups that it controls; the Kokang and the Wa. The Indian insurgents have, from time to time, used Myanmar territory to carry out their militant activities against India. To counteract these activities, the GOI and the GOB have established arrangements that enable India to carry out operational activities, from time to time, across Myanmar territory, against the insurgent camps that straddle areas alongside the Myanmar-India borders.

Understandably, India has an abiding interest in peace and tranquillity prevailing in Myanmar, favouring a nation governed by a government that has the backing of the people of Myanmar. Herein, however, lies the rub. From its inception as an independent country, while India had thrown off the British colonial yoke, political turbulence in Myanmar has been the rule rather than the exception. The current situation, which continues to rock the nation since Senior General, Min Hlaing carried out his coup some eighteen months ago, is a replica of what has prevailed in that ill-starred country since January 1948. Thus, we now visit what has caused the turbulence that most likely will continue to prevail, even as the current state of affairs has developed in a direction that spells a new and perhaps effective change in the environment between the majority of Bamar and the minority ethnic groups.

Colonial Mischief

The most compelling imperative that has governed relations between the ethnic minority and the Bamar majority has been *'distrust'*. A history lies behind this and is linked to the mischief of the then-colonial administration. Many in India are not probably aware that the colonial administration of British India, via the medium of the then Governor of Assam, Robert Reid, proposed to "combine the frontier areas of Assam and the adjacent Frontier areas of Burma into a British (Crown) colony" in November 1941.[1] The suggested area was vast, as it covered areas of India that include today's Arunachal Pradesh, Nagaland, Manipur, Meghalaya, Mizoram, Tripura, and the Chittagong Hills tract that now is a part of Bangladesh. On the Burma side, it included the frontier areas representing today's Kachin state, the Shan State, the Karenni State, etc.[2] Reid went on to state that this creation "underlined the strategic importance of India's northeast frontier in relations to Tibet, China, Burma, and Japan."

The proposal received serious attention at the levels of the Viceroy of India (Linlithgow) and Dorman-Smith (Governor of Burma). It was in more ways than one endorsed by Secretary of State Amery in London. Not surprisingly, the area comprised of the 'Excluded' areas of Northeast India and the tribal areas of Burma that had been designated as such under the 1935 Constitution, that came to govern British India and Burma (the excluded areas, in both the countries, were outside the normal provincial governance system). Fortunately, the idea remained stillborn, and the attempt to divide India further came to nought.

Frontier Areas of Burma

In Burma, the Frontier Areas were administered by the Frontier Administration Service under a commissioner. They were effectively kept outside the purview of what was designated as 'Ministerial Burma', which was demographically almost exclusively Bamar territory. Within this, the Karen and Mon minorities were denied any separate recognition. When, at the end of WW II, the freedom of Burma from colonial rule was being negotiated, Whitehall proposed that the Frontier areas also become part of Independent Burma.

The tribal areas reluctantly agreed to be part of the Union of Burma, along lines negotiated what was known as the Panglong process, ending in the Panglong Agreement, which affirmed three elements as the binding that would glue the frontier areas to an Independent Burma. The agreement was processed under the leadership of General Aung San and endorsed by him in all its finality. The three key elements agreed to were:

1. Federal Constitution, affirming the rights of the frontier peoples
2. Full autonomy
3. The right of the constituent frontier territory to secede from the union after ten years in case it did not feel comfortable to remain in the Union.

These are the issues that have continued to befog the problems faced by Burma/ Myanmar ever since Independence. The first act that created unease among the Frontier states was the draft constitution worked out under Aung San, which met the provisions of the Panglong Agreement, being substantially diluted by U Nu, who took over the leadership of the Anti-Fascist Peoples Freedom League (AFPFL) after the assassination of Aung San. This went a long way to uphold, in the minds of the ethnic groups, that they could not trust the intentions of the Bamar majority.

However, the inclusion of the Right to Secession under Chapter X of the 1947 Constitution, ten years after the date on which the Constitution "comes into operation", was an acknowledgement that satisfied the Ethnic Groups, and they went along with reservations to remain as part of the Union. It was the possibility of this provision being resorted to that became the cause celebre that Ne Win utilised to claim that the nation's territorial integrity was at stake, and it was the duty of the armed forces to ensure that this did not happen.

Considering the strong influence that the Indian nationalist movement had over the freedom struggle, carried out by the various politically active groups in Burma, there was a turn that Burma's national movement took that was entirely different from the Gandhian format of a non-violent struggle to India securing her independence. In the first instance, the combination of Burmese political parties that merged into the Forward Bloc concluded that the use of force was the way that would gain their freedom from the colonial yoke.

The Thakin 30 group, which had Aung San as one of its leaders, decided that the way was to join hands with the Japanese and gain independence under the Japanese slogan of 'Asia for the Asians.' The Japanese supported this development and trained, under the command of Colonel Meiji Suzuki, the group forming in the process the Burma Independence Army (BIA).[3] The BIA was divided into six groups that entered Burma from different directions, along with the Japanese invasion force. As the BIA established control over Burmese territory, it also established administrative control over the area. There was a gross misuse of power in many of these administrative pockets. In the Salween district and the rice bowl of the West delta, the BIA maltreated the local Karen population, adopting an openly racial approach favouring the Bamar. This resulted in many communally related deaths, laying the foundation of the long-prevailing Karen rebellion against the Bamar-controlled political dispensation that came to rule Myanmar from Independence onwards.

Military Command

The important element here was that of the BIA[4] establishing the tradition of the Burmese armed forces being part of the political landscape. Moreover, the armed forces were from Myanmar's inception as an independent nation, racist in orientation, with an open bias favouring the Bamar majority over every other racial component that composed the Myanmar geographical landscape. As insurgency, particularly by the Karen and the Than Tun-led Communist Party of Burma (CPB), almost toppled the AFPFL-led Government of Thakin U Nu, the role of the Burmese military came to be further enmeshed into the politics of the country.

The military forces, at that time under the command of the Karen General Dun Smith, were able to contain the attack on Rangoon that was being carried out by the Karen, who had reached the outskirts of the capital city, having taken over the suburb of Insein. For all the loyalty shown by Dun Smith, he was forced out as the situation was brought under a degree of control, and Ne Win, who till then was commanding one of the three divisions of the Burmese Armed Forces, was appointed the Commander-in-Chief. He also came to hold the commanding cabinet position of Minister of Defence. Since then, defence has remained under the control of the military leadership, further consolidated by the provisions to that effect granted under the 2008 Constitution.

Independent Burma/Myanmar comprising a pluralistic demography rightfully adopted a democratic system of governance backed by a Constitution. However, as the political situation turned chaotic, U Nu, an elected Prime Minister, preferred to adopt the military route to restore order and handed over the charge to General Ne Win, the Commander-in-Chief of the Burma Defence forces, to head a caretaker Government. Ne Win took two years to restore order and supported the country for fresh elections. U Nu won an absolute majority and was restored as the Prime Minister of Burma. Ne Win had hoped that the political faction that he had put in place would win the election, and he would take charge as PM. Soon enough, the pressure from the secession-seeking frontier states, particularly the Shan State, enabled Ne Win to claim that the unity and integrity of the Union were at stake, and he carried out a coup taking charge and discarding the 1947 constitution. He established a single-party system with a socialist economy.

Since 1962, the military leadership retained the upper hand in the political domain and has been the dominant force ruling the country. The military has also denied the three-fold path to democracy that Aung San had agreed to follow, as part of the Panglong process. The three-fold path included an agreement of the ethnic minority of the Frontier States to become equal partners in forming the Union of Burma/Myanmar.

The reality, ever since Aung San was assassinated, has been one where the ethnic minority has felt not just let down but also that it had to regain its rights by following the military route, including the possibility of leaving the Union. Here it is important to point out that at the centre was the lack of relationship. The Ethnic Groups have firmly stood behind the calls for true federal democracy for Myanmar based on constitutional guarantees establishing a federal system with full autonomy for the constituent tribal states/units. The Burman majority had, till the February 2021 coup against the limited democratic Government headed by Aung San Suu Kyi, gone along with the military leadership's contention, that this could be used by the ethnic states to undermine the unity and national integrity of the Union.

Significant U-turn

When the February 2021 coup by Senior General Min Aung Hlaing was carried out, the Bamar youth opposing the act also took the public position that it stood categorically in favour of Myanmar not only restoring full democracy but that the country would follow the promise of the Panglong process by ensuring that Myanmar was a federal structure with full autonomy for the states that constituted the federation.

This has created a dynamic that has been furthered by the uniting of several forces against the military junta leading to the establishment of a coalition of pro-democracy resistance groups who, along with the Chin National Front (CNF), the Karen National Union (KNU), the Karenni National Progressive Party, along with the All-Burma Students Democratic Front are fighting the junta. They have also got the backing of the political organisations opposing the junta—the National Unity Government (NUG), the NLD and the Committee Representing the Senate and House of Representatives. The People's Defence Force (PDF) is the youth's added fighting arm with training and weapons support extended by ethnic armed forces like the Kachin Independence Army (KIA).

While distrust on the part of the ethnic minority group has not entirely vanished, there is a greater understanding that has surfaced among the Bamar youth and the political entities opposing the junta, where there is an overwhelming support for discarding the 2008 Constitution that supports the dominance of the armed forces over governance and its replacement by a constitution that establishes a federal democracy with the autonomy of the states fully spelt out. This is a grounding on which a real unity of purpose could be developed that would help remove distrust and enable the establishment of a nation that would fulfil the promise of Panglong and ensure that peace finally reigns in an insurgency-ridden Myanmar. However, there is no gainsaying the fact that the *tatmadaw* (Armed

Forces) is trained to act ruthlessly against all opposition. It has tasted direct power since 1962 and is fully aware of the privileged position that it has so far occupied in both the economy and politics of Myanmar. It is not likely to return to the barracks unless it is forced to do so. Here the role that countries like China and Russia are playing in support of the authoritarian regime in supplying the arms and ammunition that the junta needs to fight the forces piled up against it shall only help prolong the violence that has come to prevail in Myanmar.

The other compelling factor has been that Chinese involvement and the quiet support India has been providing to the junta is helping it overcome the impact of the sanctions imposed on Myanmar by the Western democracies. ASEAN itself is riven into two camps over Myanmar, with one camp influenced by China preventing a united ASEAN policy from becoming an effective tool to bring about a reasonable settlement that would restore even the limited democracy that was in operation under the 2008 Constitution and peace to Myanmar. Here it is an important factor that India has extended full support to the ASEAN peace undertaking.

Developing Civil War

As the opposition to the junta gathers, a degree of momentum and the intensity of the armed opposition gathers some strength; the nation is moving in the direction of a civil war. An example of this can be gained from the developments in the Sagaing Division of Myanmar. Here cooperative action against the *tatmadaw* has developed with the PDF and the KIA working in tandem. A number of significant operations conducted jointly by the PDF forces and the KIA have forced the vacating of a number of villages and posts held by the *tatmadaw* in the north of the Division. There have been actions elsewhere by the PDF where, as in the case of the Mon State, the PDF has gained some success in its attacks on *tatmadaw* posts.

The execution of four pro-democracy activists in July 2022 has only granted added motivation to the forces that are gathering strength in their efforts to militarily and politically oppose the junta. A close examination of the developments in Myanmar implies that the differences of the past between the Bamar and the ethnic groups have to a significant extent been pushed to the back and both sides have finally arrived at an understanding that they have a commonality of interests that unites them. The Bamar majority, represented in the groups that have joined hands with the Ethnic Groups, has ensured that they are aligning their political demands in line with the cherished goals espoused by the ethnic minority groups.

They have also arrived at the conclusion that they have to jointly resist the junta and ensure that democracy based on a federal structure is put in place. As the situation continues to deteriorate towards a civil war, there appears to be little that the ASEAN can achieve. The junta that has the active support of the Chinese and the Russians has so far shown little interest in adhering to the ASEAN's five-point approach to restoring the status quo that prevailed before the coup and bringing peace to this war-torn nation. Violence has become widespread, and despite the ruthlessness displayed by the *Tatmadaw* to put down the armed opposition, the opposition to them continues.

The irony is that even if the ASEAN's attempts were to succeed, the battle lines on the type of democracy should remain at the centre of the differences that have ensured that peace and unity have continued to elude Myanmar. Every effort that has been made ever since Thein Sein assumed the Presidency in 2010 has seen the military leadership headed by Senior General Min Hlaing, stand in the way of a settlement that would be cast in the spirit of an amended Panglong process. Obviously, the differences are generic in nature, and it would require a complete change in the mindset of the military for an acceptable political arrangement to be arrived at. This indicates that a civil war is the most likely outcome that Myanmar and its neighbouring countries would be faced with. It is also likely that eventually, there could be support, both material and of equipment, that may start flowing in to assist the rebellion against the junta, and this could have an adverse spillover impact on India.

It's no secret that the security structures of Myanmar and India have, over the decades, been cooperating with each other to help contain Indian insurgents from our Northeastern states. This cooperation has, at times, led to Indian actions against insurgents being carried out on Myanmar territory adjacent to India's borders with Myanmar. The security factor has been one of the key aspects guiding the bilateral relationship. While 'Official India' has kept the lid on the consistent support that China has extended to the Indian insurgents that have taken refuge on the soil of Myanmar, the reality is that the material support being extended to the insurgents by China has never ended; it has only taken a different shape. The support is now extended by the Kokang and Wa tribal groups that are under Chinese control.

For India, given these circumstances and keeping in mind that the only way to counter the Chinese leverage would be to have whoever rules Myanmar out of Nay Pyi Taw continue to help India, and deny space to the Myanmar-located Indian insurgents and the groups within Myanmar that support them. This, however, has its own barriers as the control over large swathes of frontier territory, particularly in the Kachin State, is not being exercised by the Union Government. Any development that constrains the Union Government of Myanmar would be against India's counterterrorism efforts and interests. This is a dilemma that ensures that India does not repeat the mistakes of 1989-92 of hedging its bets against the present military takeover of Myanmar or of retaining a pragmatic relationship with the military leadership. Given these circumstances, it's obvious that a civil war that creates a seriously chaotic politico-military situation in Myanmar is something that is not in India's interests.

China-Military Junta Relations

The current close relationship between a military junta-controlled government and China is nothing new in nature. It was the securing of power by the SLORC in 1989, and the subsequent refusal to hand over power to the victorious Suu Kyi-led NLD in 1990 that had a very clearly stated support extended to it and its policies by Beijing that stood in strong contrast to India's criticism of these events. What is more, the Chinese have consistently adopted policies that would contain India by creating buffers on India's borders with Pakistan and Myanmar, supplementing their policy of pressurising India on its northern borders with Chinese-occupied Tibet. Given this intent, New Delhi can hardly afford to give Chinese relations with Myanmar a free run.

An authoritarian Myanmar suits Beijing as it fits into the Xi Jinping contestation that China's model of governance is superior to the liberal democratic model. Myanmar, in its present form of authoritarian military rule fits into the split between the world's autocracies and democracies by firmly aligning it with the autocracies. While there may have been an expectation, in some quarters, that China may hesitate to extend support to the junta-led government on account of the close relations established with the Suu Kyi-led NLD government of Myanmar, the Chinese Foreign Minister Wang Yi's statement that "no matter how the situation changes, China will support Myanmar in safeguarding its sovereignty, independence and territorial integrity, and in exploring a development path suited to its national conditions,' should set all speculation on this account at rest. It also means that the junta leadership can continue to ignore ASEAN's attempts to bring peace to Myanmar. Let it also be pointed out that the sanctions regime adopted by the Western democracies has aided the Chinese in strengthening their presence in Myanmar.

On the strategic side, the Chinese are now closer to securing their ambition to have a road and railway link between Yunnan and the Bay of Bengal through the outreach of the China-Myanmar Economic Corridor (CMEC) where they have the junta-controlled State Administrative Council's (SAC) endorsement of key rail and road highway projects that would link the Kyaukphyu Deep Sea port and the adjoining economic zone being developed by China to Ruili, the border town on the Myanmar-Yunnan border. This would fulfil Beijing's long-held strategic ambition to establish a direct link between Yunnan Province and the Indian Ocean through the Bay of Bengal.

The Chinese, however, are not blind to the fact that there is a prevailing sense of distrust of the Chinese that is native to the people of Myanmar and that is also a sentiment harboured among many in the armed forces. The thinking that lay behind the limited multi-party democracy that was provided for under the 2008 constitution and the policy followed by the Thein Sein-led Government would not have lost its import on the leadership in Beijing. One of the factors that they continued to employ to ensure that Myanmar could not go entirely into the Western camp was the leverage that they have continued to maintain over the peace process between Naypyidaw and the ethnic groups. This leverage has a concrete support base in the Kokang and Wa army groups as well as the linkages to the Shan (SSA) and the Kachin (KIA) insurgent groups. This leverage would continue to play a role unless the new alliance between the Burman rebel groups, which have both a political and an armed force combination uniting their actions, strictly holds to the promise of a federal union that guarantees full autonomy is adhered to. This is the new strategic element that has come into play in the prevailing situation in Myanmar.

India-Myanmar

It is clear that India faces a very complex situation that seriously impacts its strategic and security interests. There is little doubt that India has long-term interests best served by a peaceful and prosperous Myanmar, where the Union Government controls the entire territory. The reality of geo-political circumstances compels India to go along with whoever governs Myanmar. Democratic India, however, is sympathetic to the Myanmar people's wish for democracy to prevail in their country. Within the folds of this complexity lies the ever-questioning process that engulfed relations in the ruling emotion of distrust between the majority Burman demography and the minority ethnic groups. This has been the main cause of violence prevailing along Myanmar's frontier states with military repression being visited upon the people of Myanmar. One common result of this has been that the frontier areas have largely remained undeveloped, with their natural resources being exploited by commercial interests backed by the armed forces and select Chinese business groups. The insurgency has in itself become a major factor that has prevailed in Myanmar, with insurgent groups from India finding shelter and support in the areas of Myanmar across the India-Myanmar borders.

During the Thein Sein Presidency, a period of relative peace came to prevail in the area and in the joint statement that was issued on the visit of the then Indian Prime Minister, Dr. Manmohan Singh, there was an agreement between the two sides that India would engage itself in extending support of a socio-economic nature to help in the development of Myanmar's Frontier Areas. This, in a logical sense, implied a tying in of the development process directed at India's North-east States with the frontier areas of Myanmar along with logistical support that would ensure business and developmental linkages between the NE States and ASEAN. Within this compact lay the strategic importance of developing the Kaladan multi-modal system and the tri-state highway that would link India, Myanmar, and Thailand.

The present turmoil in Myanmar is likely to be long-lasting in nature as the *tatmadaw,* supported by increasing supplies of Chinese and Russian equipment, continues its efforts to subdue the opposing forces ruthlessly. This leaves India with very limited options; one way of securing its interests, which has both strategic and security positives embedded in it, would be to work with the Myanmar authorities to extend projects and capacity building to help develop the adjoining frontier states of the country. This would imply working with the administrative organisations put in place by the ethnic groups, particularly the Kachins, the Chins, and the Burmese Naga groups holed up in the northern Sagaing Division forested areas. This is not going to be easy, but it would certainly if suitably worked out, lend teeth to PM Modi's Act East Policy.

Concluding Observations

What is certain is that Myanmar is well set on the road to a civil war situation despite the determination of the military leadership to have its way. They are, for the first time, confronted by a determined aspirational youth who have cut the umbilical roots of the divide that had, till the takeover by General Hlaing, prevailed between the Burmese and the ethnic minorities. This is a factor that could derail the *tatmadaw's* play book. If the united efforts gain real strength, it is possible that a degree of material support may eventually support the popular fronts. Whatever the outcome, till some solution emerges that also takes this new and significant development into account, a security dilemma shall continue to confront India. ASEAN, for all practical purposes, is a house divided by the games that China has continued to play; this affects not only what is happening in Myanmar but also the claims by many of the ASEAN member-states on the South China Sea area.

ENDNOTES

1. Robert Reid "A Note on the Future of the Excluded and Partially Excluded and Tribal areas of Assam" Note: these were areas that were declared as "Backward Tracts' under section 52(A) of the GOI Act of 1919 covering the frontier areas of Assam and Burma along borders that were defined under the Indo-Tibetan Convention (Treaty) signed at Shimla in 1914.
2. The colonial administration designated the Arakan Hill tract, the Chin, Naga and Kachin hills, the Shan and Wa States and the Kareni State along with additional Karen country in the Tongoo Hills and the Salween area as Frontier area, that comprised almost 50 per cent of the land area of Burma and held at that time a population of two and a half million. Quoted from *The Journal of The Royal Society of Arts* issue of 06 December 1946, contributed by E. R. Leach.
3. Here it would be worth projecting the discriminatory policy adopted by the colonial administration that created further distrust between the Bamar majority and the Ethnic minority groups. The British Burmese Army that was a force of 22,000, comprising of 3,000 Chins, 2,000 each of Kachin and Karen tribals and only 200 Burman's (Bamar); the rest being Indians and Gurkhas. When the BIA was formed, the composition was entirely of the Bamar people.
4. Till 1930, the British colonial Administration in Rangoon completely excluded Burman's The Bamar) from the security services as they 'were thought to be "unreliable, insubordinate and unfitted generally for military services." Taken from Stephen J. Hoadley's book *Soldiers and Politics in Southeast Asia. (*Cambridge Mass.: Schenkman Publishing Co., 1975), p. 37. The BIA was entirely Burman in composition while the Kachin, Karen, and Chin Armed Forces remained loyal to the British.

21

India and Myanmar: Reimaging a Stable Borderland

Prof Sreeradha Datta

ABSTRACT

Burma was separated from the rest of the Indian Empire in 1937, just ten years before India became independent in 1947. Thus, their interaction and movement across the border were disrupted, leading to many challenges in that region. The ethnic overlap posed security issues for India, and ever since Myanmar attempted to limit the cross-border insurgency movement in the early 1990s, the neighbours have shared cordial ties. The transition to democracy that was taking place before the 2021 coup was also largely supported by India. While the coup has upset the tone of engagement to an extent, India continues to maintain its ties with Myanmar.

This chapter is an attempt to understand the changing nature of India's eastern borders with Myanmar. The environment on the Indian eastern borders has undergone changes and has possibly set the tone for a new discourse that encompasses not only improved bilateral neighbourly ties but also improved local and regional cooperation. The revamped "Act East" policies seem to promise a renewed interest in creating greater social and economic spaces for mutual prosperity. At the same time, ground-level realities challenge these top-down notions and visions of trans-regional engagement and fast-track development.

It is hoped that a return to democratic transition in Myanmar will allow for state and non-state actors to continue seeking new directions away from a past haunted by conflicts, violence, and unsettled differences. While the borders enjoy an informal interactive space, the security apparatus continues to seek a raison d'être of its continued presence. The prevalence of shadow economies, criminal activities, and illegal trade continues to limit the possibilities of opening up the borders and providing for the borderland communities living on both sides of the borders of India and Myanmar. This chapter will seek to examine how friendship ties and communal bonds can be strengthened across borders to make space for respect, recognition, and co-existence for the borderland people on both sides.

Introduction

Burma was separated from the rest of the Indian Empire in 1937, just ten years before India became an independent country in 1947. Thus, India and Myanmar share a long history with a long land border of over 1,600 km and a maritime border in the Bay of Bengal, because of which there is a strong ethnic overlap too. At the time this volume was conceived, it was hoped that the internal strife in Myanmar would settle down, giving way for not only peace and stability but also a return to the process of democratic transition, which was abruptly interrupted by the military leaders in February 2021. The military leaders overthrew the National League for Democracy (NLD) and formed the State Administrative Council (SAC), imprisoning senior NLD leaders, including State Counsellor Aung San Suu Kyi and President Win Myint. They discredited the November 2020 elections, which saw the NLD win with a strong margin—920 of the 1,117 seats—as against the Union Solidarity and Development Party (USDP) acquiring 71 seats which were even lower than its previous 2015 election performance.

The stalemate continues with periodic violence between the military and armed resistance groups that emerged after the coup. A group of elected and now deposed leaders formed the National Unity Government (NUG) but managing the disparate interests of the ethnic armed groups has not been easy for them either, and Myanmar remains fractured, violent and conflict-ridden. Thus, the contemporary state of affairs inside Myanmar does not offer many rays of hope for not only its internal stability but especially for developing better bilateral ties with India. The elections still seem up in the air, as well as the possibility of multiparty participation, making the issue of deepening engagement in the borderland seem rather distant and really confined to the realm of imagination for now.

Nevertheless, this chapter attempts to focus on the huge possibilities that the India-Myanmar border offers. Post decades of military rule, when the ruling junta, and the State Peace and Development Council announced the new constitution as part of the roadmap to democracy in 2008, it was hoped that Myanmar would finally shift from the military regime (1962 onwards) towards a participative multiparty polity. Similarly, the environment on Indian eastern borders has also undergone changes, and the economic opportunities along with the new transport connectivity that is taking shape in the North-eastern region have possibly set the tone for a new discourse that encompasses not only improved bilateral neighbourly ties but also robust local and regional cooperation. The revamped Indian "Act East" from "Look East" and the launch of the "Neighbourhood First" policy in

2014, with the coming of the NDA government to Delhi, brought a renewed interest in creating greater social and economic spaces for mutual prosperity. It is in this context that the Indo-Myanmar border holds special significance for the implementation of the above policies and helps develop comprehensive bilateral engagement.

The focus of this chapter is limited to delineating the Indo-Myanmar borders. It will also factor in how, for a rather longish period, this border has been a source of security threats, both traditional and non-traditional. This chapter will touch upon cross-border trade and seek to examine how friendship ties and communal bonds can be strengthened across borders to make space for respect, recognition, and co-existence for the borderland people on both sides. This chapter argues that ensuring greater connectivity at the borders will improve not only cross-border trade and commerce but also social interactions. Further, borders can be utilised to provide services for the borderland population on both sides. This would range from commerce that can be realised through cross-border 'haats' (local markets) as well as medical and education facilities that are much required by them. The growing engagement at the borders will ensure a secure common space that will provide a shift for people to initiate legal trade practices and shun illegal activities undertaken across the borders.

The Security and Strategic Imperatives

Given the realignment of the region with the formation of a separate Myanmar (erstwhile Burma) from India (1937) and then the subsequent partition of the subcontinent (1947), much of the earlier peoples' movements and commercial activities across the borders were ruptured. For long time, there was an easy movement of people across borders for various reasons, including similar ethnic overlap with sustained kinship and social and cultural ties. Post the 1940s, the interaction and movement across the borders were disrupted, leading to many challenges in that region. The ethnic overlap posed security issues for India, and ever since Myanmar attempted to limit the cross-border insurgency movement in the early 1990s, the neighbours have shared cordial ties.

The environment on Indian eastern borders has undergone changes and has possibly set the tone for a new discourse that encompasses not only enhanced bilateral neighbourly ties but also leads to local and regional cooperation. India has initiated bilateral initiatives with Myanmar, including building physical and digital connectivity that would bring the neighbours closer and develop strong economic and political ties for greater prosperity and progress of the people of both sides. However, the recent developments within Myanmar have once again ushered in an era of suspicion and security threats.

As is well known, India had to shift its stance of lending support to the pro-democracy forces to move towards the military given its inability to manage the cross-border ethnic insurgency movement creating instability in the Northeastern region, especially in Manipur and Nagaland. Along with the support of the junta in clearing the insurgent bases from the borderlands, India had subsequently, through negotiations, dialogue, and coercion, been able to control many of the insurgent movements, apart from one of the Naga population and their demand for greater Nagaland. Post-2014, India had made substantial progress in building peace and development in the region, and the democratic transition in Myanmar was also a critical element for building greater bilateral and regional ties.

However, the coup of February 2021 not only stalled much of the infrastructural work but also changed the nature of the border. There are several reports about the presence of non-state actors that are being used to create instability. The Myanmar junta is now resorting to using these ethnic armed groups to control its own population that has turned against the military government.[1] The problem at the border is not limited to only insurgent movements but a variety of unlawful activities. The permeable nature of the borders has enabled locals on each side to access the other side while also giving way to illegal activities and even hostility and violence. There exists a well-organised drug cartel; trafficking of small arms and humans too are known to be rampant on the borders. As summed up by Munmun Majumdar,

> "The location of India–Myanmar border throws up many challenges for effective management of the boundary and the rugged terrain; the internal dynamics of the region in terms of clan loyalties of the tribal people, inter-tribal clashes, insurgency, trans-border ethnic ties makes the situation even more complex. What can be inferred is that the Manipur–Myanmar border connections that have sustained over time and that the contingent processes (social and political) have advanced a dynamic character to boundary lines. This also means that fencing of the border with severe implications for the lives and livelihoods of diverse border communities, and the tangible and intangible flows across borders cannot be ignored".[2]

While the borders enjoy an informal interactive space, the security apparatus continues to seek a raison d'être for its continued presence. The prevalence of shadow economies, criminal activities and illegal trade continue to limit the possibilities of opening up the borders and providing for the borderland communities living on both sides of the borders of India and Myanmar. The continued traditional head-loads of goods moving across the border have been used by some elements to indulge in many malpractices. The security establishment on both sides has taken several security measures to address many of these unlawful activities. India had also constructed a border to minimise illegal movements.

Transport Connectivity Projects

In recent times, under the Border Region Development MoU, the Government of India has extended USD 5 million micro development assistance every year for five years for projects on the India-Myanmar border. Under the project plan, schools and health centres have been built. India also inaugurated the land border crossing between the two countries at Zokhawtar in August 2018 and has opened an immigration check-post in Mizoram along the border with Myanmar, which has facilitated the movement of people from Myanmar to India. However, bilateral trade has not picked up as yet. Earlier, the two governments had established the Free Movement Regime allowing for the local population to travel 16 km on each side without visas. With the restoration of stability at the borders, the Indian Government decided to give a fillip to the existing cross-border trade, especially at the Moreh-Tamu (Manipur's Chandel district) located in Sagaing in northwest Myanmar. While the border at Zhowkatar-Rih Dil is also a designated border point, it has not generated much traffic in goods. The third border at Lungwa village between Nagaland's Avakhung-Pansat and Myanmar's Somra does not have any formal structures as yet, although it is also proposed for cross-border trade. While several connectivity and infrastructural projects are being developed at these points, cross-border trade at Moreh-Tamu remains rather low.

The Integrated Check Post (ICP) inaugurated (January 2019) at Moreh has not facilitated border trade as expected; although the number of people moving across stands at 3,056 during 2018-19, marginally higher than in the past years, the Indo-Myanmar trade stands at a mere USD 2.1 billion. More importantly, the cross-border trade is even more insignificant for barley at USD 87 million (India exported goods worth USD 78 million, and imports totalled USD 9 million during 2018-19). This, in fact, dipped to USD 85.8 million in March 2019. As the figures indicate, there is a greater demand for Indian buying from across the border at Namphalong market in Tamu, with very little interest among traders to enter Moreh to buy Indian goods.[3]

India also started a weekly bus service between Imphal in Manipur and Myanmar's Mandalay in mid-2020. There is also a proposal to start a bus service between Mizoram and Tahan Township in Myanmar, given the large number of Mizos residing in that area. There are several connectivity projects that India had undertaken with Myanmar that would increase transport linkages with Myanmar as well as the region of Southeast Asia, connecting it to South Asia too. India has extended development assistance to Myanmar on generous terms, mostly grant-funded. The projects include the Kaladan Multimodal Transit Transport Project, the Trilateral Highway Project, which is an East-West corridor connecting the Indian North-east with Myanmar and Thailand; and also the Rhi-Tiddim road.[4]

The multimodal Kaladan project would facilitate loaded freight ships from Kolkata port to reach Sittwe, a port in Myanmar's Rakhine province. There, the goods will be loaded on barges that will transport them upstream on the Kaladan River to Paletwa. From Paletwa in Chin state in Myanmar to Zorinpui on the Mizoram border, and further inland into the North-east, the goods will be transported by road. On completion, the project will also connect Mizoram with the Sittwe Port in Rakhine State of Myanmar.[5] The domestic instability in Myanmar has led to the 1,600-crore road project that passes through dense forests and hilly areas remaining incomplete. Essentially this project was designed to circumvent Bangladesh during a difficult phase these two states had undergone. Now new developments that will allow NER to access closer ports have changed the ground situation substantially.

As per the latest updates, the India-Myanmar-Thailand Trilateral Highway work is now underway simultaneously in two segments. This route is designed to connect Moreh in Manipur to Mae Sot in the Tak province of Thailand via Myanmar. This would have two border crossings (India–Myanmar and Myanmar–Thailand), four customs checkpoints, three international time zones, three customs Electronic Data Interchange (EDI) systems, two different vehicle-driving standards, and three different motor vehicle laws. However, there are several challenges over convergence in standards and procedures along the corridor.[6] On the Tamu-Kalewa-Kyigone sector, as many as 69 bridges of World War II vintage are being completely reconstructed, while in the 120-km long Kalewa-Yargi sector, the track is being upgraded to national highway standard. Both these projects are fully grant-in-aid projects by the Government of India.[7]

Some of the international transport projects will supplement the cross-border Indian transport projects proposed. As proposed, the Trans Asian railway (TARN) will connect northeast India to Myanmar through the 81,000 km-long TARN. This 118-km railway track would be laid between (Manipur capital) Imphal and (border towns) Moreh and Tamu in Western Myanmar and across the border of

Moreh.[8] As part of the TARN, another 257-km railway route from north Tripura's Jawahar Nagar railway station to northern Mizoram's Kolashib and Myanmar's Darlon has been proposed.[9] Of particular importance is the proposal of an Istanbul to Dhaka rail route, also known as the ITI-DKD rail corridor. India hosts an important segment on this rail route.[10] For the Trans-Asian railway from Delhi to Hanoi to actualise India and Myanmar, railway systems have to be connected and synchronised. While India is building the Assam-Manipur rail link (scheduled for December 2020), there is no plan as yet to take the railway beyond Imphal or the Moreh-Myanmar border.[11] The feasibility of connecting Moreh to the Myanmar rail network at Kalay was assessed as well as the prospects of connecting southern Myanmar to Thailand.[12]

The connectivity projects would transform the way this region engaged. The positive effects on the Indian North-east region would be multi-fold too. From social interaction to tourism and medicine and trade and commerce, it would usher in a new era of development. Border *haat*s would be the precursor to many of the initiatives discussed in the next section.

Introducing a New Narrative at the Borders[13]

At present, the localised border *haats* on the Indo-Bangladeshi borders (two in Tripura and two in Meghalaya) are operational and have gathered momentum, providing direct contact between buyers and sellers. Nine are proposed along the Indo-Myanmar border. Although under the present impasse, with a constant flow of refugees from Myanmar into India, any new initiative for the local communities living along the border remains severely limited.[14] As understood along the Indo-Bangladeshi borders, the vendors who sell their products in border *haats* are local residents who live within a 5-km radius. These *haats* would facilitate the marketing of some locally produced items among the people living in inaccessible areas of both countries.

Thus, informal arrangements through which the local population traded goods have now been given a formal structure and have generated a specific economic activity, inadvertently opening up avenues for social interaction. The people-to-people connect is rather distinct and needs further nurturing. Although this space is yet to be fully explored, the cultural and social connection is undeniable. It is argued that the possibility of developing the *haat*s into much larger spaces for interaction is real. The people-to-people connect in this space can be given greater salience through a more creative interpretation of existing mechanisms.

As studies have revealed, these *haat*s have significantly contributed to reducing informal trade along the border areas. At the macro level, the markets are contributing towards cementing a good economic understanding and cooperation between the two vibrant economies of South Asia. Even as the frontier has divided many families, border *haats* have created a formal mechanism through which exchange of goods takes place, enabling the people to reconnect with each other.'[15]

A special outreach and capacity-building programme would be required for building foreign trade capabilities. Trade facilitation programmes to encourage local entrepreneurs to actively participate in bilateral trade would build local buy-in. A strong linkage with mainland manufacturers and traders will be a crucial ingredient for a successful export strategy. Some local value-addition near the border through packaging or assembling facilities could also be established. It is possible to locate regular exchange of trade delegations and buyer-seller meets between neighbouring areas at these junctures. Certainly, as pointed out by Asish Kundra, pre-identified verticals would serve as a useful enabler to widen the scope of commercial interaction.[16] In fact, small farmers on both sides would benefit from aggregators. Digital connectivity would be an efficient tool to enable many such limited-level activities. Local-level administration could partner such enterprises.

Border Community Zones

It is not uncommon to see fields and unused land available at borders which are not fully utilised. Border *haats*, usually held in the open space, have some limited infrastructure available, usually meant for security agencies. In the initial stages, Border Community Zones can be built with shared resources for common goods, an idea that needs greater exploration. Ranging from cultural interaction during fixed hours, it can include medical facilities as that is generally not easily available in these border areas. Limited physical space can become the delivery mechanism for many of the needs of the local populace that a peripheral region has been unable to provide for.

By and large, youth from the heartland and urban spaces have access to quality education, while children from rural areas and border zones are unable to access the same. Border areas in most states in the region are at the same level of development. Poor infrastructural facilities, given limited available resources impede the opportunities available. However, these are the very areas that can be tapped for the creation of common physical spaces for nurturing cultural and natural heritage.

Conceiving Border Community Zones for outreach to the population at the borders can address the huge gaps that remain between the urban and non-urban populations in India and Myanmar. A shared border community experience can transform the nature of lives on both sides. Even the Chakmas residing on either side of Mizoram in Thegamukh and Demagiri, though with limited contacts, have much in common. Similarly, the borders Myanmar shares with Manipur, Mizoram, Nagaland, and Arunachal are unique not only due to the ethnic overlap but also because the border zones have an environment that is distinct from the mainland for both the neighbours. On the Manipur side, the Tangluk population lives on the Myanmar border close to Moreh town, while on the Arunachal side, depending on the terrain, it takes the people 2-12 hours to come to the border, mainly on foot. While those across Mizoram can reach the border in an hour, it takes some villagers up to twelve hours. Across Nagaland, villagers from Longkwa, Chen Moho, and Chen Loisha take 2-4 hours, while from Wangti, it takes almost half a day.[17]

Apart from the ethnic overlaps, border economies are similar, and populations on both sides have limited access to services available on the mainland. In India, the concept of a creative economy as an enabler for economic value generation is finding greater acceptability and implementation. The border zones offer a ready space for a creative economy.

Towards a Creative Economy

While the media and entertainment industries have been seen as core elements of a creative economic platform as seen from practices elsewhere, along with the digital economy boom that India is experiencing, it is possible to apply creative economy to the border communities and expansion of border economy. Studies have shown how creative economy has become a powerful transformative force in the world today. This has been instrumental in not only creating income generation but also in job creation and export earnings. More importantly, human creativity and innovation at both the individual and group levels are the key drivers of these industries and have become the true wealth of nations in the twenty-first century.[18]

Indeed, the social and economic environment on both sides of borders are often similar; the livelihood patterns, the available educational opportunities, and even cultural practices. This creates an interactive space for building a common knowledge system through interaction and exchange with the local population on each side. This cannot only provide the basic amenities most required but also de-securitise the border zones to a large extent. The space would be readily available for issues of climate change and its prevention and mitigation, agricultural methods, simple vocational training and issues that are common and beneficial to all. Trans-border community living has to be incubated to create connected minds and hearts.

Further to social and economic activities getting traction, the possibility of developing a common school curriculum for children may be explored. Differences in the language would have to be bridged through a deeper understanding of the mutual needs of both sides. There would be issues over language that would require further detailing. Security concerns need to be addressed through the issuance of biometric identity cards and a full mapping of the population. The development of border zones that become interactive spaces rather than dividing lines will enable the creation of an integrated economy and stable, friendly neighbourhood.

Distance education is well established within India. The Indian apparatus can be expanded to include greater geographical and subject bandwidth for imparting quality education far and wide. Transmission of distance education can be in a variety of languages as demanded by the two countries. Given Indian technological advancement, distance education can reach out to different audiences with different needs. India has initiated a specific platform to impart content for children between ninth and twelfth standards through the Swayam programme on television channels. Given the limited internet access reach (33 per cent in India) but much larger access to television, this programme can be expanded further across the borders.

Common certifications are another area that other regional groups have successfully implemented. Integration of IT would be imperative for promoting such initiatives.[19] This is most effective for vocational courses, including common areas like tourism, culinary, yoga, etc. In India, many fraudulent practices abound, duping unsuspecting students. If formally implemented, this would address the gaps. An entrepreneurial culture can thus be encouraged through concerted efforts by both state and civil society organisations. While such schemes are available for the North East Region (NER), these could be introduced for cross-border development programmes too.

The Ministry of Skill Development and Entrepreneurship, through the National Skill Development Corporation, is implementing Capacity Building scheme for the skilling of unemployed youth of NER in various sectors.[20] The proposed scheme would encourage entrepreneurship amongst those under-represented. The cross-border population can be included in these schemes. Special efforts will also be made to enrol incubators and mentors catering to these groups within the national/bilateral entrepreneurial ecosystem. This also includes hospitality, housekeeping, and the food and beverages sector.

It is hoped that a return to democratic transition in Myanmar will allow for state and non-state actors to continue seeking new directions away from a past haunted by conflicts, violence and unsettled differences. With the borders enjoying an informal interactive space, the security apparatus continues to seek a raison d'être for its continued presence. The prevalence of shadow economies, criminal activities and illegal trade continues to limit the possibilities of opening up the borders and providing for the borderland communities living on both sides of the borders of India and Myanmar.

The transition to democracy that was taking place before the 2021 coup was also largely supported by India. While the coup has upset the tone of engagement to an extent, India continues to maintain its ties with Myanmar. Gautam Mukhopadhaya explains the rationale behind India maintaining ties with the Myanmar junta.

> "A security-first policy predicated on engagement with the Myanmar military worked as long as the *Tatmadaw* was in control of the country. That is no longer the case. India needs to enlarge and expand its options in Myanmar toward a more comprehensive relationship rooted in support of the people rather than the *Tatmadaw* alone."[21]

The political situation in Myanmar is likely to remain tense and violent-prone in the months ahead. Presently there are no leaders who can bring together disparate interest groups. Bringing down the State Administration Council (SAC) (the government established by military leaders) may seem like a common goal, but that has not induced a large section of people to set aside their differences to seek measures to establish a polity that represents the majority of the interests and stand up to the military junta. A vast number of ethnic leaders have not been able to find common ground with the National Unity Government that was formed by many of the deposed elected leaders post the coup of 2021.

Under these circumstances, India has to walk the tightrope. Given that the junta will always enjoy powers, if not in this unbridled form, India can ill afford to annoy them too much by siding with the democratic forces. India historically has always supported democracy in finding its roots in Myanmar, but it also needs to be seen as supporting those forces during the present difficult times. Security and strategic considerations have always been an overpowering incentive for India, but given the growing international recognition of its stature and capacity to find itself on the wrong side of history is not a very welcoming position. Myanmar's support is important for realising many of India's foreign policy objectives but not at the cost of partnering with a pariah government.

ENDNOTES

1. Saket Ambarkhane and Sanjay Valentine Gathia, "Over a Year Later, Myanmar's Military Coup Threatens India's National Security, United States Institute of Peace, 10 May 2022, available at https://www.usip.org/publications/2022/05/over-year-later-myanmars-military-coup-threatens-indias-national-security, last accessed on 06 December 2022
2. Munmun Majumdar, "India–Myanmar Border Fencing and India's Act East Policy", *India Quarterly*, 76(1) (2020): 58–72
3. Sreeradha Datta, *Act East Policy and Northeast India* (New Delhi: Vitastata, 2021)
4. Ministry of External Affairs, "India-Myanmar Bilateral Relations", January 2019, available at https://mea.gov.in/Portal/ForeignRelation/India_Myanmar_Bilateral_ Brief_Website_ jan_ 2019.pdf, last accessed on 06 December 2022
5. Pratim Bose, "India starts construction of [1] 1,600-cr Mizoram-Myanmar Kaladan", *Business Line*, 17 April 2018, available at https://www.thehindubusinessline.com/news/india-starts-construction-of-1600-cr-mizoram-myanmar-kaladan-road/article23577107.ece, last accessed on 06 December 2022
6. Prabir De, Sunetra Ghatak, and Durairaj Kumaraswamy, "Assessing Economic Impacts of Connectivity Corridors in North East India, An Empirical Investigation", *EPW*, Vol. 54, Issue No. 11, 16 March 2019.
7. "Development Cooperation", *Indian Embassy of Yangon*, November 2022, available at https:/ /bit.ly/3FtVip5, last accessed on 06 December 2022
8. Sujit Chakrabarty, "India's northeast to be linked to Trans-Asian Railway Network", *Business Standard*, 16 September 2013, available at https://www.business-standard.com/article/news-ians/india-s-northeast-to-be-linked-to-trans-asian-railway-network-113091600475_1.html, last accessed on 16 December 2022
9. Ibid
10. Two-Day meeting on "Strengthening Railway Transport Connectivity in South and South West Asia" *PIB*, 15 March 2018, available at http://pib.nic.in/newsite/PrintRelease.aspx?relid= 159276, last accessed on 16 December 2022
11. Subhir Bhaumik, "Delhi uncertain over Trans-Asian railway," *Look East*, 28 June 2016 https:/ /lookeast.in/delhi-uncertain-over-trans-asian-railway-plans/, last accessed on 16 December 2022
12. Report, "Assessing India's Connectivity with Its Neighbourhood: A Retrospect", *VIF*, December 2018
13. This section borrows points from my previous publication, Sreeradha Datta, *Act East Policy and Northeast India* (New Delhi: Vitastata, 2021)
14. Border *Haats* (localised cross-border marketplaces) are set upon the eastern and northern sides of the India-Bangladesh border, creating a better economic environment for the local people.
15. "Border Haats' to boost economy, people's ties: Experts," *The News Scroll*, 20 July 2020, available at https://www.outlookindia.com/newsscroll/border-haats-to-boost-economy-peoples-ties-experts/1886266, last accessed on 16 December 2022
16. Asish Kundra, "Galvanising the trade via Northeast", *Business Line*, 23 August 2018, available at https://www.thehindubusinessline.com/opinion/columns/galvanising-trade-via-the-north-east/article24762267.ece, last accessed on 16 December 2022.

17. Walter Fernandez et al., *Relation Across the Borders: Communities Separated by the Indo-Myanmar Border* (Guwahati: NERC, 2015)
18. Amlanjyoti Goswami, Aromar Revi and Shriya Anand, "India's Cultural and Creative Economy: New Imaginations and Emerging Practice," *UNDP,* 2013, available at http://www.unesco.org/culture/pdf/creative-economy-report-2013.pdf, last accessed on 16 December 2022
19. NEC, "*Vision 2020,*" May 2008, available at http://necouncil.gov.in/sites/default/files/about-us/Vision_2020.pdf, last accessed on 16 December 2022.
20. Lok Sabha Unstarred question 3012, 31 December 2018, available at http://loksabhaph.nic.in/Questions/QResult15.aspx?qref=76481&lsno=16, last accessed on 16 December 2022
21. Gautam Mukhopadhaya, "India Needs to Get Serious About the Crisis in Myanmar: The political landscape in the country has shifted. New Delhi now needs to adjust its own approach", *The Diplomat, 04* February 2022, available at https://thediplomat.com/2022/02/india-needs-to-get-serious-about-the-crisis-in-myanmar/, last accessed on 16 December 2022

SECTION SIX

The Way Forward

22

Myanmar's Path to Federacy

Khin Zaw Win

ABSTRACT

By many counts, Myanmar can be said to be in a state of frangibility. The rebellions following independence and the uprising of 1988 were serious threats to the state and union. However, these were all followed by recovery and reconsolidation of the centre. The cataclysm brought about by the coup of February 2021 differs from all that had gone before. Besides being extensive and lengthy, the present crisis is marked by an unprecedented fragmentation of the Bamar/Burman ethnopolitical majority. All things considered, the possibility of reconsolidation along the lines of the past is minimal. Even though the three Bamar 'Empires' in history are glorified by the military, there have been an equal number of interregna that few people are aware of.

The final part of this chapter explores what could emerge in the wake of this implosion. It goes without saying that this upheaval in Myanmar poses a grave threat to the region, especially to its immediate neighbours. Rushing to send humanitarian aid when a crisis hits is not going to be enough. A new entity—political, structural, and ethnic—is being born, and neighbours and others could lend a hand in accouchering it to help ensure a safe delivery that is least deleterious to all.

Introduction

When we talk about the past and history, we have to assess how those accounts came to be written and who wrote them. The seventy-odd years in which Myanmar has existed as an independent country is enough time to afford an honest look at its history and the central institutions that have shaped it. For too long, the majority of the Myanmar people had gone along with the official narratives and more or less supported those institutions. However, the past year's events have forced the entire country to engage in a fresh and urgent reckoning—to reappraise their collective past and thus reshape their future. Myanmar's sad destiny is to be saddled with its military as the primary arbiter of its fate.

Since about the 8th century CE, the Ayeyarwady Basin has been home to successive civilisations and kingdoms. The Pyu had flourished in several city-states—Sri Ksetra, Hanlin, and Beikthano (Vishnu) among them. In the 10th and 11th centuries, the Bamar (Burmans) came to the ascendant, and the capital of Bagan became the Burman-Buddhist centre par excellence. At about the same time, Mon kingdoms held sway in the country's south. In all the polities, the institution of the Buddhist Sangha (clergy) established itself, more often than not, closely associated with the state.

Official versions of history speak of three Myanmar 'Grand States' (equivalent to empires), with Bagan being the first. All three empire-builders were Burman kings, and giant statues stand beside the parade ground in the present capital, Naypyidaw. Different polities had their distinctive cultures, languages, and economies. When they went to war with each other, the extent to which ethnicity played a part can be argued. Instances of war on the grounds of religion were negligible. Overwhelmingly, it was a pattern of Buddhist monarchs fighting other Buddhist rulers. To put it in another way, Buddhism and Buddhist institutions were poor deterrents to war.

There had been invasions from China during the Yuan (Mongol), Ming, and Qing dynasties. There had been three wars with the British—first with the East India Company and later with the British crown—eventually resulting in annexation. That these encounters brought racial overtones to conflict cannot be denied. As a reaction against imperialism and from the ferment in Europe and the Empire came the imported ideology of nationalism. The Bamar majority were foremost in being drawn to it—first the intellectuals, then a significant segment of the public. The non-Burman ethnicities reacted to colonial rule in different ways.

In recent years a 'resurgence' of nationalism was seen. However, this may be too polite a term since the impetus came from inciting latent racist phobias and demonising the 'other'. The brunt of this wave fell upon a vulnerable 'foreign' community—the Muslims, particularly the Muslim Rohingyas. The year 2017 saw the most extreme and brutal manifestation of this: a horrific campaign that the UN has described as amounting to genocide.

At Independence, Myanmar had started off a little unsure of itself ideologically while threatened by a far-left armed rebellion. With the collapse of the left in

1989, the swerve in the opposite direction began with a vengeance. The 70-year-old civil war in Myanmar is only a manifestation. The real tragedy of Myanmar is that one ethnic group sees itself as the only embodiment of Burma/Myanmar and that all the other ethnicities and minorities must conform to it.

Myanmar is being subjected to forces and influences quite unlike what it has experienced in the past, and change, whether willing or unwilling, will be the order of the day. With an incompetent state and un-visionary leaders pursuing their paltry little ends, Myanmar has little chance of standing up to the winds of change. The outdated nationalism which is found so helpful now may be transformed beyond recognition. Only a diverse and resilient national identity can hold its ground.

The Divide of 2021

The cataclysm brought about by the coup of February 2021 differs from all that had gone before. This is the fourth military coup in Myanmar's 74 years of independence. Their negative impacts have been felt widely and deeply, and this present one promises more of the same. Whether the military junta manages to hang on or democracy is restored, various aspects of Myanmar have suffered irreparable damage. The country was not doing too badly in 2020, despite the pandemic. Now it faces a very uncertain future, while the prospect of decline is unmistakable.

The coup forces mounted an assault upon all who opposed them and then some more. The impact of the all-out war upon rural, agrarian Myanmar is many-sided and difficult to fathom at this point. It will certainly not go easy on the junta and its remaining forces. For 70-odd years, the civil war had been along ideological (i.e., Communism) and ethnic lines. However, it is no longer so; for the first time it is a straight fight for freedom and against tyranny.

Besides being extensive and lengthy, the present crisis is marked by an unprecedented fragmentation of the Bamar/Burman ethno-political majority. All things considered, the possibility of reconsolidation along the lines of the past is minimal. Even though the three Bamar 'Empires' in history are glorified by the military, there have been an equal number of interregna which not many people are aware of.

The centre—civil and military—had been able to hold on and assert itself because it held sway over the Burman majority population in a number of ways. Spatially and historically, the central part of the country and the broad riverine plains were occupied by the Burmans. However, in just one year, 2021, those advantages that the centre enjoyed have been irretrievably lost. Within the hearts and souls of the local people, the institution of the sit-tat (army/military in Burmese) has been smashed to smithereens.

The seemingly impregnable centre is in abject disarray now. It is a situation of its own making. In pre-colonial times, a crisis at the centre (commonly over succession) puts the state in a very vulnerable position. The usual narrative is that one of the contenders has to seize the throne and bring the situation under control. Otherwise, the strife could persist, with deleterious results. Moreover, there are instances of neighbouring polities seizing the opportunity and taking advantage of the stricken state.

In the present case, one contender for power (the military) is trying to exert control with almost blind brutality but without much effect. In a country like Burma/Myanmar, where the centre has been culpable of egregious abuses for half a century, its present debility opens up possibilities for various elements (minorities and others) to correct past wrongs and further their long-thwarted agendas. There is little doubt with regard to the legitimacy of these. We can see this happening in great measure, and there is virtually no means of reversing it.

Looking at the resistance, the leadership is local and does not spring out of any political party. Arms are in short supply, leading to a flowering of ingenuity, creativeness, and metal-working. The outcome this year hangs in the balance. As with the majority of revolutions, a slew of icons is being demolished—political leadership, senior Buddhist clergy, so-called civil society, and generally the old way of seeing and doing things. Seeing the war previous to 2021 as an ethnic war pitting the majority of Bamar against the ethnic nationalities has been turned on its head. The savagery of the attacks on Bamar Buddhist villages is without precedent and puts paid to the ethnic rationale. Even democracy and federalism are in line for leapfrogging.

Myanmar is no stranger to protracted conflict, and the present one could become a "frozen conflict". (This has been touched upon before). A smaller country like Syria becomes divided into four parts; Myanmar is more extensive and diverse, with the roots of enmity and grievance reaching deep. There are Ethnic Armed Organisations (EAOs)-controlled territories of long-standing, and now areas of bitter contestation have sprung up.

Genuine revolutions (some have called them "organic") are unpredictable events. The present one in Myanmar lacks leadership, doctrine, or a set plan.

Instead, the military has declared the population to be the enemy and deploys an "us vs them" concept. For them, it represents the continuation and refinement of half a century of domination by the military class. It is not difficult to see how it could end.

The Long and Winding Road (Talking About) Federalism

The 'peace process', as it came to be called, was launched in 2011 during President Thein Sein's term of office. Incongruously, in that same year, the eleven-year ceasefire with the Kachin Independence Organisation (KIO) broke down, and hostilities resumed. This tandem stream continued for a decade, including the National League for Democracy government's term after its victory in the 2015 elections.

For many, if not all, the EAOs and ethnic-nationality parties, peace negotiations cannot be separated from discussions regarding a future federal system. Sadly, the country is nowhere near both objectives after a decade (and this was before the coup). Ethnic leaders, in particular, have had to painfully conclude that this lack of progress stemmed from a lack of sincerity at the centre.

The coup has extinguished all glimmers of peace. Major EAOs like the Karen National Union (KNU) and KIO harboured men and women who fled the brutal suppression of peaceful protests. These recruits are now fighting in the People's Defence Forces (PDFs) formed mid-last year. junta Chief Min Aung Hlaing has rolled out a fresh call for talks beginning in May this year. Ten EAOs answered this call, and he met each group individually. However, only three small groups appeared when he recently launched a second round with all EAOs.

On the opposition side, a new federal charter is being drafted. Part I, containing the preamble and preliminaries, has been agreed upon, but Part II is bogged down. With all this evidence before them, it is not surprising that some EAOs are charting their own courses now. In place of a federal system derived from the centre, some of them are working on their own constitutions. There are also rumbles about setting up a confederation with the option of outright secession.

Deep down, there is a sense that a federal system is not going to happen as it is generally understood. So let us say the only alternative we have can be called 'variations on a theme of do-it-yourself'. Can anyone think of any agency that could prevent this—be it ideology, religion, governance, leadership, or military force? It's very late in the day, and there are not even straws that can be grasped.

Michael Breen sums it up thus:

> The modern state of Myanmar has had a tumultuous existence, punctuated by ethnic conflict, military rule and poor development. Throughout, the specter of the federal promises made during the independence process continues to preoccupy ethnic nationalities, Bamar elite and the military. The constitutional (and prior political) asymmetry, initially and now, is directly related to multinationalism. The ethnic nationalities have consistently proclaimed their distinct identities and history as independent nations, and recalled the promises made at Panglong. Furthermore, the asymmetry was derived initially from the autonomous or independent status of many of the ethnic nationalities under the British colonial system. Most non-Bamar ethnic nationalities were relatively unaffected by the countries' colonial history, retaining largely independent, self-governing, anti-feudal and anti-central traditions. However, initially only certain ethnic nationalities were recognised as such, and some (such as the Rohingya) remain almost entirely disenfranchised (Breen).

Both Relief and Remedy

At the time of writing, the civil war grinds on, civilian casualties mount, and a political solution is nowhere in sight. Quite frankly, neither the military junta nor the parallel government (National Unity Government) can offer a way out of the morass. Having to assess a civil war is a numbing business, and other than filling news columns, it is never enough. So what I lay out here is not a neat blueprint but a set of rough landmarks in a new and murky landscape which might serve as guides in a general direction. For a way has to be found.

(a) Militarily the closest description of what is happening is a 'people's war', an uprising against tyranny. But it is the kind of war where a conclusive outcome may not be possible;

(b) There are at least six theatres of war, with high attrition rates and the accompanying destruction of civilian homes, entire villages, and places of worship. The present number of internally displaced peoples (IDPs) is 1.2 million. In those six theatres, no area can be considered safe (Ye Myo Hein);

(c) The ostensible 'pathway to federalism' was a constant buzzword in the past decade. It would seem now that this has not only been reinforced but even overtaken. The final goal may be more than federalism;

(d) Despite all its brutality, the centre has been severely weakened and shall find it extremely difficult, if not impossible, to regain its former stature;

(e) Paraphrasing a remark from a retired British general about the war in Ukraine, one could say, 'the military won't win, and the PDFs/EAOs won't lose';

(f) Recognising all this, the only feasible short-to-medium-term remedy would be de facto acceptance of areas of control;

(g) For the time being, the configuration and label which would come closest to the new entities would be 'de facto federacies'.

It can be said that the Spring Revolution is bringing the political centre and majority population to their senses. Through its many 'versions', the Union of Burma/Myanmar has shown itself to be unworkable. The sequel to the coup has dispelled any doubts about it. There is now an opportunity to reshape and restructure Myanmar for the better; however, this time, it will not be a top-down process. The remnants of the fractured centre will oppose this and wheel out its time-worn prescriptions. Though it attempts to garner support for its 'vision', wide acceptance is nothing more than a pipe dream.

If the opposition's Federal Charter gathers steam, there could be another chance at establishing a federal system nationally. However, even with the best intentions, this could take years. Assuming that the present war could be brought to an end, it will take an effort, but a local version of the Dayton Accords can be considered. Myanmar has been locked on the unattained goal of federalism for decades. Other variations can be studied for their appropriateness too. However, I would say that not enough effort has been expended on this.

The recent history of violent conflict makes the establishment and functioning of the institutions of territorial pluralism difficult. Mutual distrust can be so pervasive that both sides fear that the other might renege on the mutually agreed upon deal. Under such circumstances, territorial pluralism needs to be combined with consociational democracy, with emphasis on the inclusion of representatives of all major groups in government and on their veto power over important areas of decision making. While such arrangements might foster political paralysis in the long run, without them, deeply divided states might become battlegrounds once again. States faced with powerful autonomist movements have one of two democratically acceptable solutions. One is to let the group in question become independent—a prospect not usually welcomed by central elites. The other is to implement some variant of what we have referred to in this volume as territorial pluralism. The contributors understand the challenges of managing diversity in plural states and appreciate that territorial autonomy cannot be the answer in every case. However, they also demonstrate how important it can be to achieve a modicum of stability and political inclusiveness that goes beyond simple majoritarian democracy. Territorial pluralism will remain a valuable option for those seeking to ensure stable democratic governance in complex states (Basta and Simeon).

The premise is that the military cannot be defeated throughout the country, but there are vast areas over which it would have to relinquish control. That means a divided Myanmar. The military will employ everything in its playbook to re-exert control. So the likelihood is increasing that the country moves to a patchwork of fortified territories where the two sides face off (if the military is up to it). The federacy concept comes in handy here. Ultimately, the hope is to have them merge, with full consent, into the kind of federation that a broad segment of the population can be comfortable with. That is but one goal.

Carried further, the Spring Revolution goes beyond opposing and toppling a detested military-fascist institution. One sees expressions against ethnic and religious dominance and discrimination that have plagued the country for so long. One sees opposition to patriarchy, majoritarianism, leadership cult, and finally, the military caste system. Revolutions have far-reaching impacts, and this one is also meant to be so. Myanmar's multiplicity of problems has converged, and a singular opportunity presents itself.

REFERENCES

Basta, Karlo, McGarry, John, and Simeon, Richard. *Territorial Pluralism: Managing Difference in the Multinational States.* University of British Columbia Press, 2015

Breen, M.G. *The Road to Federalism in Nepal, Myanmar and Sri Lanka: Finding the Middle Ground.* London: Routledge, 2018

Breen, M.G. The Origins of Holding-Together Federalism: Nepal, Myanmar and Sri Lanka. *Publius: Journal of Federalism* 48(1) (2018): 26–50. https://doi.org/10.1093/publius/pjx027

Breen, M. G. "Asymmetry or Equality? Ethnic Nationalities in a Bamar-Dominated State. A Country Study of Constitutional Asymmetry in Myanmar." In *Constitution Assymentry in Multinational Federalism*, edited by P. Popelier & M Sahadzic. Switzerland: Palgrave Macmillan, 2019

Breen, M.G. "Federal and Political Party Reforms in Asia: Is There a New Model of Federal Democracy Emerging in Ethnically Diverse Countries in Asia." *Government and Opposition: An International Journal of Comparative Politics* 57 (2022): 296–317. https://doi.org/10.1017/gov.2020.26

Win, Khin Zaw. "2010 and the Unfinished Task of Nation-Building." in *Ruling Myanmar: From Cyclone Nargis to National Elections*. Singapore: ISEAS, Singapore, 2010.

____ "Myanmar's malaise and an Indian emperor's message", *Mizzima Weekly*, 23 April 2015.

____ "Time for Myanmar to Grow Beyond its Nationalisms" in *Nationalism in Asia and Europe*, Panorama, Konrad Adenauer Stiftung, Singapore, 07 December 2015.

Ye Myo Hein. "One Year On: The Momentum of Myanmar's Armed Rebellion", Wilson Centre (May 2022).

23

Myanmar: Looking Back, Looking Ahead

Amb Gautam Mukhopadhaya

ABSTRACT

Two years after a legally dubious internal 'coup' against the results of an election conducted under its own military-drafted 2008 Constitution that re-elected an NLD government led by Daw Aung San Suu Kyi on 01 February 2021, the Myanmar Army has not been able to quell widespread protests against the military action that have transformed from a peaceful civil disobedience movement into a near nation-wide armed struggle. On the contrary, far from imposing a forced stability by the use of disproportionate force, the Myanmar Army has lost more and more territory to a proliferation of Peoples' Defence Forces and Ethnic Armed Organisations from Chin State in the west, through the Bamar heartland of Sagaing and Magwe to Karenni, Karen, Mon, and Thanintharyi in the east, forcing it to take recourse to increasing use of artillery, air power and arson against military and civilian targets. For all purposes, it has become a war by the Army against its own people, and vice-versa. All indications point to a total breakdown and fragmentation of the country as we know it.

The Army's efforts to force a solution within the 2008 Constitution that preserves its vanguard role in governance and security in Myanmar, including through attempting to hold elections using a proportional representation system by which it hopes to cobble together the required majority to preserve its primacy in the running of the country, appear to have failed with the National Defence and Security Council meeting on 31 January 2023, stretching the Constitution to extend the state of emergency for the fourth time. The military is clearly out of ideas on how to control the situation other than escalating the use of force. Experts estimate that anything between 50-70 per cent of Myanmar is outside the control of the military. On 02 February 2023, it imposed martial law in 37 townships and 4 Regions and 4 States, but it is far from clear that it will succeed in crushing the resistance. Rather, there are signs that the armed resistance may get succour from outside powers complicating an already volatile internal situation by geo-political rivalries. On the other hand, the National Unity Government that represents most opposition forces too has not quite been able to get its act together, and confronts serious challenges in presenting a unified command against the military, a nationwide leadership, a transition process that includes the army and all arms of the administration, international recognition, and a favourable international environment.

This chapter looks at the historical and contemporary factors that have brought the Myanmar Army to a virtual cul-de-sac where it offers simply no hope for the new generation that has emerged over ten years of democratic transition and technological transformation of Myanmar and will not give up, and the areas that the opposition, both ethnic and majority Bamar, need to address if they are to preserve Myanmar or Burma as it was known earlier, as a united, independent country.

Introduction

As should be clear to anyone following Myanmar by now, two years after the fateful military 'coup' executed by the Myanmar Army against the elected government in Myanmar on 01 February 2021, the political situation in Myanmar is far from stabilised and closer to any resolution. If anything, the portents are of a protracted low intensity, multi-sided conflict that (like Iraq, Libya, Syria, or Afghanistan) could stretch on for years without any side being able to assert nation-wide control or authority, possibly leaving in its wake a highly fractured and fragmented polity: a military government operating out of Nay Pyi Taw, Yangon, and Mandalay, some or most state capitals and other urban areas by use of its superior force but unable to control the rest and increasingly prone to attacks, sabotage, and de-legitimisation within; a patchwork of ethnic armed organisations with large areas under their control or contested by the Myanmar Army; and local 'peoples' defence forces and governments, or even small enclaves and 'state-lets' with greater or lesser capacity to provide security or governance in the Bamar heartland that could take years if not decades to merge within a single national authority, whether civilian or military, government or opposition, under the right conditions in the territory that we know today as Myanmar.

Yet, this is only part of the picture. There are silver linings that point towards sharpening and clarification of fault lines that have clouded Myanmar's journey to nationhood ever since the British overthrew the Konbaung dynasty in Burma over three Anglo-Burman wars in the 19th century (resulting in the exile of the last Burmese ruler, King Thibaw to India in 1886), that could, circumstances permitting, lead to the emergence of a new federal democratic union (or some variation of it) at greater peace with itself. This process will not be easy. It will need political imagination, leadership, and unity amongst all constituents, an enabling, if not supportive international environment, and a process of transition. None of them can be presumed presently. However, such a future is not impossible. The road ahead will depend on a hard-headed assessment of domestic and international forces at work, their relative balance over time, the direction Myanmar is likely to take, and what kind of Myanmar the people and the international community would like to see and be able to shape.

Stalemate

As of now, despite a harsh crackdown on peaceful protests led by a popular, non-party Civil Disobedience Movement (CDM) in the spring of 2021, arson and scorched earth policies against recalcitrant villages in the Bamar heartland of Sagaing and Magwe, amongst others, use of artillery and air power against rebellious People's Defence Forces (PDFs) and Ethnic Armed Organisations (EAOs) in ethnic states like the Kayah, Kayin and Chin (populated by the Karenni, Karen, and Chin ethnicities respectively); and the unleashing of army-backed vigilante groups against ordinary civilians to instil fear amongst the populace at large, the army has not been able to pacify widespread civil resistance to military rule.

It is, for all practical purposes, a war by the Myanmar Army and its cronies against its own people, and, in response, a 'peoples' war against the Army relatively untainted by the majority, minority, ethnicity, religion, 'left', 'communist', 'right' or other sectarian or partisan labels. It is not a civil war. It is, in fact, a struggle for freedom against tyranny. Outside its core of loyalists, the Myanmar Army cannot count on the support of the people, even in areas where there is relatively little fighting. Drawn from the same population pool, within the Armed Forces, recruitment is reportedly declining, and there have been scores of desertions, although few at the senior levels to open cracks within the *Tatmadaw*, a term of respect that the majority now reject in favour of the more neutral 'Sit Tat' or more derogatorily, 'terrorist'.

Unlike in the early 1990s, when the *Tatmadaw* was helped by the Chinese in reaching ceasefires with individual EAOs under its influence, an offer by the State Administration Committee[1] (SAC) to enter into a dialogue with EAOs who are signatories of the Nationwide Ceasefire Agreement (NCA) of 2015, has drawn only a tepid response from a handful of smaller outfits. The SAC has been obliged to extend its emergency *four times*, already stretching what is permissible under its self-drafted 2008 Constitution, and its efforts to hold elections on its own terms, including introducing a proportional representation system by August 2023, appear to be failing.

On the other hand, according to most analyses, despite the formation of a coalition of deposed parliamentarians, the Committee Representing Pyidaungsu Hluttaw (CRPH); the formation of a National Unity Government (NUG) with an acting President and full Cabinet (including a Foreign Minister and Defence Minister); the constitution of a National Union Consultative Committee (NUCC) comprising of major political parties, the EAOs, CDMs, the General Strikes Committees (GSC) and civil society organisations; the adoption of a Federal Union Charter by the NUCC; a resilient armed opposition made up of alienated urban youth, local, township (or higher level) PDFs that have grown in sophistication and capability with little foreign assistance, and several battle-hardened EAOs; a new empathy and solidarity between the Bamar majority and ethnic (and even religious minorities like the hapless Rohingyas) forged under brutal military operations against all of Myanmar, including the Bamar; and a Defence Minister and high military command of the NUG, the resistance does not have the organization, leadership, or equipment to realistically defeat the Myanmar Army conclusively on the battlefield.

With little political activity and its most towering leader, State Counsellor Aung San Suu Kyi, in solitary confinement in prison, the real power in Myanmar is subtly shifting to those who are fighting, particularly the more active large EAOs. However, several EAOs wary of the National League for Democracy (NLD) and Bamar majority and large enough to function on their own, or ethnically, politically or economically tied to China in the North like the Wa, Mongla, Kokang, and Shan, and some others (including the Arakan Army off and on), are sidestepping the conflict and waiting to see a clear direction before making their own moves.[2] Nor do the EAOs that have fought their separate wars with the central government for most of Myanmar's post-independence history have any tradition of fighting a common enemy together. Though some EAOs are training PDFs and other rebel forces, there is very little coordination among the different PDFs, EAOs, and fighting forces, and despite a Defence Minister and high military command of the NUG, those who are still fighting the *Tatmadaw* are still fighting on their own. Most lack access to the sea for any genuine autonomy.

Diplomatically, the international community has found it convenient to accept the primacy of the ASEAN in addressing the Myanmar problem and letting it find a resolution to the crisis rather than soil its hands. This has its merits, including cushioning and containing geo-political rivalries in the region. However, there has been no progress on the '5-point consensus'[3] announced at a special summit of the ASEAN in Jakarta in April 2021 with some fanfare despite strenuous attempts by the outgoing ASEAN Chair, Cambodia, to advance it, leading to frustration within ASEAN (notably Indonesia, the next Chair, Malaysia, and Singapore) with the military regime. Impatience with the Junta's repeated disregard of the international community's expectations over the Five-Point Consensus (FPC) and its sentiments over issues such as the politically motivated execution of four dissidents (including an MP) and trials of President Win Myint, State Counsellor Suu Kyi and others, have provoked a Security Council resolution censuring the regime for imposing a protracted state of emergency and not implementing the FPC.[4]

Nevertheless, the military government, represented by the SAC, continues to man Myanmar Embassies abroad (except Myanmar's Mission to the United Nations), although in response to Myanmar's failure to respond to ASEAN initiatives, the former's top leadership has been excluded from summit-level ASEAN meetings. Only a handful of Russian, Chinese, and ASEAN officials have visited Myanmar at the political level.[5] Russia remains the regime's principal backer providing military hardware and diplomatic cover in the UN Security Council to play its own weak Indo-Pacific card in an area where it has little other influence. China is distrusted but using its diplomatic and political leverage with a weakened *Tatmadaw*, EAOs under its influence, ASEAN and the UN Security Council, to extract the maximum strategic and economic benefits it can. The UN has a Special Envoy for Myanmar, Noyleen Heyzer from Singapore, and maintains a presence inside Myanmar, although their job has not been easy, and actions have at times provoked controversy. Meanwhile, although the NUG has been received in some Chancelleries (notably the USA and Malaysia), it has not yet been recognised by any country internationally, has no territory it can claim its own, and no official headquarters inside Myanmar.[6] As a result, the NUG is functioning more like a public relations outfit than a government-in-exile.

Looking Back

It may be tempting to look at the February 2021 coup through the prism of past democratic ruptures and uprisings in Myanmar when the military prevailed over popular or democratic opposition by the use of overwhelming force, such as in 1962 or 1988 but that would be a mistake. There are several factors behind this coup and the intensity of armed opposition that it has provoked make it different, not least the fact that it followed a 10-year period of relative political, economic and media freedoms and opening to the outside world by the USDP government of President U Thein Sein in 2011 followed by the NLD government in 2016 and the technological changes that took root in that interregnum that gave the youth new opportunities that they had been denied for nearly 50 years of military rule and that they are determined not to lose. However, several longer-term historical factors and forces and more contemporary politico-military reflexes and responses have also contributed to the current acute polarisation between the people and the Myanmar Army that has reached a breaking point.

First, a latent demographic divide between the largely Bamar plains and ethnically diverse hill areas,[7] aggravated politically by the British colonial administrative division of Burma into direct 'Ministerial' rule of the plains and loose, indirect rule of the ethnic regions like the Shan, Kachin, Chin, etc., through their rulers and chiefs, was severely aggravated with the failure of Burma's post-independence governments to fulfil the promise of equality and self-determination negotiated by Gen. Aung San and ethnic leaders in anticipation of Burma's independence in the Panglong Agreement of 1947.

Nothing that civil or military governments have done since then, whether through the use of force, periodic ceasefires, or rare political initiatives such as the Nationwide Ceasefire Agreement (NCA) of 2015 or the Panglong II process initiated by the NLD, or at the social level, intermarriages, has healed that breach. Though the NCA process was a good faith attempt to address the political and emotional gulf with the ethnic political and insurgent outfits yet that breach has only crystallised over time, not least because of later Citizenship laws, processes, and practices that privileged the Bamar.

Part of the reason for this collapse could be explained as a reaction to ethnic insurgences across the horseshoe-shaped hills of Myanmar over time, starting with the Karen uprising in the south that, in 1948, threatened the capital Rangoon, compounded by communist uprisings led by the Communist Party of Burma (CPB) and influenced by the Communist Party of China (but also to some extent by influential figures in the Indian Communist Party). Although the CPB collapsed with the withdrawal of Chinese support in the 1990s, and the Chinese brokered several individual ceasefires with a number of EAOs after the 1988 democratic agitation forcing the then Burmese military government to negotiate with them to contain the agitation in Bamar areas, ethnic insurgencies struck root under military-Bamar-Buddhist majoritarian pressure since the 1950s and consolidated themselves over the decades to a point where they have de facto authority over large swathes of Myanmar ethnic states like Kachin, Karen, Shan, Chin, and more recently, Rakhine.

Part of the Bamar-ethnic divide also had to do with the nature of British colonial administration, Burmese nationalism and the role of the Burmese Army in it. Since the weight of colonial government fell most on the largely plains-centred, Bamar-populated 'Ministerial' Burma, it was logical that nationalist opposition to British colonial rule and exploitation too incubated and grew in the Burmese 'heartland' of the Irrawaddy basin through various popular, often monks-led peasant rebellions (like the Saya San rebellion), and the student strikes of the 1930s that brought Gen. Aung San to prominence.

It was these student nationalists who went on to form the '30 Comrades' trained by the Japanese Imperial Army to form the Burmese Independence Army (BIA) led by Bogyoke Aung San to attain freedom from British colonial rule from behind the Japanese in World War II, and then join the Allied army led by Gen. Slim to liberate Burma from Japan and claim and negotiate independence from the British. Although there were leaders from Burma's ethnic constituents in positions of authority and influence, the major part of the post-independence Burmese political and military leadership was drawn from this social and ethnic base. Starting with certain measures taken as early as by Prime Minister U Nu to revitalise Burma's Buddhist traditions, they also embodied and reflected Bamar's majoritarian tendencies.

Third, as a result of the role of the *Tatmadaw* in Burma's independence, the Burmese independence movement (ostensibly 'led' by the *Tatmadaw*) never became a mass political movement led by civilian political formations like the Indian National Congress inspired by Gandhi came to be in India. It, therefore, failed to democratise and unite the large mass of Burmese around a common anti-colonial cause as it did in India and arguably replaced a British colonial elite with the basically military-backed Bamar elite organised around values of authority, discipline, and obedience (apparent in their vision of 'discipline-flourishing democracy'). Seen from this angle, one could see the widespread nationwide resistance to the military after the coup as a much-delayed denouement of an independence movement that was arrested for 75 years by the *Tatmadaw*.

Perhaps all these could have been softened politically had democratic institutions taken root or Gen. Aung San been alive, had it not been for the near 'mythic' association forged by the *Tatmadaw* with the Bamar strongmen who presided over Burma's imperial past memorialised in giant statues of the founders of the Bagan, Toungoo, and Konbaung dynasties, Anawrahta, Bayintnaung, and Alaungpaya, that grace public and military buildings all over Myanmar. As the eminent Myanmar historian Thant Myint-U reminds us,[8] they serve as props to underline that greatness can only be achieved by a near superhuman exercise of force and will be epitomised by these great leaders of the past that the military rulers of Myanmar take as their reference point. They may also be forgetting that these periods of imperial glory were interspersed with equally, if not longer, interregna of instability, anarchy, and breakdown of authority such as we may be seeing now. Buddhism, too, was pressed into service with the construction of pagodas in the remotest parts of Myanmar, often at commanding heights overlooking minority ethnicities accompanied by legends of their installation on the orders of Emperor 'Athoka' (Ashoka) or other legendary Myanmar Buddhist figures.

This 'fusion' of Bamar ethnic, linguistic, and religious nationalism may have exacerbated the Bamar-ethnic divide, but it served to forge ties with the Bamar majority every time it faced a crisis of legitimacy vis-à-vis the public and burnished the *Tatmadaw*'s self-image as the vanguard and guardians of Burma's unity and integrity. This unity was seen and shown to be threatened from all sides, first of all by ethnic rebellions, but also by the communist insurgency, the demographic and economic 'colonisation' of Myanmar by immigrant communities like the Chinese, Indian (and later 'Bengali' Rohingya), and by democratic freedoms that allowed Burma's diverse peoples their political representation and rights. The *Tatmadaw* exploited each of these sentiments in society to the full by reneging from the clause in the Panglong Agreement guaranteeing self-determination, nationalising the economy, private businesses and property owned by Chinese and Indians in the 1960s, suppressing periodic democratic expressions, notably the 1988 student agitation for democracy, and progressively disenfranchising the Rohingyas. Cumulatively, they served to mask the basic opposition between the military and the people that now stands exposed. It was also partly Daw Aung San Suu Kyi's inability to transcend her Bamar identity vis-à-vis the Rohingya that impelled her to defend the *Tatmadaw* at the International Court of Justice (ICJ) on the grounds of 'national' honour appropriating and eclipsing the nationalist credentials of the Army and burnishing her own already formidable political standing with the Myanmar people as a whole.

Over decades, the idea that the *Tatmadaw* was the guarantor of Myanmar's independence, unity, and integrity and that democracy was synonymous with the disintegration of the Union became one of the cardinal precepts of the *Tatmadaw* justifying military rule to prevent the 'non-disintegration of the Union'. Today, when the *Tatmadaw* see anarchy in the form of anti-military sentiments and acts convulsing the country and the possibility that the post-independence 'order' may disappear altogether, one can understand if they feel vindicated in thinking that they may be right. They may also be mixing the relationship between cause and effect. Ironically, it may well be the Myanmar Army that is bringing about the disintegration of the Union, except that it does not appear that the EAOs actually want independence per se, only greater equality, and autonomy under a federal, democratic Constitution as a union, federation, or confederation.

Looking Ahead: The Military

If the February 2021 coup has one virtue, it has been to clarify the issues facing Myanmar today in a clear light free of the dust of history that has obfuscated structural and self-inflicted contradictions between the Bamar majority, Myanmar Army, the ethnic constituents of Myanmar, and democracy and basic freedoms, underlined earlier. These issues are a sense of equal citizenship between the majority Bamar on the one hand and the ethnic 'races' of Myanmar on the other, with due regard to each other, and a citizenship law that does not discriminate between Myanmar's ethnic constituents (including ethnic Myanmar Indians) on racial grounds; fair representation in political structures, and a democratic civilian government with a professional army necessary for the defence, unity and integrity of the country and accountable to it; and greater decentralisation and delegation of powers and authority towards the constituent units of Myanmar in whichever form they decide—united, federal or confederal. The blueprint of this can be found in Section I of the Federal Union Charter drafted by the NUCC. There can be no going back to the authoritarianism, centralisation, and military rule of the past. The way ahead has to be a new Myanmar, nothing less.

This is, of course, easier said and done. The biggest obstacle to this is the *Tatmadaw* itself. Steeped in its own self-absorbed and insular view of Myanmar as basically ethnically and linguistically Bamar and Theravada Buddhist; harking back to its pre-colonial past as an imperial power (that, to be fair, was never ruled from outside until the shocking advent of the British) ignoring its long periods of instability and disorder; bred in an uncritical narrative of its role in Myanmar's independence struggle; carried away by a self-serving sense of historic and manifest destiny to protect the Union at any cost while exploiting the wealth of the country as its own through its business interests and cronies; infected by distorted racist and chauvinist notions of race derived from colonial and Soviet categories and classifications of ethnicities and 'nationalities'; sharing a sense of siege with the Buddhist right wing over an imagined demographic, political and cultural threat posed by Islam to Buddhism; constrained by a military culture of nationalism, hierarchy, obedience and discipline; trained in military doctrines of 'scorched earth' and the 'Four Cuts'; and unschooled in the arts of politics and negotiation, the *Tatmadaw* is simply unable to grasp that times, and Myanmar, have changed and that they have to give way to a new reality that the youth and future of

Myanmar can look forward to. Autocratic models such as those of Russia and China, major powers, too, cannot provide much succour or comfort. Nor can their protection be depended upon indefinitely. China, in particular, could change its strategy towards the various constituencies of Myanmar in its own interest at any time.[9]

Instead, the *Tatmadaw*'s only response to this upheaval is to double back and try to re-impose 'order' by fear and use of crude and excessive force. Its 'democratic' imagination is limited by the vocabulary of the 2008 military-drafted constitution to, at most, gerrymander new elections by proportional representation to yield an outcome that ensures its vanguard role in Myanmar's government that it wants at any cost, unmindful that it will be violently opposed by the resistance, next to logistically impossible to hold under present conditions, and universally dismissed as rigged, fraudulent, pre-determined and manipulated. Far from resolving the problems caused by the coup, it will only unleash another round of violence that may be worse than before. In the end, the *Tatmadaw* will have to change. It cannot see that it is in a *cul-de-sac*.

Opposition

The opposition, too, has many shortcomings and faces major challenges, some of its own making. The military and organisational limitations of the PDFs, EAOs, and other fighting forces of the resistance compared to the weaponry, equipment, logistics, firepower, and ruthlessness of the *Tatmadaw* have already been flagged.[10] While they have locally held their ground against the superior force of the Myanmar military with ingenuity, they lack the international support and arms and logistics networks to take the battle to the *Tatmadaw* and hold major urban centres and territory that they can use as a base for further operations. Moreover, despite a framework of the NUG, a Defence Minister and a partially unified military command, they lack a unified structure to coordinate and maximise their impact. Each PDF and EAO is still fighting its own individual war. They have not yet been able to elevate their struggle to a wider national or even regional one.

That is not all. Although the empathy and solidarity between the Bamar and ethnic constituents represented by ethnic political and military organisations are refreshing, there is still a substantial reserve on the part of the latter to talk of a full-fledged partnership between them. Distrust on the part of ethnic constituents of the Bamar is entrenched, as is the majoritarian mindset of the Bamar that will take more than just a common but perhaps passing sense of victimhood to overcome. In addition, several EAOs have kept a distance from the opposition, both civilian and armed, on account of such suspicions, and some have gone to the extent of making overtures to the *Tatmadaw* to balance the NLD's influence in the NUG. Lastly, there are internal differences and splits within some EAOs like the Shan, Karen, Chin, Rakhine, etc., that have also enabled the *Tatmadaw* and its supporters to exploit.

Such shortcomings and stresses are only to be expected in any situation, let alone in a context of repression, insecurity, and struggle. More serious has been the inability of long-running and established EAOs that have fought their individual wars against a common 'enemy' for 75 years to join hands to form a common front even now. It is often said that the *Tatmadaw*, Bamar majority, and ethnic constituency constitute the three pillars of power in Myanmar, and that an alliance of any two would prevail upon the third. Now that the Bamar majority, too, have turned to the EAOs for support and training, there is both reason and opportunity for the Bamar and ethnics to join forces and forge a united front to force the *Tatmadaw* to change. Yet, despite the existence of the NUG and NUCC and collaboration between important EAOs and many PDFs, this does not seem to be happening. The EAOs have not thrown their full weight behind the Bamar fighting forces, partly out of fear that once it is over, the latter would once again run Myanmar as if it is primarily their country.

This is also one reason why they prefer to work via a 'collective' leadership rather than a 'national' leader like Daw Aung San Suu Kyi. Part of the reason that this is even possible to contemplate is that Daw Suu is in solitary confinement in prison, but it is also partly to do with the disillusionment of ethnic leaders with what they perceive as Daw Suu's own Bamar-centricity. Indeed, many may secretly see her incarceration by the junta as just the opportunity to avoid such a fate; her return to politics would almost certainly turn the internal balance within the opposition even now in favour of the Bamar.

In principle, the idea of collective leadership in Myanmar is attractive. Most of the ethnic leaders are well grounded in their respective communities, better placed to meet their needs and aspirations, and many enlightened in their political thinking. Such a structure would be fresh, faithful to Myanmar's ethnic diversity, and avoid many of the pitfalls of a single, dominant, or charismatic leadership that contributes both to excessive centralisation or a personality cult around authoritarian leaders in many countries. It would also correspond more to the federal or confederal model that ethnic constituents and leaders aspire to, and the NUCC has adopted as a Charter for a Federal Union. Its weakness is that it deprives the movement of a recognisable leader who can be a rallying point for the whole country, as Daw Suu did from 1988 until the NLD victory in the 2015 elections, one who can resolve the internal frictions and rivalries that are inevitable in keeping a diverse movement together, adjudicate differences politically and nourish a new generation of leadership.

There are three other challenges that the pro-democracy movement will have to confront and should be prepared to deal with from now. One is the challenge of transition. It is a harsh reality that over 55 years of military or *quasi-military* rule from 1962 to 2016, virtually every Burmese institution, from the Presidency to the National Security Council, to the defence ministry, administration, police, border affairs, and even the big business conglomerates, was led or dominated by the military; and even during the five-year interregnum when the NLD ruled and Parliament came to its own, they were constrained by and under the shadow of the 2008 military-drafted Constitution in which a veto-wielding 25 per cent of members nominated by the *Tatmadaw* denied them the ability to amend the Constitution. Today, when in response to the oppression and excesses of military rule, the opposition is determined to decisively end the role of the military in running the country, they have to make sure that they create or inherit transitional institutions necessary in every walk of life to keep and run the country together.

Ironically, this applies most of all to the *Tatmadaw* itself. In their understandable antipathy to the *Tatmadaw*, it would be tempting for the opposition to dissolve the *Tatmadaw* altogether as the USA did with Saddam Hussein's Army in Iraq. There, it led to a vacuum that was filled by the Islamic State of Iraq and Levant. It might not be exactly the same in Myanmar, but an unemployed and disgraced army would not sit idle. Such a transition cannot be forced on an unwilling *Tatmadaw*. It would be easier if there were known divisions in the army with a part of the leadership willing to take the *Tatmadaw* to the pro-democracy movement, but notwithstanding some notable desertions, there are no signs that this is happening. There are no easy answers to this conundrum, but it is necessary to think of how to deal with a defeated military before they return to haunt them now, not in the euphoria of victory. The even more recent lessons of the Taliban in Afghanistan and Putin's Russia after their defeat and humiliations should be telling enough.

Finally, the opposition will have to take cognisance of the international situation. In the past, it was predictable that one or the other major power would support freedom movements, whether they were for self-determination, democracy or other oppressed peoples out of positions of principle, ideology, or ethnic solidarity. This was true for the USA and the Soviet Union in the context of the

Cold War, and India and what grew to be the Non-Aligned Movement with regard to de-colonisation and apartheid. The West's support for democracy in the developing world was always controversial, often selective, politically motivated, self-serving and moralising, but they became the natural beacons for freedom, democracy and human rights, not least as inheritors of the values of the French Revolution and the American War of Independence. The same could be said of India with regard to anti-colonial struggles for independence.

One of the sad ironies of our times is that the vision of countries that were once in the vanguard for freedom has shrunk and fallen back on self-interest to the point where the dominant principle of international relations now is 'my country first'. Values of, and solidarity with, movements for freedom, human rights and democracy have now taken a back seat in favour of realism, 'national' security, selfish interests and racial affinity apparent in geo-political phenomena as diverse as the AUKUS (the security arrangement between the USA, Australia and the UK) where the three democracies have fallen back on their Anglo-Saxon roots to ignore even Europe; Ukraine, where have they belatedly re-discovered the virtues of trans-continental solidarity against an old enemy; and Myanmar and Afghanistan, where these same virtues and values have been either betrayed or reduced to rhetoric and symbolic sanctions.

The struggle for basic rights and freedoms being waged by the people of Myanmar against their own Army will, for all practical purposes, have to be waged by the Myanmar people themselves. There are signs of hope that the ASEAN, which the international community has turned to in relief to handle the disastrous aftermath of a badly miscalculated military coup of February 2021, will take a stronger stand vis-à-vis Myanmar's military on behalf of its people. If so, the international community should shed its reticence to get more deeply involved in finding a solution. If not, the international community may need to think of fresh approaches to restore a future for Myanmar's youth which presently looks dark.

ENDNOTES

1. A mixed civil-military body appointed by Sr. Gen. Min Aung Hlaing to run the affairs of the country during the state of emergency
2. There are signs however that this might be changing with reports that the Northern Alliance, a coalition of four ethnic armed organisation including the powerful Kachin Independence Army, shedding their neutrality and deciding to join the struggle against the *Tatmadaw*
3. Niniek Karmini & Grant Peck, "ASEAN Foreign Ministers Urge More Progress in Myanmar Crisis", *The Diplomat*, 27 October 2022, available at https://thediplomat.com/2022/10/asean-foreign-ministers-urge-more-progress-in-myanmar-crisis/, last accessed on 24 January 2022.

4. Sebastian Strangio, "UN Security Council Adopts Rare Resolution on Myanmar," The Diplomat, 27 December 2022, available at https://thediplomat.com/2022/12/un-security-council-adopts-rare-resolution-on-myanmar/, last accessed on 24 January 2022
5. India has undertaken an official visit to Nay Pyi Taw at the level of its Foreign Secretary and maintains normal official contacts with the SAC through its Ambassador in Yangon.
6. India has also maintained discreet contacts with the NUG, including the presence of a NUG representative in India.
7. Although all the major Burmese empires were Bamar and plains-based and extended into the hill areas, such expansions were part of the ebb and flow of empires and rarely took an ethnic-Bamar character. In fact, a lot of present-day Shan state in the North East of Burma changed hands between rulers in Yunnan, Burma, the Thai, and the Lanna in northern Thailand, and Shan kingdoms often extended their rule into Bamar areas.
8. Thant Myint-U, *The River of Lost Footsteps* (USA: Farrar, Straus and Giroux, 2008).
9. "China's new special envoy to Myanmar meets representatives of seven EAOs in Yunnan," *DMG*, 29 December 2022, available at https://www.dmediag.com/news/5617-7-mb-fpncc, last accessed on 24 January 2022.
10. Although they should be seen against other situations from Vietnam to the Taliban in Afghanistan where rebel forces have forced the most powerful military in the world to pull out.

Index